THE CURRENCY OF POLITICS

The Currency of Politics

THE POLITICAL THEORY OF MONEY FROM ARISTOTLE TO KEYNES

Stefan Eich

PRINCETON UNIVERSITY PRESS

PRINCETON & OXFORD

Published by Princeton University Press
41 William Street, Princeton, New Jersey 08540
99 Banbury Road, Oxford OX2 6JX

press.princeton.edu

All Rights Reserved
ISBN 9780691191072
ISBN (e-book) 9780691235448

British Library Cataloging-in-Publication Data is available

Editorial: Rob Tempio, Matt Rohal, and Chloe Coy
Production Editorial: Mark Bellis
Jacket Design: Lauren Smith and Maria Lindenfeldar
Production: Erin Suydam
Publicity: Kate Hensley and Charlotte Coyne
Copyeditor: P. David Hornik

Jacket and frontispiece image: Kaye, Otis (1885–1974) © copyright. *Heart of the Matter*, 1963. Oil on canvas, 127×108 cm (50×42 1/2 in). Anonymous gift, 2015.419. The Art Institute of Chicago, Chicago, U.S.A. Photo credit: The Art Institute of Chicago / Art Resource, NY

This book has been composed in Miller

10 9 8 7 6 5 4 3 2 1

For Priya

Money is the necessity that frees us from necessity.

—W. H. AUDEN, "A POET OF THE ACTUAL,"
FOREWORDS AND AFTERWORDS (1973)

CONTENTS

Money is, above all, a subtle device for linking the present to the future.

—JOHN MAYNARD KEYNES[1]

IT WAS JANUARY 1924 and John Maynard Keynes found himself turning to the ancient past. Over the previous year, while watching with horror as Weimar Germany descended into hyperinflation, Keynes had published his seminal *Tract on Monetary Reform* that would eventually come to define a new age of central banking.[2] But now his mind wandered into the distant past. He was "absorbed to the point of frenzy," pursuing the history of money as far back as ancient Mesopotamian debt accounts.[3] Soon Keynes stumbled over records of ancient Athenian monetary reforms. An entire world of monetary politics unexpectedly opened up before him. Only a few decades earlier, in 1891, a papyrus manuscript of the long-lost Aristotelian *Constitution of the Athenians* had been discovered in Egypt.[4] Keynes pored over the treasure. Its history of Athenian monetary reforms and the political uses of coinage immediately caught his attention. After studying and translating parts of the text himself, Keynes concluded that money's *political* meaning—the feature that struck him as so important in his own time—could be traced back to ancient Athens.[5]

Keynes was far from the first to be sent back in time by a modern monetary impasse. He joined, for one, Karl Marx, who opened his *Capital* with a reading of Aristotle on exchange and money.[6] Indeed, as I wrote this book, I was struck by the ways in which monetary crises tended to open up historical wormholes. Over and over again I witnessed philosophers, historians, and economists returning to previous monetary disruptions in the hope of stabilizing their own present and taking stock of the conceptual resources at their disposal. The traces these time travelers left behind can often be found by following their footnotes. It was in this spirit that this book originally began by tracing Marx's notes in *Capital* to Aristotle and Locke, but also to long-forgotten monetary cranks and pamphleteers. A similar pattern emerged as I turned to other thinkers who all grappled with historical crises during their own moments of disorientation. The history of political thinking about money, I came to realize, accumulated in layers of crises.

Tracing these sedimented layers, I have conducted a kind of geological stratigraphy of the political theory of money.[7] This book is structured as a study of six historical layers of monetary crisis and their imprint on the history of political thought. Each moment ties a monetary theorist to a particular impasse while setting the stage for future episodes of contestation. Instead of forming independent readings of canonical thinkers or disconnected case studies of monetary crises, these texts and moments are intimately linked not just through lineages of contested reception but also through the repeated revisiting of prior moments of crisis. Rather than telling a single continuous history of money, my stratigraphy of money reveals a layered system of metamorphic rock in which the pressure of later layers easily affects what we can discern in earlier ones.

Money has an intimate relationship to time. It is, as Keynes observed, a device for linking the present to the future. Already Aristotle had introduced currency as a social solution to a temporal problem. The advent of modern public credit further accentuated this temporal quality of money. By establishing a network of claims that link the present to the future, a future that can be permanently deferred, public credit changed both the nature of the state and the relation of citizens to it.[8] The related rise of fiat money, backed "only" by the promise of the state, was tethered to a new conception of political time. Money is the battlefield of conflicting conceptions of the future. Suspended between an ever-expanding horizon of expectations and an increasingly unstable space of experience, monetary modernity found its purest expression in moments of crisis.[9] It was also in moments of monetary crisis that new thinking about the nature and purpose of money periodically burst forth. Whereas periods of calm continuously reproduce meaning based on repeated enactment, moments of crisis are marked by rupture and an openness to new ideas. Crises are windows for making the previously unimaginable politically possible, indeed often necessary.[10]

Understanding the ground on which we stand at the same time helps us to confront the present. Grappling with past crises by restaging their debates helped previous theorists to escape the misleading certainties of their own time and we repeat that move today, each act of escape conditioning the next. This book tells thus an episodic story that peels away some of the crushed layers that have come to define what we see—and don't see—when we look at money today. The texts I examine and the stories I tell here demonstrate a historical method by which political theorists' neglect of money can be overcome by broadening what we mean by the history of political thought and by rethinking the notion of tradition as itself formed in moments of crisis. I am at the same time myself writing from within our own ongoing moment of monetary interregnum. Not coincidentally, I started this project struggling to think through the political questions posed by the financial crisis of 2008. I wrote then about ancient Greek money during the sovereign-debt crisis of the eurozone, and I have finished the book engulfed by the extraordinary monetary measures taken during the COVID-19 pandemic.

Reading my way into past crises and the political thought of those layers gradually came to provide me with a sense of orientation. Let me highlight here one conceptual point in particular that came to guide me throughout this book. The intellectual and political struggles recounted in the subsequent chapters encourage us to move beyond narrow debates over the "depoliticization" versus "repoliticization" of money or central banking. Instead, by providing a multidimensional map of the political theory of money I will defend two fundamental claims. First, attempts to "depoliticize" money rely on a performative contradiction—a magician's sleight of hand—insofar as they disavow that such calls are themselves political moves within the politics of money. Much of what passes as "depoliticization" would be more accurately described as the de-democratization of monetary politics, which itself ought to be subjected to democratic scrutiny. I hope that this study encourages those who are either skeptical or fearful of what they take to be a "politicization" of money and monetary policy to appreciate that their own position is itself a move on the chessboard of the politics of money. Even where it announces itself in an anti-politics, money is always already political. Hence my recurring reference to the *politics* of monetary depoliticization. This does not disqualify calls for the "depoliticization" of money, but the underlying values and goals have to be articulated and defended in the language of politics. Monetary depoliticization does not void the right to justification.[11]

Inversely, calls to "politicize" money are from this perspective empty—and even potentially reckless—where they fail to articulate what kind of politics is meant to be injected. Reconstructing past monetary proposals reminds us of the radically divergent political assumptions and values that authors projected onto the politics of money. Irrespectively of how we judge these proposals, they encourage us to stop agonizing over whether money should or should not be politicized and force us instead to pose a more meaningful set of questions: What is the normative purpose of calls to repoliticize money? What is the tacit conception of politics that underwrites such calls? Is it to bundle money power in one hand or instead to open it up to democratic decision-making? I thus hope to encourage those who rightly demand more explicitly political control over money (myself included) to specify their own political values and distinguish more clearly between politicization and democratization. The underlying debate cannot be over *whether* money has or should have a political dimension but instead over *how* that politics ought to play out and what values should guide it.

My own starting point for doing so reflects a recognition of just how much our current monetary system falls short of both earlier hopes and more modest expectations. It is in this context worth posing anew fundamental democratic questions about the exercise of "money power"—both the power to create it and the power to rule it. This still leaves open how best to democratize money and I pretend in no way that the answer is easy. But despite all difficulties I recall throughout the book the aspirational promise of money to act as a tool of democratic self-rule. By the end of the book, I hope to have articulated the need for renewed democratic political thought about money that can help to overcome narratives that tend to render the politics of money invisible or unintelligible. As a first step, this means establishing the ways in which discussions of money as an institution of governance and collective value form a constitutive part of the history of political thought. This is what I have in mind when I refer to money as the "currency of politics." Having rendered the political theory of money visible, we can pose to monetary regimes the same questions we ask of political regimes: How do these regimes justify themselves, and where does their power lie? Living in a moment of monetary interregnum entails the need to pose the question of hegemony.

No one knows what lies ahead. But the story told in this book allows us to pose the crucial questions with greater precision and articulate more democratic visions of the future of money. Central banks already shape our lives and polities in a multitude of often unrecognized ways. Why not turn them into laboratories of "open democracy" and worldmaking? This may seem unlikely at first. But such demands hark back to long-standing calls to treat sites of production as fundamentally political.[12] Critiques that point to the uses of power in sites of production apply all the more to the production of credit. If there is one place of unbridled privatized power, it is in the realm of credit creation at the heart of our monetary system. Instead of naturalizing the current international monetary system with its glaring hierarchies, can we dare to think the possibility of democratic global money? How might we democratize that system? Is it possible, and desirable, to turn the normative contestation of money that always accompanies monetary crises into a feature of ordinary democratic politics? Articulating a persuasive vision of money as a public good and constitutional project of self-government will be essential if we want to reinvigorate or reinvent democracy for the twenty-first century.

Washington, DC
October 2021

THE CURRENCY OF POLITICS

INTRODUCTION

Money will not manage itself.

—WALTER BAGEHOT, *LOMBARD STREET* (1873)[1]

DURING TIMES OF TRANQUILITY, it can be hard to perceive what we have come to take for granted. The commonplace becomes invisible. "Sometimes what is most familiar," Hanna Pitkin reminds us in a different context, "can be as difficult to perceive accurately as what is wholly missing."[2] Money is one such elusive institution. But its invisibility is not inevitable. It is itself a fragile political construct and one that has a history. The closing decades of the twentieth century bestowed us with a legacy of money as a seemingly depoliticized lever of scarcity. Both the global financial crisis of 2008 and the monetary response to COVID-19 have by now unraveled this illusion of money as neutral and apolitical. It is once more possible to appreciate the neglected political face of money that had previously been rendered invisible. Even more, as we are engulfed by climate catastrophe and incessantly growing wealth inequalities, it has become ever more urgent to recover and articulate money's lost political promise. Money has once again been revealed as a construct of political power and thus—as I argue in this book—a central problem of political theory.[3]

In the course of this book I reconstruct a number of political theories of money that both build on each other and diverge from one another in crucial respects. As we will see, these layers, and the choices they afford, continue to form the material of our own tacit monetary imagination. Disentangling them, clarifying their conceptual shape, and sharpening their political implications involves an exercise of historical reconstruction but also a constant act of self-clarification. Most fundamentally, what emerges from this genealogy are two twin insights. First, money is a foundational institution of democratic self-rule. I denote this democratic aspiration throughout the book by referring to money's role as "political currency" (on which more in the next section). This is perhaps the most alien and fragile aspect of money but it is also the one that stands in greatest need of recovery. Second, and closely related, most of the time money does not rise to the level of "political currency." It all too easily can appear as naturalized or depoliticized. But this is a sleight of hand that disguises the political ramifications of the power to create money.

By reconstructing debates about the politics of money, I not only hope to recover money as a neglected site of political thought and a potential institution of democratic self-rule but also offer an account of how the politics of money came to be eclipsed in the first place. The book thus traces two parallel movements: the periodic reassertion of a political awareness of money especially at times of crisis; and a historical reconstruction of the thinkers and debates that contributed to the eclipse of the politics of money. As a study of how things become invisible, this book constitutes an attempt to understand how and why the political dimension of money became obscured—without ever fully disappearing.

We live in a moment of monetary interregnum. The myth of neutral money beyond politics is dead, but in the words of the economic historian Adam Tooze, "a fully political money that dares to speak its name has not yet been born."[4] This book unpacks this complex political predicament of contemporary capitalist monetary regimes and sketches a number of possible responses to it. To understand both the possibilities of "money power" and the binds it imposes, I turn to the tools of political theory. Despite the centrality of money in, and between, our polities, we currently lack the language to articulate these fundamental questions of democratic monetary rule, let alone to answer them. Money's political dimension has become impossible to ignore, but our vocabulary for discussing the function and purpose of money is impoverished and inert. One of my motivations is thus to contribute to overcoming this linguistic impasse.[5] Political theory and the history of political thought can help us to recover and craft a language capable of articulating the power of money and its pitfalls in democratic terms.

Central bankers find themselves today inadvertently cast into the limelight as their discretionary ability to create money became impossible to hide or deny. But we struggle to discuss the underlying political choices in democratic terms. Pressed to explain whether the $85 billion bailout of the insurance giant AIG in March 2009 put taxpayers' money at risk, Federal Reserve chairman Ben Bernanke famously described the sublimity of conjuring money out of thin air: the Federal Reserve had simply credited AIG's account with nine zeroes. No congressional approval was needed, nor any difficult arguments about taxes. "We simply use the computer," Bernanke explained to the blank stare of the CBS journalist.[6]

But if the crises of the past decade alerted us to an unexpected degree of technocratic discretion in a system that was supposed to be without alternatives, they at the same time rapidly undermined any presumption that states could exercise monetary sovereignty free from all restraints. As central banks sought to govern the international credit system, most found themselves entangled in a vast and arcane global financial structure that was, at least in part, beyond their direct control. The political authorities that wield the power to make money found themselves hamstrung in their ability to govern the new money.[7] It is not just the Federal Reserve that can create money out of thin air; the state has delegated this practice of magic for the most part to private banks.[8] This reliance on private credit money shapes the state profoundly from within. And nonetheless, despite the fact that most money today is created as bank credit, despite the fact that it circulates around the world as capital, money remains ultimately tethered to the states that guarantee it.[9] A tacit hierarchy structures the pyramid of modern money, both domestically and internationally, depending on how widely and easily a certain credit claim is accepted. At the very top of the hierarchy continues to stand money backed by the state and its central bank.

At least in Europe and the US, until recently these underlying questions concerning the politics of money remained largely beyond public debate. This is no longer the case. Money has at last reentered political debate. This is a welcome change that also reflects tireless activism—intellectual and political—by various civil society groups in the decade since the global financial crisis. With their former mystique punctured, central banks have finally begun to explain the way money works. The regained recognition of the politics of money has at the same time reopened fundamental debates about the nature of money and its proper relationship to politics. This does not mean that the end of the neoliberal mystique of neutral money has given way to more democratic forms of money power. In many ways, the COVID-induced shock revealed the exact opposite.[10] And nonetheless a window for democratic debate has been opened that did not exist before. We are consequently once more witnessing struggles over the monetary imagination that range from the full-employment demands underwritten by proponents of Modern Monetary Theory (MMT) all the way to visions of private cryptocurrencies beyond the state. As Antonio Gramsci already observed in the interwar years, during the interregnum when old thinking is no longer believed but the new cannot be born, "morbid phenomena of the most varied kind come to pass."[11] Nothing could be more true for the world of electronic money. Nor is it at all clear what a more democratic money could actually look like for a financially integrated capitalist world economy.[12]

Political theorists have a crucial role to play in these debates over the future of money. They can help to conceptualize the ambiguous place of money in democratic politics and offer a multitude of conceptual tools for exploring the possible meaning of justice and democracy under the peculiar monetary order that is financial capitalism. If money has turned out to be more political than many had come to assume, this still leaves open what kind of politics will shape it. Political theory can also provide much-needed historical orientation that helps us to better understand our own precarious moment of interregnum and possible democratic paths out of it. In this book I consequently turn to the history of political thought to explore the foundations, promises, and limitations of the politics of money.

Between Trust and Violence

It is a surprising and telltale fact that in most contemporary economics textbooks—both those published before and after the financial crisis—the status of money is ambiguous. It is both essential and irrelevant.[13] When our savvy forebears picked some (usually shiny) commodity to mediate in exchange, we are told, they enabled us to move from barter to market exchange. This is the essential precondition for any modern economy. But money appears here merely as a neutral veil behind which real economic transactions occur.[14] Money merely greases the wheels of commerce. Politics and the state are nowhere seen in this picture.

This account of money is best read as a "just so" story. Taken at face value, it is deeply mistaken—as conceptually misleading as it is ahistorical.[15] Nowhere in the world have anthropologists or historians ever been able to find examples of barter economies.[16] What they found instead were sophisticated social systems of credit.[17] Practices that may have looked like barter in fact presupposed an implicit unit of account and an invisible system of credit. Nor is money, inversely, simply a piece of metal, coin, shell, or note. To be sure, physical tokens are often used to record or discharge debts; but to mistake the token for money is, as Keynes once quipped, like "confusing a theatre ticket with the performance."[18] Rather than being a commodity of convenience, money is a technology of credit. As a social relation, it exists prior to the market.[19]

There is another widespread, and arguably more plausible, "just so" story about the origin of money that inverts the anemic economic account of monetary neutrality. In this alternative story, money emerges not out of commerce but force: money is whatever one is forced to pay in taxes in order to avoid being requisitioned at the point of a gun (or rather sword). To avoid punishment for failing to pay taxes citizens need to obtain the government's currency. Rather than emerging out of equal exchange, money here instead measures the tax debts imposed under the threat of violence. The state is, in other words, in the unique position of issuing a currency that it can then force its citizens to use. In this "chartalist" account (from *charta*, the Latin word for token), taxes exist because they allowed ancient rulers to create a demand for their own tokens.[20]

In their conscious disagreement with one another, both of the above "just so" stories have more in common than they care to admit. Both are implicitly driven by certain ideological commitments, and both are meant to promote a particular understanding of money. Both also make sweeping historical claims. Indeed, in (rightly) seeking to displace the myth of barter, chartalism risks swapping one transhistorical assumption for another.[21] Despite their theoretical juxtaposition, the two stories end up mirroring each other. Where politics is entirely absent in the barter account, it appears as an undifferentiated mass of tax power in the chartalist account. Where the state is missing in the economics textbook, in chartalism it is presupposed as fully formed. Crucially, both accounts end up sidestepping a richer political theory of money that is not reducible to commerce or force but suspended between them. My aim is not to propose yet another origin story. Instead, I hope to make explicit the underlying political stakes by laying out broader debates over the political theory of money. Deploying the tools of political theory, we can derive a more capacious understanding of money's political role and purpose. We can also better understand the political work that divergent conjectural histories of money perform.

Modern money is indeed a legal creature that cannot be understood without reference to political power and authority, including the threat of force. But money also hangs by a thin thread of trust and collective belief that can be revoked at a stroke. By helping to constitute and perpetuate social values and relationships, money is not just derivative of political power, it is also inherently a source of power.[22] Money has a political life of its own with a rich performative and communicative dimension. Tellingly, discussions of money in the history of political thought were often structured through complex analogies to law and civic speech. Money is not reducible then to either trade or taxes. Instead, it is an ambivalent political project suspended between trust and violence.[23] This means first of all that the idea of money beyond either trust or politics—a fiction peddled by cryptocurrencies and fintech—is a dangerous delusion that disguises a power grab. But nor is money merely a neutral tool of the fiscal state. Money is best understood as a fragile project of political language and it is this predicament that renders it both uniquely promising and challenging for democratic politics.

Crucially, these political possibilities and responsibilities go beyond legal tender narrowly understood and extend to modern credit money created by banks. Even where the state has become entwined with private capital markets, the state's money sits at the very top of the hierarchy of money, both domestically and internationally.[24] Even where it has delegated the provision of credit to banks, the modern state claims a monopoly on what Max Weber called the constitutional monetary order (*Geldverfassung*).[25] At the intersection of state currencies and private credit, central banks stand today as peculiar institutions of public-private money creation with an uncertain constitutional status.[26] As the legal historian Christine Desan has pointed out in her influential constitutional approach to money, while we commonly speak of "monetary regimes," we rarely consider their normative and political dimension—something we habitually do with other sets of constitutional institutions.[27] Like legal constitutions, monetary systems are both sites of distribution and debate. Modern money cannot escape fundamental questions of power and democratic governance.

Political Currency

While I work broadly from a credit conception of money, in the course of the book I introduce a normative conceptual distinction of my own: what I call money as "political currency."[28] Political currency, as I define it, does *not* refer to cash or legal tender. Instead, I use "currency" in a metaphorical sense to refer to money as a tool of democratic self-government, an idea whose genealogy I trace throughout the book. As a political theorist, I am concerned with the legitimacy of institutions. One account for understanding legitimacy—for example, the legitimacy of a particular law—is to stress the way in which an institution is not externally imposed from above but authored by those affected by it. This is the basic democratic idea of government of the people, by the people, for the people. All too often monetary systems are merely assessed based on whether they achieve certain outcomes, such as, for example, price stability; in the language of political science, they are assessed based on their output legitimacy. This is no doubt an important, indeed crucial dimension of legitimacy. But it is only one. From the perspective of political theory, a system that is legitimate because it genuinely stands to benefit everyone in a lasting sense is best achieved by giving those affected a say in the matter.

"Political currency" marks, then, a normative aspiration. But it is at the same time not entirely divorced from the history of money. Even where they ultimately failed, monetary innovations—from ancient Greek coinage to eighteenth-century paper money—time and time again sought to reorient money toward the idea of "political currency" by reconceiving of the monetary system to ensure that it would serve the citizenry rather than the other way around. To speak of money as "political currency" acts from this perspective as a reminder of the political possibilities of money and the ways in which political communities not only lay claim to govern the money circulating in them but also rely on money to govern themselves more justly.

That money has political dimensions is of course rarely denied outright. After all, most states continue to issue their own currency. But designating money as "political" more often than not means little more than pointing out that monetary policy has distributive implications and is therefore contested. A country's monetary policy and choice of currency are of course subject to intense political contestation due to their broad effects on the distribution of wealth and power.[29] This is a crucial aspect, one that has long preoccupied scholars of political economy as well as, more recently, normative political theorists.[30] But this still falls short of what I mean by the politics of money.

When I speak of the politics of money, I have a more fundamental sense of politics in mind. First, all political communities require tools of reciprocity to achieve civic relations among citizens.[31] Money is one such tool alongside law and civic speech. As such, money can help to create and maintain the preconditions for politics, especially democratic politics. Not coincidentally (as we will see below), the monetization of the ancient Greek world went hand in hand with the rise of the polis. Second, money is an essential tool for the formulation and pursuit of justice. Control over the monetary standard entails more than just whether the value of money will be stable; it also affects the very ability of political communities to define social value, distribute resources, and enact compensations, fines, and reparations. This aspect acquires a particular importance in the case of democratic regimes. Third, money is a political institution based on forms of collective imagination that connect the present to the past and the future. Arguably more than any other modern institution, ideas and expectations are foundational to the way money operates. Our monetary institutions have shaped our ideas about money, irrespectively of whether these ideas are "right" or "wrong." Indeed, whether a particular conception of money is "correct" depends itself on our collective beliefs.[32] These three dimensions that describe the political-institutional qualities of money can be recovered from the history of political thought. This book offers a first attempt at doing so.

In reconstructing historical debates over the political theory of money, I emphasize throughout their layered quality. These theories did not emerge in isolation from one another; each consciously revisited prior moments of crisis, but also prior foundational texts. Locke and Marx both grappled deeply with Aristotle's treatment of money. Fichte, Marx, and Keynes engaged closely with Locke's argument during the coinage debates of the 1690s. The monetary controversies during the Napoleonic Wars loomed large for Proudhon and Marx, but they also still cast their shadow over Keynes and interwar debates over the gold standard. Nor were the resulting responses timeless proposals; each sought to respond to their own specific moment of crisis and each used history to locate their own peculiar position in the midst of crisis. I am in the first instance similarly interested in providing orientation by taking stock of how the conceptual tools we employ to understand the politics of money were shaped by past struggles and inevitably continue to reflect these in a fragmented manner.

This genealogical exercise allows us at the same time to produce a map that can be used to capture divergent political visions of the politics of money. Despite their historical differences, the reconstructed positions of Locke, Fichte, Marx, and Keynes form an eerie prefiguration of our current moment. There is first of all the basso continuo of the Lockean orthodoxy of "sound money," which considers money to be too important politically to be left to discretionary—let alone democratic—decision-making. In critical response to this Lockean politics of monetary depoliticization, Fichte, Proudhon, Marx, and Keynes outlined a matrix of possibilities that continues to frame debates about money and politics. The

Fichtean notion of a well-ordered national state system based on monetary sovereignty continues to shape demands for a more activist approach to public finance, not least based on the insights of MMT. Proudhonist demands for popular monetary reform to republicanize credit or subject it to decentralized control have resurfaced in debates over financial citizenship and the public provision of credit. All the while, Marx's disillusioned insistence that money is in the end indissolubly associated with a power which is not that of the state but that of private capital has similarly proven hard to shake off in light of capital's extraordinary ability to benefit from even the greatest disasters. Finally, Keynes's attempt to reconcile monetary autonomy with international coordination through the founding moment of a new global monetary regime continues to shape the outer limit of our monetary imagination. Taken together, these options provide us with a grid for mapping some of the—partially divergent, partially complementary—political responses available to us.

Tracing these layered responses also helps us to understand how the political theory of money could come to be obscured over time. Both Locke and Marx had pointed in their own ways to the limits of the politics of money—one affirmatively, one critically. In the hands of their disciples, these delimitations came to take on lives of their own. Their original political quality was all too easily lost and over time they contributed to the gradual obfuscation of money as a topic of political thought. As a result, both the Lockean and the Marxist positions fed—as mirror images of one another—into a symmetrical liberal and left neglect of the politics of money that rendered it long invisible and that continues to exercise its sway over us.

Keynes battled against these elisions of the politics of money, both in its liberal and its Marxist variant. Yet he shared at the same time elements of all of the earlier responses and consciously sought to respond to the resulting predicament. It is for this reason that he can serve as a sympathetic, though not entirely disinterested, guide to the various options offered by Locke, Fichte, and Marx. Against those who presented money as a spontaneous order brought about by the natural forces of the market, Keynes stressed its political preconditions. Against those who shrugged at the unequal burdens of adjustment imposed by the gold standard, he sought to tie money to social justice. Like Fichte, Keynes moreover stressed that modern money was in a number of direct and indirect ways ultimately tied to the state. Yet Keynes was simultaneously distinctly aware of the technical and political limits of monetary politics. He shared with Locke a commitment to economic depoliticization and with Marx an appreciation for the underlying logic of capital and financial markets; but for Keynes, depoliticization did not preclude an awareness of the political foundations of economic life. Instead, depoliticization precisely required the ability to repoliticize when necessary. As a result, he argued for the need to bring money under deliberate and politically legitimate control by removing it from the naturalistic illusion that obscured its political foundations. Keynes was at the same time aware of the futility of solely relying on monetary reform or better monetary management. Instead, he sketched the limit conditions under which monetary policy would cease to be effective and more direct forms of socialization, in particular of investment, would be necessary.

Through Keynes we thus encounter one way—there are numerous others—to navigate the options sketched by Locke, Fichte, and Marx. My hope is that mapping the various options will provide some orientation to political theorists who have been hesitant to enter the seemingly perilous terrain of the politics of money. But I also hope that such a map or grid will allow us to think more creatively, more dialectically in Albert Hirschman's sense, about the tacit relations between the various options and the ways in which they are not mutually exclusive choices but also overlap, each capturing a different element.[33] The grid invites us to explore productive contradictions by reestablishing contact between different ideological formations.

Layers of Crises

Instead of such a layered genealogy, the history of monetary thought is often read as the clash between two competing theoretical camps: orthodox theories of commodity money and heterodox theories of credit money.[34] The former—closely associated with the above economics-textbook account—regard money primarily as an exchangeable commodity of convenience.[35] Heterodox accounts, by contrast, see money primarily as a way of recording credit claims. Money is here a "nominalist" system for naming things.[36] Distinguishing between orthodox and heterodox accounts has obvious classificatory benefits and it can provide an initial handle on a vast history of monetary thought. But much is also lost in this process of bifurcation. To begin with, many historical authors fail to fit neatly in one of the two categories. In the course of our investigation we will encounter several such instances, most notably in the case of Marx. In addition, a bifurcation between two opposing camps gives a misleading impression of homogeneity within each. There are crucial differences, for example, between the economics-textbook account for which the entire topic of money is a neuralgic blind spot and the committed defenses of monetary orthodoxy by Austrian School economists or interwar central bankers. Similarly within the heterodox camp, it would be a mistake to reduce nominalism to only the chartalist state theory of money.[37] The broad tent of credit can accommodate radically different conceptions of money.

There is another, more subtle conceptual drawback. Any classificatory scheme between orthodox and heterodox theories revolves around divergent accounts of the *nature* of money. But this is only one dimension of debate, or rather only one way to look at money. What it misses is the way in which disagreements about the nature of money often reflect underlying political disagreements about the *purpose* of money. Indeed, even a shared understanding of the nature of money can translate into radically different political uses depending on one's conception of the state, freedom, or justice. In this book I read debates within the history of monetary thought instead as based on divergent *political* theories of money.

What is ultimately lost in the bifurcation between orthodox and heterodox accounts is a crisis-driven narrative that recovers existing conceptions of money as themselves products of various political struggles over the purpose of money. Instead of constructing a static choice between two or more divergent conceptions of the nature of money, I here cut into the geological metaphorical ground on which we are standing to locate discrete layers of monetary politics, to trace connections between them, and to provide a sense of how prior responses conditioned and elicited later ones. My geological probe is at the same time necessarily selective and itself constrained by the very ground on which I happen to stand. It does not claim to be exhaustive, nor indeed to offer a comprehensive continuous history of money. Instead, what ultimately holds Aristotle, Fichte, Marx, and Keynes together are footnotes—those wormholes through which we can travel between crises.

Both the orthodox and the heterodox positions mentioned above are often traced back to Aristotle, whose engagement with money in the *Politics* and the *Nicomachean Ethics* formed the starting point for a hundred generations of scholars.[38] While modern readers of Aristotle—at least since the eighteenth century—have tended to stress passages that appear to portray him as an early commodity theorist, I argue in the first chapter that

Aristotle instead provided an early articulation of the political conventionalism of money and as such was an early theorist of money as "political currency." This was an insight that attended the emergence of coined
money in the Mediterranean world since the sixth century BC. While
money had existed for millennia, the first coins in the Eastern Mediterranean coincided with the emergence of the Greek polis.[39] The proliferation of coinage went hand in hand with a new conception of the political
community and it gave money a new political dimension closely tied to the
notion of self-governance.

In the opening book of his *Politics*, Aristotle speculated that precious
metals had come to be used as money in response to the inconveniences of
long-distance trade.[40] This is the passage that is usually cited to support
readings of Aristotle as a commodity theorist of money. But he immediately contrasted this view with a second one that posited money as "wholly
conventional, not natural at all."[41] Where the *Politics* appeared to link
money to metal, his *Nicomachean Ethics* presented an account of coinage
as a civic institution of reciprocity. By attending to the political meaning
of currency (*nomisma*) and in disentangling it from Aristotle's critique of
wealth accumulation, we can shed light on his seemingly contradictory
account. For Aristotle, as for the Athenians in particular, currency was
not only a means of commercial exchange but also a pillar of the specifically political community and a crucial tool of justice.[42] Placing money at
the heart of politics has far-reaching consequences. The idea of money
as political currency poses foundational questions of what characterizes
a political community, what allows citizens to relate to one another as
citizens, and what enables them to make collective decisions of value and
justice. In Aristotle's idealized analysis, currency formed a political institution of reciprocity and justice.

Much of this original aspiration was disappointed and eclipsed over
time. But Aristotelian monetary nominalism nonetheless had far-reaching
repercussions and left its mark on Roman law, scholastic thought, and
early modern legal practice.[43] Retracing Aristotle's argument in his *Ethics* during the second half of the thirteenth century, Thomas Aquinas
affirmed that money originated by "a kind of agreement among men."[44]
It was not a measure by nature but by law and convention (*nomos*). This
was widely interpreted to mean that the value of money flowed from the
discretionary power of the sovereign. Yet this royal prerogative at the same
time imposed a strict duty on the sovereign to keep the standard of value
stable.[45] Throughout ancient, medieval, and early modern Western political thought, currency was considered a constitutive political institution

marked by this crucial ambiguity. Was money conventional in the sense of a social institution that gradually arose over time or could the sovereign change it at will? Who owned the money—the sovereign or the people?

We can witness the political and philosophical struggles over these questions come to the fore in periodic moments of crisis. In the midst of a great wave of French debasements during the fourteenth century, Nicolas Oresme counseled that while alteration of the currency—*mutacio monetarum*—may at times be inevitable, it ought be undertaken only under eminent necessity or if it were to the obvious benefit of all.[46] While conceding that the duty to mint coins was the monarch's, he maintained it was the community that exercised the right to control money's value.[47] Like Oresme, much commentary continued to be torn between legal nominalism (often tracing itself back to Aristotle) and an insistence on the limits of justified debasements. The relation of money to the political community posed a thorny set of puzzles that was only further compounded by the rise of the early modern state and an unprecedented inflow of bullion from the New World driven by colonial expansion. In the context of early modern religious war, these debates reached a new fever pitch even though they remained stuck in the same impasse. In his *Six Books of the Commonwealth* (1576), for example, the French jurist Jean Bodin explained that the right of coining money was not just analogous but "of the same nature as law."[48] The right to coin money (*nummus*) was as much a mark of sovereignty as the right to give law (*nomos*). But invoking the principles of Roman law, Bodin at the same time issued a stern moral stricture against debasements in a series of pointed interventions.[49] While the right of coinage was a sovereign prerogative, the prince could not alter the weight of coins at will—neither the welfare of his subjects, nor that of strangers trading with him and his subjects could be violated.

Recognizing early modern money's role as a powerful tool of rule thus went hand in hand with an acknowledgment of profound limitations on how such an institution could be shaped. If sovereigns could pride themselves on their royal prerogative to be able to make money, they also faced a reality in which that right was curtailed, morally and practically.[50] Coinage was sovereign, yet its reach was decidedly constrained by the parallel existence of more and more sophisticated international banking networks.[51] This meant that medieval and early modern money existed in a bifurcated system.[52] Nominalist currencies and debt systems administered by rulers were accompanied by various informal credit systems for small-scale local transactions, as well as bills of exchange and promissory notes (often denoted in precious metals as units of account) for merchant transactions beyond the realm of the ruler.[53] Money would soon leave behind this patchwork of partially overlapping currencies and credit networks and step into a more recognizable realm of modern money.

Constitutional Project and Fictitious Commodity

The tension between an ever more powerful state with its own currency and a patchwork of local credit and international specie came to a head in the seventeenth century. Whereas there had been two parallel monetary systems across Europe for much of the Middle Ages—a nominalist one for local and domestic transactions, a commodity-denominated one for transactions with foreigners—in the late seventeenth century the two became entwined. The old bifurcated system began to take on a radically different shape in England, and what has become known as the Financial Revolution was in the first place an upheaval in the way in which money was created and, in turn, understood.[54] Most importantly, modern capitalist money combines and entwines the two previously distinct monetary systems of state money and private monies. Capitalist money is in this sense characterized by the monetization of private debts through a banking system that is in turn backed by the state.[55] Relatedly, whereas states had previously charged for the minting of metal into coins, they now paid interest on public debt.[56] This placed the state at the heart of the monetary system while at the same time obscuring that centrality and binding the state's invisible hands.

Put in terms of political theory, the modern state essentially came to rely on private actors to provide the public good of money. Modern money, even in the form of bank loans or deposits, is at the same time never fully private but ultimately guaranteed by the central bank as the supervisor of the banking system. A purely private financial system, just as much as purely private money, is by necessity a fiction—even where that fiction is seemingly a necessity of the modern financial regime.[57] The hierarchy of capitalist money, like money itself, remains ultimately a creature of the law.[58] Capitalism must thus be considered a unique epoch in the history of money. Indeed, capitalism is in an important sense defined by a peculiar form of money creation: public and private credit are deeply entwined—with often paradoxical and illusory effects.[59]

This new system began to be forged in a moment of crisis in the closing decade of the seventeenth century.[60] One particularly influential reconceptualization that reshaped the politics of money and became itself foundational was that advanced by John Locke (who forms the subject of chapter 2). Instead of having to mobilize moral strictures against discretionary debasements, Locke set out to derive a novel conclusion from the old Aristotelian premises. Locke famously described the monetary contract as a tacit, prepolitical agreement of all mankind, thereby seemingly placing money outside of political control. This unspoken bond between all humans was furthermore said to have given license to the inequalities that inevitably followed commercial development.[61] In his view, the cosmopolitan nature of the tacit compact of metal money entailed a duty to maintain monetary stability, while supporting the expansion of overseas trade and even colonial settlement. Consequently, for Locke monetary justice meant first and foremost a duty to guard the inviolability of metal money that was also a covenant of trust between the sovereign and his subjects. In the background of Locke's intervention stood a new fiscal constitution that made taxation dependent on representation.[62] But this only further highlighted the awkward constitutional role of monetary power. Irrespectively of whether it was left in the hands of the sovereign or placed into the lap of Parliament, the power to create money would seem to render the fiscal constitution moot. To avoid such monetary excesses, the point now was to check monetary power and disentangle it as much as possible from the fiscal state. This was one way of closing off the great turmoil of the seventeenth century and redefining the relation between sovereignty and money.

But it was at most a temporary solution. The development of capitalism and the rise of the fiscal-military state built on public debt in the eighteenth century soon found its expression in proposals for paper money that tested Locke's orthodoxy. The age of revolutions and the British suspension of gold during the Napoleonic Wars became another laboratory for discussion of monetary, commercial, and fiscal order. This produced intense debate in Britain and France, but also in the war-torn German lands. The author who pushed this furthest was Johann Gottlieb Fichte, who distanced himself from Locke's assertion of a tacit universal assent to metal money and instead drew a close analogy between money and the social contract (explored in chapter 3).[63] Where Locke had sought to place money outside of the direct political control of the commonwealth, Fichte argued that currency had to facilitate the same demands of rationality and coordinated autonomy that underpinned the social contract.[64] Monetary justice implied not only the enforcement of private contracts but also the realization of civic equality and the right to work. Economic justice hinged on radically altering the monetary system.

Fichte's radical proposal was stillborn. Instead, global capitalism took off and the age of commercial revolution between the 1820s and the

1870s sparked a new phase of debate. Although Britain returned to the gold standard after the Congress of Vienna and the end of the Suspension Period, there was nonetheless no single hegemonic monetary order. Calls for credit reform became in this context a recurring socialist demand, in particular in France where Pierre-Joseph Proudhon pursued the establishment of a People's Bank in the course of the 1848 revolution.[65] Even the *Communist Manifesto* demanded the centralized provision of credit and the founding of a national bank.[66]

Yet Marx, during the decade following publication of the *Manifesto*, developed an extended critique of the promises of monetary reform (reconstructed in chapter 4).[67] Against Proudhon, he argued that proposals for credit reform mistook cause for effect. Rather than introducing a contradiction, money merely mirrored a prior one since under capitalism money merely embodied all the tensions of capitalist exchange. Proudhon peddled, in Marx's words, dangerous "money nonsense."[68] In his own analysis Marx cautioned both against Proudhonist credit reforms and against Fichte's vision of malleable national fiat currencies. Instead he pointed toward the intimate link between the capitalist mode of production and the development of new forms of credit money.[69] To reform money without touching the productive system was a contradiction in terms. As "crystalized labor power," money as capital did not obey the word of the state but instead spoke "the language of commodities."[70] Under capitalism, the public good and social relation of money had been transformed into a fictitious commodity, as Karl Polanyi put it in *The Great Transformation*.[71] But for Marx, this fictitious quality was not simply a false belief or a kind of illusion to be overcome. It was a real aspect of the way in which under capitalism the social relation of money had come to be commodified. As the "necessary form of appearance" of value, money did not straightforwardly bend to political will.[72] Global capital—even when dressed in national garbs as state-issued currency—was decidedly less malleable than Fichte or Proudhon envisioned.

What are we to make of this peculiarly Janus-faced character of modern money as both malleable constitutional project and crystallized private commodity? If money is a constitutional undertaking, as Desan has persuasively insisted, what kind of constitution is it?[73] What kind of constitution should it be? What kind of constitution could it be? Locke, Fichte, and Keynes all appreciated modern money's significance as a constitutional project, but each had a distinct conception of the nature and purpose of that constitution. I read their disagreements here consequently as expressions of divergent *political* theories of money based in particular on divergent understandings of the ultimate purpose and nature of the state. The following chapters trace, then, an interlocking set of analogies between money and speech, and between the bond of currency and the social contract. In reconstructing these debates I further extend the vocabulary of political theory and the scope of the history of political thought into ostensibly economic matters. This is more urgent than ever in our own moment of disorientation. Such an extension has in turn the power to challenge our existing conceptions of language, trust, and the social contract. To recast credit creation as based on an implicit social contract also allows us to interrogate existing conceptions of contractualism, dispense with overly static understandings, and enrich our political vocabulary in the process. Societies are not created in a single moment; they are built, over time, by complex relationships of trust and reciprocity.[74] They are built on promissory notes, on collateral, on credit. Conversely money is underpinned by social trust: "habit congealed through repetition into faith," as the historian Rebecca Spang has put it.[75]

This emphasis on trust and credit, as well as the dangers of breaking those ties might be taken in the first instance as tying the politics of money to conservatism. Just as Locke derived from his emphasis on trust an uncompromising need to secure the inviolability of property and the unalterability of coin's metal value, the classic defense of the gold standard perpetuated that project into the twentieth century as an anchor against the gyrations of an increasingly unpredictable politics, be it in the form of new democratic demands or efforts at armament by nationalist governments during the interwar years. The promise of sound money became the mantra for a nostalgic search for lost stability. Already Locke's narrative of monetary fragility had been held together—like Hobbes's state—by tales of trauma. In the second half of the twentieth century, central banks themselves became the master spinners of such stories of fear and fragility.[76]

But this conservative construction of the politics of monetary trust as too fragile for democratic politics is only one of many options opened up to us by modernity. As critics of Locke pointed out, keeping promises at any cost spells the end of trust. To insist with Shylock on getting repaid, even in an equal pound of fair flesh if necessary, is a sure path to disaster. Formulating an alternative position more suitable to a democratic age is what gives such central significance to Keynes (to whom I turn in chapter 5). Responding to those who insisted on the sacredness of the gold standard during the interwar years, Keynes argued that where sacrifices had grown so unbalanced the result would be class war—the twentieth-century version of civil war. It was thus the duty of responsible statecraft and a precondition for the functioning of democratic politics to ensure a more just distribution of burdens. Devising more or less roundabout methods for achieving this balancing is the political project of Keynes's monetary thought. Monetary trust then does not simply imply the enforcement of existing contracts but the realization of a more fundamental, and more equitable, social contract that requires a sharing of sacrifices and benefits. As the political theorist Danielle Allen has put it, democratic society demands that the loser can trust that his or her loss is transient and not a persistent feature of society.[77] In a democratic society monetary trust must be tied to a negotiation over justice. The absolute defense of price stability implies either a repression of democracy or a social hegemony so complete that the problem of justice is no longer posed.

Depoliticization as De-Democratization

If these arguments about money as a central political institution appear unfamiliar, one reason is that political theory has recently tended to sidestep them. Even historians of political thought have more often than not handed money to the history of economic thought for safekeeping. Money constitutes in this sense a privileged case for studying the politics of depoliticization of the economy.[78] There are few ostensibly economic institutions that experience a mystification and naturalization as complete as money. Part of this simultaneous centrality and invisibility of the politics of money derives no doubt from money's peculiar relation to the modern distinction between politics and economics. Narratives of the separation of economics and politics are a long-standing—perhaps even constitutive—feature of modern political thought. Yet money does not fit neatly into such delineations. Precisely for that reason, it can serve as a rewarding object of study.

Despite its seeming political invisibility during periods of calm, money remains tightly tied to politics and the state. As we will see throughout, monetary depoliticization is not an innocent description of the world but always a political strategy itself. I consequently take care to speak of a *politics* of monetary depoliticization. Politics does not disappear; it changes shape and is modulated. Money cannot be removed from politics but only be "encased" against democracy.[79] This means that much of what passes as the depoliticization of money is a sleight of hand that would be more accurately described as the de-democratization of money. Unsurprisingly, this antidemocratic politics is rarely spelled out openly. After all, doing so would likely be counterproductive in the realm of democratic politics. But occasionally the underlying sentiment is blurted out, either inadvertently or as a sign of complacency. Perhaps the most famous such instance involves the influential monetary economist Rudi Dornbusch pronouncing in 2000 with spectacular bluntness that "democratic money is bad money."[80]

The seeming antipolitics of neutral money should then not be taken at face value but is instead best understood as a peculiarly modern antidemocratic politics of monetary depoliticization.[81] By recovering discussions of money in the history of political thought, we can as a first step crack the false pretense of naturalization and defamiliarize what has become too familiar. Who gets to create money and who gets to decide who gets to create money reflect themselves the contingent outcomes of political struggles. They are not theoretical givens or structural necessities.[82] But from studying the past we can also learn to better understand the appeal of different political strategies of depoliticization that themselves emerged as weapons in such struggles. Depoliticization, even as a peculiar kind of politics of its own, is deeply real. That means critiques of depoliticization risk being limited by a failure to take appearances seriously. This is fatal in the case of money. Money is a metaphor that demands to be taken literally. Like language, money does not merely represent reality but constitutes it.[83] Even where the political side of money is often shrouded in myth or disavows itself, these appearances are as powerful as they are deceptive. What is lost in either ignoring or giving in to the illusion is an appreciation of the ambiguous political status of money and the way in which it constitutes itself the plane on which divergent conceptions of democracy are locked into a struggle with one another.

As I argue in the concluding sixth chapter, political theory has in this sense itself been implicated in the most recent wave of monetary depoliticization since the collapse of the Bretton Woods system in the 1970s. Over the past forty years, momentous changes in the politics of money have radically reshaped societies and polities. These decades, which witnessed a renaissance of theories of justice in the academy, now also stand for the gradual erosion of the welfarist institutions and policies advocated by many of those very theorists.[84] The rise of liberal theories of social justice coincided with the acceptance of permanent unemployment, new forms of financialization, and widening income and wealth disparities—often along markedly racialized lines. The radical reshaping of the monetary order and monetary policy since the 1970s has been crucial to all three dimensions of this silent revolution.[85]

Political theorists have since become vocal critics of the ways in which money's corrosive effect can corrupt civic norms and political institutions. Confronted with the economic developments of the past decades, they developed powerful arguments against commodification and lamented what the philosopher Jürgen Habermas dubbed the "colonization of the lifeworld."[86] In the hope of pushing money back into its place, political theorists repeatedly drew lines in the sand, each soon to be erased by the next wave of financialization and commodification. The implicit flip side of this defensive posture is rarely considered. In attempting to contain the political reach of money, political theorists often unwittingly accepted the premise that money is merely economic in the first place, thereby equating it with commodification and immunizing the disinflationary depoliticization of money against critique.[87]

This is doubly tragic because it forestalled an alternative money modernity. What happened in the 1970s was not so much a passive fading away of Keynes's original vision but rather its forcible suppression by a truly violent process of depoliticization. Precisely at the moment at which Keynes's clear-sighted vision of a different politics of money became most relevant again, it was denied. We have still not been able to respond to his challenge of how to conceive of an adequate democratic politics of capitalism and how to reconcile the pull of financial globalization with the ideal of legitimate self-government. The bitter irony of our own current moment in the early twenty-first century is that we find ourselves back in the Keynesian conversation but with only a partial understanding of his monetary thought and on a ground shaped by supercharged financial capitalism that seems to leave little room for democracy or indeed experimentation.

⟨⟫⟩

Overcoming the current impoverishment of our political language concerning questions of monetary rule and justice requires as a first step rendering money power visible again. Instead of pitting money against democracy, we will have to craft alternative visions for a more democratic politics of money and articulate a better democratic language of money power. This will be an economic as much as a political challenge. It will have to entail new work in monetary economics as well as renewed thought about the deep interactions between politics and economics. But if I am right, the vocabulary and institutional imagination of political theory are much needed in the realm of these monetary debates. Only by bringing political theory into questions of money will we be able to live up to this challenge in our current moment of interregnum.

While I write as a political theorist, I hope that my reconstructions and arguments also resonate with those already thinking about money from other vantage points. This includes those who are already looking for a better language to articulate underlying questions of legitimacy and justice, but I also hope to reach those who might not yet realize that they are indeed in need of such conceptual resources. Whether we acknowledge it or not, money is a conduit of power. An adequate understanding of the effects of monetary policy and of proposals for monetary reform require an articulation of questions of power, rule, and justice. Today, this is most immediately the case for central banks. Despite their powerful status, central banks—and the private banks they supervise—exist in a peculiar constitutional blind spot of our polities. The mantle of neutrality with which central bankers used to shroud their actions has been revealed as a convenient myth.[88] Old narratives and templates have run their course. As we step into a world of rapid technological change and climate catastrophe, the global politics of money is up for grabs—perhaps more than ever before.

This does not mean that money is malleable in any straightforward sense. Indeed, it can easily seem as if money works most effectively precisely when it can be taken for granted, when it is unthought and its social construction hidden from view.[89] The indispensable but fragile social fiction of money as a commodity is essential to capitalism and nonetheless constantly at risk from its own tendencies toward commodification on the one hand and depoliticization on the other. Money is always more than a simple tool. We never simply make money. Money also makes us. It is within this tension that the politics of money plays out.

CHAPTER ONE

The Political Institution of Currency

ARISTOTLE AND THE COINAGE OF THE POLITICAL COMMUNITY

Money is the true bond of society.

—JEAN-JACQUES ROUSSEAU[1]

THE STARE OF THE OWL'S enormous eyes would have been a familiar sight for every Athenian. More than 2,500 years later it has lost none of its intensity. Athenian *tetradrachm* (four-*drachma*) coins are perhaps the most familiar of all ancient coins. Worth roughly a week's wages, they were referred to as "owls" after the image of Athena's big-eyed bird stamped on their reverse side. Next to the owl they depicted a crescent moon, an olive branch, and the Greek letters Alpha Theta Epsilon—abbreviated "of the Athenians." On their obverse side the coins carried an image of Athena, goddess of wisdom and patron deity of the city. *Tetradrachms* were prized throughout antiquity for their quality and uniformity. Each weighed around seventeen grams and was made from nearly pure silver, mined by slaves at Laurion on the southeastern tip of Attica.[2]

And yet there was much more to the coin than its silver value. It is easy to miss what truly made an "owl" special. The *tetradrachm* was the proud symbol of Athenian power; indeed it embodied the political community itself. As the classicist and political scientist Josiah Ober has put it, Athenian owls possessed a "fiduciary value added."[3] Like most Greek silver coins, they traded at slightly more than the worth of the silver alone. This has long been a mystery. According to economists, the "value added"

FIGURE 1.1: Athenian silver *tetradrachm* (four-drachma) coin from the late fifth century (450 BC–420 BC) (ANS 1968.34.40). The obverse side shows Athena in profile wearing a crested helmet. The reverse side depicts Athena's owl next to a crescent moon and an olive sprig as well as the inscription AΘE, which was short for "of the Athenians." Photo: Courtesy of the American Numismatics Society.

reflected the ease with which the coins allowed parties of exchange to transact without having to weigh and assess the metal.[4] But there looms another, altogether more political dimension behind the fiduciary value of Athenian owls. In trusting the coin, one trusted the Athenian polis.

The classical Greek world featured a striking abundance and diversity of coinage. The earliest known coins in the Western world were minted in Lydia, in present-day Turkey, sometime in the mid- to late seventh century BCE.[5] Solon's mythical visit to the king of Lydia, Croesus, formed part of ancient Athenian lore and was frequently linked to Solon's monetary reforms.[6] Over the following centuries, coinage spread rapidly throughout the Greek world. At its peak close to five hundred Greek poleis issued their own coins.[7] In Athens, by the end of the fifth century BCE uncoined metal had ceased to be legal tender in the agora and almost all payments had to be made in local coinage or a small number of approved coins from other poleis.[8]

While the Greek passion for coins is well-known, its meaning and significance remains disputed. Confronted with the fragmentary monetary map of the classical Greek world, economic historians have puzzled over the obvious "inefficiencies" of constant foreign currency exchange. Bewilderment over hundreds of Greek city-states issuing their own coinage only grows once we appreciate that both domestic and external trade had for centuries been conducted perfectly well with older forms of money such as uncoined metals based on weight.[9] What those puzzled by the proliferation of coinage had missed, the classicist Moses Finley pointed out in *The Ancient Economy* (1973), was that ancient Greek coins were "essentially a political phenomenon."[10] Instead of seeing the fragmented Hellenic monetary map as a nuisance, the Greeks proudly celebrated their local coinages and established ferocious penalties for counterfeiting by treating it not merely as a commercial offense but a form of treason punishable by death.

Where Finley had still left the precise political role of coinage somewhat vague, over the past two decades scholars have since recovered the symbolic dimensions of exchange, drawn attention to the contentious political struggles behind the spread of coinage, and traced its profound philosophical implications.[11] Despite important differences in emphasis, it is now clear that the adoption of coins bearing the stamp of individual city-states was closely related to a number of crucial intellectual, social, and political changes in the transition from the archaic Greek world to that of the classical polis. Specifically, the rapid spread of the new institution of coinage went hand in hand with the development of a new form of political rule. The birth of politics had a pronounced monetary dimension.[12] By minting their own coins, citizens of Athens, Corinth, Delphi, and other city-states were distinguishing themselves from each other but also tying each other together. In an age before the printing press, circulating coins were reproducible symbols that inscribed the polity into social memory.[13] Ancient coins functioned as a medium for the construction of the social and symbolic imaginary of the polis, just as the rise of modern imagined communities would be tied to new technologies of print and mechanical reproduction.[14]

The spread of coinage throughout the ancient Greek world had of course an important economic dimension since coined money saved ponderous weighing and removed uncertainty. But on its own such an economic approach struggles to explain both the extraordinary monetary fragmentation of the Greek world as well as the wider social and political meaning of coinage. Ancient monetary exchange had instead a wide range of symbolic functions beyond any narrow economic logic.[15] Most broadly, the introduction of coinage was linked to a shift in the conception of political authority and how it was wielded; a shift away from divine justice and toward a form of political authority that was more terrestrial, more conventional, more political. Coinage accompanied and enabled the development of more abstract forms of reciprocity, a new philosophical interest in an impersonal universe, and a more autonomous conception of the individual.[16] Polis and coinage developed in parallel, and both marked

a shift in the conception and practices of reciprocity away from the tribu-
tary gift exchange that had characterized the archaic world depicted by
Homer and toward more abstract monetized forms of redistribution and
exchange conducted in the currency of the polis. Recovering the politics
of coinage serves then as a reminder that the Greek polis was structured
around the agora—not as a purely commercial space but also as a communal and political one in which the exchange of words and coins mirrored and complemented each other.[17] As the classicist Alain Bresson
puts it, Greek coins "were a value that circulated, just like words."[18] This
ancient politics of coinage forms the neglected background to Aristotle's ambivalent account of monetary reciprocity. I turn to it here as the
foundational but also forgotten—indeed repressed—layer of my genealogical inquiry.

The political centrality of currency in the ancient world was most fully
reflected in Aristotle's account of reciprocal justice in the *Nicomachean
Ethics*. "A polis," he asserted there, "is maintained by doing things in return
according to proportion."[19] Similarly, in the *Politics* he wrote, "Reciprocal
equality preserves city-states."[20] Political theorists have recently begun
to give reciprocity the attention it deserves as a crucial part of Aristotle's
answer to the problem of political justice and civic equality. In doing so,
they have tended to focus on how law and speech can foster relations of
reciprocal justice.[21] When they acknowledge the role of coinage at all, it is
often moved into the background, be it out of suspicion of its crass commercial connotations or incredulity that the great philosopher would stoop
to such a tawdry consideration.[22] Perhaps thanks to its association with
exchanges of gifts in modern anthropology, reciprocity is often assumed
to be opposed to monetary exchange. As a result, it is tempting to read
references to reciprocal exchange as implying nonmonetary forms of gift
exchange.[23] But Aristotle's discussion of reciprocal justice pivots around
the correct use of currency (*nomisma*).[24]

There are also conceptual obstacles. Most English editions of Aristotle
tend to translate two distinct terms as "money": *chrēmata*, which signified material wealth in general, and *nomisma*, which meant coinage in
particular. Translating both as "money" elides the conceptual distinction
between wealth and currency, and risks obscuring Aristotle's argument. In
attending to the ancient meaning of currency (*nomisma*) and in disentangling Aristotle's account of currency from related but distinct discussions

of wealth accumulation, this chapter focuses on how a well-used currency can contribute to reciprocal justice. This was the case in three interrelated ways. According to Aristotle, currency can ground civic relations by equalizing citizens, maintain the polity by serving as a measure of political justice, and cultivate practical wisdom and deliberation.

Recovering the political purpose of currency allows us to reframe the role of money in a subtle but far-reaching manner with implications that point far beyond Aristotle. Many influential readings of Aristotle's political thought contrast the political world of speech in the polis with the private realm of domination in the household.[25] After all, Aristotle rebuked Socrates in the *Politics* for having insufficiently distinguished between households and the polis.[26] While households are structured hierarchically and satisfy daily needs, the polis is a community of equals based on difference. Sometimes readers have radicalized this distinction into a bifurcated view by elevating the polis as a space in which citizens debate about justice by means of speech, while marginalizing exchange and currency as belonging to the household. But just as the household was also characterized by speech about the just and advantageous, exchange and currency were central to maintaining reciprocal political justice. According to Aristotle, when used correctly (a crucial qualifier as we will see), currency could bond society, bringing citizens together rather than dividing them, serving justice rather than corrupting it. Reconstructing the role of currency (*nomisma*) in analogy to law (*nomos*) highlights Aristotle's expectation that money could be an institution that would contribute to the cohesiveness of the polis—but one that was also insufficient, imperfect, and laden with potentially tragic consequences for a self-governing political community striving for justice.

Aristotle held high hopes for currency. But what is perhaps most striking in recovering these promises is how greatly they have since been disappointed. Even by Aristotle's own account, currency was necessary yet deeply ambivalent. Indeed, his account of monetary reciprocity as a tool of justice in the *Nicomachean Ethics* can appear to be in tension with his critique of wealth accumulation in book 1 of the *Politics*. As many commentators have remarked, Aristotle seems torn between two radically divergent approaches to money.[27]

But the two can be reconciled and indeed complement each other. To be sure, conceptually and practically money is entangled with wealth. Wealth is measured in money and it will in turn be deployed to accumulate yet greater riches. Money appears from this perspective as the great corrupter. But according to Aristotle, monetary exchange was not inherently inimical to political justice and can even serve it. At the least, it was a mistake to think of currency as necessarily, inextricably, and inevitably tied to unjust exchange.[28] Currency becomes unjust only if and when it deviates from just use by fueling the accumulation of wealth for its own sake.[29] Put to ill use, money can become a serious threat to any political community. Employed as a tool of reciprocity, however, currency serves political justice. The point is not that the institution of money cannot lead to distortions—it obviously can and does. But it also allows us to recognize those injustices and, possibly, amend them. Currency contains within itself the necessary condition for its own improvement.

Reemphasizing money's role in furthering equality and reciprocity instead of undermining them is a significant challenge for our own time. All too often, contemporary political theorists and historians of political thought have projected a distinction between politics and economics into the past.[30] This easily obscures the political dimension of currency in Aristotle's thought. As I will argue in the subsequent chapters, once the political significance of currency is brought back into the frame, not only ancient but also modern political thought on money takes on a different cast.

Law and Currency

If we approach Aristotle's account with a preformed and anachronistic idea of money in mind, his argument of currency as a political tool of reciprocity is easily obscured.[31] A first hint of how to substantiate the link between currency and polis is embedded in the Greek word for coinage (*nomisma*), which shares a linguistic root with the conventional law of the polis (*nomos*). Both derive from *nomizein*, to acknowledge or to sanction something by established belief or custom. *Nomisma*, a plural noun, means "what is sanctioned" and could indicate anything customarily and collectively affirmed. The term gradually came to refer to coinage but it never fully lost its broader meaning.[32]

The earliest surviving occurrences of *nomisma* all refer to acts of collective confidence, often based on divine inspiration.[33] Aeschylus referred, for example, to a certain "Hellenic *nomisma*" to describe the Greek collective practice of shrieking during battle and sacrifice, which inspired collective confidence and helped to overcome fear.[34] Such ritualistic, onomatopoeic ululations (*ololugē*) are widely attested in numerous plays and almost always uttered by women.[35] They can be cries of joy but, as

Herodotus observed, ululation is usually associated with acts of sacrifice, often accompanying the very instant the animal's throat was cut.[36] *Nomisma* here stood for divinely inspired acts of collective confidence. "Whether in sacrifice, battle, or coinage," the classicist Richard Seaford explains, the collective practice of *nomisma* "depends on and objectifies the collective confidence of the community, for whom it introduces order into potential chaos."[37] The linguistic origin of *nomisma* thus captures a shared element of communal faith and speech but also the way in which coinage mirrored the role of sacrifice in fostering the bonds of community.[38] Indeed, ancient Greek coinage's link to sacrifice and sharing echoed through the denomination of *obols* (one *drachma* was worth six *obols*), which invoked the roasting spits (*obeloi*) used in the preparation and sharing of sacrificial meat.[39]

By the end of the fifth century BCE, the second meaning of *nomisma* as coinage was circulating widely in common language. But the older connotation was never fully displaced and could be exploited by witticisms. In Aristophanes's *Clouds*, for example, Strepsiades asks Socrates to teach him how to reason. In exchange he promises to pay any fee ("May the gods bear witness"). But Socrates replies that "the gods are not current [*nomisma*] with us." Strepsiades responds with confusion: "What do you swear by? Iron coins like in Byzantium?"[40] While Socrates puns on the broader meaning of *nomisma* as collective belief, Strepsiades takes it to be a literal reference to coinage. This double meaning comes out in numerous other places in Greek culture, including for example in relation to the Cynics, in particular Diogenes of Sinope, who was said to have received the Delphic maxim "*parakharattein to nomisma*": deface the currency, but also violate the customs.[41]

As a conventional institution, *nomisma* shared then not just a linguistic root but also the political ambition with the conventional law of the polis (*nomos*). Both operated in the triangle of custom, rule, and law. *Nomos* and *nomisma* were no longer immutably given by the gods, but instead were a subject of constant public debate in the assembly, the theater, and the agora. The way the Athenians related to currency was "strictly parallel to the way they used the laws," the classicist Sitta von Reden has observed.[42] *Nomisma* retained a connotation of collective political choice and conventionalism absent from the modern English "money," though partially preserved in the term "currency." As we will see, this connotation was central to Aristotle's conceptualization of the political promises of currency in analogy to law and speech.

Once we pay close attention to the actual Greek terms underlying Aristotle's discussion of reciprocity in the *Nicomachean Ethics*, the political dimension of his discussion of currency emerges. Arguing against the limitless pursuit of wealth, Aristotle usually spoke of *chrēmata*, material wealth, or *ploutos*, wealth in the abstract. When he concluded, for example, that "the love of honor and the love of wealth are the causes of most voluntary wrong-doings among human beings," the phrase "love of wealth" (*philochrēmatia*) is often misleadingly translated as "love of money" when it in fact stands for the love of all material wealth.[43] In his discussion of political justice and reciprocity, by contrast, the term Aristotle used was always *nomisma*, which designates not any kind of money but specifically coinage issued by the polis.[44] To be sure, as I will argue in the next section, *chrēmata* can certainly mean money, just as currency is a form of physical wealth. *Nomisma*'s association with the political community does not mean that it is immune from potentially tragic cycles of destructive insatiability.

The Two Sides of the Coin

Before I turn to Aristotle's account of reciprocal justice in the *Nicomachean Ethics*, it is important to anticipate an objection. Far from describing currency as a necessary political institution, in book 1 of the *Politics* Aristotle drew a link between currency and the excessive accumulation of wealth that threatens to corrupt both the individual and the city. In the same passage he conjectures that the need for *nomisma* seems to have first arisen out of foreign trade and that the art of accumulation appears to have come into existence as a result of the invention of *nomisma*.[45] When Joseph Schumpeter described Aristotle as a proto–commodity theorist of money, this was the passage he pointed to.[46] Aristotle's seeming emphasis on the link between commerce and currency moreover associates money with wealth accumulation. As he explained, "That is why it seems that the craft of wealth acquisition [*chrēmatistikē*] is most of all concerned with *nomisma*, and that its function is to be able to get a theoretical grasp of the sources from which a quantity of wealth will come. . . . For wealth is often assumed to be a quantity of *nomisma*."[47] Unsurprisingly, this has often been read as a critique of money tout court. But note, to begin with, that Aristotle used indirect speech ("it seems [*dokei*]") when introducing the idea of wealth-getting as dealing specifically with *nomisma*. Furthermore, to illustrate that he was merely passing on a widespread opinion—not his own—he immediately contrasted this first view with a second one: "But sometimes, contrariwise, *nomisma* is also held to be nonsense and wholly conventional, not natural at all."[48] Characteristically, having presented two common views, Aristotle went on to partially reject and vindicate both. First, while *nomisma* was conventional in origin, its uses need not be contrary to nature and ought to remain linked to natural use. Second, while currency was entangled in unnatural wealth accumulation, its just use pointed in a radically different direction.

Aristotle himself offered a clue as to the origin of the confusion. As he explained in the *Politics*, those who tended to link *nomisma* to the art of wealth accumulation raised an important point, but the link was not a direct one, nor could it be collapsed into one of necessity. Instead, it was a complicatedly contingent one. "This kind of exchange is not contrary to nature, nor is it any kind of wealth acquisition; for its purpose was to fill a lack in a natural self-sufficiency. Nonetheless, wealth acquisition arose out of it, and in an intelligible manner."[49] Part of the problem seems to be Aristotle's shifting definition. In the passage he used the same word (*chrēmatistikē*) to denote both a genus and a particular species within it. Initially, he proposed the term for both natural and unnatural exchange, but he then narrowed it down to the unnatural accumulation of wealth for its own sake.[50]

It is nonetheless a confusion to think that the art of wealth accumulation "deals specially" with currency. Instead, as von Reden has stressed, "the idea that money is a danger to political exchange rests on a tradition which associated the acquisition of *chrēmata* (not money) with the violation of the political order."[51] Wealth (*chrēmata*) might very well consist of currency and trade will often, though not inevitably, be conducted in currency. But this does not mean that currency and the art of wealth accumulation can be collapsed into each other. Some of the best commentators have been tempted into such a conflation that threatens to obscure Aristotle's very point about the ambivalence of money. Karl Polanyi, for example, hailed Aristotle's critique of wealth accumulation as "probably the most prophetic pointer ever made in the realm of the social sciences" but then translated *chrēmatistikē* as "*money*-making."[52] Instead of distinguishing more sharply between wealth and money, Polanyi concluded that "the genius of commonsense . . . failed to see how impracticable it was to ignore the existence of markets."[53] The ambivalent account of wealth and currency Aristotle had in mind was thereby obscured.

Importantly, Aristotle never directly blamed *nomisma* for the corruption associated with unmoderated desires. Instead, what mattered was the purpose to which currency was put. Did it serve the satisfaction of needs or the excessive accumulation of wealth? Aristotle structured his critique of unnatural wealth accumulation (*chrēmatistikē*) around an investigation of the psychological and ethical pitfalls of striving for material wealth (*chrēmata*) for its own sake. An excessive enchantment with wealth and a tendency to chase the fleeting promises of limitless gratification were moral and psychological failures that resulted from a badly habituated character prey to excessive desires.[54] Even Aristotle's critique of wealth accumulation differed thus crucially from early modern narratives, so familiar not least from John Locke, that firmly pivot around the invention of money as a moment of fateful corruption.

To conceptually disentangle money from unnatural wealth accumulation, we can instead build on the linguistic distinction between currency and wealth, a distinction not unique to Aristotle but found in many ancient texts. The Athenian visitor in Plato's *Laws*, for example, voiced his worry about the accumulation of wealth (*chrēmatōn*), not currency (*nomisma*).[55] The guardians in the *Republic* are banned from handling any precious metals, but the citizens of Kallipolis rely on currency (*nomisma*) as an institution essential for civic coexistence.[56] Even the city of utmost necessity—so basic that Glaucon considered it at best fit for pigs—was said by Socrates to already use currency (*nomisma*) as a token for exchange.[57] The first city's feverish path to ruin was thus not linked to the introduction of money but instead to the perverted use to which money was put once nonnecessary desires took hold. Indeed, as Solon already suggested, the excessive and insatiable desire for material riches predates the invention of coinage.[58] Translating both *nomisma* and *chrēmata* as "money" elides the conceptual distinction between currency and wealth, and ultimately obscures Aristotle's argument.

It is at the same time futile to attempt to fully disentangle the two concepts. Currency is after all itself a form of wealth and Aristotle defined *chrēmata* as "anything whose worth can be measured by *nomisma*."[59] From this perspective, any conceptual delineation between the accumulation of wealth (*chrēmata*) and currency (*nomisma*) begins to look like a distinction without a difference.[60] Instead, *nomisma* contains in itself the tension between reciprocal justice and the unnatural accumulation of wealth. Insofar as currency is a form of material wealth, it is a potential tool of acquisitiveness. The use of money appears to involve from this perspective an act of abstraction that risks corrupting the satisfaction of our genuine needs by instead fueling excessive wants.[61] I will return in a moment to the paradoxical, and potentially tragic, status of *nomisma* as an instrument of both justice and accumulation. Let me state for now that recovering the political significance of currency does not do away with Aristotle's influential critique of wealth accumulation, which also partially incriminates currency. But nor does acknowledging the possibility of corruption obviate the need to recover the lost argument of currency as a tool of political justice.

Reciprocity and Equality

We can now turn to Aristotle's account of the positive uses of money. The concept of reciprocity lies at the heart of his treatment of political justice in book 5 of the *Nicomachean Ethics*, but the relationship between reciprocity and justice has nonetheless often perplexed readers. Aristotle distinguished between two kinds of justice that establish and maintain relations of equality among citizens concerning external goods: distributive and corrective justice. Distributive justice is concerned with the distribution of honor, wealth (*chrēmatōn*), and "anything else that can be divided among members of a community who share in a political system."[62] Corrective justice relates to the "corrective principle in transactions" and can apply in different ways to voluntary or involuntary transactions. Some have consequently argued that reciprocity is simply that part of corrective justice that has to do with voluntary actions.[63] Others have by contrast detected in the turn to reciprocity the introduction of a third and distinct kind of justice: perhaps a more primitive form;[64] a separate ethical account of fair exchange;[65] or even an awkward early theory of exchange value.[66] Read as such, the passage has left interpreters deeply frustrated.

But far from being a protoeconomic digression, reciprocity is central to the account of political justice.[67] When turning to reciprocity in book 5, chapter 5 of the *Nicomachean Ethics*, Aristotle first brought up a view associated with the Pythagoreans: "Some people think reciprocity [*to antipeponthos*] is just without qualification [*haplōs dikaion*]."[68] This is sometimes interpreted as "Simple reciprocity is justice," suggesting that the Pythagoreans regarded justice as a simple kind of reciprocity. Others, more plausibly, have interpreted it as "reciprocity is simply justice," suggesting that the Pythagoreans took justice to be exhausted by reciprocity.[69] Part of this may even reflect an intentional ambiguity, for Aristotle went on to reject both interpretations while making room for a new notion of proportional reciprocity or, more literally, reciprocity by analogy. The Greek term Aristotle employed for his discussion of reciprocity, *to antipeponthos*, typically connoted the negative reciprocity of retribution.[70] But

Aristotle stressed that the kind of reciprocity he had in mind was not the simple reciprocity of retribution. Instead, it was a more complex form of reciprocity according to analogy.[71] This use of the term had a geometric connotation and one of the ancient texts to employ it not as retribution was Euclid's *Elements*.[72]

There is a way to respect Aristotle's classification of two kinds of particular justice while restoring the centrality of reciprocity. Instead of seeing the turn to reciprocity as a digression or a third kind of particular justice, it constitutes a shift of perspective.[73] Aristotelian reciprocity emerges not as a separate kind of justice but as a fundamental aspect of all political justice made visible by a shift in perspective.[74] As Aristotle declared, "In communities of exchange, this way of being just, reciprocity based on analogy not equality, holds people together [*sunekhei*]; for a polis is maintained [*summenei*] by doing things in return according to proportion [*tō antipoiein analogon*]."[75] While the polis does not exist for the sake of exchange, it is itself a community based on exchange and reciprocity is central to its maintenance.[76]

For Aristotle reciprocity had a material and specifically monetary dimension that deserves greater attention. A number of recent readers of Aristotle have persuasively begun to correct for the neglect of Aristotelian reciprocity.[77] This chapter builds on them and extends their account to currency. "Most contemporary legal and political philosophers," laments Jill Frank, "neglect his account of reciprocal justice entirely and few Aristotle scholars take it very seriously. . . . That is unfortunate, for . . . Aristotle's expectations of reciprocal justice are high."[78] Danielle Allen has similarly placed reciprocity at the center of her reading of Aristotle, arguing that Aristotelian citizenship revolves around "a developed discourse of reciprocity."[79] To find likeness in difference and to compare like to unlike, reciprocal justice requires elaborate tools of analogy.[80] The civic use of speech is a crucial Aristotelian tool for affirming relations of civic equality among citizens. But currency also serves as an analogous tool of reciprocity.

To appreciate the wider political significance of monetary reciprocity, it is necessary to read *nomisma* in light of Aristotle's account of political justice that forms its immediate textual context. Political justice, Aristotle explained, "belongs to those who share in common a life aimed at self-sufficiency, who are free [*eleutherōn*] and equal [*isōn*] either proportionately [*kat' analogian*] or arithmetically [*kat' arithmon*]."[81] While household justice is based on hierarchy, political justice rests on an attempt to reconcile difference with civic equality and shared mutuality.

Law (*nomos*) exists consequently only among those "who have equality in ruling and being ruled."[82] As Allen notes, Aristotelian political justice is thus itself an example of comparing incommensurables and discovering similitude in difference.[83] "The just [*to dikaion*]," Aristotle tells us, "is some kind of analogy [*analogon*]."[84] Reciprocity requires comparison and comparison requires commensurability. If things and people are by nature different, as they are for Aristotle, their differences need to be bridged in order to allow for reciprocity. This is where analogy enters as a method of discovering likeness in difference. Like reciprocity, the concept of analogy is mathematical in origin and it enables Aristotle to reason that A is to B as C is to D.[85] In the *Poetics*, analogy structures his conceptualization of metaphor as itself an act of exchange.[86] In his biology, it allows him to conclude that feathers are to a bird as scales are to a fish.[87] Reasoning by analogy means making two terms commensurate by bridging their difference without erasing it.

Commensurability is in this sense required for exchange. Aristotle considers two possibilities. "In truth," he pointed out, "the measure is use [*chreia*]."[88] If you happen to need what I offer and I need what you offer, our respective uses are commensurable. But we can hardly count on this coincidence, especially not in political communities. More often than not our uses will not be perfectly compatible. What we need is a tool that can achieve commensurability on a higher plane. "Currency [*nomisma*] came along to do exactly this, and in a way it becomes an intermediate, since it measures all things [*panta gar metrei*], and so measures excess and deficiency."[89] As Aristotle explained, "By convention *nomisma* has come to serve as a pledge for use [*chreia*]. And this is why *nomisma* is called *nomisma*, because it exists not by nature but by the current law [*nomos*], and it is within our power to alter it and to make it useless."[90] Currency is a conventional stand-in for use that enables exchange. It achieves commensurability not "in truth" but "by stipulation."[91] While this tied currency to use, its role as a mere proxy of use at the same time contained a potential for abuse that always threatens to remove currency from proper use.

Aristotle defined both speech and currency then as tools of analogy that can bridge difference. Reciprocal justice, according to him, functioned through acts of symbolic, civic, and material analogy conducted via currency. Specifically, according to Aristotle, currency could enable three political functions. First, it served as a powerful medium of civic commensurability to equalize citizens. Currency introduced new habitual bonds of reciprocity among citizens who had left behind the close-knit familial communities of the archaic world and now encountered each other as strangers in the polis. Second, money coined by the polis asserted the authority of the community over questions of value and justice. By denoting legal fines in the city's currency, paying a monetary compensation to those attending the law courts and the assembly, as well as awarding coins to celebrated poets and athletes, currency acted as a constitutive medium of the Athenian polis through which a civic bond was sustained, injustice assessed, and equity dispensed. Currency is in this sense a measure of political justice through which distributive and corrective justice are assessed and administered. Third, currency could enable a range of activities that helped to cultivate virtues of citizenship, practical wisdom, and deliberation. As such, for Aristotle currency was a necessary political institution—even where it was insufficient by itself.

Aristotle's account of monetary reciprocity at the same time hinted at a complex conception of equality. *Nomisma*, he summarized, "makes things commensurate [*summetros*] as a measure does, and equates them [*isazō*]; for there would be no association without exchange, no exchange without equality [*isotēs*], no equality without commensuration [*summetria*]."[92] While commentators agree that acts of exchange were, as described by Aristotle, in some sense exchanges between equals, they disagree on the precise logic of equalization.[93] Indeed, Aristotle's oscillating references to equality and difference—what the philosopher Gregory Vlastos once called his "acrobatic linguistic posture"—have often frustrated commentators.[94] Yet, if we understand equality (*to ison*) here not as arithmetic equality but as proportional or fair equality, a first share of the puzzle disappears. Once we conceive of political justice as aiming to achieve or preserve a status of fair equality, it becomes clear why Aristotle repeatedly describes justice as a form of analogy and a kind of mean. "Doing justice," he wrote, "is intermediate between doing injustice and suffering injustice, since doing injustice is having too much and suffering injustice is having too little."[95] Aristotle evidently conceived of political justice as a state of balance. As he put it, "Since equality [*to ison*] is a mean [*meson*], the just [*to dikaion*] is some sort of mean [*meson*]."[96] But to find that mean, excesses and insufficiencies have to be measured and currency is one such measure.

Commentators have similarly wondered about Aristotle's claim that in making goods commensurable, currency also equalized the parties of exchange. Some have, for example, forcefully argued that the parties of exchange are equal from the outset and therefore do not need to be equalized.[97] But Aristotle suggested that monetary exchange also affirms conventional relations of equality between the parties of exchange. "The relation between the people will be the same as the relation between the things involved."⁹⁸ This does not mean, however, that currency always introduces arithmetic equality. Instead, as we saw, reciprocal exchange is based on proportional equality. The terms of political justice, furthermore, did not reflect universal rules but varied by regime, as did systems of measurement and currencies.⁹⁹ Different regimes assigned different worth (*axia*) to their citizens. In an aristocracy, for example, some had greater worth than others, whereas in a democracy all citizens were free and equal.¹⁰⁰ In our context this means that the terms of monetary exchange reflect the relative social standing of the parties involved. This seems puzzling to modern ears since monetary exchange and prices are usually thought to reflect only demand and supply, not the worth or honor of the parties of exchange. But there was nothing in ancient monetary exchange that would rule out differential terms of exchange.

Aristotle encoded such social relativity—the importance of social standing—in his discussion of friendship (*philia*), by which, though conventionally translated as friendship, he meant social relations more broadly. He described political friendship as the bond (*sunekhein*) of the polis in terms that explicitly echoed his account of reciprocity.¹⁰¹ One of the hallmarks of such political friendships was their reliance on monetary reciprocity.¹⁰² This helps to shed light on the above question of unequal equalization. For in friendships among unequals, the terms of exchange involve both money and honor.¹⁰³ The superior party will receive less (or give more) in monetary terms to reflect their greater worth; that loss will be made up in honor. "Friendship must be equalized [*anisasai*] and analogy [*analogon*] secured by some other means," he explained, "and this means is honor."¹⁰⁴ Aristotle described this reciprocal equalization here as a "diagonal conjunction [*diametron suzeuxis*]," the exact expression he used in the *Nicomachean Ethics* to describe the relation between farmer and physician. In the special case of two parties with equal standing— for example, two citizens in a democracy—proportional equality collapses into arithmetic equality. But in the case of exchange among unequals, monetary exchange will reflect such differences. What was fair in terms of reciprocal justice thus depended on the kind of regime and the standing of the parties of exchange.

Currency also contained a surprising moment of ethical deliberation. We might not expect deliberation (*bouleusis*), moral choice (*prohairesis*), and practical wisdom (*phronesis*) in acts of monetary exchange. But, according to Aristotle, monetary exchange, if approached correctly, could practice an element of deliberation and judgment about what is just and what constitutes just use.¹⁰⁵ Reining in unmoderated desires (*pleonexia*) was of course primarily a question of a well-habituated character and a virtuous disposition. But in Aristotle's account, virtue required actions formed in patterns of habituation, and such virtuous habits required in turn a political frame. The purpose of the polis was precisely to enable a virtuous life based on proper habituation. Currency was one such institution that, when used correctly, could support virtuous activities and help cultivate both deliberation and judgment. It was, however, precisely because of this moment of ethical deliberation that monetary exchange can also fail to be just.

❧

The centrality of coinage, with its flaws and its possibilities, was prominently on display in Athens. Indeed, the polis with the most extensively attested and widely circulating coinage in the Greek world was democratic Athens, an inherently flawed regime from Aristotle's perspective. Once alerted to the political significance of currency, its central role in Athenian democracy—a deeply ambivalent role from Aristotle's perspective— becomes visible in a number of contexts.

In Athens, the public assessment of justice in the sense of excess and deficiency was closely tied to coinage. As far as we can tell, the redistribution of wealth from the rich to the poor seems to have been at least partially mediated by currency through the financing of public goods, festivities, and communal feasts—including the one famously alluded to in book 3 of the *Politics*.[106] Taxes for public festivals and the fleet were usually raised in coin and came in addition to the property tax (*eisphora*) levied on citizens above a certain level of property. Currency also partook in Athenian corrective justice. Ever since the Solonian introduction of legal fines, punishment and compensation were tied to the city's coinage.[107] Moreover, according to the pseudo-Aristotelian *Athenian Constitution*, which we witnessed Keynes reading in the preface, the introduction of monetary payments for attendance of the assembly and especially the jury courts was an important part of the shift from aristocratic to democratic values.[108] Among the institutions listed in the *Politics* as distinctly democratic in character, Aristotle mentioned "having pay provided, preferably for everyone, for the assembly, courts, and public offices."[109] Jury service was often referred to as "the *triobol*," after the three *obol* coins awarded for it.[110]

Coinage may even have acted as a tool for the spread of a specifically egalitarian political ideology. The classicist Leslie Kurke, for example, has described coinage as a tool for the spread of such an ideology. Coinage, Kurke writes,

> represents a tremendous threat to a stable hierarchy of aristocrats and others, in which the aristocrats maintain a monopoly on precious metals and other prestige goods. With the introduction of coinage looms the prospect of indiscriminate distribution, exchange between strangers that subverts the ranked spheres of exchange-goods operative in a gift-exchange culture. . . . As stamped civic token, coinage challenges the naturalized claim to power of the aristocratic elite.[111]

The introduction of coinage paved the way for new forms of exchange between strangers that subverted previous hierarchies embedded in gift exchange.[112] As poleis issued currency, they asserted the city's authority over questions of exchange and value. As circulating symbols, the coins contributed to the collective imaginary of the polis. The ideology of reciprocity, which the classicist Paul Millett has described as the cement of classical Athenian society, was distinctly monetary.[113] The reciprocal ties between Athenian citizens were rooted in monetary exchange and patterns of monetary redistribution, and currency fulfilled an important role in those exchanges.[114] Currency, alongside rhetoric and law, preserved the abstract reciprocity on which the polis depended.[115] Aristotle was no doubt suspicious of many of these democratic uses of coinage, not least because they tended to conflate proportional and arithmetic equality. But these historical examples nonetheless provide an illustration for why he treated currency as a crucial tool of politics and placed such high hopes in it as a possible bond of reciprocity.

From the Best Regime to Democracy

Much of what I have said so far has consciously bracketed any distinction between Aristotle's ideal polity and actually existing regimes. Before turning to the tragic side of money, let me briefly deepen this aspect of the discussion by asking what role currency plays in the best regime and how Aristotle's account of currency relates specifically to Athenian democracy. According to book 7 of the *Politics*, there is one regime type that is by nature the best. Given its ethical ambivalence, would currency still be desirable, or even necessary, in this best city? As an institution that makes divergent needs compatible, currency will have some role in any city. The principle of reciprocity seems similarly as important for the best regime as it is for others. Even the best regime operates, for example, according to the principle that all who share in the constitution "share alike in ruling and being ruled in turn" based on the principle of proportional equality.[116] But Aristotle left no doubt that the best regime and those striving to live the truly best life would limit the importance of monetary relations. The use of money might be necessary to satisfy needs, but bonds of friendship would also be needed.[117] Reciprocity made citizenship possible but it had to be partially transcended to reach the truly best life.[118] In the best regime, friendships based on like-mindedness and a shared pursuit of the good (not mutual advantage) would complement political justice and political friendships.[119] This also seems to be reflected in Aristotle's orientation toward the realm of intellectual virtues in the concluding chapters of the *Nicomachean Ethics* and his turn toward psychological considerations in the final two books of the *Politics*.[120]

Aristotle was, however, also concerned with constitutions that had flaws but might nonetheless be second-best given certain limitations. Along these lines, the *Politics* also studied existing regimes and constitutions that were good but not ideal.[121] In his discussion of actually existing constitutions Aristotle isolated their positive characteristics, while stressing the importance of improving such regimes.[122] What was the role of currency in these unjust or imperfectly just communities? Admittedly, Aristotle never said about currency what he said about speech at the very beginning of the *Politics*, namely that sharing in speech about what is just or unjust makes the polis.[123] But as we have seen, he described reciprocity as the bond of cities, enabling commensurability and sustaining polities when used correctly. Given their inflamed desires and defective institutions, it was likely that certain flawed regimes would extensively use currency for unjust purposes. This produces a paradox. In the best regime, in which currency would function best because it was aligned with use and justice, citizens will likely rely least on it—though even in the best political community, currency will be required. In flawed regimes, by contrast, in which currency was most removed from use, citizens will likely rely on currency all the more but in unjust ways. Currency seems needed least when it functions best and used most when it functions worst.

Tragic Money

That money might fail to live up to its political promises was, then, always more than a theoretical possibility. To recover the ways in which ancient money was made politically and carried weighty political hopes does not imply that it succeeded in holding the city together. Emphasizing the

political promise of money as a tool of reciprocity and as a possible institution for ethical deliberation should not prevent us from appreciating
its paradoxical quality. Money's collective faith depends on communality,
and yet money often ends up being isolating. Money quantifies by assign-
ing specific numerical values, and yet it seems to have no limits. Currency
equalized previously hierarchical relationships, and yet it introduced its
own forms of inequality. It is this double-sided ambivalence of money—
suspended between vaunted hopes and disappointments—that partially
accounts for its tragic potential.[124]

Alongside any emphasis on monetary reciprocity as a tool of political
justice there always runs the violence of money. When Michel Foucault
turned to the ancient Greek invention of truth, law, and tragedy in his first
Collège de France lectures in 1970–71, he placed the emergence of coined
money at the heart of his account and stressed its underlying paradox.[125]
On the one hand, coinage served to undermine archaic relations of hierarchy and was constitutive of a new sense of the self and of equality. *Nomisma* enabled foundational acts of redistribution that would not have been
possible in kind. By repaying creditors, taxing wealth, and dispersing it to
the poor, the polis used coinage to stabilize social conflict. As such, coined
money prevented excessive wealth and excessive poverty. It enabled the
political community to measure, tax, and redistribute wealth, while allowing the poor to redeem their debts and engage in wage work. But precisely
because coined money acted as a pacifying instrument it created new
class alliances that not only transformed power but preserved hierarchies.
Money allowed for new patterns of distribution, yet it also limited social
demands and preserved property. While coinage imposed limits on wealth
and poverty, it ensured at the same time "the preservation of class domination."[126] Coinage acted as a substitute for violence that allowed the rich to
avoid major political upheaval and preserved the greater part of their land
and wealth.[127] As Foucault put it memorably, inscribed in the stamp was
a struggle for and around political power.[128]

Emphasizing *nomisma*'s possible role in serving reciprocal justice must
then not lead us to overlook the persistence of power, the inevitability of
losers, and the hidden violence of money. The double bind of money was a
recurring theme in Greek tragedy. Where the comedies teased their audience with portrayals of the self-defeating effects of wealth, several of the
tragedies explored the deep-seated ambivalence of money. In his *Antigone*,
for example, Sophocles portrayed Creon's ill-fated pursuit of a single all-
encompassing standard of value in the metaphorical language of currency
and exchange—a point noted with great delight by Marx.[129] Throughout

the *Oresteia*, the theme of retribution is subtly expressed by metaphors of monetary exchange and reciprocity that present blood vengeance in analogy to the commercial accumulation of wealth.[130] The Furies or Erinyes are similarly not only symbols of blood revenge but also act as collectors of the metaphorical debt Orestes has incurred by killing his mother.[131] Both revenge and acquisitiveness are presented as giving great satisfaction while threatening to undermine the ties of political justice among citizens.[132] As a result, when the jury acquits Orestes and bans the Erinyes from the heart of city, they are led to their new dwelling place at the margin of the city in the ceremonial red garments worn by the metic commercial traders during the Panathenaic festivals.[133] Ares, the god of war, who had earlier been introduced as a money changer is banned from the city entirely.[134] With the force of its conventional law, the city sought to tame both blood revenge and wealth accumulation by banning them from its midst. But as the ending of the *Oresteia* implied, this ban can never be complete, leaving the resolution open to a precarious balance that always threatens to undo itself and easily cuts against itself.

And yet unlike in tragedy, where protagonists are irreversibly compelled to self-destructive action, much of money's possible tragedy depends on the psychology of desire and the political framing we give money.[135] None of this is inevitable. In holding together money's simultaneous political potential and cognitive seduction, Aristotle thus suggested a path for harnessing the benefits of currency while limiting its use to the right kind of ends. We can see this most clearly by placing currency alongside law and speech as institutions that can either contribute to justice or fatally undermine it. Like the law, currency can encourage ethical deliberation and judgment. But it can also, like the law, be a vehicle of power and exploitation. Both the law (*nomos*) and currency (*nomisma*) are powerful civic standards that aim to control violence and exchange, and yet both can at the same time allow for class power to be preserved. In the wrong hands, currency and law are moreover powerful tools of tyrannical rule. Currency thus mirrors the larger tension of the polity between new forms of individual autonomy and the communal life of political justice.

What, if anything, can check currency from exceeding its limits and becoming a vehicle for the limitless pursuit of wealth that entrenches existing inequalities? Aristotle gestured toward one possible answer by emphasizing the role of institutions, which can remind citizens of the correct purpose of currency. Aristotle tied most activities of moral choice to the just political community and several related directly to the administration of money. He highlighted the offices of market regulation and the inspection of transactions as "first among the necessary offices" without which "a city-state cannot exist."[136] To ensure that exchange satisfies "each other's necessary needs," it was crucial to inspect and regulate it.[137] Monetary exchange was thus neither banned from Aristotle's polis nor presented as contrary to natural use. Instead, just exchange would involve money but, as Melissa Lane has succinctly observed, only a "limited supply of money necessary to live the good life."[138] Whereas wealth accumulation was limitless, *nomisma* could serve as "its limiting factor."[139]

Aristotle tellingly concluded his discussion of money in the *Politics* with a reference to Midas. "It would be absurd," he explained, "for something to count as wealth [*plouton*] if someone who has lots of it will perish of starvation, like Midas in the fable, when everything set before him turned to gold in answer to his own greedy prayer."[140] Confusing precious metal or coinage for actual wealth meant mistaking the means for the end. Despite being entangled in the confusions of wealth accumulation, the purpose of money was to act as an abstract stand-in for need (*chreia*) and, as such, serve as a measure of deficiency and excess in the just political community. Aristotle's invocation of Midas functioned in this context both as a reminder of the true purpose of money while acknowledging the potentially tragic consequences of insatiability. But Midas also takes us back all the way to the origin of Mediterranean coinage where we began. The electrum deposits in the river Pactolus in Lydia—the source, as we saw above, of the first minted coins in the Mediterranean world—were said to have been the mythical residues of King Midas having washed away his golden touch in its waters.

Conclusion

It was always easy to forget about the political side of money. Suspicion of monetary abstraction runs deep. Socrates's first line of defense in the *Apology* was after all not that he had been a good citizen but that he had never charged money for his teachings.[141] In Plato's *Republic* the guardians are emblematically banned from handling money altogether. Instead, they carry in their souls divine gold and silver that, unlike money, does not pollute their desires. "Many impious deeds," Socrates explains, "have been done for the sake of the currency of the multitude [*pollōn nomisma*], while theirs is untainted."[142] Currency, like democracy, reflected from this perspective the rule of corrupted desires. This line of thought inaugurated a tradition that sought to ban money from the political community and even contemplated its complete abolition.[143] Self-consciously following

Plato's lead, Thomas More's tale of *Utopia* (1516) culminated in an account of the transformative effect achieved by the abolition of money. According to Raphael Hythloday, More's fictional protagonist, the Utopian abolition of money amounted to nothing less than the end of all "fraud, theft, robbery, quarrels, brawls, altercations, seditions, murders, treasons, and poisonings." The very moment money goes, "so would fear, anxiety, worry, toil, and sleepless nights."[144] Invoking Plato, Hythloday appealed to his interlocutor, and thereby the reader, "Wherever you have private property and money is the measure of all things it is hardly ever possible for a commonwealth to be just or prosperous."[145] The tantalizing thought of abolishing money for good runs through the utopian tradition like a red thread. As Fredric Jameson has remarked, utopia *is* the abolition of money.[146]

What this familiar suspicion of money's abstraction and acquisitiveness obscures, however, is that ancient political thought also acknowledged currency as a central political institution. Ever since the introduction of coinage into the classical Greek world, citizens of poleis saw money as both a fraught vehicle of abstraction as well as an institution of societal value closely associated with the political community. Once this neglected side of money as political currency comes back into view, many familiar accounts of monetary suspicion appear as merely one side of an ambivalent Janus-faced account of money. Like coins themselves, the institution of political currency is two-sided. Alongside the well-known suspicion toward money, we can often find extensive acknowledgments of the political character of currency. In Plato's *Republic*, the citizens of Kallipolis are, for example, explicitly allowed to handle the city's currency.[147] Currency was an essential institution for coexistence in any city, and the spread of coinage formed the neglected background to Aristotle's account of reciprocity and exchange in the just polis.[148]

The Athenian politics of money left a lasting—if often misunderstood—imprint on subsequent monetary and political thought. Despite its neglect today, Aristotle's analysis of *nomisma* as a conventional token of reciprocal justice proved vastly influential. It represented the beginning of the study of money as an institution central to political rule. As Keynes recognized two millennia later, behind Athenian democracy there loomed another political innovation: currency issued by the polis. In modulated form, Aristotle's nominalist account of money profoundly shaped Roman law; it became a backbone of scholastic accounts of exchange and the just-price doctrine; and it played an important part in the ethical analysis of money in the Islamic Aristotelian tradition and its critique of usury.[149] The Aristotelian tradition bequeathed at the same time a crucial ambiguity. If money originated by "a kind of agreement among men," as Thomas Aquinas put it in the thirteenth century in his commentary on the *Nicomachean Ethics*, did this mean it was a conventional institution that belonged to the members of the political community or could the sovereign control the value of money at will?[150] More specifically, under what circumstances was it permissible to alter the value of money through debasements? A century after Aquinas, the French philosopher Nicolas Oresme posed this question starkly when he asked: Who owned the money—the sovereign or the people?[151]

While the nominalist account set out in the *Nicomachean Ethics*, with its repercussions of currency as a contested if ambiguous political institution, had long shaped conceptions of money, in the course of the seventeenth century the Aristotelian emphasis on money's conventionality and its associated political tasks was gradually eclipsed. Conjectural histories of money in the natural law tradition increasingly turned to the *Politics* instead and extrapolated an account of money as born out of commerce.[152] Where scholastic accounts had primarily drawn on the *Ethics*, eighteenth-century political economy grounded its discussion of money's origins not in the political community but in long-distance trade and economic accumulation. At the threshold of modernity, the long-standing recognition of money's conventional nature began to be displaced by new attempts to constrain the ability of sovereigns to engage in discretionary interventions. Tying the hands of the sovereign provided an effective check on devaluations, but it also meant a gradual loss of awareness of money as a lawlike institution that should live up to expectations of justice. Rather than translating into an embrace of money as a tool of emancipation and collective agency, modernity brought new forms of monetary self-binding. The result was a politics of monetary depoliticization that I trace in the next chapter on John Locke.

And yet Aristotle's account of *nomisma* as a political institution of reciprocity and justice forms part of our genealogy of modern money. We can detect the traces of Aristotle's positive argument alongside the more familiar suspicion of money. Consider the unlikely example of Jean-Jacques Rousseau, whose critique of money's moral and civic corruption has become paradigmatic. As Rousseau lamented in his *First Discourse*, "With money, one has everything, except morals and citizens."[153] "Give money," he put it in the *Social Contract*, "and soon you will have chains."[154]

But in describing Emile's curriculum, Rousseau also outlined the political face of money and acknowledged the foundational character of currency as a bond of society in words that directly echoed Aristotle's argument in the *Nicomachean Ethics* and that contain this chapter's epigraph:

> No society can exist without exchange, no exchange without a common measure and no common measure without equality. Thus all society has as its first law some conventional equality, whether of men or of things. . . . Conventional equality among things prompted the invention of money, for money is only a term of comparison for the value of things of different kinds, and in this sense money is the true bond of society [*le vrai lien de la société*].[155]

As Rousseau immediately added, this positive side had of course since been overshadowed by money's adverse moral effects, originating in its potential for abuse and confusion. But according to his account in *Emile*, in order to understand money's deleterious effects one first had to grasp its intended positive function as a bond of society and a token of conventional equality.[156] Recovering the political centrality of currency should not lead us to sidestep the fact that Rousseau's ultimate verdict was that money's overwhelming effect was not as a bond of society but as an instrument of corruption. Just as Rousseau's paraphrasing of the Aristotelian hope for money in *Emile* was meant to illustrate its subsequent failure all the more starkly, measuring the gap between ideal and real is worthwhile in itself and provides orientation for restoring a fuller appreciation of money with all its ambiguities. Despite its vast historical distance from us, Aristotle's account of political currency constitutes the silent sedimentary layer of our genealogy of money.

Recovering the political aspirations once placed in money, even where these were disappointed, reminds us that money can never be fully removed from the quest for justice. This is not because we can return to Aristotle or because his argument somehow shows us the way forward. Rather, we begin our genealogical journey with Aristotle precisely because he seems most removed from us today. His positive argument for currency as a conventional political institution has largely disappeared from view, even though subsequent modern arguments all engaged with him in one way or another as interlocutor and foil. In order to appreciate these modern responses to Aristotle, we need to be able to ground them in the lost conventionality of money that once defined its latent possibilities. It might nonetheless seem perverse to recover across such a vast distance in time an idea that seemingly failed. But as Albert Hirschman put it in his

perceptive intellectual history of the eighteenth-century origins of capitalism, while we should surely study triumphant ideas that shaped our world,
we can learn as much, perhaps more, from recovering ideas that failed.[157]
Indeed, obscured and buried by their seeming failure, these intended but
unrealized ideas stand in much greater need of being made visible again.
Precisely because their once hoped-for result had refused to come into the
world, Hirschman explained, "the fact that they were originally counted
on is likely to be not only forgotten but actively repressed."[158]

CHAPTER TWO

The Modern
Depoliticization of Money

JOHN LOCKE AND THE GREAT
RECOINAGE OF 1696

Till you writ, we used money as the Indians do their wampompeek.

—WILLIAM MOLYNEUX TO JOHN LOCKE, JUNE 1696[1]

THE SITUATION SEEMED DESPERATE AND DIRE. In the wake of the Glorious Revolution of 1688, the English state found itself in a near-permanent state of crisis. It was engaged in an intense war against France that stretched from the Rhineland to the Hudson Bay. At home, loyalty to the new king could not be taken for granted, and rumors of rebellion constantly roiled the polity.[2] Meanwhile a deeply entrenched monetary crisis haunted the realm. The amount and quality of circulating silver coins had been deteriorating for years, indeed for decades as silver discoveries in the Americas had dried up. But by the mid-1690s the shortage of silver reached unprecedented levels. In response, the practice of coin clipping had taken on ever-larger proportions, whereby the edges of coins were shaved off or clipped off and the silver sold for profit while the coins were returned into circulation at their face value (see figs. 2.1 and 2.2).

By 1695 English coins in circulation lacked more than half of their original silver content.[3] What was a nuisance at first had come to pose a serious threat to the trust and legitimacy of English money. All agreed that the whole monetary system soon threatened to come to a grinding halt, cutting off the military and bringing down the new government with it.[4] "The Business of our Money," recalled John Locke (1632–1704), "has so near

FIGURE 2.1: Unclipped (almost) silver shilling coined during the reign of Charles I (Nicholas Briot's second milled issue, coined 1638–39). The XII refers to the twelve pence that make up one shilling. Photo: Courtesy of Spink.

brought us to Ruin that . . . it was every Body's Talk, every Body's Uneasiness."[5] Blame fell variously on villainous clippers, conspiratorial counterfeiters, or the government itself, but all could agree that the currency had suffered such severe damage that the fate of the country itself was at stake.[6] The man on whom the fate of the nation would come to depend—at least in his own estimation and that of subsequent generations—was Locke himself. Notoriously anxious to guard his authorial anonymity, during his lifetime Locke published only three texts in his name. The first two were his *Essay Concerning Human Understanding* (1690) and his *Thoughts Concerning Education* (1693).[7] The third owed its existence to the altogether more unforeseen and politically charged circumstances of the Coinage Crisis. At the height of the crisis, in December 1695, Locke published a pamphlet calling for a full recoinage at the old value, hoping to sway public opinion and the concurrent deliberations in Parliament.

A year before, in January 1695, when the House of Commons had appointed a committee to consider the matter of coinage, Locke had sought to influence the debate by anonymously publishing an earlier pamphlet on the matter.[8] In the course of 1695 matters deteriorated substantially. As the Lords Justices began to seek expert advice, Locke, alongside Isaac Newton, Christopher Wren, and Charles Davenant, was asked to submit a proposal.[9] The debate dragged on for several more months but when it transpired in late November 1695 that the government might not heed his advice for full revaluation at the old rate, Locke broke with his self-imposed anonymity in order to throw in his lot and good reputation for the cause. He rushed *Further Considerations concerning Raising the*

FIGURE 2.2: Heavily clipped and pierced silver shilling of Charles I
(Tower Mint, 1641–43). According to Locke's proposal for the recoinage
of 1696, owners of clipped coins were to be compensated based only on
weight rather than the face value of the coins, implying heavy losses.
Photo: Courtesy of Civitas Galleries.

Value of Money to the printer with his name prominent on the title page.[10]
It appeared on December 27, 1695, riddled with errata that testified to the
great haste under which it was printed. In the end, to the surprise of many,
Locke's radical proposal won out against plans for a devaluation. In the
summer of 1696 the government instituted a wholesale recoinage at the
Elizabethan old rate, just as Locke had demanded.[11] It was an exercise of
enormous scale, the first full recoinage since 1299.

Despite Locke's towering presence in liberal political thought today, political theorists rarely engage with his monetary writings.[12] But money was a
linchpin of Locke's political philosophy. Throughout his works, his prose is
consciously saturated with monetary metaphors. Money, as is well-known,
plays a transformative role in his history of property and civil society in the
Second Treatise. Locke's monetary thought in many ways determined
his approach to politics, and reconsidering his writings on the subject allows
in turn a reevaluation of his political thought. But for his contemporaries it was Locke's advice during the postrevolutionary Coinage Crisis
of 1695 that, more than anything else, sealed his reputation and that most
immediately affected their lives.[13]

Locke's argument set a precedent. His contemporaries and many
subsequent generations hailed the coinage writings as his seminal contribution to the art of statecraft. Up until his liberal refashioning in the twentieth century, Locke was remembered in the Whig tradition primarily as

an epistemologist and a monetary thinker.[14] Scottish political economists, Whig politicians, and nineteenth-century liberals all celebrated Locke as the patron saint of "sound money." His insistence on coins' fixed metal content and the resultant protection of creditors was read as having paved the way for the Financial Revolution and Britain's rise as a world power.[15] Locke's nineteenth-century biographer Lord King (himself a man with decided views on currency) emphasized the significance of Locke's monetary thought, crediting him with saving the country from impending ruin by restoring the monetary standard.[16] In his *History of England*, Thomas Macaulay similarly praised Locke's writings on currency, remarking that "it may be doubted whether in any of his writings, even in those ingenious and deeply meditated chapters on language which form perhaps the most valuable part of the *Essay on the Human Understanding*, the force of his mind appears more conspicuously."[17] Karl Marx's choice to open volume 1 of *Capital* with a series of references to Locke's coinage pamphlets mirrored this influence.[18] The esteem of the coinage pamphlets was itself reflected in the very structure of Locke's collected works, which prominently included the coinage essays and afforded them a special place often ahead of the *Two Treatises of Government*.[19]

Yet if the coinage writings once held a special place in Locke's works, they always posed an interpretative puzzle. Locke's rise to the status of patron saint of political liberalism has only raised the stakes further. According to one influential reading, developed by the historian Joyce Appleby during another period of monetary turmoil in the 1970s, Locke constituted an early illustration of what Karl Polanyi had described in *The Great Transformation* as the commodification and naturalization of money.[20] Locke, Appleby argued, removed money from the realm of politics and rooted it instead in nature. From this perspective, Locke asserted the existence of certain natural laws of the market and thus foreshadowed economic liberalism. While Appleby presented Locke as a precursor of nineteenth-century invocations of natural economic laws, she simultaneously presented his position as a throwback. According to her, Locke simply "reasserted the bullionist position."[21] As a result, his argument was "circular and outdated."[22] While Appleby captured the depoliticizing effect of Lockeanism (on which more below), Locke's own position is both more intriguingly paradoxical and more political than this allowed.[23] Locke broke with the reigning precedent of nominalist monetary regimes in which the denomination was set by a sovereign fiat largely independent of coins' metal value. But he also differed from bullionist monetary regimes in which silver was simply stamped according to weight and quality.

Instead, coins' denominations were according to Locke based on particular quantities of metal that were set by fiat but then solidified over time until they were—paradoxically—declared beyond sovereign meddling. Rather than being a throwback, Locke's proposal broke with both earlier nominalist practices and the bullionist practice of pricing unstamped silver at market value. He espoused neither pure nominalism nor pure metallism but instead sought to erase the distinction between weight and unit. Locke did not simply invoke the market; instead he advanced a novel political theory of monetary depoliticization.

At the heart of the confusion surrounding Locke's politics of money stands his puzzling invocation of "intrinsick value." While Locke insisted in his coinage essays that money derives its "natural intrinsick value" from its metallic content, elsewhere he presented money as conventional and even tacitly consensual, having arisen out of the mutual agreement of mankind. Locke's monetary writings have thus often appeared, in the words of one scholar, as "an unaccountable turn to essentialism on the part of a theorist usually thought of as being comfortable with the notion that signs have conventional, rather than natural values."[24] This seeming contradiction actually hints at an important truth about Locke's politics of money. It was precisely the malleable conventionality of money that led Locke to advocate safeguarding the monetary contract by linking it to an initially arbitrary but then unalterable quantity of silver. Placing Locke's understanding of the shared semantic fragility of money and language in the context of his political thought restores the importance of trust for Locke and opens up a path toward dissolving the paradox of his politics of monetary depoliticization.

In the previous chapter, we explored Aristotle's foundational account of currency and his understanding of *nomisma* as a conventional tool of commensurability and civic reciprocity. Readers of Locke's monetary thought have often detected remnants and traces of this Aristotelian account.[25] Like Aristotle, Locke began from an emphasis on the conventional origins of money. But he derived from them a radically different argument and a novel political conclusion. Instead of considering currency a malleable tool of justice, Locke attempted to stabilize what he took to be a dangerous nominalist instability. As we will see, Locke thought that language and money shared a pervasive instability and corruptibility.[26] But money—unlike language—could be stabilized by tying it to the empirical concept of a substance in the form of silver or gold. This would remove money from discretionary political meddling, thereby effectively depoliticizing it.[27]

Locke's argument for the absolute sanctity of the monetary standard constituted a radical break in the way political thought had treated money. Despite its Aristotelian roots, it was filtered through the lens of seventeenth-century natural law debates that sought to preserve political stability at home while at the same time furthering colonial trade. In describing the monetary covenant as not congruous with the political one but predating it, Locke argued for a depoliticized metallist money of global reach that could ensure the stability of contracts at home and fuel colonial expansion and settlement overseas. Precisely because money was a tool for governing, Locke insisted, no government could meddle with it. Reconstructing this Lockean argument allows us to better understand the political framing of depoliticization that has been key to modern money and the debates surrounding it.

Excavating Locke's political philosophy of money along these lines thus reveals a far-reaching irony. Stabilizing money by linking it to an arbitrary but then unalterable quantity of metal required itself an act of sovereignty even while Locke insisted that no future sovereign ought to be allowed to meddle with the standard thus set. This means that what came to be seen as the naturalization of money originated, paradoxically, in an act of fiat that tied a specific quantity of metal to a certain denomination. Restoring the monetary contract did not imply a curtailment of sovereign power but rather its invocation in a peculiar way. As Polanyi famously quipped in a different context, "Laissez-faire was planned."[28] This act of intervention in the name of noninterventionism forced two distinct conceptions of money as measure and metal into coincidence. As a result, Locke ended up altering the very meaning of the word "money," as his friend, the Irish scientist and politician William Molyneux, observed in the peculiar line that serves as the epigraph for this chapter. Precisely because of the enormous sway of his intervention, money came to be disassociated from politics in the minds of observers and subsequent generations.[29] If the politics of money has been largely invisible in liberal political thought, we can trace one set of origins of this eclipse back to Locke.

Monetary Crisis

Far from ushering in a new age of stability, the Glorious Revolution produced a profound state of crisis. For much of the 1690s England was engaged in an intense war against France that extended from the Rhineland and the Low Countries as far as Madras in the east and the Hudson Bay in the west. At home, loyalty to the new king, William III, was similarly under threat, with constant rumors of Jacobite rebellion and counterrevolution. The turmoil was made worse by a deeply entrenched monetary crisis. The amount and quality of circulating silver coins had been deteriorating for years, but during the Nine Years' War (1688–97) the shortage of silver reached unprecedented levels and affected both everyday transactions and the public purse. Coin clipping, the most visible sign of the crisis, intensified dramatically. Although clipping had affected much of seventeenth-century English money, by the end of 1695 almost all coins in circulation were noticeably clipped and reduced in size, with sometimes as little as half of their original silver content left.[30] While coins with milled edges that could not be easily clipped had been introduced in 1662, these represented only a small share of the overall amount of coins.[31] Moreover, the unclipped milled coins rapidly disappeared from circulation and were either hoarded or sold abroad as bullion.[32] On one level clipping was an intelligible response to the shortage of silver, but by 1695 it had reached such extreme levels that it had introduced a sense of confusion and corruption, based on the large divergence between clipped coins' nominal and metal values.[33] The problem was thus an uneasy compound of two distinct but related problems. First, there was the pronounced shortage of silver, stemming from merchants' exports and from government expenses for troops abroad. Second, there was the uncertainty and confusion of clipping. As Macaulay put it later, "Nothing could be purchased without a dispute."[34] This constant state of confusion compounded the effects of the shortage of silver and threatened to bring the whole monetary system to a grinding halt.[35] If clipping could not be stopped, Locke's friend John Evelyn warned, "all Pacts and Covenants, Bargains, Obligations, Estates, Rents, Goods, Credit and Correspondences whatsoever (becoming dubious and uncertain) must sink and be at an end."[36]

It was the Nine Years' War that turned a troubling nuisance into an existential threat. The war pitted Louis XIV's expansionist plans against a broad European coalition of England, Austria, the Holy Roman Empire, the Dutch Republic, and Spain. But for postrevolutionary England the war had an even more existential political dimension and it quickly became a daunting undertaking. Not only was it the country's first major military involvement on the continent since the Hundred Years' War nearly four hundred years earlier, but—given France's active support of Jacobite forces and its preference for the restoration of the Stuart monarchy—it was also a war of succession over the future of the new political order in England.[37] By the mid-1690s, 80 percent of the public revenue of the English state went into the war effort. While maritime battles stretched the navy, much of the war on the continent was fought in slow land campaigns and protracted sieges that required standing armies in the field on a scale not seen before, not even during the Thirty Years' War earlier in the century.[38] The French army eventually counted more than four hundred thousand men.[39] One in seven adult English males served in the army during the war, on top of large numbers of foreign mercenaries.[40]

Such a resource-intensive war with a large standing army placed a heavy strain on the public finances and fundamentally altered the patterns and balance of trade. But above all, it "exposed the weaknesses of a chronically ill-functioning currency and credit system."[41] This is where the Coinage Crisis compounded an already difficult financial situation, which in turn intensified the monetary ills. Most of the revenue raised in taxes reached the Treasury in the form of underweight, clipped coins that had become, for practical purposes, the only coins in circulation. Meanwhile the troops abroad—and the resources necessary to feed, house, and clothe them—had to be paid in unclipped coins, few of which found their way back to England.[42] While taxes had to be raised at home, they were spent abroad. All fiscal and monetary resources were stretched and William's army in Flanders felt the resulting shortage of coins directly.[43]

Both the war effort and the fragile state of the public finances came to a head in the summer of 1695. King William had joined his troops on the continent in May, arriving in The Hague from Gravesend before taking personal command of more than fifty thousand troops in Flanders in June and besieging the fortress city of Namur, lost to the French in 1692.[44] But to support and sustain the siege the army's paymaster had to shuttle to Brussels to try to raise loans from local bankers. After months of negotiations overshadowed by the state of English finances, he eventually managed to extract 300,000 florins, and on September 5, 1695, Namur fell.[45] But the war was far from over. Indeed, William's paymaster judged the victory at Namur to have come at a cost that was hard to justify. As William declared to Parliament in November upon his return, unfortunately the funds that had already been given had proven "very deficient."[46] He directly linked these financial difficulties to "the ill State of the Coin."[47] This was a matter of such profound and general concern, "of so very great importance," that he asked Parliament to address the problem at last.[48] It was in this fraught context that Locke, as one voice among many, advanced his monetary proposal.

The crisis thus arose at the intersection of several distinct but related problems, including the pressures of war finance and the fact that the international price for silver exceeded its nominal value in England. Each aspect allowed for divergent interpretations and each provoked deep disagreement. While some argued that the intensity of the war meant that any remedy would have to wait, others insisted that it was precisely the precarious military situation that demanded swift action.[49] In the course of 1695 the Secretary to the Treasury, William Lowndes, was tasked with drafting an official response. In his report, which appeared in the fall of 1695, Lowndes proposed that the Treasury raise the nominal value of coins through a recoinage.[50] As Lowndes demonstrated (with extensive use of historical evidence), such sovereign adjustments were a long-standing practice. Up to the seventeenth century there had been nothing sacred about the metallic value of the unit; instead, successive devaluations through nominal adjustments had saved Europe from a perpetual fall of prices as the silver discoveries in the New World slowed down. As the legal historian of money Christine Desan has illustrated, the monetary nominalism undergirding such adjustments was a hallmark of English medieval and early modern monetary thought and practice.[51] In Lowndes's words, it was "a Policy constantly Practised in the mints of England . . . to Raise the Value of the Coin in its Extrinsick Denomination from time to time, as Exigence or Occasion required."[52] Raising the nominal value to bring the new price in line with the market price of silver, Lowndes promised, would immediately eliminate the disastrous gap between the price of silver and coins' nominal value and put an end to the profitability of clipping.[53] Locke could not have disagreed more strongly with this practice. He set out his views in detail in *Further Considerations concerning Raising the Value of Money*, which appeared in late December 1695.[54]

Locke's views were generally positively received among Whigs, though not universally so. His harshest critics on the coinage were Tories, ranging from Charles Davenant to Nicholas Barbon.[55] As Barbon explained, Locke's entire argument rested on the peculiar supposition that there was an "intrinsick value" in silver. If this notion "should not be true, then all his Consequences must be mistaken."[56] Instead of being intrinsic or derived from the tacit consent of mankind (two notions that, as we will see, converged in Locke's mind), Barbon insisted that "Money has its Value from the Authority of the Government, which makes it currant, and fixes the price of each piece of Metal."[57] Locke's worries about a devaluation were thus "imaginary Mischiefs." By contrast, "if the *Money* be not Rais'd," Barbon proclaimed, "the *Mischiefs* will be real, and Consequences very fatal to the Nation."[58]

Charles Davenant shared with Locke an appreciation of the constraints of foreign trade on the coinage. More than Locke, however, Davenant placed the Coinage Crisis as a result squarely in the context of trade imbalances and bullion outflows necessitated by war finance.[59] Addressing the shortage of coinage could not proceed by some easy fix but required an improvement in the balance of trade, which was almost impossible during wartime. "Trade and Money," Davenant explained in deploying a Hobbesian bodily metaphor, "are like Blood and Serum, who tho Different Juices, yet runn through the veins mingled together. And this present Corruption of our Coyn is like a dangerous Ulcer in the Body Politick which is never to be thoroughly Cured by applying Remedies to the Part, but by mending the whole Mass of Blood which is corrupted."[60] Also employing a similar set of medical metaphors, Christopher Wren concurred with Davenant: while the current "Consumption of the Mony (The Nerves of Warr) . . . requires a Speedy Consultation before the Disease be Fatal," the culprit was not clipping itself but instead the adverse balance of trade under conditions of war.[61] Davenant went even further. Clipping, he claimed, was not a harmful or corrupt practice but instead a perfectly rational and, indeed, welcome means for increasing the supply of money. Furthermore, heavily clipped coins, whose nominal value exceeded their metal value, were immune to being melted down and exported as silver.[62] This was as much a critique of Lowndes's proposal as it was of Locke's. At the same time, its conclusion of resigned futility rendered it profoundly unhelpful for a Parliament bent on fixing the state of the coin while committed to war.

While many of Locke's most formidable critics were affiliated in one way or another with the Tories, in his opposition to devaluation he also clashed with other Whigs. Like Lowndes, Locke's friend Isaac Newton, for example, favored a recoinage at a lower denomination.[63] If the goal was to end the ruinous export of coins as bullion by aligning the nominal value of money once more with its intrinsic value, Newton explained, "it seems more reasonable to Alter the extrinsick than the Intrinsick Value of Milled Money that is, to raise a Crown Piece to the Value of an Ounce of Bullion."[64] In his submission to the Lords Justices, Newton acknowledged as the only "reall objection" to his own position the worry that "the raising of Bullion and the Corruption of Our Coyn have mutually promoted one another."[65] Newton did not mention him here but it was a worry that would have resonated with Locke, who similarly derided the prospect of an official devaluation as an act of "public clipping."

Despite formidable opposition, Locke was not alone in insisting on the inviolability of the standard.[66] Besides his friends and acquaintances, many of whom had been decisively influenced by his argument, Locke could find vindication in the late William Petty, who had died in 1687.[67] Indeed, at the height of the campaign for recoinage, Locke helped to publish a previously privately circulating essay of Petty's from 1682.[68] Brief and aphoristic in style, Petty's *Quantulumcunque concerning Money* converged in a number of ways with Locke's own recommendations and it appeared in the fall of 1695 with the publisher that also printed Locke's own monetary pamphlets. Responding to a series of hypothetical questions, Petty insisted on the preservation and restoration of the Elizabethan standard and stressed the need to settle ancient debts at the ancient rate.[69] Although nowhere in his monetary pamphlets did Locke cite Petty directly, he was clearly familiar with Petty's arguments given his hand in publishing *Quantulumcunque* and the presence of Petty's works in his library.[70] A more surprising source of support emerged from the court of the new Bank of England that had been founded the previous year with Locke as one of its original subscribers. While Lowndes's devaluation plans did gather support from London bankers, the governor of the Bank of England—Sir John Houblou—in fact favored Locke's solution.[71] Traders might indeed benefit from devaluation, but Houblou pointed out that landlords and the landed gentry that backed the Whig regime stood to suffer most since they could not easily adjust their rents.[72] This offers a first glimpse at some of Locke's own implicit political motivations, but to appreciate his long-standing preoccupation with the political theory of money it is necessary to take a step back.

The Nature of Money

When Locke first dedicated himself to the study of money in the late 1660s, he had recently left Oxford and joined the household of Anthony Ashley Cooper, later the first Earl of Shaftesbury. In 1667 Locke had decided to leave Christ Church and enter Ashley's services, where he initially worked as a tutor and physician but was soon tasked with much broader responsibilities. Ashley was as influential as he was wealthy. At the time he was chancellor of the exchequer and since 1663 one of eight Lords Proprietors with title to what would become the Province of Carolina. It was in this context that Locke began advising Ashley on commercial and political matters, both domestically and concerning his venture in Carolina. Locke's emergent thinking on money and interest was shaped by this involvement with matters of trade and empire.

Little more than a year after having joined the household, Locke penned a memorandum to Ashley entitled "Some of the Consequences that are likely to follow upon Lessening of Interest to 4 Per Cent."[73] Locke was primarily concerned with critiquing demands for lowering the legal rate of interest from 6 to 4 percent—demands prominently supported by

Sir Josiah Child, whose pamphlet in favor of reduction was circulating widely.[74] The matter had also been put forward in a Commons bill that failed to find support. Locke's position on the question remained relatively uninfluential at the time, but it provides an important glimpse at his evolving monetary thought. Money, Locke explained, always has two roles: it is necessary as nominal "counters" for "even reconing," but it also acts as "pledge" or "security."[75] It achieves the former "by its stamp and Denomination" and the latter "by its intrinsick value which is noe thing else but its durableness, scarcity and not being apt to be counterfeited."[76] While domestically money may pass as counters or tokens, what mattered for foreign trade was money as a pledge. Locke's very framing of the question and his related focus on foreign trade betrayed his new involvement with commercial matters that the association with Ashley had opened up.

Only a few years earlier, still teaching at Oxford, this emphasis on foreign trade had been an alien world to Locke. In his *Two Tracts* manuscript from the early 1660s, coinage had appeared in a more conventional light. Drawing on the standard account expounded in medieval and early modern political commentary, Locke explained—in a characteristic monetary metaphor—that the authority to coin money was one of the "tokens of sovereignty."[77] Coinage had long been a sovereign prerogative and the rise of the early modern state had only furthered such claims.[78] The 1668 manuscript did not abandon this argument but it marked a first shift of emphasis. Coinage was still a sovereign prerogative but its administration was now severely curtailed by the necessities and pressures of overseas trade and the challenges of colonial administration. Navigation and commerce, Locke explained, had brought far-flung corners of the world into contact with each other, as well as with the use of gold and silver. This imposed strict limitations. "In a Country that hath Commerce with the rest of the world it is almost Impossible now, to have any Coyne, but of Gold and Silver, and haveing mony of that it is Impossible to have any standing unalterable measure of the value of things."[79] Overseas trade made it imperative to have money of gold or silver. But this meant in turn that it was increasingly difficult to maintain a stable measure of value domestically since the price of metal money would fluctuate with its international supply and demand. Not coincidentally, at the same time as Locke made his first serious foray into questions of money he was also tasked by Ashley with writing "The Fundamental Constitutions of Carolina" and preparing a new decimal currency for the colony based on the sterling penny.[80]

A decade later, at the height of the Exclusion Crisis as Whigs sought to bar James, Duke of York, from the succession in the early 1680s, Locke returned to these questions in his *Second Treatise*, trying to work out the role of money and property in his account of the emergence of civil society and the state. It was now in particular the work of Samuel Pufendorf, born the same year as Locke, which helped him to clarify his own position.[81] In Pufendorf's magisterial eight-volume *De Jure Naturae et Gentium* (1672), the German jurist and philosopher defended two familiar claims.[82] First, like Jean Bodin and Thomas Hobbes, he considered coinage to be a sovereign prerogative. Second, like Bodin and Locke himself, Pufendorf placed strict limits on the sovereign's right and ability to exercise this prerogative. It is worth quoting Pufendorf's account here at length:

> In states the sovereign has the right to establish the value of the currency [*nummi*]; hence it is usually stamped with official symbols. In establishing the value of the currency we must take notice of the common valuation of neighbouring nations or trading partners. For otherwise if a state puts too high a value on its currency [*nummis*] or if it does not mix the alloy properly, it will impede that part of its trade with its neighbours which cannot be conducted by simple exchange of goods. This is precisely the reason why a change in the value of the currency [*valore nummorum*] should not be made lightly, but only if required by a very severe crisis in the country.[83]

Commercial interdependence, in other words, heavily constrained interference with the currency and rendered an alteration of its value appropriate only as a crisis measure.

Following a detailed exposition of the scholastic distinction between use and exchange value, in *De Jure Naturae et Gentium* Pufendorf subsequently turned his attention to a speculative history of money.[84] The resulting narrative pivoted around the emergence of "luxurious desires" (*cupiditates*) that had led most nations to give up on their "primitive simplicity" and, no longer content with what was produced at home, develop a yearning for the delights of other climes.[85] The result, Pufendorf concluded, was that "it has seemed best to most nations, which have enjoyed a higher level of culture, to set by agreement [*conventione*] an *eminent* price on a particular thing, which would serve as a measure for the proper prices of other things, and in which they would be fully contained, so that by it as a medium a man could secure for himself anything that was for sale and carry on all commerce and fulfill every agreement [*contractus*] with perfect convenience."[86] In Pufendorf's conjectural history, money was born as a convention for the purpose of convenience to satisfy increasing material desires. Money was thus introduced only after the embrace of acquisitiveness. The introduction of money *followed* the loss of "primitive simplicity" and the associated rise of "luxurious desires." In support of his narrative, Pufendorf turned to book 1 of Aristotle's *Politics* (1257a32–41).[87] As we have already seen, this was of course not Aristotle's only discussion of money; in the *Nicomachean Ethics* he provided a more explicitly political account. Pufendorf did in fact go on to reproduce two short passages from book 5 of the *Nicomachean Ethics* (1133a26–32 and 1133b15–20) that emphasized the role of *nomisma* as a conventional measure of need that facilitates the formation of associations, but he left these excerpts uncommented.[88] Instead, he affirmed that when needs were simple, money was not yet necessary, but that with the growing complexity of desires the demand for money eventually arose. Since we cannot know in the present what we will want in the future, Pufendorf explained, *nomisma*—or money—was introduced as the means to secure our future wants.[89] The emergence of money allowed, in other words, for our newly expanded tastes to be satisfied as they changed over time.

In line with this emphasis on the invention of money for foreign trade based on luxurious desires (instead of the use of currency within political communities, implied by the *Nicomachean Ethics*), Pufendorf turned next to the importance of trade with other nations and the associated use of bullion.[90] What followed was a delicate balancing act between accounting for the conventionality of money (so heavily emphasized by Aristotle) while denying much of its practical relevance. The use of metal, Pufendorf acknowledged, was not natural but based on agreement. "Since this function of money [as metal] is not given it by any necessity arising from its nature, but by the imposition and agreement of men, . . . it is obvious that other materials can be and are used under stress of circumstances or by preference."[91] Leather, paper, and many other materials had for this reason at various times been used in cases of great necessity. But despite these theoretical possibilities, in normal times the material of choice was metal and foreign trade placed strict practical limits on its alterability.[92] For although the value of gold and silver was conventional and had sprung from the agreement of men, governments were not free to change it at will. Instead they were bound to uphold money's purpose of furthering commerce, not merely between citizens of the same state but also, as Pufendorf stressed, between those of different states.[93]

Locke read all this with great attention. He first closely studied Pufendorf's *De Jure Naturae et Gentium* in 1681 and the encounter left an indelible mark—not that he found himself entirely in agreement. Despite

Pufendorf's formative sway, in the *Second Treatise* Locke developed a twofold revision. First, where Pufendorf had argued that money was introduced as a result of mankind departing from its primitive simplicity, Locke reversed the chronology. Second, where Pufendorf had made room for the acquisition of property to be conducted based on either express consent or tacit consent by the parties of exchange, Locke narrowed this to a most tacit form of consent to the introduction of money, which he then furthermore took to imply consent to all the inequalities that followed.[94] According to Locke, there were thus two distinct prepolitical states. In the first, man cultivated nature through his labor in line with God's command but without yet having recourse to money.[95] This implied an imperative for cultivation but it also specified strict natural laws that constrained accumulation.

The introduction of money disrupted this first state of relative equality by circumventing natural law limitations, thus unshackling men's covetous desires and in turn introducing the need for a social contract to guard life and property. Locke summarized the tumultuous development in a memorably compressed passage in the *Second Treatise*.

> Men, at first, for the most part, contented themselves with what unassisted Nature offered to their Necessities: and though afterwards, in some parts of the World, (where the Increase of People and Stock, with the *Use of Money*), had made Land scarce, and so of some Value, the several *Communities* settled the Bounds of their distinct Territories, and by Laws within themselves regulated the Properties of the private Men of their Society, and so, *by Compact* and Agreement, *settled the Property* which Labour and Industry began.[96]

With the use of money came thus an increase in population that made land scarce and raised its value. In its wake followed material inequality, disorder, and dispute. "The invention of money," as the historian of political thought Istvan Hont summarized Locke's account, "broke all the natural limits of primitive society."[97] Through the invention of money, men were able to live up to God's command for the cultivation of the earth in hitherto unimaginable ways without violating God's simultaneous provisions.[98] The circumvention of the previous natural law constraints ushered mankind into an age of unheard-of riches, unequal possessions, and inevitable strife, which eventually produced the necessity for civil government.

This account of money deviated subtly but decisively from Pufendorf's treatment of property and consent in prepolitical society, and Locke's

[62] CHAPTER 2

deviation spoke directly to a pressing problem of colonial administration.[99] Money was, in Pufendorf's narrative, important but largely epiphenomenal. In Locke's account, money acquired by contrast a pivotal significance at the threshold of civilization. The absence of metal money was no longer just a sign of backwardness but its very cause.[100] From Locke's perspective, this placed the entire Americas in a prepolitical state before the rule of contract. Behind Locke's claim that "in the beginning all the World was *America*" stands thus not just a vague reference to the state of nature, but instead the idea that the Americas still lacked money—based on the mistaken idea that only precious metal could be money—and thus operated outside the realm of civil government.[101] In his account, Locke thus distinguished between three stages: first, a premonetary state of nature which he described as one of relative plenty and, because of strict natural law constraints, relative equality; second, after the introduction of money a brief transitional state of nature with money (what I call "the state of money"); and, finally, a state of civil society founded by political compact.

It is worth spelling out the colonial dimension of this argument. Focusing on this unstable intermediary state of metal money highlights Locke's narrowing of Pufendorf's account of consent for the acquisition of property.[102] For the acquisition of property in the commonwealth, Locke followed Pufendorf in insisting on express consent. "In land that is common in England, or any other country, where there is plenty of people under government, who have money and commerce, no one can enclose or appropriate any part without the consent of all his fellow-commoners."[103] For Locke property rights by cultivation could never override existing contractual relations under civil government.[104] But Locke's argument at the same time upended the nature of money and property in the state of nature. First, his emphasis on productivity and labor-mixing denied any prior Native American land rights. According to Locke, property in land in the Americas could be acquired based on labor mixing and it did not require any contractual consent by its previous indigenous owners. Second, where Pufendorf had left room for both tacit and express consent, Locke presented an account of the invention of metal money as rooted solely in a hypothetical tacit universal prepolitical consent of "mankind." The resulting argument has long perplexed commentators.[105]

> Since Gold and Silver, being little useful to the life of man in proportion to food, raiment, and carriages, has its *value* only from the consent of Men, . . . it is plain, that Men have agreed to a disproportionate

and unequal *Possession of the earth*, they having by a tacit and voluntary consent found out a way how a man may fairly possess more land
than he himself can use the product of, by receiving in exchange for
the overplus gold and silver, which may be hoarded up without injury
to any one; these metals not spoiling or decaying in the hands of the
possessor.[106]

Locke thus located the origin of money's conventionalism in an age before
the emergence of civil government while leaving open the question of
whether subsequent civil governments could alter the conventionality.
Money was neither merely private nor did it result from the explicit political covenant that founded civil government. Instead, as an artificial store
of value and labor to prevent spoilage, money was established by mere
"Fancy or Agreement" in an age before the formation of civil society.[107]

Crucially, this means that money is for Locke not natural. Monetary
riches are "none of nature's goods, they have but a fantastical imaginary
value: nature has put no such upon them."[108] Readings of Locke's monetary thought as an attempt at naturalization often acknowledge these
conventional origins of money in the *Second Treatise*, but they sidestep
the way in which Locke's argument hinged on money's in-betweenness as
a conventional institution that was nonetheless to be removed from political discretion. Far from money being natural, Locke pursued a political
strategy of depoliticizing the *appearance* of money by rooting its "intrinsick value" in the "common consent" of mankind that had selected precious metals to serve as money on account of their "fitnesse."[109] Locke's
analogies between money and language—and, crucially, the differences he
draws—shed light on the paradoxical notion of money's conventionality
and Locke's attempted naturalization of it.[110]

Linguistic Instability

In the *Essay Concerning Human Understanding*, Locke took up money's
artificiality by analogizing it to the malleability of language. Throughout
the *Essay*, Locke sought to accommodate the new natural sciences by
distinguishing the naming of natural objects and phenomena (which followed empirical laws) from the more malleable naming of ideas as "mixed
modes."[111] Mixed modes, he explained in book 3, are "voluntary Collections" of ideas, "assemblages of *Ideas* put together at the pleasure of the
Mind."[112] Not grounded in nature, they have no fixed interpretation but
are "very various and doubtful." As a result, Locke concluded, linguistic

ambiguity "hath invaded the great concernments of humane life and soci ety" and "brought confusion, disorder, and uncertainty into the affairs of mankind."[113] As the historian of political thought Hannah Dawson puts it in her work on Locke's philosophy of language, for Locke "words act more like a painting than a window."[114] If mixed modes are mental constructs that can and will vary substantially between and even within linguistic communities, any kind of linguistic exchange of ideas that was not merely based on observations about the natural world—thus, all of moral and political discourse and philosophy—was fraught with fragility and could potentially lead to confusion. Language was opaque; mixed modes were semantically malleable. Linguistic exchange, Locke implied, was unstable.

In contrast to Hobbes, who had appealed to sovereignty as the only way to solve the underlying coordination problem, Locke considered this semantic problem essentially impossible to solve. At best it could only be contained, and linguistic clarity was imperative for doing so. Words that failed to signify a unique idea or that signified no idea at all were to be avoided.[115] Furthermore, men were to take care to use words as closely as possible to the sense that common use had given to them.[116] "'Tis true," he explained, "*common Use*, that is the Rule of Propriety, may be supposed here to afford some aid, to settle the signification of Language; and it cannot be denied, but that in some measure it does. Common use *regulates the Meaning of Words* pretty well for common Conversation."[117] For philosophical discourse, however, the soft standards of common use were often insufficient. Common use was after all almost impervious to any intentional alteration, as might be required for philosophical clarification. This was a frustrating limitation for philosophers but a blessing for everyone else. For just as common use was largely resistant to interventions by philosophers, it was similarly impervious to the influence of abusers of words.

If the mentally constructed nature of mixed modes was responsible for a certain fragility of language, it also implied enormous difficulties for translating mixed-mode terms. The difficulties compounded when it came to the translation of complex ideas of mixed modes, such as measures of time, distance, and weight.[118] This posed particularly serious epistemological challenges to imperial rule and international trade, which Locke flagged repeatedly. "The terms of our Law," he argued, "which are not empty Sounds, will hardly find Words that answer them in the Spanish or Italian, no scanty Languages; much less, I think, could any one translate them into the *Caribee* or *Westoe* Tongues."[119] No more, Locke thought, could societies straightforwardly translate their respective measures of money—another mixed mode.

In the *Essay Concerning Human Understanding*, Locke introduced language as the "great Instrument and common Tye of Society."[120] It was, after all, only through the performative use of language that we were able to make promises and oaths to each other. Promises and covenants bound us together and committed us to each other; they constituted the true bonds (*vincula*) of our social existence.[121] This meant that language was based on consent in two distinct senses: an act of semantic consent that allowed for mixed modes to acquire meaning in the first place and a kind of moral consent not to abuse language.[122] The use of words also entailed a moral dimension that obliged us to speak the truth, refrain from abusing words, and not break promises. This moral command was a clear case of natural law and contravention constituted a violation of God's will. One significant conclusion Locke derived from this worry about the fragility and variability of language was the need to standardize English spelling, punctuation, and capitalization rules as much as possible—a linguistic reform he vigorously demanded and practiced.[123]

Money mirrored for Locke these anxieties about linguistic fragility. As a "mixed mode" in his philosophical system, with all this implied in terms of a proneness to abuse, money faced the same conundrum as language: "We must trust untrustworthy men," as Dawson puts it.[124] Money, Locke feared, risked in this light being little more than a precariously floating mixed mode with ill-defined patterns of common use and strong temptations for devious abuse. And such abuse ranged for Locke from clipping and counterfeiting all the way to the government itself "raising" the coin by reducing its silver content, that is, "devaluing" its money. Precisely because the idea of money resulted from "Fancy and Agreement" it was all the more important to somehow ground it. Money had to be stabilized and Locke proposed doing so in two ways. First, he insisted on tying money, like the mixed modes of moral concepts, to natural law and the divine intentions embodied therein. Locke's interest in oaths and his stern insistence on promise-keeping fell into this register. Second, and more importantly, Locke sought to stabilize the mixed mode of money by tying it to the substance of silver (or gold in the case of guineas). Substances, in contrast to mixed modes, "carry with them the supposition of some real Being, from which they are taken, and to which they are conformable."[125] Rooted in natural patterns that could be ascertained empirically, substances were not subject to the whims of linguistic construction.

> In our *Ideas* of Substances, we have not the liberty, as in mixed Modes, to frame what Combinations we think fit, to be the characteristical

Notes, to rank and denominate Things by. In these we must follow Nature, suit our complex *Ideas* to real Existences, and regulate the signification of their Names, by the Things themselves, if we will have our Names to be signs of them, and stand for them.[126]

Where mixed modes were made, substances were discovered. Only if linked to a metallic substance, whose weight and fineness could be empirically verified according to the natural sciences, could the fragile mixed mode of money serve as the stable bond of society across time, a crucial matter in postrevolutionary England.[127]

Money, like language, relies on fragile acts of semantic consent backed up by a moral imperative of honoring one's words. But unlike language, money's semantic fragility can be stabilized—and Locke insists it *must* be—by tying it to metal.[128] This was Locke's great hope. It was this complex argument that motivated his uncompromising insistence on money's "intrinsick value" that has so often puzzled commentators who saw in it a contradiction of Locke's simultaneous insistence on the conventional character of money and his emphasis on the tacit consent involved in its introduction. As Locke already pointed out in his early writings on interest, "intrinsick value" was not to be misunderstood as simply natural. Instead, it was "onely in the opinion of men consenting to it, yet being universall has generally but not allways . . . the same effect as if it were natural."[129] Philosophically, intrinsic value derived from the notion of near-universal tacit consent that had elevated gold and silver to the status of money. With money tied to metal, it was empirically possible to test whether a given substance was in fact the precious metal it pretended to be and if so, how much.[130]

Locke's comparison of money to language is helpful both for the similarities and differences it brings to the fore. Playful analogies on coins and words were of course a trope with a distinguished ancient pedigree. In the seventeenth century, however, these quips found themselves at the heart of a number of new philosophical systems.[131] What had long been a mere metaphor came to be taken literally. Pufendorf had already prepared his account of the origin of property and money by way of a long discussion of language and oaths. In book 4 of *De Iure*, Pufendorf made the link explicit. Quoting Sextus Empiricus, he pointed out that just as words had conventional local meanings associated with them, so coins had their conventional values.[132] This nominalism was a standard interpretation. But Sextus Empiricus's aphorism contained a further lesson. It not only portrayed money as a conventional institution that varied by country depending on whatever was "current," it also indicated the constraints of such a nominalism. Just as issuing one's own private money will most likely prove disappointing when attempting to get it accepted, failure to adhere to the common language use of the community similarly rendered one "a fool."[133] When presenting his own list of examples of linguistic abuse, Locke tellingly used a monetary metaphor when referring to "the school-men and metaphysicians" as "the great mint-masters" of linguistic confusion.[134] The abuse of language for purposes of obfuscation appeared from this perspective akin to the clipping and counterfeiting of coins.

The Recoinage of Trust

In February 1689 Locke returned to England from his Dutch exile. Once more questions of coinage were being widely discussed, and Locke immediately recognized that their resolution was essential for stabilizing the postrevolutionary order. He anonymously published a revised version of his earlier manuscript, opening it with a direct link between money and the politics of trust.[135] "Faith and Truth," Locke asserted, "especially in all Occasions of attesting it upon the solemn Appeal to Heaven by an Oath, is the great Bond of Society: This it becomes the Wisdom of Magistrates carefully to support, and render as sacred and awful in the Minds of the People as they can."[136] As a result, "It will always be worthy the Care and Consideration of Law-makers, to keep up the Opinion of an Oath High and Sacred, as it ought to be, in the Minds of the People."[137] This was a carefully considered statement implying a specific program of action.

In the context of the Coinage Crisis five years later, this stance formed the foundation of Locke's rejection of Lowndes's proposal for devaluation, which he considered a dangerous violation of a public pledge. For Locke, far from putting an end to clipping, devaluation would amount to an official sanctioning of the lower metal content that had become an unfortunate reality through clipping and forgery. By raising the nominal value of coins, the government would lower itself to the level of the clippers and undermine its trustworthiness by repeating on a large scale what it had previously condemned as fraud. Devaluation was nothing less than "a publick failure of Justice," arbitrarily giving one man's rights and possessions to another.[138] Lowndes's proposal thus amounted from Locke's perspective to a breaking of contracts and a violation of property that would weaken, if not totally destroy, public faith.[139]

Instead, Locke proposed that the government call in all the circulating currency and recoin it to affirm its official silver content as originally set

FIGURE 2.3: Silver shilling coined as part of the Great Recoinage during the reign of William III (first bust, 1696) (S. 3497, ESC 1104). The Great Recoinage restored coins to their old Elizabethan weight. Photo: Courtesy of Spink.

in Elizabethan times. For Locke, a pound sterling was and had to remain neither more nor less than three ounces, seventeen pennyweights, and ten grains of sterling silver—regardless, crucially, of the actual world market price for silver.[140] To be sure, this would produce fewer coins but it would restore trust in the monetary and political system. To the surprise of many, Locke's novel insistence on the unalterability of the standard carried the day. Lord Somers and other Whigs influenced by Locke worked tirelessly in assembling parliamentary support and even won over the king to their cause.[141] Parliament passed the act in January 1696 and the date for the recoinage, an enterprise of enormous scope, was set first for May, then moved to June. In the summer of 1696 clipped and worn coins were removed from circulation and replaced by newly minted coins with milled edges (fig. 2.3).

To enforce the new emphasis on coins' inviolable intrinsic value, anyone found with counterfeit coins would have to pay and no punishment could be too severe. Isaac Newton, appointed warden of the Royal Mint in the course of the recoinage in 1696, affirmed this zeal for prosecuting and executing criminal abusers of the coinage.[142] The burden of the recoinage fell, however, not only on counterfeiters. As many skeptical voices had warned, while the recoinage largely stopped the clipping of coins it did not prevent the new coins from disappearing once more abroad for profit as quickly as they left the mint. The amount of money in circulation in fact contracted sharply with the recoinage (fig. 2.4).[143]

As damaged old coins that had been clipped or broadened were removed (alongside counterfeits), it took agonizingly long for the newly minted coins to enter circulation. This has long been a point of

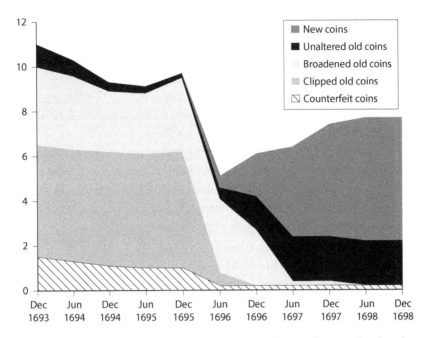

FIGURE 2.4: Silver coins in circulation, 1663–98. £ million sterling, as at last day of month. Source: Patrick Hyde Kelly, "General Introduction," in John Locke, *Locke on Money*, ed. Patrick Hyde Kelly, 2 vols., Clarendon Edition of the Works of John Locke (Oxford: Oxford University Press, 1991), 1:112–13.

consternation among economic historians of the recoinage.[144] It remains disputed, for example, whether Locke should shoulder the full blame for the shortage of coin after the recoinage. While his advice won out, the implementation of the recoinage deviated procedurally from his recommendations in a number of important ways.[145] Most significantly, Locke had argued for an immediate demonetization, but the implemented plan opted for a gradual demonetization over several months and chose to compensate holders of clipped coins, encouraging further clipping at the state's expense in the meantime. Locke had also believed that large amounts of hoarded unaltered old coins would be returned into circulation after a recoinage, but this happened only slowly and to a limited extent.

Locke's primary concern was in any case always with trust, not simply the quantity of money, and he accepted the significant costs that would be associated with the restoration of trust. The recoinage entailed great hardships for many and the pain of restoring trust was strikingly unevenly distributed. As Locke himself acknowledged, his prescription specifically privileged the welfare of creditors over that of debtors. The effect of the recoinage on the domestic economy and the war effort was disastrous.

Demonetization spelled "near-disaster" for England's finances.[146] The burden of the cash shortages affected every trade and every part of the country. The London cloth markets shrank by nearly a fifth in the course of 1696–97 and, as one contemporary source remarks, "many self-murders happen in several families for want, and all things look very black."[147] While the fiscal situation had been undeniably fragile throughout 1695, the protracted deflationary recoinage proved an even greater military burden. As one recent military historian has put it, the recoinage "emasculated William's martial ambitions" and reduced the armies in the Low Countries to minimalist defensive operations.[148] Davenant concluded at the time that the economic exhaustion of the recoinage tied England's hands and forced it into a series of peace treaties, such as the Peace of Ryswick in September 1697.[149] Ultimately, only an improvement in the English balance of trade could address the state of the English coin. This in turn required the kind of intensified colonial expansion that came to mark the eighteenth century. Locke's own appointment in 1696 to the Board of Trade, then the backbone of English colonial administration, reflected this shift of priorities.[150]

The Politics of Monetary Depoliticization

While Locke's proposal passed itself off as mere common sense, it was always bound to appear paradoxical if not deceitful. For what Locke called "intrinsick value" originated, paradoxically, in fiat. Intrinsic value, it turns out, refers in Locke's account to "the quantity of Silver by publick Authority warranted to be in pieces of such denominations."[151] Where Locke had earlier defined "intrinsick value" based on universal consent, he now tied it to the sovereign as the embodiment of civil consent. Intrinsic value was consequently defined as a fixed quantity of silver that was itself set by the sovereign. Locke, then, did not simply turn the market against the state. Nor was enforcing the monetary contract a curtailment of sovereign power but instead a novel invocation of it. The recoinage intervened in the name of nonintervention.

For Locke, as we saw, the issue at stake in the Coinage Crisis was never just the material shortage of silver but the erosion of trust and the proliferation of monetary confusion, both between citizens and toward the government. Precisely because of the fragility of the postrevolutionary order, Locke was concerned about a collapse of societal trust and insisted on tying the mixed mode of money to metal. At numerous points throughout his three essays on coinage Locke brought up this threat of an erosion of the monetary standard—through clipping but even more so through a potential nominal adjustment—leading to an implosion of societal faith as such.[152] If clipping could not be stopped and clipped coins continued to circulate, Locke wrote in a characteristic passage, "all must break in Pieces, and run to Confusion."[153] The Coinage Crisis, he feared, risked exposing not just money but society as dangling by a fragile thread of trust.

The monetary dimension of Locke's thought thus serves as an illustration of the centrality of trust and faith to his political thought: trust in our fellow human beings, trust in the government that rules us, but also faith in an even higher authority. As the historian of political thought John Dunn has long stressed (without, however, pointing to its crucial monetary dimension), the question of trust is pivotal in Locke's political philosophy.[154] It came to form a key pillar of Locke's thought, first tentatively in his early lectures, then in a constitutive form in his mature political philosophy. Where the *Two Treatises of Government* gave a political account of the centrality of trust in civil society, the *Essay Concerning Human Understanding* provided an epistemological and normative grounding.[155] But as Locke recognized, trust was fragile. Humankind's fall from grace in the Garden of Eden—itself equated in his account with the introduction of money—had brought not only the disintegration of the original community of man but also introduced the threat of distrust that came from the breaking of promises.[156] Persistent violations of promises and oaths, if left unchecked, sooner or later entailed the collapse of society. As Hobbes pithily put it, "Where's no trust, there can be no Contract."[157] In Locke, the point acquired a further vertical dimension whereby trust not only bound the members to each other but was also the proper relation between a people and its government. Citizens not only entered a covenant with each other, Locke insisted, but also placed their trust in the ruler. Trust was in this double sense—among citizens and between the citizenry and the ruler—the bond of society, the *vinculum societatis*.[158] From the monetary essays Locke thus emerges as preoccupied first and foremost by the fragility of societal trust and consequently insisting on the need for a strict enforcement of oaths, public promises, and contracts, including in particular property contracts. Conversely, Locke licensed the dissolution of the political compact when the government itself violated the trust placed in it, as he feared it was about to do during the Coinage Crisis.

Rather than an attempt to straightforwardly naturalize money, Locke's plan was a political strategy to depoliticize money's *appearance*, flowing from an understanding of money as all too artificial and malleable. Locke's embrace of unalterable metal money was itself an attempt to tame the consequences of this account of money as supremely malleable and his assessment of postrevolutionary society as prone to a fatal collapse of trust. The issue at stake was thus not so much the material shortage of silver money but the erosion of trust, both between citizens and toward the government. Building on the centrality of trust, it was Locke's insistence on the keeping of promises and the preservation of the public faith that served as the central anchor for his argument during the Coinage Crisis.

The result was a performative contradiction: rooting "intrinsick value" in fiat and having to persuade his contemporaries that money's value did not depend on their opinions. Money (defined as silver and measured by weight) was property, Locke insisted, and as he had argued both in the *Second Treatise* and his *Letter Concerning Toleration* it was a governmental duty to secure property, just as tampering with contracts was always an abuse of governmental power.[159] Applied to the recoinage this meant that since contracts had been made on the basis of the publicly announced value of money (in this case the Elizabethan mint price for silver), no government could rightfully alter the nominal standard of money without violating property and with it social trust. Instead, Locke insisted, "the Standard, once thus settled, should be Inviolably and Immutably kept to perpetuity."[160] The reason the monetary standard should not be changed, he summarized, "is this: because the publick Authority is Guarantee for the performance of all legal Contracts."[161] After the rate was set and pledged, public faith demanded that no government should be able to alter the standard of the mint.[162]

Conclusion

As was the case for Aristotle, Locke began by emphasizing the conventional origins of money. But instead of building on this nominalist foundation an account of currency as a malleable political institution, he derived from it a radically novel argument. In attempting to stabilize money's nominalist instability he sought to tie it to an arbitrary but then unalterable quantity of metal. Once set by fiat, Locke insisted, no future government should meddle with the monetary standard. This attempt to force measure and metal to coincide ushered in something else entirely. Forced into coincidence, measure and metal seemed identical and the glitter of gold easily obscured the measure's conventional origins. The resulting optical illusion continues to confuse our understanding of Locke's project and, arguably, of modern money at large. Locke's intervention ended up changing the very meaning of the word "money" by conflating the distinction between money as counters and money as pledges that had formed his own starting point.

This conflation was not entirely innocent. As we saw, it derived from an insistence on the limits of the politics of money that was itself politically motivated even where it sought to hide its own politics. No doubt unintentionally, this Lockean politics of monetary depoliticization was a strategy that proved essential for the development of capital. Mirroring the earlier Whig gospel of Lockean metallism, Marxist political theorists have long read Locke as an early theorist of capitalist society. While historians of political thought have since picked over such readings, their monetary dimension has received relatively little attention. But as the political theorist C. B. Macpherson already put it, for Locke "the characteristic purpose of money is to serve as capital."[163] Variations of this claim have recently resurfaced, for example, in the work of Christine Desan who has argued that "Locke made money into capital."[164] Locke may not have been a theorist of "possessive individualism." He did, however, capture the way in which modern money was not just political currency but also increasingly served as capital.[165] The specific nature of his argument was nonetheless easy to miss and turns out to be more paradoxical. Just as the radicalism of the Glorious Revolution had been dressed in the colors of continuity and moderation, Locke portrayed his monetary argument as the commonsensical wisdom of the most judicious thinkers of the past. But his monetary argument *was* radical and novel. Its influence was moreover enormous. Locke's insistence on the unalterability of metal money even in the face of changing silver prices led to a wholesale reversal of standard government policy. Most importantly for our purpose, Locke's intervention not only affected the policy of his day, it also profoundly altered the way subsequent generations understood money.[166]

Macaulay's later claim that it had been the Lockean gospel of "sound money" that had laid the financial foundation for Britain's rise to world power is no doubt an exaggeration.[167] We can acknowledge the vast influence of Locke's doctrine without drawing a misleading direct link between Locke's coinage advice and the financialization of the British state in the course of the eighteenth century. Placing the credit for the Financial Revolution on Locke's shoulders obscures the specifically political logic of his argument but also the unintended consequences of his advice. Locke's impact was more ironic than most Whig and Marxist readings allow for. Concerning credit in particular, Locke was always far more ambivalent than later Whig readings of the Financial Revolution allowed.

Public credit was but in its infancy in Locke's time. Its meteoric rise that marked the prospects and anxieties of the eighteenth century would have undoubtedly shocked him.[168] Despite being an original subscriber to the Bank of England, Locke was always skeptical. He thought credit's reliance on opinion far too fickle to reliably carry the enterprise of money and the state.[169] But in insisting on restoring the Elizabethan standard in order to tame the fictitious quality of money, Locke ironically achieved the opposite: the even greater shortage of silver money as a result of the recoinage further fueled the need for private and public credit. What eventually eased the shortage of money was not the recoinage but the widespread proliferation of credit notes in its wake, as well as the aggressive exploitation of silver in India.

Reconstructing Locke's reasoning in his monetary writings and recognizing their enormous influence brings to light a further irony. It was the very political success of his insistence on the unalterability of metal money that has since rendered invisible and almost unintelligible the political nature of his argument. To the frustration of his contemporary critics, Locke's deceptively simple and seemingly tautological position rapidly became conventional wisdom. The Scottish pamphleteer James Hodges, in describing his frustration, noted that already by 1697 Locke's argument formed a "fixed perswasion" in the minds of many. Daring to argue against it felt like claiming "that twice two is not four, or that, taking two from four ther remaineth not two."[170] Locke claimed to substitute clarity for confusion. As he put it in the dedication to his *Further Considerations*, his purpose was to strip "the mysterious Business of Money" of its "obscure and doubtful Words" that had "artificially perplexed" it.[171] But the intellectual rupture he effected set into motion a modern forgetting of the politics of money that continues to cloud our view both of Locke's argument and the politically constructed nature of money more generally.

Precisely because Locke's political theory of money succeeded so widely, it effaced its own political character. Adam Smith, for example, while praising Locke's strictures against devaluations, naturalized what had for Locke still been a political argument. "The debasing of the coin," Smith explained in his *Lectures on Jurisprudence*, "takes away the public faith."[172] But in arriving at Locke's conclusion, Smith further naturalized what had for Locke still been a political argument necessary to stabilize money's conventionality. Instead, Smith now concluded that money's value "is not as Mr. Locke imagines founded on an agreement of men to put it upon them; they have what we may call a naturall value."[173] The old Aristotelian premise of conventionality, still shared by Locke, was thereby lost. In denying money's conventionality, this also obscured the implied political possibilities. Where discussions of currency were once central to the canon of political thought, today they have been largely eclipsed. Instead of taking Locke's depoliticizing argument at face value, we should detect in his concept of "intrinsick value" a particular politics of monetary depoliticization. Locke's intervention was itself political, even where it removed political discretion. This strategy is reminiscent of a larger paradox inherent in much subsequent liberal thought about the economy: economic relations are structured and enforced by the state, but they are at the same time shielded against discretionary political interference. Naturalizing Locke's conclusion ignores that his depoliticizing conclusions had themselves been derived from a political theory of money.

CHAPTER THREE

The Monetary Social Contract

JOHANN GOTTLIEB FICHTE AND THE
POLITICS OF PAPER MONEY

The peculiarities of a nation are like its language and its currency: they
make communication easier, indeed they enable it in the first place.

—JOHANN WOLFGANG VON GOETHE
TO THOMAS CARLYLE, JULY 1827[1]

IT WAS A SATURDAY AFTERNOON, February 25, 1797, when an unprecedented request reached King George III. His prime minister, William Pitt the Younger, urgently asked that he come into London to attend an emergency Privy Council meeting the following day. This was a first. Even during the most tumultuous phase of the American War of Independence there had never arisen the need for an emergency meeting of the kind. This time, however, the specter of financial crisis hovered over the country and threatened to fatally compound the already tense political and military situation in the war against revolutionary France.

Over the previous days, reports of landings by French troops had arrived in London. On Wednesday, more than a thousand French troops had landed near the Welsh port of Fishguard, led by American republican generals and backed up by Irish insurgents. By the time Pitt called the king to London, British troops had been able to gain the upper hand, but only bad weather in the Irish Sea kept more French ships away from the shores. Meanwhile a series of mutinies rippled through the Royal Navy. Edmund Burke, writing from his sickbed in Bath, described the seriousness of the situation in frank words: "It is not the invasion of Ireland only that is threatened, but of this Kingdom also."[2] For Burke the threat was serious enough for him to insist on being buried in an unmarked grave,

separated from his wife and son, "on Account of the French Revolution-
ists" who would surely desecrate his grave.[3]

Faced with this existential threat, Pitt was slowly running out of the
gold necessary to maintain the British position. Without it, paying the
rebelling troops and hiring more mercenaries would be impossible.
Although Pitt had managed to win the previous summer's general election, the financial pressures of the war weighed by now heavily on his
government.[4] The mounting fiscal constraints and the bleak military out-
look filled the daily papers, stirring up a climate of profound uncertainty;
a financial reckoning and military collapse were on everyone's mind.
Reports of a rivulet of people converting their bills of exchange for gold
could at any moment easily turn into a mighty current. A run on the Bank
of England's dwindling gold reserves was no longer just a distant theoretical possibility.

On Sunday evening (February 26), after long hours of deliberation in
the Privy Council, the government issued a breathtaking proclamation:
"too delicate a subject to anticipate," as one Monday paper put it on its
front page.[5] The Bank of England had suspended the convertibility of
paper into gold. Circulating promissory notes would no longer constitute
a claim to gold and had become pure fiat money overnight. The pound
sterling, still in name referring to the weight measure of silver, had become a
piece of paper backed only by the word of the state. That weekend in February 1797 marked the dramatic opening of a now largely forgotten episode
in global monetary affairs that would last for the following quarter century
and separate the era of metal monies of the eighteenth century from the
gold standard of the nineteenth.[6] The gold standard continues to dominate
our monetary imagination, having taken on mythical proportions, and it
is often closely associated with the rise of Britain as an imperial maritime
power.[7] But for two foundational decades, from 1797 until 1821, Britain
experimented with the most advanced monetary practice in the world—
pure fiat money—and with it the politics of modern central banking. Both
sets of practices challenged and transformed not only reigning conceptions
of money but also the nature and role of the modern state. Political thinkers and philosophers across the continent keenly perceived these changes
and sought to capture the new possibilities of state and money.

The closing decade of the eighteenth century was a period of great
social and intellectual upheavals that has often been described as a portal
to modernity.[8] Political and philosophical revolutions became intimately
entwined, and at the heart of that tangle was a series of extraordinary
monetary experiments—a fact that weighed heavily on the minds of

contemporaries. The British suspension of gold during the Napoleonic Wars soon became a touchstone of all subsequent monetary thought. But the experience also left a distinct philosophical imprint. One of the most incisive commentators on the British Suspension Period and the new possibilities of fiat money was the German philosopher Johann Gottlieb Fichte (1762–1814).[9] Like many others, Fichte detected in the British suspension of gold both the promises and anxieties of the unfinished project of philosophical and political modernity. Unlike others, he developed a radical sketch for how the new powers of fiat money decoupled from gold could be put to new philosophical uses. In reconstructing Fichte's proposal for harnessing the power of fiat money to complete the social contract we can capture this philosophical ambition that continues to inform, in diluted ways, our own contemporary monetary imagination.

※

In the first two chapters on Aristotle and Locke I reconstructed two seminal accounts of the politics of money—more than two millennia apart—that formed frequent reference points in discussions of money during the late eighteenth century and beyond. Both Aristotle and Locke treated money as conventional in nature while stressing its political significance—albeit with crucially divergent conclusions. In Aristotle's influential nominalist account, *nomisma* emerged ambivalently as an essential institution of civic reciprocity in the ancient polis as well as the medium of unnatural accumulation. In Locke's protoliberal account of money, coinage was instead presented as an essential pillar of societal trust that guaranteed the stability of the early modern state just as the state served as the harsh guarantor of the inviolability of metal money. In reconstructing Locke's argument, I emphasized the roots of what I take to be a key paradox of all modern liberal political theories of money: namely, that the political and conventional nature of money is enforced by the state but at the same time shielded against direct political interference in an attempt to establish money as somehow beyond politics. Where Aristotle's account of *nomisma* brought to the fore an ambivalence between currency's role as a political institution and a tool of accumulation, Locke's theory compounded this ambivalence by highlighting the paradox of modern money's deceptively self-effacing political nature.

If currency in the form of coinage was considered one of the institutions that constituted, in its own ways, both the ancient polis and the early modern state, then the nexus of politics and money intensified and transmogrified in the course of the eighteenth century. As Michael Sonenscher has shown, much of eighteenth-century political thought was marked by the spectacular rise of public credit which frequently appeared as a predicament of overwhelming proportions.[10] In the course of a single century British public debt had exploded from little more than one million pounds in 1694 to more than half a billion pounds by 1800, approximately twice the size of the national income.[11] Alongside this vast expansion of public credit, the spectacular bursting of the South Sea Bubble in 1720 and the rapid spread of private banking operations in the second half of the century generated anxious talk about the fictitious nature of credit.[12] Skepticism toward the modern state's reliance on credit came in various shades, ranging from Jean-Jacques Rousseau's broad admonitions against public and private finance to David Hume's dire predicament regarding the specific forces of public credit.[13] As Hume famously put it, "Either the nation must destroy public credit, or public credit will destroy the nation. It is impossible that they can both subsist."[14]

Such apocalyptic predictions crystallized in profound debates concerning the sublime relation between money, state, and time.[15] The stunning advent of public credit was, in J.G.A. Pocock's words, "a momentous intellectual event" in the history of political thought, nothing less than "a sudden and traumatic discovery of historical transformation."[16] The growth of public credit, Pocock explained, required societies to develop something they had never possessed before: the image of a secular and historical future.[17] Two aspects of this assessment are particularly striking. First, the credit revolution was, in Pocock's account, not merely a development of financial significance but an epistemological revolution with wide-ranging repercussions. Second, it tied public credit to a new sense of historical temporality and secular change.[18] By placing value into a permanently postponed future, the new pervasiveness of public credit altered both the nature of the state and citizens' relation to it. Sovereignty, and the imagined community it mirrored, had become inescapably temporalized. This revolution resonated with a conception of modernity whose temporal horizon now extended into an open-ended future tied to promises of the betterment of mankind. But public credit was at the same time a powerful tool for binding future generations to the choices of the present. As Richard Tuck has observed, public credit posed on this account problems of legitimation that parallel those of written constitutions, another eighteenth-century rage.[19] Both public credit and constitutions acted as forms of intergenerational self-binding that confronted politics with the problem of time.

While some detected in the rise of public credit the threat of debt-fueled military escalation and a dangerous hollowing out of the principle of property, others saw in it undreamt-of possibilities for reconciling republican aspirations with the modern world of commerce. To some—not least Fichte—public credit and paper money appeared even as the missing pieces to complete Rousseau's challenge of how to constitute an internally rational state in a pacified international political economy.[20] To others, monetary experimentation was primarily a tool of revolution. As observers had recognized at least since the American Revolution's issuance of Continentals in 1775, revolutionary wars could be financed through paper money. The circulation of French Revolutionary *assignats* some fifteen years later only underscored that impression. But both were primarily remembered for the loss in value they underwent. While paper money and public debt had entered late eighteenth-century discourse, the political nature of money itself could nonetheless remain obscure, not least because of the self-effacing political logic of Locke's influential argument. As long as international trade was conducted in gold and silver, or at least in promissory notes convertible into gold and silver, it was tempting to oppose credit to "real value," and see promissory notes or paper money as mere representations of metal. The Suspension Period directly challenged such presumptions and opened the door to a radically new understanding of fiat money and its relation to the modern state.

Fichte's proposal formed the most daring vanguard of such a reconceptualization of modern money as a self-referential token backed by the promise of the state. For Fichte, this new understanding of money had far-reaching implications not just for the domestic structure of the state but also for debates about peace and external commerce. A century earlier, Locke's defense of the unalterability of metal money had already reflected the pressures of settler colonialism and the imperial aspirations of the postrevolutionary English state. In the increasingly international politics of money of the late eighteenth century, questions of gold and public credit were now intimately tied to considerations concerning international economic integration, the European state system, and in particular the prospects of commercial empire. It was against this background that Fichte advanced his sketch of fiat money as a guarantee against colonial exploitation and international economic competition. This Enlightenment critique of empire implied the vision of a radically different state system and it did so by perfectly aligning the monetary system with the modern state.

An Ocean of Boundless Debt

To appreciate the eventual impact of the British suspension of gold in 1797 and to capture the broader context of debates over public debt and paper money in the closing decade of the eighteenth century, it is helpful to briefly recall Edmund Burke's critique of the French assignats and read it alongside Immanuel Kant's late reflections on paper money and public debt.

Burke's *Reflections on the Revolution in France* (1790) are today primarily known and read for their comprehensive critique of the French Revolution. But Burke's more immediate target, as he emphasized in the text, was the French paper-money assignats that had been issued in 1789 by the National Assembly as a temporary measure to address the pressing need to repay the nation's outstanding credit.[21] The assignats functioned in this context as a synecdoche for the entire French Revolution, symbolizing all that Burke found objectionable in it condensed into a single piece of paper. As J. G. A. Pocock pointed out in his seminal reading of the *Reflections*, Burke's visceral critique of the assignats constitutes the key to understanding his broader assessment of the revolution.[22] "When Burke's eyes turned to the French Revolution," Pocock summarized, "he saw a monstrous paper-money despotism being installed on the ruins of the Church."[23] The second half of the *Reflections* offered consequently a detailed chronicle of why the revolution's experiment in public finance was doomed to failure. For Burke, irresponsible paper-money speculators had struck at the Church by destroying its property and brought down the nobility by destroying chivalry. With the first two historical pillars of manners gone, there could be no doubt that the next step would be the ultimate subversion of commerce.[24] As he put it programmatically in a letter from 1793, "The utter destruction of assignats, and the restoration of order in Europe, are one and the same thing."[25]

For Burke, the assignats were tainted from the beginning by their origin in expropriated Church property.[26] As "Symbols of publick Robbery" they could "never have the Sanction and the currency that belong exclusively to the Symbols of publick faith."[27] Through their fraudulent origin, the assignats amounted to a challenge to the principle of property.[28] If land was the ultimate form of property that secured the social order, the assignats exemplified a nightmarish "continual transmutation of paper into land, and land into paper" that ultimately dissolved any stable system of property.[29] A more "unnatural and monstrous activity" could scarcely be imagined. It constituted "the worst and most pernicious part of the evil of a paper circulation."[30]

It is tempting to extend this critique of the assignats to public credit in general, not least because Burke had opened by remarking that "nations are wading deeper and deeper into an ocean of boundless debt."[31] Yet Burke was careful to distinguish between the assignats and public debt. His reasoning for why the assignats were fraudulent and destined to fail was far subtler than that of many other observers who derived from the spurious nature of the assignats a sweeping denunciation of all credit. It was a mistake, Burke retorted, to equate public credit with doom. Instead, credit was a "great but ambiguous principle, which has so often been predicted as the cause of our certain ruin, but which for a century has been the constant companion, and often the means, of our prosperity and greatness."[32] As a Whig familiar with the British state's finances, Burke recognized the hazardous abuses of public debt but nonetheless saw the benefits provided by the Bank of England's credit since its foundation in the 1690s.[33] Public debt may subsequently have grown excessive, Burke explained, but it had originally secured governments by turning public tranquility into an object of widespread financial interest.[34] In Burke's account the assignats thus constituted not only a violation of property but also of the principle of credit itself.[35] This meant that the elimination of the revolutionary notes was a necessary step precisely to restore public credit. "A reasonable publick Credit, and some retribution to those who have suffered by its destruction," Burke explained in a letter, "may be hoped for, when this immense mass of fraud and violence, which has usurped its place, is totally destroyd, so as not to leave the slightest trace of its ever having existed."[36] Despite his visceral critique of the assignats— and despite his occasional apocalyptic pronouncements on the "ocean of boundless debt" that threatened to engulf the nations of Europe—Burke was far less perturbed by the rise of public credit than Smith or Hume had been.

In the *Reflections*, Burke even acknowledged that a paper currency may, in principle and for a while, successfully act as the "cement" of social life.[37] The French revolutionaries had only doomed their endeavor from the beginning by basing their attempt to create a land bank on the confiscation of Church land. The problem in their case was not the principle of credit itself, or even the use of paper money, but the fact that its collateral—confiscated Church land—had been gained by injurious means that violated the trust necessary to sustain credit. "If the confiscation should so far succeed as to sink the paper currency, the cement is gone with the circulation. In the meantime, its binding force will be very uncertain, and it will straiten or relax with every variation in the credit of the paper."[38] What ultimately mattered for Burke was "the credit of the paper," and the French revolutionary regime had done everything it could to destroy faith in that credit. It was this lack of faith that constituted the ground on which Burke arrived at his pessimistic verdict. This insistence on the monetary contract recalled Locke's argument from the 1690s, but Burke's intimate familiarity with the state's finances and the workings of the Bank of England led him to a defense of English statecraft with its reliance on public credit—credit in which, he assumed, the public would have faith. The suspension of gold during the last months of Burke's life would come to test this cautionary embrace of the principle of credit.

The "great but ambiguous principle" of public credit and the peculiar status of the French assignats can similarly be detected in Immanuel Kant's contemporary account of money and debt. In January 1797, at the height of the assignats' hyperinflationary bonfire and less than three weeks before the British suspension of gold, Kant published the first part of his *Metaphysics of Morals*.[39] The *Metaphysical Foundations of the Doctrine of Right*, or in short the *Rechtslehre*, also contained a brief excursus on the question "What is money?"[40] The section, easily skipped and frequently disregarded, was appended to the table of rights that can be acquired by contract and Kant opened it by initially providing a nominal working definition of money: "*Money* is a thing that can be *used* only by being *alienated* [*veräussert*]," he explained in using the precise legal term for selling.[41] The exchange of money was not intended as a gift but "for *reciprocal* acquisition." This implied, secondly, that money was a "mere *means* of commerce" without value in itself. In moving toward a first definition of money, Kant employed the notion of industriousness to capture the Lockean sense in which money was stored-up labor power. Money was consequently "the universal means by which men exchange their industriousness [*Fleiß*] with one another."[42] "Thus a nation's wealth," Kant argued, "insofar as it is acquired by means of money, is really only the sum of the industry with which men pay one another and which is represented by the money in circulation within."[43] Money was a representation of the nation's wealth embodied in its industriousness and labor. Its value, he explained, must have cost as much industry to mine as the industry that had gone into the goods one was hoping to acquire with said money.[44]

To support his claim, Kant invoked the authority of Adam Smith— itself an indication of how deeply Scottish political economy had begun to permeate European philosophy by the end of the eighteenth century.[45]

"'Money is therefore' (according to Adam Smith) 'that material thing the alienation of which is the means and at the same time the measure of the industry by which men and nations carry on trade with one another.'"[46] This was a loose paraphrasing of Smith's account of money in the *Wealth of Nations* as the universal instrument of commerce between all civilized nations.[47] More telling was Kant's commentary on the Smithian definition he endorsed. Smith's account, Kant pointed out, could be seen as a bridge between the materiality of species and money's formal purpose. This meant first that banknotes and promissory notes (*Assignaten*) could not be regarded as money for they involved too little industry to produce value. Their value was, according to Kant, "based solely on the opinion that they will continue as before to be convertible into *hard cash* [*Baarschaft*]; but if it is eventually discovered that there is not enough hard cash for which they can be readily and securely exchanged, this opinion suddenly collapses and makes failure of payment inevitable."[48] No wonder the French assignats were collapsing in value. This was a widely accepted assessment at the time that could make sense of the circulation of promissory notes and paper money but dismissed them as fickle, epiphenomenal representations of metal. Only the labor invested in finding gold or silver gives money its value, Kant insisted. Directly echoing Locke's argument from the Coinage Crisis, Kant explained that the stamp that comes with coinage matters only because it confirms the weight and content of a certain piece of metal.[49]

But Kant added a further twist to this analysis that unwittingly anticipated the events of the Suspension Period. Having set out an initial definition of money as a material representation of industry, Kant gestured in conclusion toward a more formal conception. This was meant as a definition that sought to grasp money as an intellectual concept abstracted from mere empirical materiality.[50] Smith's definition, Kant explained, "brings the empirical concept of money to an intellectual concept by looking only to the *form* of what each party provides in return for the other in onerous contracts (and abstracting from their matter), thereby bringing it to the concept of Right in the exchange of what is mine or yours generally (*commutatio late sic dicta*), so as to present the table above as a dogmatic division a priori, which is appropriate to the metaphysics of Right as a system."[51] In drawing a parallel between money and books, Kant elaborated on these formal qualities. "The concept of money, as the greatest and most useful means for the commerce [*Verkehr*] of men with things, called buying and selling (trade), similar to that of a book, the greatest means for exchanging thoughts, can be dissolved into manifold intellectual relations."[52] While the empirical definition pushed Kant to a substantivist account of money rooted in specie and industry, his formal definition emphasized that money was never merely matter but also form.

The ambivalence that characterized Kant's position on money between form and matter had an important political dimension that was not spelled out in the *Rechtslehre*. Though Kant stressed there that money was characterized by being universally accepted, he added in brackets that this universal acceptability was limited to "within a nation."[53] Kant's parenthetical insertion betrayed a broader tension between universality and particularity. His emphasis on specie as derived from the universal value of industriousness translated into a preference for gold as a cosmopolitan currency of free trade. But the formal character of money could easily pull in a different direction, as we will see below. On Kant's account, this possible disjuncture was still contained by an attempt to align the universalism of industry with the formal dimension of money by tying both to a cosmopolitan concept of commerce.

As Kant had explained in his philosophical sketch on *Perpetual Peace* from 1795, commerce was the most reliable driver of morality in bringing nations together.

> It is the *spirit of trade* [*Handelsgeist*], which cannot coexist with war, which will, sooner or later, take hold of every people. Since, among all of the powers (means) subordinate to state authority, the *power of money* [*Geldmacht*] is likely the most reliable, states find themselves forced (admittedly not by motivations of morality [*Triebfedern der Moralität*]) to promote a noble peace and, wherever in the world war threatens to break out, to prevent it by means of negotiations, just as if they were therefore members of a lasting alliance.[54]

But there also lurked a worry behind the promises of commerce and its instruments. As Kant noted, commerce could also produce the kind of monetary wealth that motivated envy—the jealousy of trade, in Hume's words—and in turn paid for war.[55] The power of money (*Geldmacht*), Kant explained, may well be the most reliable tool of war.[56] Only the difficulty of actually assessing another state's wealth provided a check on the accumulation of riches being in all cases perceived as a threat of war.

This ambivalence also found expression in Kant's stance on public credit in the essay's fourth preliminary article. While the section has sometimes been misread as a blanket ban on public debt, it specifically bans only the use of debt in relation to the state's "foreign affairs [*äußere Staatshändel*]."[57] Kant's opening caution against public credit was immediately followed up by its embrace when used for welfare or infrastructure purposes.[58] Debt posed "a dangerous monetary power" only if it was used to finance military endeavors.[59] Kant ambiguously suspended the political implications of public debt between welfare and warfare, just as he had suspended money conceptually between matter and form. The Bank of England's suspension of gold in the context of European war a mere three weeks after the publication of Kant's *Rechtslehre* would come to further deepen these ambiguities.

A Weekend in February 1797

The suspension of gold in February 1797 stunned the entire political punditry in London and across the Channel. The weekend was the most condensed form of the epistemological revelation of credit Pocock had in mind. Overnight, conventional monetary wisdom evaporated as astonished observers struggled to comprehend what had happened. Where money had previously been seen as having a stable commodity value, it was now revealed to be a circulating sign, a collective cultural and political project of artificially created value.

Despite a growing wariness of public credit, over the course of the eighteenth century the Bank of England's reputation and influence had grown in leaps. Trust that the Bank's notes were reliably redeemable in hard coin meant it was able to slowly displace most of its smaller, private country-bank competitors. By the 1770s the Bank had become the near sole source of bills of exchange in London.[60] Bills had been in circulation for almost a hundred years, issued both by private banks and the Bank itself, but these had, at least nominally, always been backed by gold, silver, or land. They were precisely not (yet) fiat money. In the minds of contemporaries, recording claims to deposited gold on paper was merely a shortcut of convenience whose entire value continued to derive from claims to actual metal, safely stored away in a bank vault but redeemable at will. It was this link that was broken in February 1797, not by fraud but by design.[61] On Monday, February 27, 1797, British money was no longer based on bullion but had instead been revealed as a token of credit. Notes that had promised payment in gold were now fiat money, a form of circulating debt backed solely by the promise of the state. With money no longer rooted in precious metal, it had become a self-referential fiction based on the credit of the state that could either be self-confirming in the form of circulating trust or self-undermining in the case of panic-fueled bank runs. More perplexing, the British transition to fiat money also revealed to contemporary observers that even commodity money had always been a form of credit. Coins had been money not merely because of their materiality—the gold or silver from which they were minted—but because of the sign stamped on them, a sign of trust in the modern state.

For us, citizens of modern commercial states, this point is easily understood and uncontroversial. In an age of credit cards and electronic payments it is plainly obvious that what we call money is in fact credit. For the English citizen hoping to buy a loaf of bread on the Monday morning after suspension in February 1797, the thought was far more alien and frightening. The suspension of convertibility must have appeared all the more remarkable, not to say audacious, in light of French monetary events earlier that very same month. On February 4, 1797 (16 Pluviôse V), the French assignats had met a disastrous end. After a gradual decline in value the notes had finally collapsed entirely, having lost almost all of their value in an inflationary spiral as the link between paper and land had become spurious. The British suspension of gold less than three weeks later seemed to many observers a tragic repetition of the French events.

But things were not quite as they seemed. Interpretations as to what precisely had happened varied dramatically and left observers baffled.[62] Perhaps the most widely expected scenario involved a rapid rise in prices, yet for the first three years prices stayed almost completely stable despite being no longer tied to gold.[63] Much of existing monetary theory found itself shortchanged. Many had equated the suspension of gold with immediate and apocalyptic disaster. But prophecy failed. Soon the new notes came to illustrate the changing nature of sovereignty and government, of the linkages between the modern state and the monetary economy. For while the French assignats had still been backed by expropriated Church land, the new English notes were backed only by public credit. Paradoxically, it was this leap that allowed the suspension notes to succeed where the French notes had failed.

The British suspension of gold was at once more radical and, oddly enough, more stable than earlier attempts to issue paper money based on land. Apart from the French Revolutionary assignats, the other eighteenth-century paper-money experiment based on land that would have been on the minds of observers was the French issuance of promissory notes during the 1720s by a royalist Mississippi land bank associated with the Scottish monetary reformer John Law.[64] But both Law's project as well as the assignats some seventy years later ended in a spiral of default as the notes lost their value. Both projects had carried a whiff of fraud precisely because they did not break the underlying link to "real value" but merely

FIGURE 3.1: Bank of England, £1 note, March 2, 1797 (serial number 2). This is the earliest known Bank of England £1 note still in existence. Signed by Abraham Newland, the Bank of England's chief cashier at the time, the note carries serial number 2 (the whereabouts of the first note is unknown). In the top left is a crowned vignette of Britannia. The text reads "I promise to pay to Mr A[braham] Newland or bearer on demand the sum of One Pound." The note was sold most recently for £40,000. Photo: Courtesy of Spink, London.

shifted it from metal to land, before then gradually softening it through overissuance. The British turn to fiat money in 1797, by contrast, rested on trust alone. It quickly found widespread support among those whose opinion mattered—notwithstanding severe criticism that compared the shift to earlier experiments. Already on the very day of its announcement the London banking community immediately issued a note of full support for the suspension by vowing to honor the paper money and conduct all its own domestic transactions, as far as possible, in it. Popular reaction to the decision thus coalesced into a curious state of numb shock. Gold coins, of course, quickly disappeared from circulation. New notes in small denominations were issued in their stead. For the first time, one- and two-pound notes entered circulation (see fig. 3.1). An immediate financial meltdown was avoided and on May 3, 1797, Parliament confirmed the suspension.

Unlike the preceding crises of the last quarter of the eighteenth century, the crisis of 1797 brought together the precarious role of government war financing with the fragility of the largely unregulated private banking system outside of London—the so-called country banks. At the juncture of the two stood a relatively new institution that the crisis pushed into the limelight: the Bank of England, which throughout the crisis established itself fully as the first modern central bank. The Bank succeeded in staving off the slow strangulation of the British fiscal-military machine by standing the entire monetary system on its head. Suspension was presented as but a temporary, cautionary measure, to be revoked six months after a victory over the French. None of this calmed the critics and a lively debate about the relative merits of the radical measures emerged.

James Gillray, one of the most popular caricaturists of the time, took up the suspension of specie with unprecedented vigor. In a print from March 9, 1797 (see fig. 3.2), Gillray presented the Bank of England as a reverse Midas whose touch turned everything into paper. Standing in front of approaching French ships and marked by an inflated belly that held the "key of public prosperity," the Anti-Midas farted and belched out paper notes. Ironically, the new printing techniques that allowed for the mass printing of the new notes also made possible Gillray's satirical sketches as well as widespread attempts at counterfeiting.[65] Indeed, some of the very same engravers commissioned to print the new notes likely used the same presses in the evening to produce political caricatures against them. Indeed, quite a few of the same printing presses likely spat out forged notes at night. While printing drove the political economy of suspension, the simple design and the rushed production invited counterfeiters. The monetized state responded with violence. Counterfeiting paper money was declared treason and as such a capital crime, punishable by hanging—even for the mere possession of a single forged bill.[66] Forgery made visible the larger contradictions of suspension. A world in which so much hinged on one's ability to tell fiat from forgery elevated anxieties of authenticity to unprecedented levels. The distinction between truth and fiction was destabilized.[67] In an ironic public sphere, printing presses were simultaneously printing banknotes, forgeries, and caricatures. Indeed, some of the most ingenious caricatures themselves resembled forged banknotes (see fig. 3.3).[68]

As we have seen, Burke had contrasted his case against the French assignats with the stability of the English system of finances. As he intimated in numerous letters during the last months of his life before his death in July 1797, suspension barely altered his assessment, at least not initially. Unlike the doomsayers of public credit, Burke insisted on "the good State" of the Bank of England and its credit, "the late disturbances" notwithstanding.[69] The Bank's credit, he explained, "cannot be affected but by invasion."[70] As Burke recognized, despite his unease

FIGURE 3.2: James Gillray, *Midas, transmuting all into gold paper* (March 9, 1797).
Hand-colored etching, 40.8 × 29 cm. Washington, DC: National Gallery of Art. Photo:
Courtesy of the National Gallery of Art, Washington.

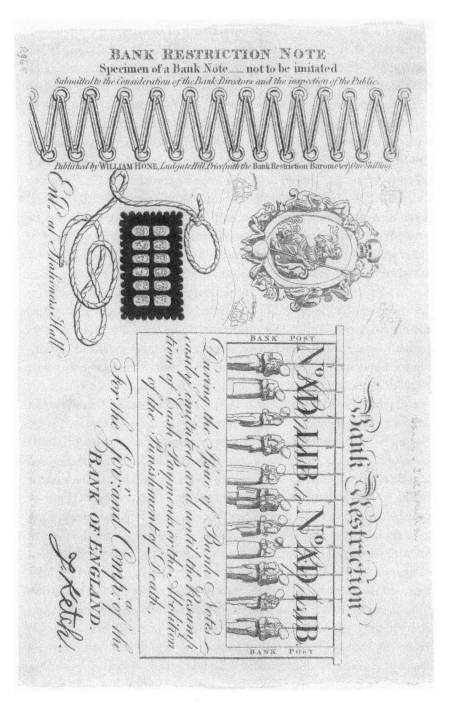

FIGURE 3.3: George Cruikshank and William Hone, *Bank Restriction Note* (1819). Etching, 12.4 × 19.5 cm. London: British Museum. Photo: The Trustees of the British Museum.

about the military situation, what mattered was not the question of gold or paper but instead the fundamental health of the English political system and its ability to sustain the nation's credit. "I do not altogether like the complexion of Monday's debate," Burke admitted in commenting on the Commons debate of Monday, February 27, following the suspension of gold announced by the Privy Council over the weekend.[71] But this, he explained, had more to do with Pitt's lackluster defense of suspension than with the act of suspension itself. "As to the present flurry about publick Credit, there is no cause, I think, for alarm, unless the means that are taken to support it, should not undermine its foundations."[72] There was little reason to doubt the soundness of England's credit. "For the present, if the general interest is appealed to in support of Credit, Credit will be supported," Burke concluded.[73] Suspension placed the burden of the war effort and the public finances squarely on the shoulders of public credit, and thereby on faith in the nation's creditworthiness.

Like Locke, Burke understood that money was conventional and thus depended on trust and faith.[74] But while Locke had concluded from this the need to irrevocably tie money to metal as a means of stabilizing its semantic uncertainty, Burke allowed for more flexible means of sustaining trust and stability.[75] This also expressed itself in his *First Letter on a Regicide Peace* (1796) where Burke sketched a Whiggish account of the rise of public credit since Locke's days.[76] The emergence of public credit was in Burke's account a direct response to the Coinage Crisis of 1695. Gazing back at the Bank of England's founding and subsequent ability to expand its credit successfully over more than a century, Burke argued that Britain's rise as a maritime empire had been built on the back of the Bank's credit. Credit could be stabilized as long as property was vigorously guarded. *This* was the principle the French revolutionaries had so egregiously violated in attempting to build circulating credit on the basis of an initial act of expropriation.[77] And yet, despite this acknowledgment of the possibilities of credit, Burke never fully lost sight of Locke's insistence on metal money. He drew part of his support for Pitt's decision from the belief that it was a temporary act and that, paradoxically, confidence in the Bank's credit would soon lead to the reappearance of coins.[78] When confronted with the realization that this would not be the case and that new notes in low denominations would instead come to replace coins, Burke was dismayed. "I am exceedingly mortified at this scheme of issuing small paper," he confided to a friend.[79]

In the late spring of 1797, as the suspension of gold gradually took on a more permanent character, Burke, sick and no longer able to write, dictated what would prove to be his last work, the *Third Letter on a Regicide Peace.*[80] Despite his subtle accommodation to the forces of public credit, he remained indebted to a set of Lockean arguments concerning the unalterability of the price of money. Criticizing attempts to set the rate of interest, Burke concurred with Locke that "the value of money must be judged, like every thing else, from it's [sic] rate at market. To force that market, or any market, is of all things the most dangerous."[81] To alter the monetary contract, Burke explained, "would amount to a tax on that peculiar species of property. In effect, it would be the most unjust and impolitick of all things, unequal taxation. It would throw upon one description of persons in the community, that burthen which ought by fair and equitable distribution to rest upon the whole."[82] This verdict now expressed itself in Burke's assessment of the broader monetary situation. His opinion tilted from an initial cautious optimism to the kind of predictions of doom that had begun to characterize his assessment of the war with France in general. Burke was now, as he put it himself, "in a strange kind of harmony of discord, between both sides of the House" that left room only for "melancholy reflections."[83] He died in July 1797 with fears of a French invasion on his mind.[84]

Despite the lingering military threat, the suspension of gold succeeded in stabilizing the British financial system and the war finances. The notes, even the new small denominations, remained largely in parity with the gold that no longer backed them. Though prices began to rise somewhat after 1800 under the intensified need for war financing and increased gold hoarding on the continent, inflation never reached anything like the dramatic depreciations experienced in the earlier French cases (or indeed the American Revolutionary currency). Fears that the pound might follow a hyperinflationary spiral proved unfounded.[85]

Fichte's Sign of All Value

Once it became clear that the Bank of England's audacious move had succeeded in easing the wartime financial situation while maintaining a broadly stable currency—despite being no longer tied to gold—a lively debate ensued.[86] In the late 1790s monetary experiments became a broadly shared contemporary reference point across Europe, in particular among the newspaper culture that flourished in the patchwork of German states and principalities. Printed alongside Kant's famous late essays in the *Neue Berlinische Monatsschrift* readers could find accounts of the latest monetary developments across the Rhine and the Channel.[87] A whole generation of critical Kantians, young Romantics, and Hanoverian Anglo-philes began to interest themselves in the latest monetary politics. Novalis, the Schlegel brothers, and Friedrich von Gentz all contributed to the discourse. But it was Johann Gottlieb Fichte who set out the most incisive plea for the need to think through the political and philosophical implications of the new possibilities of fiat money.[88]

As we saw above, Kant had already immersed himself in a reading of Scottish political economy in the 1790s that allowed him to incorporate a discussion of commerce and debt into his vision of perpetual peace. Fichte and the young Romantics took this recognition of the new philosophical centrality of political economy still further, emphasizing in particular its monetary dimension. As Isaac Nakhimovsky has shown in his pathbreaking study, Fichte's *Closed Commercial State* (1800) was a radical contribution to debates about war and peace that dominated postrevolutionary European politics and pushed the theory of the modern state and the social contract to its economic conclusion.[89] What drove Fichte's spirited argument for closing the state to external commerce was a twofold reconsideration of the internal and external constitution of the state. Externally, Fichte detected a pervasive web of international conflict and commercial competition between states that was triggered, or at least fueled by, considerations of foreign trade, in particular if these took on colonial aspirations. Far from being the bond of peace, commerce between nations was by this account a threatening obstacle to a stable state system consisting of rationally constituted republics. Domestically, Fichte insisted that the rational state, based on the principle of autonomous individuals brought together by a social covenant, had to move beyond the preservation of bare life toward a guarantee of the economic conditions of autonomy. In response to economic inequality within the state and the jealousy characterizing trade between states, Fichte thus argued for extending the social contract to include a right to work, while closing off commerce beyond the bounds of the state in order to escape the pressures of international economic competition.

Fiat money played a central role in Fichte's proposal.[90] His outline for the rational state contained an elaborate discussion of the nature of fiat money, how the transition from specie to fiat money would have to be effected, and how the rational state would subsequently be able to control the money supply to achieve its domestic goals. I will return to all three dimensions. As we will see, fiat money perfectly encapsulated and exemplified Fichte's solution to the problem of perpetual peace. Closure of international commerce and the introduction of fiat money went hand in hand in his scheme.[91] This was true in two related senses. First, only the new possibilities of fiat money allowed for the commercial closure of the state that now no longer had to rely on the inflow of bullion from abroad or fear its outflow. Second, only with external commerce banned could fiat money become the kind of fully self-referential medium of value Fichte intended it to be. As long as there was foreign trade, merchants would always compare the value of local fiat money to the international price of bullion, as indeed happened in Britain during the Suspension Period (and as came to be cited in arguing for the eventual return to gold in 1821). Only once specie was fully demonetized would commercial autarky be feasible, just as commercial autarky would be required to fully effect the demonetization of specie. The new fiat money issued to replace the old coinage would likely be refused as payment for international transactions and could no longer be converted into gold for this purpose.

In addition to reconstructing the immediate Prussian context for Fichte's essay, Nakhimovsky has elegantly situated the proposal within longstanding French debates about political economy and the possibility for amicable relations among the nations of Europe.[92] For Nakhimovsky the historical backdrop for Fichte's fiat-money proposal comes primarily in the form of prior French monetary experiments, ranging from Law's Mississippi scheme to the revolutionary assignats. But Fichte's fiat money was strikingly different. The key to appreciating Fichte's confident embrace of fiat money is thus the British suspension of specie in 1797. For while the two earlier French cases continued to link paper to land (only to undermine that link gradually through overissuance), the British suspension experiment constituted a genuine leap to fiat money. While specie had continued to circulate alongside the French assignats, Fichte commended the British decision to fully displace it by fiat money domestically.[93] In contrast to the two earlier French cases, the more radical British move of tying money solely to the credit of the state turned out to be vastly more successful and consistent. In particular during the first three years of the Suspension Period, the years during which Fichte was working on his proposal, observers began to marvel at the unexpected stability of fiat money as prices remained almost perfectly stable.

When Fichte summarized his argument to his publisher Cotta and to his friend Friedrich Schlegel, he not only made explicit reference to the immediate contemporary relevance of his proposal but also emphasized debates about the potential introduction of paper money that had reached the Court in Berlin.[94] The debate had aroused in him so much indignation that he set out to clarify the attendant questions of "trade and change, money, national wealth."⁹⁵ This interest in money—and with it a first imprint of the British suspension of gold—can already be detected in Fichte's two-part *Foundations of Natural Right* (1796–97). Its first part, published in March 1796, did not mention money at all.⁹⁶ But the second part, published in September 1797 after the suspension weekend, abounds with observations about money, both as a form of property and a central institution of the rational state.⁹⁷ Money, Fichte now explained, is "the universal sign of the value of things [*das allgemeine Zeichen des Werths der Dinge*]."⁹⁸ Crucially, it was the state that guaranteed the sign's validity. "At any time, each person must be able to acquire, in exchange for his money, anything whose enjoyment in general the state has guaranteed; for every piece of money in the hands of a private person is a sign of the state's indebtedness [*Zeichen einer Schuld des Staats*]."⁹⁹ The state alone had the authority to coin money "because only it can guarantee to everyone the value of this money. For this reason, the mines are necessarily a royal prerogative."¹⁰⁰ In *The Closed Commercial State* Fichte would radicalize this position by embracing the possibility that a state could be well ordered and cut off from foreign commerce, indeed that the truly rational state would *have* to be so constituted.

Some aspects of this process of radicalization are further on display in a short note on political economy (entitled "Über StaatsWirthschaft") that Fichte likely wrote in early 1800 in preparation for *The Closed Commercial State*.¹⁰¹ As he explained there, to insist on metal money's intrinsic value was to fall prey to an illusion. Like other forms of money and despite its shiny appearance, it had value only thanks to its universal acknowledgment (*allgemeines Gelten*).¹⁰² Moreover, as Fichte sketched in quick but precise strokes, a rational state could take advantage of this fact and substitute necessity for mere capriciousness (*Willkühr*). This moral principle applied no less to money than to relations of power in general. For a system of trade to be truly rational and free, its capriciousness had to be eliminated. Problems of political economy thus fell directly in the realm of moral necessity, "where an 'ought' is transformed into an 'is.'"¹⁰³ If the existence of money as an intermediary of exchange complicated the state's ability to ensure how much each citizen would receive for his or her labor, the realization that money was a sign guaranteed by the state also opened the door to new possibilities of imposing reason onto political economy.¹⁰⁴

As Fichte pointed out, this still begged the question of why paper money, as a sign, had been ordinarily backed by metal. Retracing Locke's logic, Fichte explained that the insistence on metal as a collateral should be understood not merely as an illusion but "a protection against suspicious governments."[105] A lack of trust in governments prevented the full utilization of paper money's potential. A second reason, as he had already explained in part 2 of the *Foundations of Natural Right* (1797), was the prevalence of foreign trade. Since most well-governed states (*policirte Staaten*) were now engaged in commerce with one another and since foreigners were unlikely to accept a state's money if it had been "arbitrarily increased *ad infinitum*," it followed that the value of paper money would be discounted even domestically relative to gold and silver.[106] The greater a state's reliance on importing and exporting, the more its national currency—its *Landesgeld*—was exposed to the pressures of the foreign exchange markets. As long as states depended on foreign trade, their ability to control the value of fiat money was severely constrained.

Closing the Fiat-Money State

In the *Foundations of Natural Right* this double predicament still served as a check against a move toward fiat money. In *The Closed Commercial State*, by contrast, Fichte sketched a countervision of a rational state that had the full confidence of its citizens and was no longer entangled in foreign trade.[107] As he sought to assure his readers, once the state was understood as the reconciliation of the individual autonomy of its citizens, its interest could be seen to converge with those of its members. A state that enjoyed the trust of its citizens had at its disposal the full powers of modern money. A national fiat currency combined with commercial closure, Fichte explained, was the solution to the problem of political economy. "A closed commercial state whose citizen engages in no direct commerce with the foreigner *can make absolutely whatever it wants into money*. All it has to do is declare that it will let itself be paid with this money alone and absolutely none other."[108] After all, money had only an "artificial value."[109]

Given the state's growing influence over economic life in the form of taxation (the previous year, 1799, had seen the introduction of the first income tax in Britain), whatever the state accepted for the servicing of taxes would almost by default become legal tender. If the state were to collect taxes in the form of the new fiat money, this alone would secure the universal validity of the new national currency.[110] To effect the transition from bullion to the new fiat money, Fichte recommended firm and decisive action. "Hence, the solution of our task is as follows: all the world currency that is found in the hands of the citizens, viz., all gold and all silver, should be brought out of circulation and converted into a new national currency."¹¹¹ The demonetization of specie had to come in the form of an abrupt break—"all in one stroke."¹¹²

Interestingly, Fichte insisted that the new fiat money ideally should not be paper. However irrationally motivated, in the wake of the French assignats disaster and the persistence of general skepticism, paper money still suffered from too much prejudice. Doubts about the viability of paper could, however, be circumvented by resort to a wholly different and possibly even cheaper material. Instead of paper, Fichte thus advocated that fiat money should be made from an unknown and otherwise useless material.¹¹³ "The more useless this sign is in and for itself, the less intrinsic value it has, the more fitting it will be to serve as a mere sign, since everything that can be utilized belongs to the nation's intrinsic wealth, and should be enjoyed by the nation and not applied to other ends."¹¹⁴ Besides its ability to escape the prejudices of the people, to please the eye, to be largely useless otherwise, and cheap to manufacture, the new currency had to fulfill one crucial criterion: it had to be difficult to counterfeit.¹¹⁵ To make the currency as inimitable as possible, Fichte insisted that the material or at least some essential constituent part of it would have to be treated as a state secret. Conveniently enough, this gave Fichte license to evade any further queries concerning what material he had in mind, if any. "It should be evident why I cannot express myself more clearly on this point, even supposing that I knew how this would be carried out."¹¹⁶

If popular opinion concerning paper could be suitably deflected, what mattered far more was to escape the mistaken belief in the intrinsic value of metal. It was—and remains—a genuine puzzle how and why people began to endow gold and silver with a unique intrinsic value instead of recognizing that even precious metals derive their worth from the opinion of people. But as Fichte added:

> To investigate how it came about that men agreed to grant the validity of gold and silver, and nothing in their place, as the sign of all value would take us too far afield. At the very least the reason offered by a famous writer will not do. He claims that because the extraction of a certain amount of gold or silver costs just as much time and effort as the extraction or manufacture of some other specific ware, we are able to accept the one as an equivalent for the other.¹¹⁷

This was a knowing nod to Adam Smith's account of the history of money in the *Wealth of Nations*—indeed, most likely a reference to the same passage Kant had already cited in the *Rechtslehre*.¹¹⁸ As Fichte pointed out in response, even the value of precious metals "rests merely in the general agreement about their value."[119] Usefulness as a raw material alone could hardly account for the extraordinary value these commodities were able to command when used as specie. The scarcity of metals was a social phenomenon brought on by the artificial demand of monetary convention, not because of metals' use value. The monetary value of metal, just like that of paper, derived from opinion—even if the fact was easily overlooked. With a keen eye to how the forces of convention tend to obscure their own conventionality, Fichte even speculated that if the situation had been reversed, "the same public would still ask: How then can this piece of silver be worth my good paper?"[120]

This observation suggested not only the extraordinary force of historical contingency but also that a supreme coordinating function accrued to the state in matters that could be settled only by conventionality, of which currency was a signal example. Fichte's argument here recalled Hobbes's line of reasoning that only the sovereign could solve the complicated coordination challenges that either had no intrinsically correct solution or allowed for too much disagreement over the correct solution.[121] If conventionality decided what counted as money and if the state was in a unique position to steer underlying patterns of conventionality, however imperfectly, it was the state that could decide what counted as money. "Money, in and for itself, is nothing at all," Fichte exclaimed in a statement that also served as one of his chapter epigraphs. "Only through the will of the state does it represent something."[122] If previous metal money had obscured this conventionality, a national fiat money made it abundantly clear that money rested on opinion (*Meinung*).[123] Fiat money rendered visible the underlying link between opinion and money that was easily obscured in the case of specie despite the fact that metallist currency hinged just as much on conventionality and opinion.

Fichte went even further in suggesting that specie rested *more* arbitrarily on opinion than a national fiat currency backed by the state.

> Precisely because . . . the value of world currency to goods has no other guarantee than public opinion, this ratio is just as fluctuating and variable as public opinion itself. . . . The national currency described above would, in contrast, have an entirely different guarantee, since it would have to be a fundamental law of the state that it will forever accept the money it gives out at the same value in relation to commodities and maintain it at this value among the fellow citizens.[124]

This was no trivial point. It implied that a fiat currency was more rational than specie precisely because it allowed for the intentional and self-conscious ability of the state to control the value of money instead of being the largely helpless recipient of whatever the fickle opinions of the world market determined the price of gold or silver to be. The commercial closure of the state would thus validate the independent worth of things that had previously rested only on opinion.[125] Once a national fiat currency had been introduced and the commercial state been closed, the rational state was free to conduct its independent monetary policy.

> Since the prosperity of an industrious and well-governed nation will grow from year to year, an ever greater number of goods of an ever higher value relative to the primary means of nourishment will enter into circulation. The state will keep a precise watch on this increase, since it occurs under its own direction. Therefore, the state can and will determine the ratio of money according to this increase in the value of goods. If the prices in money of the goods are to remain as they were, it will increase the amount of circulating money in proportion to the additional value of goods.[126]

Fichte was prescient. It would take more than a hundred years for John Maynard Keynes to set out a similar path for how to manage money based on the deliberate control of one's currency.[127]

All this still begged one profound political question, as Fichte himself acknowledged. How was the state to guarantee the stability of its new fiat money in the absence of external constraints imposed by specie and international trade? Fichte, rightly, predicted that his critics would insist that money had precisely been kept independent of governments in order to prevent abuse. This was one of the reasons Locke had argued that money had been guaranteed by the agreement of all of mankind.[128] As Locke might have asked, who would watch over governments that were now able to issue national fiat monies as they pleased? Fichte's response to these queries turned on the acknowledgment that the rational state would have to police itself somehow. The closed commercial state had to stand by its word that it would "ensure for all time the value of the money distributed by it."[129] Already in book 1, Fichte had explained that in the rational state the value of fiat money must remain invariable. This meant the state had to follow "firm principles."[130] How was this to be achieved? Fichte's response echoed Rousseau in this regard, as Nakhimovsky has pointed out: "The only way to prevent abuse by the government was to ensure that its interest was aligned with the common good."[131] Fichte thus specified that the imperative of safeguarding the currency's value had to be fixed in constitutional law. But such a constitutional constraint itself had to be grounded by an even deeper alignment of the state's interest with that of the public. Only such an alignment could produce a check powerful enough to prevent the motivation to transgress.[132]

Fichte's most fundamental point, however, was to force his readers to look with different eyes at the state and the money issued by it. The purpose of the rational state, he insisted, was not to serve itself or its rulers but to advance the autonomy of its citizens. This meant inversely that the social contract was not merely a pact of mutual self-preservation but instead required the state to guarantee the availability of work as a precondition for a "pleasant" life.[133] It was the profound duty of the state "to put each in possession of what is his due."[134] Gazing out onto an open-ended future, Fichte sketched on this basis a contingent philosophical "history of the present" (*Zeitgeschichte*)—as he entitled book 2 of *The Closed Commercial State*—that portrayed a divided mankind striving toward a more rational existence.[135] As we saw, Fichte derived from this in the first place a new need for the rational state to control its own currency so that it could secure a set of economic rights. But fiat money also acquired in his sketch a more philosophical role as nothing less than the engine of historical progress.[136]

Conclusion

By 1810 the rise in British prices, modest as it may have been initially, had nonetheless attracted ire. Despite the immediate success of suspension in keeping London's state finances flowing, ships sailing, and troops marching, the very fact that prices were fluctuating became a source of discontent, especially among those trading with Hamburg, Amsterdam, or the like. In 1810 Parliament took the unprecedented step of charging a Select Committee with investigating the rise in the price of bullion or, conversely, paper's loss of value. The Bullion Committee's daily hearings of bankers and brokers were accompanied by a flurry of pamphlets (including by a hitherto unknown banker named David Ricardo).[137] The resulting debate on money became, in John Kenneth Galbraith's words, "the most famous indeed in all history."[138]

The events of February 1797 had excited the imagination of an entire generation of political observers and thinkers in Britain, on the European continent, and across the Atlantic. Fiat paper money had crossed a hitherto unimaginable threshold of respectability and significance. It had arrived at the core of the modern state. What surfaced in February 1797 was the seemingly illusory but extraordinarily powerful force of modern credit money and the politics that accompany it. Even more miraculous perhaps was that paper money had become a tool not of revolution but of an antirevolutionary defense of the status quo. For Fichte, this was a decidedly double-edged sword. The gain in acceptance that fiat money had experienced had come at the expense of its transformative political potential, domestically as well as internationally. Instead, as we saw, Fichte set out to provide a philosophical sketch for how fiat money could be harnessed in far more radical ways to complete the social contract and allow a rational state to secure the universal right to work.

⟨⟩

I ended the previous chapter by alluding to Locke's hesitant caution concerning the incipient forces of public credit that would come to mark the eighteenth century. The turn to fiat paper money during the British Suspension Period was one logical end point of the groundswell of public credit. But it was Fichte who offered the most radical and prescient account of the possibilities of fiat money as the completion of the social contract. With the events of 1797 it had become clear that—as the German publicist Adam Müller put it—money was an idea in the Kantian sense, neither tied to metal nor adequately captured as a mere representation thereof. As Müller stressed in 1816, the emergence of fiat money confronted eighteenth-century theories of the state with notions of self-referentiality that could either be seen as the ultimate culmination of the social-contract tradition or, as Müller intimated, its collapse.[139] More generally, it was in this context of British paper money at the turn of the nineteenth century that arguments about reality and mere semblance, *Sein und Schein*, left their imprint on German idealism. The new possibilities of creating value by fiat produced a generational concern with authenticity and provoked playful amazement as much as they stoked dark suspicions of Mephistophelian foul play explored in Goethe's *Faust*.[140] The well-traveled road from Kant to Hegel leads through territory marked by monetary innovation and experimentation. The concept of negation (*Aufhebung*), for example, was first deployed by Fichte as a technical term in his discussion of credit money and national income accounting.[141]

Where Locke had adapted classical tropes and analogies between language and coinage to develop his argument for an unalterable metal standard to stabilize linguistic fragility, Fichte and other young Romantics gave this theme an entirely different twist by posing the question anew in a way that celebrated the poetic potential of paper money and the forces of collective imagination sustaining it. Money had been revealed as a pure sign that gained its value only from being circulated. Like language, money was a complex cultural artifact whose validity and utility depended on its wide circulation and acceptance. As circulating sovereignty, fiat paper money highlighted both the fluidity and the reach of the modern state as it broke out of earlier attempts to bind it by fixed representations. February 1797 opened a Pandora's box of modern monetary politics.

And yet the box was closed again in the end. The suspension of gold was itself suspended in 1821. After a long series of intense parliamentary sessions about the future of the currency, pressed by a new merchant class worried about its external trading position, it was Napoleon's defeat at Waterloo in 1815 that paved the way for a return to gold. In July 1819 Parliament decided against paper currency and ordered the return to gold at the old exchange rate before its suspension in February 1797. The experiment was over; or in any case it would be over once practice could be forced again to follow theory. This meant a harsh and uneven reduction in prices and wages with enormous distributive consequences in the event that the two did not fall fully in line with each other, as predictably they did not. Within two years wages were brutally brought down to prewar levels while prices only followed slowly. This contractionary episode and the labor unrest it created provided the context for the "Peterloo" massacre of August 1819 in St. Peter's Field in Manchester.[142] Only in the wake of Waterloo and Peterloo could the gold standard be reintroduced in 1821. As Keynes later sarcastically quipped in the *General Theory*, Ricardo's view had won out, conquering England in due course "as completely as the Holy Inquisition conquered Spain."[143] Within less than a generation the gold standard would acquire an air of quasi-religious writ; it was a self-evident and permanent reality. For the next century it would be easy to forget that the return to gold masked a two-decades-long experiment with fiat money. The memory of the potent political forces unleashed by the suspension was far too unsettling for those who were looking to gold to act as the natural moral anchor of the international trading system under British hegemony. The political dimension of the episode, both at its inception and its ending, eventually faded away.[144] With it disappeared the plausibility of Fichte's philosophical sketch.

In his lectures on the *Philosophy of Right*, published in 1821 just as Britain returned to gold, Georg Wilhelm Friedrich Hegel swiftly dismissed Fichte's proposal to close the commercial state through a fiat currency.[145] Fichte, who had become the first rector of the newly founded University of Berlin, had already passed away in January 1814 from an infection indirectly contracted in the liberation wars against Napoleon. Instead of the closed commercial state, Hegel built his system on the tenets of Scottish political economy that placed man first into civil society and only then in relation to the state. Echoing Aristotle's argument, Hegel did acknowledge the significance of monetary commensurability for the state's ability to achieve "the justice of equality [*die Gerechtigkeit der Gleichheit*]."[146] But what fell to the wayside was Fichte's insistence that money's specific institutional form would have far-reaching consequences both for the nature of the state and the kind of justice it would be able to administer.

Instead, the forces of capital were stirring. Rather than public debt as an intertemporal expression of the sovereignty of the rational state, credit now came to be seen first and foremost as a commercial force of restraint. As Benjamin Constant observed in his 1819 lecture on the *Liberty of the Ancients Compared to That of the Moderns*, commerce not only emancipated individuals but in "creating credit, it places authority itself in a position of dependence."[147] In basing itself on the forces of credit, the modern state had rendered itself dependent on the opinion of those holding its debt. In this realm of credit, blunt force was as useless as it was counterproductive. Tied to private credit and gold, money was no longer an agent of revolutionary forces but instead, Constant observed, the "most powerful restraint" on the state. If money were to flee, all operations of the state would be suspended.[148] The modern fiscal-military state built on the sublime powers of public debt now found itself entangled in a net of credit claims and dependent on the favorable opinion of its investors.

CHAPTER FOUR

Money as Capital

KARL MARX AND THE LIMITS
OF MONETARY POLITICS

All the illusions of the monetary system arise from the failure to perceive
that money, though a physical object with distinct properties, represents a
social relation of production.

—KARL MARX, 1859[1]

WHEN FRIEDRICH ENGELS returned home from the Manchester Stock
Exchange on Friday, September 26, 1856, he was brimming with excitement. As a successful investor on behalf of his family business, Engels had
been a respected member of the exchange for years. But that day the ordinary hum of the market had taken on a different tune. Having kept an
ear to the floor of the stock exchange for weeks, Engels was sure a storm
was brewing in the transatlantic credit markets. He immediately dashed
off a letter to his friend and political confrère Karl Marx in London. "The
money market clouds [*Geldmarktswolken*] are gathering in a very som-
bre way indeed," Engels announced with delight. "This time there'll be
a day of wrath [*dies irae*] such as has never been seen before . . . all the
propertied classes in the soup, complete bankruptcy of the bourgeoisie,
war and profligacy to the *nth* degree."[2] Upon receiving the letter, Marx
could barely hold back his excitement. "The anxiety of the upper classes
in Europe is as intense as their disappointment. . . . A general bankruptcy is staring them in the face."[3] Marx discerned a monetary crisis as
large as that of 1847, which had preceded the wave of revolutions of 1848.[4]
Indeed, the gathering crisis was taking on an even larger scale through
the newly created transatlantic credit networks that he had been keenly

following in his journalism over the past years.[5] This time, Marx was con-vinced, financial and political crises would truly converge. Where 1848 had proven to be incomplete, now a full social and economic revolution was on the horizon.

It took another twelve months for the long-anticipated crisis to arrive with all its force. In the fall of 1857, the loss of a cargo steamer triggered a panic in New York that immediately swept across the Atlantic. The *Central America*, a 280-foot side-wheel steamer, had left the Panama-nian port of Aspinwall (now Colón) on September 3 and was expected to reach New York three weeks later. It was carrying four hundred passen-gers as well as a vast haul of gold, twenty-one tons' worth, most of it pros-pected in California.[6] As the end of September neared and the uninsured ship had failed to arrive in New York, unease began to spread. The ship's loss in a hurricane off the coast of the Carolinas was confirmed two days later. Gone with it was its gold that had been eagerly awaited by banks all along the East Coast. Panic ensued. In the last week of September 1857 alone, more than 150 banks in Pennsylvania, Maryland, Rhode Island, and Virginia failed.[7] By October more than a thousand banks across the United States had collapsed and interest rates reached an astonishing 100 percent per annum.[8] Moreover, by 1857 the international banking system had become so tightly interlaced that the resulting shock almost immediately reverberated across the Atlantic. Within days the panic reached Germany, France, Austria, and England. This was, in the words of the economic historian Charles Kindleberger, the first "world crisis."[9]

For Marx and Engels, the arrival of the crisis in the fall of 1857 consti-tuted the most exciting news in years.[10] Finally, the clouds that had long been on the horizon had brought a financial thunderstorm. As Engels gleefully related from Manchester, "The general appearance of the stock exchange here last week was truly delightful. The fellows are utterly infu-riated by my sudden and inexplicable onset of high spirits. . . . This crisis will be as physically soothing as a swim in the sea, I can feel it already."[11] Factory owners in Manchester were forced to let their mansions and sell their foxhounds. "Another fortnight, and the dance will really be in full swing," Engels crowed.[12] He exhorted Marx to take meticulous notes on the balance sheets of the failed banks and to collect as much material on the crisis as possible.[13] He would meanwhile keep Marx in the loop about the latest gyrations of the stock exchange.[14]

The crisis also meant that Marx's long-promised analysis of capital was now in more urgent demand than ever. It was in the winter of 1857–58 that Marx for the first time pulled together all the various components of his critique of political economy that he had first envisioned in Paris some thirteen years earlier and started in earnest upon his arrival in London.[15] "The present commercial crisis," he announced in December 1857 in a letter to Ferdinand Lasalle, "has impelled me to set to work seriously on my outline of political economy [*Grundzüge der Ökonomie*] and also to prepare something on the present crisis."[16] Earning his living as a journalist during the day, Marx was working on his critique of political economy at night, staying up till four in the morning and living off a scholarly diet of lemonade and tobacco.[17]

It was no coincidence that it was a credit panic and the accompanying debates over monetary policy that spurred Marx to finally bring together his wide-ranging studies of political economy. Much of his journalistic writing for the *New-York Tribune* during the 1850s dealt with financial questions, chasing the politics of credit and bullion around the world from Paris to India, and from Australia to China.[18] His extensive notes on money and crisis from the period, which have only recently become available for the first time, make it clear that the history of monetary theories and debates over currency policy were Marx's central object of study during the formative decade of the 1850s.[19]

Already Marx's first book, published in 1847, had been an extended critique of Pierre-Joseph Proudhon's economic theories and his resulting proposal for monetary reform.[20] Marx's second book (*A Contribution to the Critique of Political Economy*, 1859) had been a direct outgrowth of the productive winter of 1857–58 and it appeared to contemporary readers to be primarily a historical survey of theories of money, coupled to a similar critique of socialist calls for monetary reform.[21] In the two decades building up to the publication of the first volume of *Capital* in 1867, Marx had developed a long-standing interest in the history of money, proposals for monetary reform, and the politics of currency legislation. If monetary policy and credit markets are seemingly absent from volume 1 of *Capital* it was not because of a lack of familiarity on Marx's part or because his interest rested solely with production. As he himself stressed in volume 3 of *Capital* (based on a manuscript Marx wrote during the early 1860s but that was published only posthumously by Engels), capitalism was intimately linked to the development of new forms of credit money.[22] Instead, the puzzle is more profound and interesting: Why did Marx seemingly erase the politics of money from at least the surface of *Capital*?

The effect of the omission has been confounding and deeply unfortunate. Many who otherwise praise Marx for having unlocked the secrets of industrial capitalism lament that he neglected crucial monetary phenomena and failed to anticipate the financialized credit economy.[23] Historians of money have been no more kind to Marx. At least since Joseph Schumpeter, Marx is often seen as a more or less closeted adherent of metallism who essentially accepted the Victorian gold-standard presumptions of his age as the background for his account of capital.[24] Building on Schumpeter's verdict, the sociologist Geoffrey Ingham consequently categorizes Marx in his justly celebrated guide to debates over the nature of money as a commodity theorist.[25] The labor theory of value, Ingham laments, committed Marx to a version of the commodity theory of money "with all its attendant errors" while preventing him from realizing that money—like capital—was ultimately a disguised social relation.[26]

The standard critique of Marx, from at least Schumpeter on, has prevented a true appreciation of Marx's analysis of money under capitalism and precluded a reconstruction of his attendant critique of monetary policy. In fact, Marx's account of capital emerged out of a close study of the history of money and monetary theory, as well as the emergence of credit markets. For Marx, the shift from monetary theory to an analysis of the value form was a self-conscious decision based on a sophisticated critique of managed money. (As we will see below, it was also in part a self-critique.) But the conceptual shift to capital nonetheless meant that what was intended as a conscious critique of modern money's malleability all too easily resulted in an elision of the history of political debates over money that has since at times mirrored on the left the liberal Lockean elision of the politics of money.

To understand Marx's rejection of the politics of monetary reform and currency legislation, it is necessary to first retrace his gradual disenchantment with the monetary dimension of French utopian socialism and in particular his critique of contemporary proposals for credit reform. When Marx in 1844 first turned to the questions of political economy (and with it, from the beginning, the nature of money), his initial position seemed to align him with Proudhon and his followers. But, as William Clare Roberts has recently shown, Marx soon turned against Proudhon by pointing out that exploitation did not originate in the monetary system and instead preceded exchange.[27] As Roberts puts it, "Marx agrees, in a sense, that force and fraud lurk 'behind' the apparently free and fair exchanges in the marketplace, but he denies that this obscurity of the market is a feature of money."[28] Proposals for monetary reform were as a result at best a confused distraction that mistook cause for effect by failing to grasp the nature of the capitalist system. Proudhon in France, but also the father of British socialism Robert Owen, and the American businessman and monetary reformer Edward Kellogg consequently peddled, in Marx's own words, "money nonsense" (*Geldunsinn*).[29]

Restoring Marx's engagement with socialist credit reforms and his understanding of capitalist money highlights the reasoning behind his ultimate rejection of both monetary reform and the power of monetary policy. Far from determining the movement of commodities, money was for Marx yet another capitalist commodity. As we will see, this does not render him a commodity theorist of money, nor does it imply that he conceived of money as somehow neutral. Indeed, he intended to criticize both of these positions. But Marx's argument in *Capital* nonetheless implied that any activist monetary policy to alter the level of investment, let alone the ability of monetary policy to shake off exploitation, was futile and ultimately misguided. Instead, according to Marx, monetary policy was heavily constrained and could at most alter the relative concentration and liquidity of capital in periods of crisis (a view interestingly not much different from that offered by Walter Bagehot, the onetime banker and *Economist* editor, in his 1873 bible of central-bank crisis management *Lombard Street*).[30] Marx's analysis thus forms an important challenge to one of the positions I have thus far reconstructed in this book, namely an understanding of money not only as a public good but also as a malleable lawlike institution. Marx chided monetary management and currency legislation as theoretically confused and politically naive. In this chapter I trace how Marx arrived at his critique through an engagement with both French utopian-socialist debates on credit reform and British debates about currency and banking.

Proudhon, Credit Reform, and Labor Money

During the 1840s proposals for credit experiments left a lasting mark on utopian socialism.[31] Marx's early economic thought initially took shape most immediately in this context of socialist debates about monetary reform.[32] Pierre-Joseph Proudhon and his followers in France, as well as Robert Owen and the Owenites in England, advocated monetary and banking reforms that ranged from an expansion of credit to the introduction of labor notes.[33] Already in *What Is Property?* (1840), Proudhon had described the overall aspiration of his philosophy as a shift away from the "fetishism of gold" toward a "realism of existence" that stressed the reciprocal nature of exchange.[34] Money was meant to enable exchange, but instead restrictions on credit and the scarcity of bullion had become obstacles to reciprocal exchange.

Proudhon synthesized and extended this analysis in his *System of Economic Contradictions*, published in October 1846.[35] As he summarized there, "Credit . . . should be the provider of work; in practice it oppresses and kills it."[36] This was an indictment of credit as it existed, tied to a celebration of its untapped potential. "Credit is . . . the most precious of all money [*l'argent*], money which holds in suspense all exchangeable values; . . . money measures, dominates and subordinates all other products [*produits*]; money with which alone one discharges one's debts and frees oneself from one's obligations; money which assures nations, as well as individuals, well-being and independence; money, finally, that not only is power, but liberty, equality, property, everything."[37] Proudhon consequently called for credit to be no longer tied to specie and issued by commercial banks but instead be made freely available based on labor productivity. The logical conclusion of this analysis was a system of labor money. As Proudhon explained, "Credit was invented to assist labour, to bring into the hands of the worker the instrument that destroys him, money."[38] Now it was time to make good on the promise of credit by breaking the hold of monetary scarcity. To realize this end, Proudhon's biographer explains, "the actual products of the workers should become, in a sense, current money."[39] Free credit would be extended to workers by rewarding them with a certain amount of coupons on the basis of their labor productivity.[40] Rather than leaving private banks in charge of rationing credit, in Proudhon's mutualism labor would furnish the basis for the extension of free credit to all those who worked.[41]

In his *Solution to the Social Problem* (1848), Proudhon expanded on this indictment of metal money. "Gold is the talisman which congeals life in society," he exclaimed in characteristically colorful language, "which binds circulation, kills labor and credit, and places all men into mutual slavery [*un esclavage mutuel*]. We must destroy the royalty of gold; we must republicanize the currency [*républicaniser le numéraire*], by making every product of labor ready money."[42] Equity in exchange was to be achieved through a reorganization of credit, Proudhon declared in one of his influential pamphlets of June 1848.[43] Speaking in the Constitutional National Assembly in Paris in July 1848, he consequently called for the creation of a republican national credit bank—a Banque du Peuple. A People's Bank, Proudhon insisted, was the only way to guarantee the meaningfulness of the right to work that had been enshrined in the new constitution.[44]

Remarkably, the People's Bank did get off the ground in early 1849 and quickly attracted more than twenty-seven thousand members, primarily workers in labor associations and individual craftsmen.[45] But only a few months later, Proudhon was forced to liquidate the scheme after he was exiled from France.[46] He nonetheless later described the three months in which its fate dominated French politics as "the finest time" of his life.[47] Nor was Proudhon's call to "republicanize the currency" a lone aberration; his demand for credit reform joined a plethora of competing socialist proposals. During the late 1840s, calls for free credit, labor exchanges, and credit cooperatives abounded in France, England, and the US. Various calls for "time chits" or other monies denominated in labor time circulated in reformist and utopian-socialist circles.[48] What united them was a rejection of the straitjacket of gold and silver. Despite important disagreements about the details of their credit reform schemes, Proudhon, Owen, and their respective followers converged on a shared hope to "demystify" money and democratize access to credit.[49] As the Chartist John Francis Bray put it, money is "that first great element of the power of the capitalist, . . . the secret of the almost omnipotent might of the capitalist."[50] Money became for Proudhon and others the ultimate shibboleth for unlocking the secrets of exchange and for opening a path to economic reform. Liberating the worker meant breaking the spell of money.

Marx too hoped to decipher the puzzle of money. When he first turned to the study of political economy in Paris in 1844, he began his economic self-education with French translations of James Mill's *Elements of Political Economy* (1821) and David Ricardo's *On the Principles of Political Economy* (1817). In his notes on Mill, Marx initially simply reproduced lengthy excerpts with short summaries appended. But as the text turned to money, Marx excitedly shifted from excerpting to commentary, praising Mill for elaborating on money's many powers and especially its ability to alter the very nature of exchange.[51] The essence of money, Marx explained, "is not initially that property is alienated [*entäußert*] in it, but that the *mediating activity* or movement, the *human*, social act through which the products of man reciprocally complement each other, is *estranged* [*entfremdet*] and the feature of a *material object* external to man becomes money."[52]

Money was an "estranged mediator [*fremder Mittler*]" and monetary exchange consequently produced a "dehumanized [*entmenschter*

Mensch]."[53] This account of money's transformative capacity as an engine of alienation forms the well-known backbone of some of Marx's most famous passages in the *Economic and Philosophical Manuscripts*, written the same year. But this discussion of money did not occur in a vacuum. Marx's observations about money's alienating force were from the beginning influenced by his critical engagement with contemporary French proposals for monetary reform.

While he had initially been impressed by Proudhon's *What Is Property?*, Marx grew increasingly suspicious of its analysis as he found his way deeper into the classics of British political economy.[54] Although he agreed with Proudhon about the alienating power of capitalist money, he was wary of Saint-Simonian and Proudhonist attempts to elevate credit above the fray. "In the credit system, of which banking is the fullest expression, it *appears* as if the power of the alien, material force is broken, the relationship of self-estrangement [*Selbstentfremdung*] abolished and man had once more human relations to man."[55] But the appearance (*Schein*) that credit might allow for an escape from the alienating forces of exchange was a mirage. As a result, the Saint-Simonians and Proudhonists had mistakenly concluded that the development of paper money, bills of exchange, new forms of credit, and banking in general constituted "a gradual abolition of the separation of man from things, of capital from labour, of private property from money and of money from man, and of the separation of man from man."[56] In declaring as their highest ideal and political goal the reorganization of the banking system, Proudhon had been deceived by the apparent disappearance of direct relations of power in credit.

It was against these French proposals for monetary reform that Marx gradually developed his own account of money and, eventually, capital. Instead of ushering in a "sublation of alienation [*Aufhebung der Entfremdung*]," Marx argued that new forms of credit instead produced an "all the more *infamous* and *extreme* self-alienation and dehumanization."[57] What was alienated in credit money was no longer merely an object, be it a particular commodity or metal, but man's very moral and social existence. Operating under the appearance of people's trust in each other and promising liberation, credit instead sowed the highest form of distrust and a more complete form of alienation. In the credit relationship, money was not transcended but humanity itself was turned into money. Credit resolved the value of money "into human flesh and the human heart."[58] Far from delivering salvation, credit money was merely the next logical step in the development of capitalist money's ability to exploit.

This also meant that the more abstract paper money and other forms of credit money ("money as money," as Marx put it) became, the more they corresponded to the essence of money. The less money shared a relationship to other commodities, the more it was created by man.[59] The development of money was in other words marked by an inverse relationship between the exchange value of money and the value of the material in which it existed. This meant that "paper money and the whole number of paper representatives of money (such as bills of exchange, mandates, promissory notes, etc.) are the *more perfect* mode of existence of *money as money* and a necessary factor in the progressive development of the money system."[60] Rather than writing in an age before credit or finance, as he is sometimes presumed to have done even by sympathetic readers, already by the mid-1840s Marx looked upon paper money and credit as constitutive features of advanced capitalism. As he declared in the *Economic and Philosophical Manuscripts*, "The nations which are still dazzled by the sensuous glitter of precious metals and are therefore still fetish worshippers [*Fetischdiener*] of metal money, are not yet fully developed money nations [*Geldnationen*]."[61] Marx was consequently sympathetic to Proudhon's critique of the "fetishism of gold" and he agreed with Proudhon that credit was the most fully developed form of money. But unlike Proudhon, Marx did not see credit and paper money as possible tools of human emancipation.

Reading Proudhon's *System of Economic Contradictions* in late 1846, Marx saw all his suspicions confirmed. After an aborted correspondence, his first elaborate response to Proudhon came in 1847 in the form of the anti-Proudhonist polemic *The Poverty of Philosophy*, which inverted Proudhon's own subtitle.[62] Writing in French and addressing himself to a French audience, Marx declared in the foreword that

> M. Proudhon has the misfortune of being peculiarly misunderstood in Europe. In France, he has the right to be a bad economist, because he is reputed to be a good German philosopher. In Germany, he has the right to be a bad philosopher, because he is reputed to be one of the ablest of French economists. Being both a German and an economist at the same time, we desire to protest against this double error.[63]

According to Marx, Proudhon's belief that the value of gold simply reflected the "labor time" it took to mine and transport it reflected "more naiveté than malice."[64] In international trade, where gold and silver ruled supreme, specie was the "means of exchange as products and not as money."[65] Contrary to Proudhon's claim that money derived its value in any straightforward sense from labor time, Marx explained, "gold and silver, as money are of all commodities the only ones not determined by their cost of production; and this is so true that in circulation they can be replaced by paper."[66] To illustrate Proudhon's lack of familiarity with the basic principles of political economy, Marx approvingly quoted Ricardo to show that paper money had no intrinsic value but derived its value instead from its scarcity.[67] Not labor time but demand and supply determined the value of paper money. More seriously wrongheaded was Proudhon's declaration that gold and silver somehow had the privilege of embodying "constituted value."

Money, Marx protested, "is not a thing, it is a social relation."[68] Proudhon had presupposed the existence of money rather than explaining its emergence. In his critique, Marx placed Proudhon in a longer lineage of earlier English socialists and communists advocating monetary reform, ranging from Owen to John Francis Bray, who had all become "deluded by appearances."[69] In a fit of confusion, Proudhon had turned "the *illusion* of the respectable bourgeois into an *ideal* he would like to attain."[70] Instead, Marx argued, "the constitution of the value of gold and silver presupposes an already completed constitution of a number of other products. . . . It is then not the commodity that has attained, in gold and silver, the status of 'constituted value,' it is M. Proudhon's 'constituted value' that has attained, in gold and silver, the status of money."[71] Proudhon had not only reduced money to labor time, he had also argued that money was "born of sovereign consecration" since it was sovereigns who "take possession of gold and silver and affix their seal to them."[72] Marx dismissed this focus on the state's agency in monetary matters by accusing Proudhon of having elevated "the whims of sovereigns" to the highest reason in political economy. "Truly, one must be destitute of all historical knowledge not to know that it is the sovereigns who in all ages have been subject to economic conditions, but they have never dictated laws to them. Legislation, whether political or civil, never does more than proclaim, express in words, the will of economic relations."[73] Instead, Marx followed Locke in insisting that the stamp "given to silver is not that of its value but of its weight."[74] Money's "intrinsic value" rested in the weight and standard of metal alone. Echoing (and historicizing) Locke, Marx consequently warned against the futility and fraud of devaluations. It had been proven time and again that if a prince decided to debase the currency, it was he who lost.[75] A debased coinage was essentially "falsified" and constituted a form of fraud. "If King Philip had decreed that one muid of wheat was in future to be called two muids of wheat, he would have been a swindler." Paraphrasing Locke, Marx declared that "by changing the name we do not change the thing."[76]

By the late 1840s Marx had thus developed a sustained critique of Proudhon's monetary thought, including his specific proposal of labor money, while also arguing against competing socialist proposals that hoped to eliminate the very institution of money. His critique was at this point still largely based on his close study of Ricardo. Marx was consequently defending a Ricardian position that regarded paper money and central banking as constitutive features of capitalist exchange. While he harshly ridiculed Proudhon's enthusiasm for credit mutualism, Marx nonetheless thought that the nationalization of credit might have a role to play in the political struggle against capitalism. The polemical disagreement with Proudhon thus obscured the subtlety of Marx's political position, the imprint of which can be detected in *The Communist Manifesto* from February 1848. Its fifth demand explicitly called for the "centralization of credit in the hands of the state, by means of a national bank with state capital and an exclusive monopoly."[77] The underlying political aim was similarly repeated in the "Demands of the Communist Party in Germany," written in March 1848, in which Marx and Engels once more called for all private banks to be replaced "by a state bank whose paper will be legal tender."[78] Unlike in the *Manifesto*, Marx and Engels helpfully elaborated the upshot of the demand. A state bank, they explained,

> will make it possible to regulate the credit system in the interest of the people *as a whole*, and will thus undermine the dominion of the great money men [*große Geldmänner*]. Further, by gradually substituting paper money for gold and silver coin, the universal means of exchange (that indispensable prerequisite of bourgeois trade and commerce) will be cheapened, and gold and silver will be set free for use in foreign trade. Finally, this measure is necessary in order to bind the interests of the conservative bourgeoisie to the government.[79]

To dismiss Proudhon's monetary schemes did not obviate the role of a state bank in smoothing the transition to communism.

As Marx explained in Ricardian terms, while arbitrarily increasing the amount of money in circulation—be it paper notes or metal coins—would not simply increase production, if production was by contrast inhibited by a lack of money, any increase in the means of exchange would imply an increase in production.[80] Thus, to insist that production was logically prior to money did not rule out the possibility of alleviating monetary bottlenecks. Furthermore, a national bank issuing mortgages and paper notes as legal tender would be a welcome attempt to move away from "the regulation of credit through a private monopoly" toward "the regulation of credit according to the general interest of society as represented in the state."[81] This was not Proudhon's promise of human emancipation through free credit. But nor did Marx dismiss all monetary reform as futile or reduce all money to metal.

Banking on Crisis

Over the next decade Marx further fleshed out his intellectual and political distance from French utopian socialism's moralizing focus on the deception of money and its attendant promises of credit reform.[82] By the mid-1850s he had come to distance himself from even his own earlier flirtations with a nonconvertible paper money issued by a state bank.[83] In his polemic against Proudhon, Marx had still mainly relied on Ricardo's *Principles of Political Economy and Taxation*.[84] When he reread Ricardo in 1851, he copied and annotated extensive excerpts in particular on money and currency. In the process, as Alex Callinicos has observed, Marx "became increasingly aware of serious weaknesses in Ricardo's theory" and in response turned to representatives of the British Banking School, such as Thomas Tooke and John Fullarton.[85] As Marx would remark during the 1860s, "the most significant [*erwähnenswerthe*] economic literature since 1830 has been mainly that on currency, credit, and crises."[86] It was in the process of compiling extensive notes on these advances in monetary theory, his so-called London Notebooks of the early 1850s, that Marx shed his earlier support of paper money and further radicalized his critique of monetary reform.[87]

Marx's full rejection of monetary reformism went hand in hand with his embrace of the Banking School and Tooke, who had emerged as the leading critics of the Bank Act of 1844.[88] Peel's Bank Act (as it also came to be known after Prime Minister Robert Peel) restricted the amount of currency in circulation to the quantity of gold in the country. Public and expert opinion was bitterly divided into two opposing camps over the issue. For the act's main advocates—known as the Currency School and represented by the likes of Robert Torrens and John Gellibrand Hubbard—the law constituted "the most important and the most salutary [measure], as regards the reform of our monetary system, which has been brought under the consideration of parliament since the act of 1819 for the resumption of cash payments."[89] As John Stuart Mill skeptically summarized in 1844, the Bank Act's supporters promised that it would "greatly diminish both in frequency and in severity . . . the calamity of almost periodical recurrence, commonly known by the name of a 'commercial crisis.'"[90] The main opposing voices to the Bank Act came from the Banking School, led by Tooke.

Where the Currency School in defense of the Peel Act traced its heritage back to the bullionists of the Suspension Period, Tooke similarly returned to the Napoleonic Wars. His six-volume *History of Prices*, published over two decades between 1838 and 1857, staked out a detailed survey of British financial history since the outbreak of the French Revolutionary Wars in 1793 and established him as the foremost expert on the nature of the modern banking system.[91] In the later volumes Tooke chronicled his own conversion from an erstwhile adherent of the Currency School and its emphasis on metal money to an ardent defender of the heresies of the Banking School.[92] Rather than fully backing each note with metal, Tooke argued that the Bank of England should simply be required to keep a large reserve of bullion for liquidity crises.[93] According to Tooke, it was a mistake to think that controlling the amount of bullion could determine the amount of banknotes in circulation and that the number of notes in circulation in turn determined prices. Instead, the amount of money in circulation was "endogenous" to the economic system rather than externally determined. The money supply could not be fixed from the outside but instead depended on the public's and industry's demand for money to which banks responded by creating credit; hence the name Banking School.[94] This revelatory argument was to have a momentous effect on Marx who came to rely heavily on both Tooke and Fullarton in all his subsequent work, including the *Contribution to the Critique of Political Economy* and all three volumes of *Capital*.[95]

In a short essay from March 1851 entitled "Reflection" (in English), in Notebook 7 of the London Notebooks, Marx similarly returned to the foundational disputes of British monetary thought during the Suspension Period.[96] He excerpted both the 1810 Select Committee report on the high price of bullion and Ricardo's response.[97] But then he immediately turned to the monetary reform schemes advocated in France by Proudhon and in England by the Birmingham School around the banker and political campaigner Thomas Atwood. Where Marx described Proudhon as a fool (*Esel*) who had "stupidly oversimplified" political economy by wanting to keep money without it having any of the properties of money, the Birmingham men were fools for wanting to "do away with the inconveniences of money altogether by making more of it or by lowering the standard of money."[98]

Both were deeply misguided, according to Marx. "Nothing is simpler to understand than that these narrow-minded reformers who remain on bourgeois grounds want to reform money."[99] It was in the money markets, to be sure, that all crises erupted, but these were merely symptoms of bourgeois production that only through a crisis became "incidental" causes.

In their correspondence in the course of 1851, Marx and Engels reiterated these shared sentiments as they grappled with the mysteries of central banking and paper money. Currency theory, Marx joked, was such an intricately "theological" matter that a Hegelian would no doubt describe it as the "study of 'otherness' [*Andersseins*], the 'alien' [*Fremden*]—in short, the 'holy.'"[100] Over the course of the year, Marx had shared with Engels his notes and extracts from Proudhon. In their correspondence Marx and Engels worked through the issues arising from their reading of Proudhon. Public banks? Workers' credit cooperatives? Proudhon was "altogether too naïve," while his proposals were quite simply "impracticable," Engels concurred.[101] More important, Marx was relaying to Engels the importance of Tooke's recent insights. "What I wish to elucidate here," he explained to Engels, "goes to the fundamental principles [*Elementargrundlagen*] of the matter."

> For my contention is that, even with a purely metallic currency, the quantity thereof, its expansion or contraction, has nothing to do with the outflow and inflow of precious metals, with the favourable or unfavourable balance of trade, with the favourable or unfavourable rate of exchange, except in the most extreme cases, which practically never occur but are theoretically determinable. . . . As you can see, it's an important matter.[102]

Marx did not claim originality on this point but credited Tooke, whom he described as having revealed the implausibility of the entire classical theory of circulation. The Peel Act was consequently based on a false theory of money and unwisely empowered banks.[103] Moreover, if Tooke was right, "the progress of crises, even though the *credit system* be a condition of the same, is concerned with *currency* [in English] only in so far as crazy meddling by the authorities in its regulation may aggravate an existing crisis, as in 1847."[104] Responding to Marx's letter, Engels brought up a recent discussion about an earlier scheme of Marx's for reducing the interest rate by setting up a national bank with a monopoly of paper currency while taking gold and silver out of circulation.[105] Now Engels himself channeled Tooke by voicing skepticism about Marx's earlier idea:

I believe that any attempt to lower the interest rate rapidly and steadily would inevitably fail because of the growing need, at a time of revolution and stagnating business, for usury, for the granting of credit to people who are momentarily in a tight corner, at a loss what to do, in other words, momentarily unsound financially. . . . The constant harping by the socialists and Proudhon on the reduction of interest is, in my opinion, no more than a glorified pious wish of the bourgeoisie and petty bourgeoisie.[106]

As long as the structures of ownership were left unchanged, Engels asserted, a reduction of interest would lead only to an increase in profit, not a social transformation. Moreover, surely the administration of such credit cooperatives and certainly of public banks called for the state, which Proudhon rejected. As Engels put it: "Hence the dilemma: either management and finally administration and regulation of these companies by the State, which Proudhon doesn't want, or the organisation of the most splendid association fraud, the fraud of 1825 and 1845, reproduced at the level of the proletariat, *Lumpenproletariat* and petty bourgeoisie."[107] Engels conceded that, of course, *after* the revolution a "monopolist state bank [*Monopol-Staatsbank*]" had a conceivable role to play in abolishing interest or keeping it very low (Engels proposed a quarter of a percent) but also in enabling the state to compulsorily purchase all real estate at its current tax value while paying for it over twenty years at 5 percent interest. "Such might perhaps one day serve as the final and immediate precursor of undisguised confiscation," he concluded. "But it would be pure speculation to ponder on the when, where and how."[108] Marx concurred. While a state bank might have a role to play after the revolution, it could not be the source of societal change. Already by 1852 Marx had thus broken with his earlier views on central banking and currency policy—just as he had done before with various forms of Owenite and Proudhonist monetary schemes. He now distanced himself more and more from the conclusion that monetary policy and credit could offer even temporary relief.

While the 1850s would come to be one of the intellectually most formative decades for Marx, they also came with a withdrawal from immediate revolutionary politics that had marked his exile in France and Belgium until 1849. Instead, he now covered high politics but also the global flows of gold and credit for the *New-York Tribune* from London. Political economy was reduced to the evenings. Behind this turn away from political engagement stood not just pragmatic concerns but also a growing conviction that the true political revolution would come only in the wake of economic and social revolution.[109] As Marx explained in 1853, one of the lessons of 1848 had been that economic crises preceded revolutions. "Since the commencement of the eighteenth century," Marx insisted, "there has been no serious revolution in Europe which had not been preceded by a commercial and financial crisis."[110] Grasping the latest monetary and financial developments was thus crucial for a deeper understanding of the political moment. Journalism was a fitting occupation from this perspective. Marx first wrote for the *New-York Tribune* in early August 1851, ten years after the paper's founding.[111] Over the next decade the *Tribune*, with its politics of abolitionism and protectionism, became the most widely circulated newspaper in the US, playing an important role in the formation of the Republican Party in 1854.[112] Marx eventually contributed around four hundred articles, at least a dozen of which were coauthored with Engels.[113] He wrote on a broad range of topics, often highlighting the links between them: English party politics and foreign policy, especially the Crimean War of 1853–56; British imperialism in East Asia, ranging from Indian uprisings to the Second Opium War with China in 1856–60; and, unsurprisingly, the commercial dimension of these political conflicts, especially the rapidly evolving status of transatlantic and colonial commerce and finance.[114]

Writing from his desk in the capital of the world, Marx began to follow the global flow of capital. During the 1850s questions of finance and commerce dominated the headlines.[115] Especially contemporary innovations in credit and banking, such as the French Crédit Mobilier, attracted Marx's attention.[116] For his articles, he moreover closely followed all the major financial publications, ranging from *The Economist* to purely financial papers such as *Money Markets*. He quickly built up a considerable knowledge of the practical machinations of both the Bank of England and the international credit markets. As he explained in the preface to the *Contribution to the Critique of Political Economy* (1859), "Since a considerable part of my contributions [to the *New-York Tribune*] consisted of articles dealing with important economic events in Britain and on the Continent, I was compelled to become conversant with practical details which, strictly speaking, lie outside the sphere of political economy."[117]

Marx followed the explosion of French credit and banking with particular alacrity. The number of joint-stock banks in Paris alone, he observed in a column in 1855, had increased sixfold since the February Revolution of 1848, many of them betting on intensified French colonization (such as the Martinique Bank, the Banque de Guadeloupe, the Banque de l'île de la Réunion, the Bank of Algiers, and the Banque de Sénégal).[118] As Marx pointed out, the ability of these banks to produce fabulous profits depended on the fact that they were heavily undercapitalized—implicitly relying on the state for support. But the most notorious and flagrant innovation in this regard was a new type of French shadow bank, the Crédit Mobilier. In a three-part series of articles from the summer of 1856, Marx turned his attention directly to the new institution.[119] Without such a comprehensive analysis, he explained, it was simply impossible either to grasp the logic of the French empire or "to understand the symptoms of the general convulsion of society manifesting themselves throughout Europe."[120]

The Crédit Mobilier had been founded in 1852 by Émile and Isaac Pereire, two brothers who claimed to have been inspired by Saint-Simon's belief that credit reform would pave the path to socialism.[121] But far from being a selfless endeavor of social reform, the Crédit Mobilier essentially functioned as a hedge fund. Its underlying principle, according to Isaac Pereire, was that "of multiplying its action and diminishing its risks by embarking in the greatest possible variety of enterprises, and withdrawing from them in the shortest possible time."[122] Being directly dependent on the favor of Louis-Napoléon Bonaparte, who in 1852 had proclaimed himself emperor of the Second French Empire as Napoleon III, the Crédit Mobilier did not neglect to present itself as an engine of the state. As it bought up titles, shares, and debt in French companies, its ambition seemed to be to turn Napoleon III into the "supreme director" of all French industry.[123] The Crédit Mobilier thus aspired not only to be a major proprietor of industry but also, as Marx put it, "the slave of the Treasury, and the despot of commercial credit."[124] As a result, the Crédit Mobilier combined for Marx all the worst tendencies of French politics by forming a "curious mixture of Imperial Socialism, St. Simonistic stockjobbing and philosophical swindling."[125]

What allowed Napoleon III to momentarily reconcile all his contradictory political pledges was the combination of private speculation and "some new-fangled scheme of public credit."[126] Here was an example of all that Marx had found faulty in Saint-Simon's and Proudhon's credit schemes, tied up with the distasteful politics of the French empire. "What was called Napoleon's democratization of credit," Marx summarized, "was in fact but the generalization of stockjobbing."[127] There had been many gambling manias before but what distinguished the present period was the universality of the rage. The Crédit Mobilier was no longer content to speculate on a particular commodity or industry but instead sought "to speculate in speculation, and to universalize swindling at the same rate that it centralizes it."[128] The inevitable result, Marx prophesied, would be a rapidly approaching "crash in Bonapartist finance."[129] This would not be an isolated French event. It was in particular English capital, he observed, that supplied "the great arteries of the European Crédits Mobiliers with the heavenly moisture."[130] The impending crisis would shake all of Europe. Moreover, unlike in 1848, this time it would not be clandestine underground plots of the working classes but the "public contrivances of the Crédits Mobiliers of the ruling classes" themselves that had sown the seed for their own downfall.[131] The very constitution of the Crédit Mobilier had made its own collapse unavoidable. "History is already at work realizing our predictions."[132]

Marx's interest in a brewing European monetary crisis must be seen in light of a broader reappraisal on his part of the sources of revolutionary change. As mentioned above, in the course of the 1850s Marx had become increasingly convinced of a relationship between economic crisis and revolution. It had been in the context of studying the sources of the revolutions of 1848 that Marx first recognized the importance of the link.[133] Alongside his monetary revisionism, Marx had consequently begun to develop a complex crisis theory of social change. A new revolution, he explained, "is possible only in consequence of a new crisis."[134] This was as certain as the fact that a new commercial crisis was inevitable. As he put it by the end of the decade in his *Contribution to the Critique of Political Economy*, all the great revolutions in history—from the collapse of the Roman Republic to the revolutions of the seventeenth and eighteenth centuries—had been triggered (*herbeigeführt*) by the conflict between money's role as a commodity and its function as a medium of exchange.[135] As the value of precious metals either collapsed or skyrocketed, societal convulsions inevitably followed. A monetary panic, he recounted in October 1857, was usually at once "the symptom and the forerunner" of a more general commercial crisis.[136] Studying the nature of monetary crisis, Marx insisted, would thus allow him to root his politics in science and snuff out the romantic voluntarism of the utopian socialists. All strands of Marx's research and journalism now converged in expectations of an imminent panic.

The Panic of 1857

In the fall of 1856, Marx claimed to have detected the first signs of the crisis in the form of a gradually increasing drain of bullion, "the common harbinger of commercial disasters."[137] Now it was time to lean back and enjoy the spectacle. Having predicted an imminent collapse, Marx was soon forced to concede that the final crisis had once more been postponed.[138]

But the "collapse is none the less sure from this postponement; indeed, the chronic character assumed by the existing financial crisis only forebodes for it a more violent and destructive end."[139] It took another year for the panic to arrive and when it did it came not from France but from across the Atlantic.

As the convulsions finally reached Europe, they constituted a moment of extraordinary satisfaction for Marx, who felt vindicated at last.[140] The Panic of 1857 was the first global economic crisis that engulfed both sides of the Atlantic at once. The historian Hans Rosenberg famously called it "the first worldwide crisis."[141] For Kindleberger, it was similarly the first world crisis.[142] Discoveries of gold in California and Australia over the previous decade had fueled a global boom that spun new transatlantic credit networks to finance railroads and other infrastructure projects. At the heart of all these developments, as Marx himself had stressed in his *Tribune* articles, was a new breed of French joint-stock banks that had become international providers of credit. During the 1850s Paris had grown into an increasingly prominent hub of the international monetary system.[143] If French banks were at the center of an overextended global credit boom, in the end the crisis was triggered in the US by a series of unrelated incidents that came together to form an explosive mixture. In March 1857, when the US Supreme Court's Dred Scott judgment denied legal standing to African Americans and ruled that the federal government could not prohibit slavery, the decision also threw into doubt the availability and pricing of land in the American West.[144] The already heavily indebted railways immediately felt the increased financial uncertainty over land prices in the West, and banks from New York to Philadelphia and from Chicago to Cincinnati began to get nervous. In the summer of 1857, a case of fraud and embezzlement at the New York branch of the Ohio Life and Trust Company led to a bank run that claimed the company as its first casualty. In the end, the loss of the uninsured steamer filled with gold from California in September was enough to trigger a full panic.[145] From New York an enormous wave of bank bankruptcies rippled along the East Coast of the US before leaping the Atlantic to Paris, London, Liverpool, Hamburg, Oslo, and Stockholm.[146] The intensity, speed, and reach of the crisis were unprecedented.

For Marx, the crisis struck at the heart of the system, just as he had hoped, and it offered a gratifying vindication of the doomsday visions he had dished up in his columns for more than a year. "Every connoisseur," he exulted in his correspondence, "must savour the earthquake-like effects of the general crisis."[147] Tooke had been proven right that the 1844 Bank

Charter Act had failed to stop or even alleviate the crisis. Marx explained all this to the readers of the *New-York Tribune* in the summer of 1858 by dedicating a series of articles to the Bank Act. Just as Tooke had predicted, the act had not only failed to prevent the crisis but had itself become one of the downturn's first victims when on November 12, 1857, the prime minister, Lord Palmerston, had been forced to suspend it.[148]

Marx followed the financial commentary on the events closely and one of his main sources was *The Economist*.[149] Most commentators saw the crisis as straightforwardly bound up with the overextension of transatlantic credit. As Walter Bagehot (then also writing under the moniker "A Banker" for *The Economist*) put it in the *National Review* in January 1858, "This crisis throws a more remarkable light on our banking practice and currency legislation. . . . The trade of the North of Europe has been conducted for a very considerable period on a most unwholesome system of fictitious credit."[150] If Marx concurred that the Panic of 1857 was, as he put it, "the most regular and classical example of a monetary crisis that ever existed," he nonetheless refused to resort to a purely monetary explanation.[151] Marx aligned himself instead with those who stressed a too-rapid expansion of fixed capital. Among these was Benjamin Disraeli—then in the opposition—who argued in Parliament in December 1857 that the heart of the crisis was not the disruption of credit and currency; its main cause was commercial and thus to be found in the realm of capital.[152] "The fact is," Disraeli elaborated, "we are mistaking, and have for a long time too easily mistaken, in all these discussions, capital for currency."[153] Marx concurred. For him, too, the crisis may have been triggered through the overextension of credit but this pointed in turn to a commercial overextension in the form of saturated overseas export markets. The problem was structural and inescapably global.[154]

Not only had the panic originated in America, but the increasingly global flow of capital had gone hand in hand with British colonial and commercial expansion in the East. As a result, British firms were stuck in a cycle of overproduction and overaccumulation. "The idea that the banks had unduly expanded the currency, thus producing an inflation of prices violently to be readjusted by a final collapse," Marx explained, "is too cheap a method of accounting for every crisis not to be eagerly caught at."[155] The question was not whether the banks had been instrumental in "fostering a fictitious system of credit" but whether they possessed "the power of determining the amount of circulation in the hands of the public."[156] Banks could extend fictitious credit, but the underlying demand for credit was determined in the productive sector and reflected a broader commercial crisis. This was one of the key tenets of the Banking School and Marx added it to his repertoire. He had come to believe that the attempt to control and contain money panics was a noble goal, but that no currency legislation could eliminate structural commercial crises based on the recurrent problem of overproduction. In his notebooks Marx had gradually shifted from theoretical reflections on monetary policy to a dissection of the shibboleth of capital.

The Riddle of Value

The initial result of Marx's attempt at synthesis during the Panic of 1857 was a loose collection of notes spread over seven notebooks. The "manuscript"—only published in the twentieth century as the *Grundrisse*—consisted of an unfinished introduction and two "chapters": a first section on money (around 120 pages) and a much longer discussion of capital (almost 700 pages).[157] The transition from money to capital took up a central position in this unfinished heap of notes. "We have here reached the fundamental question," Marx announced at the point of transition:

> Can the existing relations of production and the relations of distribution which correspond to them be revolutionized by a change in the instrument of circulation, in the organization of circulation? Further question: Can such a transformation of circulation be undertaken without touching the existing relations of production and the social relations which rest on them?[158]

In the *Grundrisse* Marx's answer still meandered; there was a need for further examination. But he was more than skeptical of whether one could change the form of money (metal money, paper money, or indeed socialist labor money) independently of the relation of production.[159] As long as money remained an essential relation of capitalist production, it seemed difficult to comprehend how any of these proposals—essentially "tricks of circulation," as Marx put it—would be capable of overcoming the contradictions inherent in the capitalist money relation.[160]

Marx eventually decided to rework and publish a small subsection of the notes the following year as a *Contribution to the Critique of Political Economy* (1859).[161] The book, now rarely read beyond the preface, returned once more to Marx's critique of Proudhonist monetary reform but now based the critique on his reading of Tooke and the Banking School instead of Ricardo.[162] Marx summarized the book's programmatic intent in a letter as follows: "In these two chapters the Proudhonist socialism now fashionable in France—which wants to retain private production but *organize* the exchange of private products, which wants *commodities* but not *money*—is demolished [*caput gemacht*] to its very foundations. Communism must above all rid itself of this 'false brother.'"[163] This was then an exercise in clearing the undergrowth for a more fundamental argument. But the book tellingly broke off quite abruptly after its long second chapter on the history of monetary theory; its third chapter on capital never appeared, and readers found themselves shortchanged.[164] For the next decade Marx set himself the task of overcoming that disappointment, and one way of doing so was to cut himself loose from all this "money shit [*Geldscheisse*]," as he put it to Engels.[165]

By 1865, addressing the First International Working Men's Association, Marx confidently insisted that "this currency question has nothing at all to do with the subject before us."[166] By the time of volume 1 of *Capital*, published ten years after the crisis of 1857, Marx's suspicion of monetary reform had not only further hardened but was now accompanied by a radical change in the way in which he presented his analysis. Where both the *Grundrisse* and the *Contribution to the Critique of Political Economy* had retraced the history of money and had drawn on a rich historiography of debates over monetary theory, in *Capital* Marx cut the Gordian knot and adopted a radically formal mode of presentation. The obsession over the nature of money was a distraction from the actual problem of value, Marx now argued. In a passage added to the second German edition (which forms the basis for most translations into English), he celebrated this moment of revelation to maximum effect.

> Now, however, we have to perform a task never even attempted by bourgeois economics. That is, we have to show the origin [*Genesis*] of the money form, we have to trace the development of the expression of value contained in the value-relation of commodities from its simplest, almost imperceptible outline to the dazzling money form. When this has been done, the mystery of money will disappear.[167]

For more than two thousand years, Marx recounted, human ingenuity had unsuccessfully attempted to crack the question of value by focusing on the nature of money. Instead, in the opening pages of volume 1 of *Capital*, Marx proudly claimed to have solved—or, rather, dissolved—the riddle. Under capitalism, he explained, money embodied all the tensions of capitalist exchange and the commodification of human labor. Value was not to be found in the nature of money but in the capitalist transformation of human labor power into a commodity. Properly understood, this meant that the mystery of money simply melted away.

It was this breakthrough that accounts for the peculiarly abstract quality of the opening chapters in which Marx stripped away all historical material to present the concept of value under capitalism. The book still opened with a discussion of commodities and money, but it now no longer dealt with the history of actually existing monies. It was now instead an abstract analysis of the value form, as well as its relationship to what Marx termed the commodity form and the money form. As a result, as he casually remarked in the preface, "the sections on the history of the theories of value and of money are now, of course, left out altogether."[168] Instead, the book opened with a close reading of the peculiar social life of the commodity (*die Ware*) under capitalism. Only in the footnotes was the reader pointed to the historiography of monetary theories.

⟨⟨⟨⟩⟩⟩

Before I delve deeper into debates over Marx's account of value and money, it is worth stepping back for a moment. Why did Marx relegate the history and politics of money to the notes? It was this question that first motivated this book. In the process, I discovered that part of the reason reflected Marx's decision to escalate his long-standing critique of socialist monetary reform proposals into an attempt to sidestep the entire money question by focusing instead on the value form. What would happen, I wondered, if we followed the footnotes and restored the displaced history and politics of money? In these chapters I have consequently taken up the search for the marginalized politics of money, and many of the authors we have so far encountered—not least Aristotle and Locke—appear in Marx's footnotes to the opening chapters of *Capital*. These footnotes disrupt Marx's formal analysis and take us back to Aristotle's discussion of *nomisma*, to Locke's coinage pamphlets, to the British suspension of gold during the Napoleonic Wars, and to nineteenth-century debates over socialist monetary reform, banking regulation, and currency laws. Reconstructing these moments allows us to understand the political history of money with which Marx himself grappled even where he later turned away from it.

But an awareness of this conceptual and historical background concerning Marx's own monetary self-education, his deep familiarity with these historical episodes, and in particular the kinds of political struggles over money that he himself sought to intervene in, also puts a range of exegetical debates over Marx's corpus in a different light by highlighting his extensive familiarity with monetary debates and the critique he developed out of his engagement with them. This is particularly promising today because recent readers of Marx associated with the "New Marx Reading" have started to pay close attention to the monetary dimension of his value-form analysis of capital.[169] As Samuel Chambers has observed, however, if this revisionist reading of value theory has turned Marx scholarship upside down, it is striking that its emphasis on Marx's monetary theory of value has so far largely avoided engaging with existing scholarship on money.[170] Despite restoring money to its central place in Marx's theory, value-form theorists have thus been remarkably uninterested in relating their own revisionism to recent accounts of money as a unit of account (Ingham), as an institution of societal value (Aglietta), or as a constitutional project (Desan). In the remainder of this chapter I will instead mobilize aspects of the new reading of Marx and place it in conversation with his own response to the monetary politics of his time, as well as that of his sources, to shed light on the ambivalent role of politics in his account of capitalist money. This allows us not only to overcome the limitations of older orthodox readings of Marx, but it also recovers Marx's political economy as an intervention in nineteenth-century debates over monetary reform (both socialist and conservative).

The money question serves then as a reminder that Marx was not just addressing claims of monetary neutrality on the part of classical political economy, but that he simultaneously sought to respond to socialist proposals for monetary reform. As the above overview of Marx's engagement with Proudhon already intimated, this was not just a question of scholarly merit. A wide range of utopian-socialist proposals at the time set out visions of the abolition of money or its reform into labor money, without, however, changing the underlying structures of production. Marx consequently focused his critical energies on establishing that commodity production and money were two sides of the same coin under capitalism.[171] Marx's favorite image to illustrate the point—both in the *Grundrisse* and in volume 1 of *Capital*—was to joke that socialist proposals for the abolition of money while leaving wage labor untouched amounted to calls for the abolition of the Pope while leaving Catholicism in place.[172]

Staying within the same image, Marx similarly ridiculed demands for the demonetization of gold (as issued by Proudhon and his disciples) as amounting to the equally absurd suggestion that all Catholics should be popes.[173] As Marx quipped in response to Alfred Darimon's Proudhonist proposals for monetary reform: "Let the pope remain, but make everybody pope. Abolish money by making every commodity money and by equipping it with the specific attributes of money."[174] Demonetizing gold would turn it into a commodity like any other, but this amounted from Marx's perspective not to a form of economic emancipation but merely to the elevation of all other commodities to the status previously enjoyed by gold. Rather than abolishing the ills of money it would merely make every commodity into money. This political background is crucial for understanding Marx's polemics in the footnotes that accompanied the radical formalism of the main body of the opening chapters of *Capital*.

Instead of beginning with an enumeration of the various functions of money, as was and is standard in textbooks of political economy, Marx decided to proceed instead in a "form-analytical" manner by setting out the relation between the value form and the money form under capitalism.[175] Most concretely, Marx did so by sketching the emergence of the money form as a general equivalent that allowed for commodities to be "valued" by relating them to other commodities. As Marx explained, while every commodity producer would like for his or her commodity to emerge as the universal equivalent, "only an act of society can turn a particular commodity into the universal equivalent."[176] The money form emerged thereby as one—and indeed the decisive—embodiment of the general form of value. Understood in this way, one of the implications was that money was a strictly necessary feature for the ability to relate commodities to one another. In other words, money was indispensable for valuation.[177]

Marx was here distancing himself from any attempt to locate value "intrinsically" or "naturally" either in specific objects or indeed productive activities prior to exchange—what one might call "substantialist" conceptions of value. To speak of value independently of prices, and thus independently of money, was for Marx simply nonsensical. Value is not something that inheres in the commodity or in labor. Instead, value arises only in the process of valuation: that is, in the process of measuring. And this social act of measuring can at the same time be conducted only by means of money.[178] Value is thus the product of a process of social validation of abstract labor by means of exchange.[179] Money serves as a general measure of value and it allows us to relate different commodities to one another. Unlike in classical political economy, money was thus a constitutive necessity. And unlike in Proudhonist socialism, money did not introduce exploitation but was a necessary aspect of commodified wage labor. It is in this specific but fundamental sense that Marx's value theory can be said to be a monetary theory of value.[180]

This meant that any quest to root the value of money in nature was profoundly misguided. "Nature," Marx had explained in the *Contribution to the Critique of Political Economy*, "no more produces money than it produces bankers or a rate of exchange."[181] But at the same time, Marx similarly rejected the idea that value was simply imposed or imaginary. Therefore, both naturalizing theories of commodity money and nominalist theories of monetary value were wrong. As Marx put it in *Capital*:

> That money is a commodity is therefore only a discovery for those who proceed from its finished shape in order to analyse it afterwards. The process of exchange gives to the commodity which it has converted into money not its value but its specific value-form. Confusion between these two attributes has misled some writers into maintaining that the value of gold and silver is *imaginary*.[182]

As an example of such confusion, Marx pointed to Locke's claim that the value of silver derived from "the universal consent of mankind" and was thus grounded in fancy.[183] There was a second and equally mistaken confusion. "The fact that money can, in certain functions, be replaced by mere symbols of itself," Marx explained, "gave rise to another mistaken notion, that it is itself a mere sign [*Zeichen*]."[184] As we saw in the previous chapter, the idea of money as a representation or even a pure sign had become a commonplace in eighteenth-century thought and its influence stretched from Forbonnais to Fichte, while its earliest roots could be found, as Marx remarked, in earlier theories of legal nominalism. But just as the value of gold and silver was not grounded in the imagination, money was not simply a sign. Marx's theory of the money form thus rejected both sides in the debate between nominalist credit theories and metallist commodity theories, and it did so not just simply because Marx's question operated at a different level of analysis but because he consciously sought to criticize both commodity theorists and credit theorists.[185]

Money as Capital

We now have a better grasp of why Schumpeter and Ingham thought they had detected in Marx a commodity theorist but also why this fundamentally misunderstands the logic and intent of Marx's argument.[186] Marx's analysis of the money commodity (*Geldware*) can at first sight appear reminiscent of an account of commodity money. After all, Marx draws a close connection between what he calls the commodity form and the money form in a way that is alien to credit theories of money. But Marx's logic runs precisely contrary to that of the commodity theorists. While he posited a money commodity as the foundation of the monetary system, he did not ground the value of money in commodities. Instead his account of the money commodity was meant to stress the social conditions under which commodities themselves could rise to the level of becoming money. "The difficulty lies not in comprehending that money is a commodity," he put it at the end of the second chapter of *Capital*, "but how, why and by what means a commodity becomes money."[187] Money was a commodity only in the sense that all commodities are money. The money form was in this sense "the reflection thrown upon a single commodity by the relations between all other commodities."[188] Under capitalism, as William Clare Roberts has put it, any commodity in the equivalent form always already functions as protomoney.[189] The money form thus merely reflected the peculiar nature of commodities under capitalism. Unlike the commodity theorist for which Schumpeter and Ingham mistook him, Marx's point was precisely that the general equivalent is not intrinsically valuable but instead comes to be seen as an expression of wealth through a social act of abstraction.

This still leaves us with a number of thorny questions about the precise relation between abstract labor, commodities, and the money form. As Marx put it when discussing the functions of money in chapter 3 of *Capital*, abstract labor is the measure of value "immanent" in commodities.[190] What renders commodities thus commensurable is, pace Aristotle, not money. "Quite the contrary," Marx insists.

> Because all commodities, as values, are objectified [*vergegenständlichte*] human labor, and therefore in themselves commensurable, their values can be communally measured in one and the same specific commodity and this commodity can be converted into the common measure of their values, that is into money. Money as a measure of value is the necessary form of appearance [*Erscheinungsform*] of the measure of value which is immanent in commodities, namely labor-time.[191]

But if it is not money itself that renders commodities commensurable, what allows money to work as a measure of value?

The passage, not found in the first edition of *Capital*, has given rise to radically divergent readings. Read on its own, it does at first sight seem to suggest a more "substantialist" reading of value as being *really* rooted in abstract labor. But such a reading would fail to take seriously the centrality of appearances to Marx's underlying analysis. Despite labor time being the immanent measure of value under capitalism, Marx's account is not a labor theory of value but a critique of such a transhistorical theory, because, for Marx, value does not simply inhere in laboring. The double character of labor was from his perspective not something inherent in labor as such but a peculiar doubling that applies only under capitalism, when labor is represented in commodities.[192] This not only means that value does not straightforwardly originate in labor but also that the value of commodities has a peculiar quality in Marx's analysis. What substantialist readings of value miss is not only the specificity of abstract labor to capitalism but that value is a "social substance" (*gesellschaftliche Substanz*) with a "ghost-like objectivity" (*gespenstige Gegenständlichkeit*).[193]

Throughout *Capital*, the metaphor Marx chose to express this point was that of "crystallization." Commodities and money were both "crystals" of abstract labor.[194] Crystals were not static or without a history, but nor were they malleable organisms to be changed at will. Though grown over time, crystals were harder than stone. In the preface to *Capital*, Marx had juxtaposed crystals in this sense to living organisms when summarizing the political upshot of his analysis as having shown "that the present society is no solid crystal, but an organism capable of change, and constantly engaged in a process of change."[195] If society was not a crystal, it is interesting that money appeared to Marx by contrast as one. For Marx, capitalist production, circulation, and the money form could not be separated from one another. Instead, they formed a mutually constitutive "crystallized" set of social relations. The "money-crystal" (*Geldkrystall*) was thus at once hard and nonetheless continuously undergoing a circulatory process of almost magical metamorphosis. "Circulation becomes the great social retort into which everything is thrown, to come out again as the money crystal. Nothing is immune from this alchemy."[196] While seemingly alchemical in its appearance as value, money did not bend to political will.

As the "necessary form of appearance" of value under capitalism, money is thus no mere veil or superficial disguise to be freely molded.[197] Instead, it is the only real measure of value under capitalism and its crystallized form has an objective quality.[198] The fetishization of money (and other commodities) is from this perspective not simply a false belief or a kind of illusion to be overcome. It is a real aspect of the way in which individuals actually relate to one another under capitalism. Human interaction is here mediated through commodified products and that means that just as the social relations between producers appear to us as commodified because they are commodified, so money appears as a kind of commodity under capitalism because it is a kind of commodity.[199] This is crucially different from a commodity theory of money. Instead, Marx's theory of value, and its related theory of the money form, are social theories for a context in which the social has come to be commodified.

Marx thereby allows us to analyze the ways in which the appearance of capitalist money, however absurd, deranged, or nonsensical it may seem, constitutes an essential aspect of modern money under capitalism.[200] The form of appearance is more than a surface and constitutes an important aspect of money itself. This helps to shed light on the stubborn persistence of commodity theories of money.[201] As Christine Desan has perceptively observed, one reason why the orthodox view of money as a kind of commodity remains so indefatigable is that it seems to be part of capitalism itself.[202] Marx made a closely related point, though he went further in arguing that the form of appearance is not simply a form of deception or a self-imposed myth but an accurate depiction of what commodified social relations under capitalism actually are like.

Grasping money "in its fully developed character" as capital requires an appreciation of the way in which, under capitalism, social relations between individuals appear in the distorted form of a material object (a commodity) external to them.[203] Capitalist money is thus the way in which commodified labor appears to us. It is in this sense a constitutive part of the productive relations, and one can only exercise true control over money by controlling the productive relations.[204] To see money as simply posited by society was the result of an "illusion" that mistook cause for effect. As Marx had affirmed with reference to Sismondi in the *Grundrisse*, capitalism thrives on a kind of objective illusion that separates the shadow from the body.[205] To grasp capitalism as a historical phenomenon implied for Marx not only placing it into a larger frame of historical development but also reckoning with these objective illusions produced by one's own vantage point within the capitalist hall of mirrors.[206] One had to somehow take appearances seriously and simultaneously glimpse behind them.

Conclusion

In November 1883, nine months after Marx's death, Engels issued the third German edition of the first volume of *Capital*.[207] Based on the French edition of 1873 and incorporating Marx's marginal corrections of the second German edition of 1872, Engels executed Marx's changes. In one of the notes to the third chapter on money that Marx had wished to revise and clarify, he now distinguished even more clearly than before between two different kinds of "monetary crisis" (*Geldkrise*).[208] While in the main body of the text he had referred to a monetary crisis as merely a particular phase in a general commercial crisis of production, Marx now explained that there was also a special kind of monetary crisis that could arise independently but then affect industry and trade. Such autonomous monetary crises were driven by money capital (*Geld-Kapital*) and their sphere was that of banks, the stock exchange, and finance.

When Engels turned after Marx's death to the manuscript of volume 3 of *Capital*, which Marx had written in 1864–65 but then abandoned, he found more evidence of Marx's persistent interest in credit and monetary crises.[209] It took eleven more years until Engels was pleased to announce in 1894 that after an enormous editorial effort he was finally ready to publish the third volume of *Capital*.[210] He himself died the following year. As Engels confessed in the preface to the book, when he started his editorial work on the third volume a decade earlier, he had little idea just how much trouble the unfinished manuscript draft from 1864–65 would give him. While some chapters were in relatively finished form, others consisted of open-ended reflections that captured Marx's unfinished thought in motion. This was in particular the case for the fifth (and longest) section on the credit system, which presented Engels with "the greatest difficulty."[211] Alongside the volume's seminal discussion of profit and rent, it was this extended discussion of credit that perhaps most puzzled readers. Generations of interpreters have since wondered how precisely the treatment of credit related to Marx's analysis of the mode of production. Was Marx more interested in credit than volume 1 had led many to believe? Or did the seeming turn to credit reflect Engels's editorial hand? Was it perhaps even a misleading distortion on his part?[212]

As we have seen, Marx's deep interest in the credit system during the early 1860s should not have come as a surprise. Even where the possibility of a true monetary crisis appeared only in the footnotes of volume 1 of *Capital*, the vicissitudes of contemporary credit money loomed large for Marx in the decade preceding its publication. In his notes he returned again and again to the crisis of 1857 and also followed any subsequent credit crises in obsessive detail, including that of May 1866 when the largest British bank, Overend, Gurney & Co., collapsed (the original "Black Friday" that prompted Walter Bagehot to write his classic account of central banks as emergency providers of liquidity).[213] The underlying question that seemed to have preoccupied Marx in these notes on monetary crises was whether the dynamics of credit could always be fully captured by the abstract analysis of capitalist value or whether they contained a further dynamic of their own.[214] Marx remained beset by doubts concerning the precise relation of credit crises to the kinds of commercial crises characteristic of the capitalist mode of production. In the manuscript draft from 1864–65, Marx left the question unanswered. Instead, he sidestepped the issue by insisting that "as long as the *social* [*gesellschaftliche*] character of labor appears as the *money-existence* of commodities [*Gelddasein der Waare*], and thus as a *thing* external to actual production, money crises—independent of or as an intensification of actual crises—are inevitable."[215] Irrespectively of their precise origin (the parenthetical insertion functioned here as a hedge), monetary crises were an inevitable feature of the capitalist mode of production. No monetary reform, no reengineering of the credit system, no superior monetary management by central banks could prevent them as long as the underlying structures of production remained unchanged.

For Marx the confused futility of the Peel Act was a supreme illustration of the point, and he offered a close analysis of the act in what became under Engels's direction chapter 34 of volume 3 of *Capital*.[216] The hope of eliminating the potential for future crises by fixing the amount of currency was not just wrong on technical grounds but betrayed a more fundamental delusion—a "monstrous error" as Marx put it.[217] Though he never returned to the unfinished manuscript, each suspension of the Peel Act consequently filled Marx with delight. Until the end of his life, he predicted that laws to reform the monetary system would prove to be unworkable as long as the pervasive rule of capital had not been fully grasped and, indeed, overcome. Behind his theory of value and his account of the endogeneity of capitalist money stood a broader, and altogether more political, point about the futility of preventative monetary management and the ultimate inability of the law to shape capitalist money.

It is helpful to relate this critical rebuke to our earlier accounts of monetary order advanced by Locke and Fichte. If capitalist money was the ultimate commodity and capital was money realized to its full extent, it was similarly the world market that constituted the full realization of capitalism's productive powers. It was only on the world market, Marx explained, "that money first functions to its full extent as the commodity whose natural form is also the directly social form of realization of human labour in the abstract. Its mode of existence becomes adequate to its concept."[218] Marx's critique was in this context meant to apply as much to the Fichtean vision of malleable national fiat currencies that I reconstructed in the previous chapter as it was intended as a response to Proudhonist schemes for credit reform. To be sure, Marx conceded, "the business of coining, like the establishing of a standard measure of prices, is an attribute proper to the state."[219] But national coins were merely "different national uniforms worn at home by gold and silver as coins, taken off again when they appear on the world market."[220] This meant that money as capital, even where it circulated as national currency, was decidedly less malleable than Fichte envisioned. Under capitalism money did not straightforwardly obey the word of the state. Instead, it spoke the "language of commodities [*Waarensprache*]."[221]

Marx's critique of voluntarist monetary politics entailed at the same time an underappreciated and to some extent unintended implication. Shifting the analytic focus from money to the value form all too easily obscured that the emergence of capital did not, in fact, lead to the vanishing of the politics of money.[222] Marx's emphatic contention that no monetary reform could eliminate capitalism's central crisis tendency of overaccumulation through the extraction of surplus value easily elided that there still were better or worse ways to operate a capitalist monetary system. While Marx himself never lost interest in the operation of credit markets and central banks' role in them, many twentieth-century Marxists dismissed monetary policy and rejected it as an implausible site of political struggle. What was easily lost on many of Marx's readers was the way in which his reduction of money to a "crystal of value" had itself grown out of a deep familiarity with and appreciation for the history of money—including political struggles fought over the constitution of the monetary system. Ironically, it had been precisely this body of knowledge that had allowed Marx himself to move along the path from money to capital in the course of the 1850s. If Marx hoped to cut through the Gordian knot of socialist monetary debates, many of his tools for doing so were themselves honed in these very debates.

This was compounded by a further difficulty brought about by Marx's method. In insisting that a scientific critique of political economy had to inhabit a historicized vantage point from within capitalism, Marx consciously forced himself to ventriloquize the objective illusions of capitalism—such as the reduction of money to a commodity—precisely in order to reveal their deceptive peculiarity to the capitalist mode of production. In the case of money this meant arguing from the widely shared premises of money as gold in order to reveal that the underlying conception of the money commodity was precisely not natural but unique to capitalism. But this crucial subtlety was easily lost on many readers of *Capital* who more often than not ended up reifying capitalist money rather than demystifying its fetishistic character. As a result, far more than placing limits on monetary policy and monetary reform, readers of Marx often eclipsed the politics of money tout court. At its most extreme, one effect of Marx's intervention has in this sense been an elision of monetary politics on the left that has at times mirrored the liberal elision in Locke's wake.

There are nonetheless ways of capturing Marx's powerful critique of the limits of monetary policy and reform without eliding the politics of money. The extreme version of the Marxian claim—that legislation on monetary matters simply does not matter—cannot hold and Marx himself never thought it did.[223] Monetary legislation and the structure of the domestic and international monetary system have proven remarkably consequential. Even under conditions of global financial markets the law makes, and continually remakes, money.[224] And yet Marx was surely right to caution against excessively voluntarist conceptions of monetary management, and to point out that schemes of monetary reform need to engage with the underlying peculiarities of production and circulation under capitalism. This does not deny that different monetary regimes have distributional implications or that the allocation of credit can alleviate or deepen crises. Instead Marx forces us to grapple with the relative autonomy of monetary policy, which recalls earlier state-derivation debates about the relative autonomy of the state.[225] The relative autonomy of the political that can be seen to emerge out of these debates extends to the relative autonomy of monetary politics. The state, it is important to recognize, is not simply the agent of capital; but nor is it removed from societal conflicts over the value form.[226] There can be no doubt that the state has a special status concerning the circulation of money. Its fiscal prerogatives allow it to enforce the circulation of its own money and this comes with certain powers. But the state also reflects the class conflicts that themselves constitute the constant circulation and transformation of capital.[227] Marx's account serves then as a reminder that the monetary autonomy of the state is real and nonetheless only relative in a system in which money is endogenously created by banks and circulates as capital.

Behind this substantive technical point looms a second, more strategic question: Are monetary politics and the allocation of credit promising arenas for political mobilization and contestation? Marx's answer was resoundingly negative. This was not an unreasonable conclusion to draw in an age in which central banks were still private institutions and in which the extension of the franchise focused on areas more immediate political reach. Reducing the length of the working day seemed a far more promising and immediately tangible arena of political mobilization and struggle. To focus one's intellectual and political resources on monetary policy would appear in this light as a fruitless distraction.[228] But the answer to this question is no longer obvious. Not only are there important historical examples of electoral politics dramatically pivoting around monetary policy, but in the contemporary context of financialized capitalism and radically shrunk labor unions the allocation of credit has rightly shifted back into the light of political struggles. Just as there are ongoing political struggles within capitalist production (ranging, for example, from the exercise of power within firms to the lack of control over labor time by many workers in zero-hours contracts), so are there important political struggles over a more egalitarian provision of credit and a more progressive monetary policy. None of this amounts to the end of the capitalist value form, but nor should we simply write off any of these struggles—and the political mobilizations necessary to wage them—as pointless or hopeless.

A better reading of Marx would take on board his powerful critique of monetary reform and his careful delineation of the limits of monetary policy, while acknowledging at the same time that even under capitalism money oscillates between currency and capital, between malleability and constraint, between law and commodity. States make money even if they do not always do so as they please.

CHAPTER FIVE

Managing Modern Money

JOHN MAYNARD KEYNES AND GLOBAL
MONETARY GOVERNANCE

My little proposals are too modest and moderate for this lunatic world.

—JOHN MAYNARD KEYNES, APRIL 1933[1]

ON MONDAY, JULY 13, 1931, John Maynard Keynes was on the prewar ocean liner RMS *Adriatic,* sailing home after a six-week visit to the United States.[2] The official purpose of his trip had been to give a series of lectures on the Great Depression and the problem of unemployment. But Keynes had also come to listen and observe. He was eager to learn about the American political response to the dire economic situation that engulfed both sides of the Atlantic. In Chicago, where he had been invited to give the annual Harris Foundation lectures in June, no fewer than fifty small banks had suspended payments over the previous two months alone.[3] In Europe, already two weeks before Keynes's departure for America, Austria's largest bank, *Creditanstalt,* had collapsed. An aggressive German threat to default on all pending reparations had meanwhile triggered a run on the German mark. With its international reserves rapidly dwindling, the German Reichsbank was soon approaching levels that endangered its continued participation in the interwar gold standard. In response, President Hoover proposed a one-year moratorium on all German reparations and international war-debt payments.

Speaking in Chicago on June 22, two days after Hoover's moratorium had been announced, Keynes took stock. "We are today in the middle of the greatest catastrophe—the greatest catastrophe due almost to entirely economic causes—of the modern world. I am told that the view is held in

Moscow that this is the last, the culminating crisis of capitalism, and that our existing order of society will not survive it."[4] Things did not improve over the subsequent three weeks. On Monday, July 13, as Keynes was on his way back aboard the RMS *Adriatic*, two more dominoes fell on the European continent. In the early hours of trading the giant German *Danat Bank* collapsed, threatening to take the entire German banking system with it.[5] In response, the conservative chancellor (and later Harvard professor of government) Heinrich Brüning suspended repayment of Germany's short-term foreign debt, then the largest in the world. The very same day, the Macmillan Committee on Finance and Industry, of which Keynes had been a member, published its long-awaited report, which confirmed Britain's significant exposure to Germany's debt. With Keynes still at sea, the pound sterling dropped sharply.

How was Britain supposed to stay on gold with its German claims frozen? As Keynes insisted, to make further sacrifices for the sake of gold was both futile and perverse.[6] "The game's up," he put it to Prime Minister Ramsay MacDonald upon arrival.[7] By August the crisis had forced MacDonald to abandon his Labour government in order to form a coalition government with the Tories and Liberals (the so-called National Government). The Bank of England meanwhile confirmed reports that its governor, Montagu Norman, had suffered a nervous breakdown and, acting on medical advice, would temporarily abandon his duties. As his last act before disappearing to Canada, Norman had ration books printed in case the monetary system collapsed in its entirety.[8]

It took until Friday, September 18, when the Bank of England lost another £18 million in a single day, for the last threads of the orthodoxy to fray. Without consultation, the Bank essentially initiated a suspension of the gold standard.[9] The new National Government formalized the decision the following day in an emergency meeting, before MacDonald announced the stunning news in a public broadcast on Sunday. The necessary legislation was rushed through Parliament on Monday.[10] To describe Keynes as elated would have been an understatement: his friend Virginia Woolf found him in a wild state of exultation, talking politics and economics "like people in the war."[11] As Keynes famously rejoiced, the "gold fetters" had been broken.[12] "We have regained our freedom," he declared in November 1931 in the preface to his new collection of *Essays in Persuasion*.[13]

The end of the interwar gold standard during the early 1930s is by now widely seen as a decisive inflection point in the history of money and the modern state. In many ways 1931 was the ultimate economic and political crisis.[14] Britain going off gold came as a shock to the entire world's monetary imagination. As Sidney Webb, a minister in the fallen Labour government, protested: "Nobody told us we could do this."[15] Ever since the end of the Suspension Period in 1821, Britain's commitment to gold had been the anchor of the global financial and economic system. With the world's leading currency unmoored, now the entire system was in question. A dozen countries immediately followed Britain, and eleven more devalued their currencies.[16] In the spring of 1933 the US, too, abandoned gold. Over the next three years, the last holdouts of the old gold bloc caved in.[17]

From one influential perspective, self-consciously fashioned by Keynes himself at the time, the British suspension of gold convertibility in September 1931 illustrated the need for domestic policy to break out of the rigid imperatives of an international monetary standard.[18] Keynes, it is often thought, chose domestic policy autonomy over internationalism. But this standard interpretation is too simplistic. While he is rightly associated with the struggle to regain national control over the monetary forces of sociability, Keynes was at the same time striving to develop a new nonorthodox international solution that could ensure real monetary autonomy domestically while preventing imbalances, crises, and strife internationally.[19] Liberating the pound and other currencies from gold in 1931 was never an end in itself for Keynes, nor did it reflect a parochial economic nationalism.[20] Instead, it raised the question of how the unchained currencies could be stabilized again while avoiding the constraining rigidities of the gold standard. Rather than pitting national monetary autonomy against international monetary coordination, Keynes sought to transform the problem of how to govern modern money from an agonizing dilemma into a daring attempt to find a new internationalism that could, in turn, ensure genuine monetary autonomy. He was striving for a new and better internationalism that would be able to reconcile domestic autonomy with global cooperation.[21] Instead of merely embracing the unilateral suspension of gold, Keynes sought to develop a new template for international coordination that would—unlike the gold standard—allow for substantial domestic policy autonomy.

Keynes's reconceptualization of money and his constitutional theory of monetary management thus sought to reconcile national policy autonomy with the promises of international trade and coordination. Crucially, as he had already stressed in the *Treatise on Money* (1930), this possible international solution to the problem of how to govern money would have to be based in turn on a fundamental rethinking of what modern money was in the first place. Tellingly, already in August 1931 while he was pushing for Britain to go off the gold standard, Keynes floated the idea of a new international currency union that could follow suspension.[22] These ideas eventually culminated in his proposal for an International Clearing Union during the 1940s. The Bretton Woods monetary agreement that shaped the postwar world is sometimes seen as an embodiment of this vision, but Keynes's international proposals were largely rejected at the Bretton Woods conference and they remain unrealized to this day.

⁙

In the preceding three chapters we encountered three possible responses to the central problem of international politics posed by modern money. Was it possible, and desirable, to ground the value of money in the prepolitical consent of all mankind, as Locke had argued, and thereby delimit the discretionary powers of sovereigns? A global monetary standard, like that provided by gold or silver, appeared to furnish from this perspective a cosmopolitan tool of international trade and global commercial sociability, as Kant had emphasized. Or should money instead be an outgrowth of the sovereignty of the modern state that mirrors the domestic social contract, as Fichte had proposed? The constraints of gold after all heavily curtailed the ability of states to conduct domestic economic policy, while the monetary hierarchies of the gold standard compounded the inequalities of an already hierarchical international state system. Or was it pointless, as Marx had cautioned, to even try to shape the nature of money and manage the flow of capital through legislation? Was the universal commodity of gold not just a tool of commercial cosmopolitanism but also the purest embodiment of a fully commodified capitalist world economy? John Maynard Keynes, I argue in this chapter, navigated between these competing visions of monetary justice and sought to reconcile their respective attractions while dispensing with their downsides.

The disagreement between Locke and Fichte in particular raised a profound question of domestic monetary politics: If money is not merely an economic tool but also a political institution, what should its political purpose and constitutional status be? Where Locke had insisted on shielding money from devaluations by placing the measure, once established, beyond legislative reach, Fichte had contemplated the possibilities that could derive from a state being able to fully control the value of its own currency. Keynes was keenly aware of both sides of this argument: the political dimension of money with its need for political justification and control, and the Lockean argument insisting on the need to remove money from direct political interference. His response was to propose, and sketch out, a new need to manage money by placing it on an updated constitutional footing. Money was from this perspective not simply analogous to law in the abstract, but instead stood in close analogy to constitutional law.

For Keynes, the management of money was a public task tied to social justice. It derived its legitimacy from the implicit political covenant that also grounded the state. But it was nonetheless removed by at least one degree from popular politics since it relied on management by a group of experts who had to carefully navigate between democratic legitimacy and the political uses of their expertise. Keynes was, in other words, sympathetic to the depoliticization of economic relations while recognizing that depoliticization was itself a political project that required not only justification but also ingenious institutional solutions. But, not unlike Marx, Keynes furthermore came to appreciate the limits of monetary policy when pointing in *The General Theory of Employment, Interest and Money* (1936) to the need to socialize investment. Keynes thus shifted from an initial focus on interest-rate policy to instead emphasize the comprehensive need to manage investment. During tranquil times monetary policy might be sufficient for doing so, but in a slump of confidence more concerted actions would be required. This was neither planning nor state socialism, but it reflected a vision of how to alter capitalism from within by gradually driving down the return on capital.

Managing Money

Keynes was a child of the gold standard. Born in 1883, he had grown up in that "extraordinary episode in the economic progress of man," as he later put it in *The Economic Consequences of the Peace* (1919), that had been shaped by a mutually reinforcing faith in free trade and gold.[23] Among the Victorian certainties of the age, few towered as tall as the gold standard. Since the United States had restored gold convertibility in 1879 after the Civil War, all of Europe and most of the non-European world had been on gold.[24] At the turn of the century, gold was the fulcrum of the first wave of economic globalization. Precious metal functioned as the fetters of economic discipline. But they also worked on the political imagination by seemingly naturalizing economic relations around the scarcity of precious metal. It was only slowly that Keynes gradually came to suspect that, as he put it later, the foundations of the age had been "sandy and false."[25] He had first begun to question some of the key tenets of laissez-faire economics in a long essay on Edmund Burke, written during his undergraduate days in Cambridge.[26] As he explained in that essay in criticizing Burke, to read economic life through a lens of natural order and laissez-faire was to fall victim to a naturalistic illusion.[27]

Money was at first seemingly sidelined in this critique. When it came to the gold standard, Keynes continued to largely share the faith of his Edwardian contemporaries. But he soon found himself inhabiting a peculiarly productive vantage point. Having joined the India Office in 1906, he made his career before World War I within the machinery of Britain's imperial finances.[28] Paradoxically, precisely because of its exceptional status at the heart of the British Empire, India's "intricate and highly artificial system" of money was an excellent training ground and laboratory for monetary heterodoxy.[29] While London championed the gold standard elsewhere, it kept British India on a rupee exchange standard.[30] As Eric Hobsbawm once quipped, no doubt exaggerating, India was "the only part of the British Empire to which laissez-faire never applied."[31] Describing himself at the time as an unabashed "apologist of our Indian administration," Keynes looked favorably at the introduction of a token silver and paper currency in India after 1893 as a way to use the gold reserves of the British Empire more efficiently.[32] In his first book, *Indian Currency and Finance* (1913), he consequently provided the most articulate defense of the India Office view.[33] By preventing bullion from circulating in India, London was able to use India's substantial gold reserves as a large mass of maneuver in support of British short-term finances.[34] Where Indian nationalists lamented the way in which their domestic price stability was sacrificed for the empire, Keynes rejected such critiques and instead praised the more efficient use (from London's perspective) of having a token currency circulate in India while keeping the subcontinent's gold reserves in London.[35]

At home, meanwhile, Keynes defended the virtues of gold. When war broke out in 1914, gold was soon suspended as a matter of war emergency. Events only seemed to confirm the adherents of gold who had long warned that any loosening of the fetters of gold would lead to monetary profligacy. As gold came to be widely suspended, all European countries experienced substantial inflation. Indeed, the wartime inflation was on a scale so vast and unprecedented, Keynes later explained, as to constitute "in itself one of the most significant events in the economic history of the modern world."[36] The only possible historical analogy—the suspension of gold during the Napoleonic Wars—paled in comparison. Moreover, while American political discourse had long been saturated with intense struggles over money, for many Europeans—certainly the inhabitants of the British Isles—the gyration of prices came as a genuine shock. Suddenly national politics revolved around the state of the currency. Karl Polanyi captured the effect memorably in *The Great Transformation*: "Nobody could fail to experience daily the shrinking or expanding of the financial yardstick; populations became currency-conscious."[37] As revolutions, constitutional crises, and civil wars swept across Europe, several countries saw wartime inflation accelerate, before moving in the opposite direction into vortexes of deflation. Wartime inflation was followed by the great deflation of 1920–21.[38] A world of deeply interdependent economies that had not too long ago been held together by golden chains had given way to an explosive mix of radically divergent monetary paths.

Keynes, like the orthodoxy, longed for the price stability that was now gone and he stressed the dangers of both inflation and deflation. He was deeply troubled by the economic, social, and political effects of escalating double-digit inflation, but also by the less overt but all the more insidious threat of a deflationary spiral that rendered economic life stale and reduced politics to strife. Where inflation engaged "all the hidden forces of economic law on the side of destruction," wiped out creditors, and threatened to pave the way toward revolution, the effects of deflation were arguably even worse.[39] In sucking all debtors into a vortex of spiraling debt, deflation turned economic life into a protracted zero-sum game at the brink of civil war. Both society and capitalism, Keynes explained, presumed "a stable measuring-rod of value."[40] Neither could function very effectively—perhaps not at all—without monetary stability. This "monetary disorder of society" was the context in which Keynes famously quipped in *The Economic Consequences of the Peace* that Lenin was said to have declared, "The best way to destroy the capitalist system was to debauch the currency."[41] Though stability was undoubtedly the best path, Keynes nonetheless weighed up the deleterious consequences of inflation and deflation respectively and concluded that when forced to choose, inflation might be the lesser evil.[42]

Initially, this growing awareness of the political ramifications of radical changes in the price level only seemed to affirm Keynes in siding with conventional wisdom in contemplating a restoration of the gold standard. But in the course of 1922, as inflation gave way to deflation, he gradually came to question his own prior commitment to gold. Where the champions of orthodoxy clung to the restoration of gold as the guarantee of stability, Keynes realized that the longing for a return to gold had itself become a source of deflationary instability. Not coincidentally, this realization was closely related to a growing awareness that monetary hegemony had shifted decisively West across the Atlantic. The value of gold was not simply given by nature but reflected international politics. Where Keynes had previously both ignored and conveniently downplayed the hierarchical quality of the gold standard and the British imperial monetary system, he now became attuned to Britain's own new inferior position.[43] It would no longer be London but now Wall Street—or worse, Washington—that would sit at the center of the new gold system. "I see grave objections to reinstating gold in the pious hope that international co-operation will keep it in order. With the existing distribution of the world's gold, the reinstatement of the gold standard means, inevitably, that we surrender the regulation of our price level and the handling of the credit cycle to the Federal Reserve Board of the United States."[44] To tie oneself once more to gold now meant to surrender London's "freedom of action." In its stead, Keynes began a sustained intellectual and political campaign calling for "deliberate control" over the monetary standard as a tool of stabilization.

Keynes's *Tract on Monetary Reform*, published in late 1923, first detailed this vision of managed money.[45] In an argument that seemed deeply paradoxical to his contemporaries, Keynes insisted that true monetary stability called for the active discretionary management of the currency. Orthodoxy dictated that an internationally integrated economy imported price stability by ensuring a stable exchange rate in the form of the gold standard. Keynes challenged this logic. From his perspective the commitment to exchange rate stability in the form of the gold standard suddenly looked like an instance of haplessly chaining oneself to a fluctuating standard. Instead of targeting the exchange rate or simply holding the money supply constant, Keynes deployed an amended quantity theory to illustrate that keeping prices stable required managing the money supply directly and altering it if necessary.[46] "The remedy would lie," he explained, "in so controlling the standard of value that, whenever something occurred which, left to itself, would create an expectation of a change in the general level of prices, the controlling authority should take steps to counteract this expectation by setting in motion some factor of a contrary tendency."[47] Even if such a policy were not wholly successful, it would be a vast improvement on merely sitting by quietly as the standard of value, "governed by chance," spun out of control.[48]

This required a holistic rethinking of money's place in the political system. "We must free ourselves," Keynes argued in the *Tract*, "from the deep distrust which exists against allowing the regulation of the standard of value to be the subject of *deliberate decision.*"[49] It was necessary to abandon the fetishization of gold as intrinsically valuable and somehow beyond politics by instead rooting monetary trust in the central bank itself. This was also an argument for the Bank of England—still a private entity at the time—to change its own self-understanding. The matter touched for Keynes on some of the most fundamental questions concerning the purpose of the state. The Lockean defenders of "sound money," he lamented, opposed devaluations and a managed currency by insisting on the inviolability of the monetary contract, both concerning the value of debts contracted between private individuals but even more profoundly concerning the monetary contract between citizens and the state. For Keynes, these critics not only misunderstood the crucial distinction between private contracts among individuals and the state's role in guaranteeing these contracts, they failed to appreciate the pragmatic nature of political stability. Not only did the state have every *right* to break contracts that ran counter to the higher social purpose of justice (since this was the purpose for which contracts existed in the first place) but, ironically, nothing could better preserve the integrity of contracts between individuals than the state's discretionary authority "to revise what has become intolerable."[50] Keynes clearly delighted in deploying his Burkean sense of expediency against the Lockean defenders of sound money. It was precisely those who cited the liberal inviolability of the monetary contract who gravely misunderstood the political foundations of liberalism. The self-declared defenders of individual liberty and contract, Keynes maintained, were "the real parents of Revolution" and posed the greatest threat to the continuance of a free society.[51]

Keynes's call for the standard of monetary value to be brought under deliberate control formed part of a broader rethinking of the relationship between state and economy. As he argued in the 1920s, the laissez-faire separation between the two that had characterized the old liberalism of the nineteenth century was no longer able to capture reality, nor was it any longer politically palatable in an age of mass democracy.[52] Instead, a new liberalism would have to address itself squarely to the economic question. This meant for Keynes nothing less than effecting a transition from economic anarchy to a regime that would deliberately direct economic forces "in the interests of social justice and social stability."[53] There was no denying that the functions and purposes of the state had to be enlarged. What to take into the public hand and what to leave to individual decisions were far from foregone conclusions. Indeed, as Keynes put it in quoting Burke, the distinction between the two was "one of the finest problems in legislation."[54] But it was clear that the line had to be redrawn and that the ability of the state to govern economic processes had to be expanded. Crucially, though, Keynes envisaged such deliberate control over the economy not in terms of planning but through what would come to be called macroeconomic policy; that is, monetary and fiscal policy. For Keynes, the management and, ideally, prevention of economic crises called for "the deliberate control of the currency and of credit by a central institution."[55] This was not planning but indirect steering.

Such steering nonetheless required the conscious exercise of "directive intelligence," which in turn depended on new tools of administration, not least the state's ability to gather and interpret extensive statistical data.[56] This demand for technical expertise, however, all too easily cut against the very processes of democratic opinion formation that made it necessary in the first place. There was no guarantee that mass politics would produce the economic policies Keynes thought necessary; in fact, there was plenty of evidence to the contrary. The discretionary rule of experts thus always implied for Keynes an important degree of political insulation from the democratic noise outside the policy machine.[57] The resulting paradox entailed persuading an electorate to reject the pretenses of impotence on the part of the Bank of England while continuing to entrust monetary power to that small elite of policymakers.[58] In a speech in August 1925 that formed the basis for his essay "Am I a Liberal?," Keynes elaborated on this tension between the epistemic demands of economic steering and the currents of democratic politics based on the whims of opinion.

> I believe that in the future, more than ever, questions about the economic framework of society will be far and away the most important of political issues. I believe that the right solution will involve intellectual and scientific elements which must be above the heads of the vast majority of more or less illiterate voters. Now, in a democracy, every party alike has to depend on this mass of ill-understanding voters, and no party will attain power unless it can win the confidence of those by persuading them in a general way that it intends to promote their interests or that it intends to gratify their passions.[59]

The increasing importance of economic questions in politics rendered even otherwise well-educated citizens practically illiterate, leaving them and the polity they shared vulnerable to manipulation and demagoguery. At the same time, in a democracy it was only possible to attain the levers of economic steering by persuading the mass of ill-understanding voters in whose interest the new captains of credit were, after all, claiming to act.

The resulting difficulties of how to discuss monetary policy in a democracy are well illustrated by the eventual struggle in 1925 over whether Britain should return to gold and if so, whether it should do so at the old rate.[60] Winston Churchill as chancellor of the exchequer was strongly urged by the Bank of England, as well as by his advisers at the Treasury, to restore the value of the pound by returning to the prewar exchange rate.[61] Keynes turned all his intellectual and rhetorical firepower on Churchill.[62] Whether one was for or against gold, Keynes argued, a commitment to the old rate implied that the government would somehow have to bring down all money wages and all money values. But no plan existed for how to do so.[63] Instead of daring to explain the policy to the public in the hope of lowering all wages (and hence prices) simultaneously through a negotiated agreement, the Treasury and the Bank of England were plotting to proceed by stealth and force. In the absence of an agreement, the only way to reduce money wages was to restrict credit and thereby cause an artificial recession. Not only was there no guarantee that the final result would be fair, but the policy pitted debtors against creditors, and stronger groups against weaker ones.[64] As Keynes observed in astonishment, to force down wages in this manner amounted to "deliberately intensifying unemployment."[65] This was a policy "from which any humane or judicious person must shrink."[66] No democratic government could ever state openly that its goal was to intentionally increase unemployment, and both the Treasury and the Bank consequently had gone to great lengths to carefully conceal their true intent. Keynes was thus not merely throwing his weight behind this or that policy; he was advancing a moral argument that monetary policy should be publicly debated.[67]

In failing to describe the perverse intent of the policy, Keynes felt that the Treasury Committee on the Currency had essentially misled Churchill in painting a rosy picture of quick adjustment. Instead, the committee ought to have dared to admit to the Chancellor that the recommended policy required political mendacity. "We ought to warn you," Keynes ventriloquized the imaginary advice, "that it will not be safe politically to admit that you are intensifying unemployment deliberately in order to reduce wages. Thus you will have to ascribe what is happening to every conceivable cause except the true one. We estimate that about two years may elapse before it will be safe for you to utter in public one single word of truth."[68] As Keynes pointed out, monetary orthodoxy and democratic debate did not mix. The infamous secrecy of the Bank of England and its systematic concealment of important statistics did not help either. And yet, Keynes insisted, educating the public and revealing the government's strategy of concealment to public opinion was the only possible hope for still preventing such an act of "social injustice."[69] The public rightly judged policies not only by standards of expediency but also by justice. It would never permit the deliberate creation of unemployment for the sake of a return to gold if only it knew what was being done.[70]

In the end, Keynes failed to persuade his contemporaries. Churchill ultimately sided with the monetary orthodoxy of the Bank and Britain returned to gold at the old rate. The forced downward adjustment of wages provoked fierce opposition and brought on the only general strike in British history in May 1926.[71] Churchill is said to have described his decision to go along with the Bank's advice as the single worst political misjudgment of his life.[72]

Accounting for Money

With the immediate battle over gold lost, Keynes played the long game and returned with great vigor to his scholarship on the nature of money. If he had by the mid-1920s become the leading voice for the exercise of more direct control over the standard of value, he had at the same time not strayed far beyond the confines of Cambridge orthodoxy when it came to conceptualizing what money was in the first place.[73] He was still relying on the conceptual tools developed by Alfred Marshall and Arthur Cecil Pigou, including a quantity theory with only minor modifications.[74] The persuasive power of the *Tract on Monetary Reform*, after all, derived from its ability to show how widely accepted premises could yield an unexpected conclusion in the form of the need to actively manage the standard of value to ensure its stability.[75] As we saw in the Preface, almost immediately after the publication of the *Tract*, Keynes began to question some of these conventional premises. In early 1924 he turned to the deep history of money and the foundations of monetary theory, going all the way back to Babylonian credit practices and Athenian monetary reforms.[76] By the following year he had produced the first outline of a new book to be entitled "The Theory of Money and Credit."[77] In the fall and winter of 1925, with the lost gold-standard battle behind him, Keynes's attention moved once more into the realm of ancient monies and the historical origins of credit. By 1927 the title of the project had changed to *A Treatise on Money*.[78] It took another three years, and several rounds of agonizing revisions, for the book to appear in two volumes in the fall of 1930.[79]

Keynes opened the first volume of the *Treatise on Money* with a definitional distinction between "money" and "money of account." It was the latter that primarily interested him. Money of account, he explained, was the unit in which debts (defined as contracts for deferred payment) were expressed.[80] Money itself was merely the tool by which such debts were discharged—be it "by word of mouth or by book entry on baked bricks or paper documents"—or through which purchasing power could be held.[81] From this fundamental observation Keynes derived two main points. First, for debts to be discharged through money they first must have been expressed in terms of a money of account. To focus on the substance of money thus missed the underlying network of credit and units of account. To think that the value of currency somehow derived from the value of its material was "like confusing a theatre ticket with the performance."[82] Instead, a relationship in which a debt was incurred preceded the exchange of what was commonly seen as money. Put differently, money of account denoted a particular kind of debt relationship that was logically and historically prior to the market.[83] The second point Keynes emphasized was the way in which this framing of money in terms of debts and contracts immediately introduced custom and the law, and with them the state and the community, into any discussion of monetary affairs. Not only did the state enforce property rights to ensure the delivery of money contracts, it also decided *what* it was that must be delivered as "a lawful or customary discharge of a contract which has been concluded in terms of the money of account."[84] It was the state, therefore, that set the money of account.

Keynes here developed and historicized a series of claims usually associated with the chartalism of Georg Friedrich Knapp's *State Theory of Money* (1905).[85] Keynes had been familiar with Knapp's argument at least since 1914 when he had reviewed a book by a disciple of Knapp's in the *Economic Journal*.[86] While left somewhat perplexed by the Knappian proliferation of neologisms, Keynes's impression was generally positive. If there was a problem with Knapp's work it was that its idiosyncratic terminology exaggerated the novelty of the underlying ideas. For Keynes, much of it seemed uncontroversial and even intuitive. Money did not have value itself but was only a measure of value. Whether or not this meant that "money is a creature of the state," as Knapp had asserted, was in some sense a "purely dialectical" question.[87] Knapp's single-minded emphasis on the state seemed a little too "Hegelian and German" for Keynes's taste, but the underlying argument was, he thought, "a great intellectual advance on what preceded it."[88]

In *The State Theory of Money*, published in German in 1905 and translated into English in 1924, Knapp had derived his conception of state money from a nominalist account of money as a particular kind of token.

The terminology he coined for this view was "chartalism" after the Latin word for ticket or token.[89] Tying this account of money as a token back to the state, Knapp explained that the state in its capacity as the guardian and maintainer of law created the "nominality" of the unit of value.[90] Knapp's historically steeped discussion of money as a legal form tied to the modern state proved enormously influential in the context of the German Historical School. When Max Weber, for example, discussed the basic sociological categories of economic action in the second chapter of *Economy and Society*, his intricate definitional discussion of the theory of money was heavily indebted to Knapp.[91] In following Knapp, Weber defined money as a "chartal means of payment" that functioned essentially as a nominal means of exchange.[92] Not coincidentally, Weber observed, the modern state claims not only a monopoly on the legitimate use of violence but also a universal monopoly on the monetary order (*Geldordnung*).[93] A country's monetary system amounted from this perspective to a constitutional order (*Geldverfassung*).[94]

Keynes followed this historical literature on monetary nominalism closely and it came to form one important starting point in the *Treatise*. Where he had earlier still described Knapp's emphasis on the state as a "dialectical" distraction, by 1930 the monetary role of the state had become far more tangible for Keynes. He now embraced the Knappian account without major caveats.[95] In addition to enforcing contracts and property rights, Keynes explained, the state "claims the right to determine and declare *what thing* corresponds to the name, and to vary its declaration from time to time—when, that is to say, it claims the right to re-edit the dictionary."[96] All modern money ("civilized money," Keynes called it) was ultimately tied to the state "beyond the possibility of dispute."[97]

After having opened the first chapter of the *Treatise* with a definitional summary of monetary nominalism and the state theory of money, Keynes turned next to "Bank Money" in order to elaborate on the role of private credit in his theory of money.[98] The result was a hierarchical pyramid of monies. While all modern money was ultimately rooted in the state, most money was in fact bank money.[99] Drawing on various accounts of credit money, including that of the Swedish economist Knut Wicksell, Keynes illustrated the way in which banks "created" money quite independently of savers' deposits.[100] Crucially, bank money was not externally given or a mere reflection of deposits but instead socially constructed by the discretionary lending decisions made by banks.[101] Keynes's *Treatise* thus drew on both German state theory of money and on contemporary credit theories of money to challenge the kinds of commodity-exchange theories of money that had become a staple of classical political economy and still influenced the thought of many of his more traditional Cambridge colleagues. The *Treatise of Money* was in this sense a showcase for the need to incorporate the perspectives offered by nominalist, state, and credit theories of money into modern monetary economics.[102]

The book immediately attracted broad attention and, because of Keynes's role on the Macmillan Committee, it was also widely read in the Treasury.[103] One of those reviewing the book in the summer of 1931 in the pages of *Economica*, the house journal of the London School of Economics (LSE), was a young lecturer named Friedrich August Hayek who had been invited from Vienna earlier in the year to give a series of lectures at the LSE and who was promptly—and to everyone's surprise—offered the Tooke Chair of Economic Science and Statistics.[104] Focusing on volume 1 of the *Treatise*, in his review Hayek primarily complained at length about Keynes's confusing terminology, his seemingly shifting definitions of profit and investment, and the lack of a concept of capital.[105] But Hayek also flagged for the British reader that continental economists had long been familiar with many of the credit theories Keynes had recently discovered for himself. Especially Wicksell's work had long formed a part of Austrian economic theorizing, not least because Wicksell had built his own theories at the beginning of the century on the classic insights of Austrian capital theory, in particular the work of Eugen von Böhm-Bawerk, an aspect—Hayek charged—Keynes had conveniently ignored in his own synthesis. In the next issue of the journal, Keynes immediately shot back. All Hayek had done in his review, Keynes complained, was pedantically "pick over the precise words I have used with a view to discovering some verbal contradiction or insidious ambiguity," while sidestepping the obvious and substantial theoretical and political disagreements.[106] Having defended himself against the charges of inconsistency, Keynes turned his response into a vicious review of his own by taking on Hayek's *Prices and Production*, which had just appeared based on his LSE lectures earlier in 1931.[107] Keynes described the book contemptuously as "one of the most frightful muddles I have ever read." It was "an extraordinary example of how, starting with a mistake, a remorseless logician can end up in Bedlam."[108] Hayek got a chance to respond in turn but the debate soon fizzled out.

Behind the peculiar mixture of definitional quibbles and personal attacks stood profound differences in philosophical perspective and in politics that translated into radically different conclusions. Part of the seemingly technical disagreement had thus no doubt to do with this clash of divergent premises and divergent practical implications. Hayek, like

Keynes, was concerned about the ways in which modern credit money destabilized the economy. But his ideal solution was to heavily restrict private and public credit creation by tying both banks and the state to gold. This was an unorthodox defense of the orthodoxy. If that was politically impossible, Hayek thought there was simply very little that could be done to prevent slumps. One of the peculiarities of this Hayekian position, as Robert Skidelsky has pointed out, was that it essentially arrived at Marx's answer concerning the futility of monetary policy from different premises and via a different route.[109] Ironically, Hayek's somber vision of the follies of capitalist credit creation seemed peculiarly attractive to a certain kind of socialist during the early 1930s, and his students at the LSE included a fair number of socialist converts to the cause of Austrian economics.

Keynes, by contrast, had a very different response to the irrationalities of private credit creation. As he saw it, his new theory of money was meant to lay the groundwork for a reconceptualization of central banking that was urgent because it held the key to how to manage credit. Indeed, in his review of the first volume of the *Treatise*, Hayek had jabbed that it must have been the urgency Keynes attributed to the practical proposals he derived from his theoretical reasoning that had led him to rush the work and publish it in an "unfinished state."[110] Keynes had of course worked on the *Treatise* on and off for the better part of five years and these swipes no doubt motivated his vindictive review of Hayek's work in turn. But it was true that Keynes thought that the theoretical insights of the "pure theory" of money had far-reaching and urgent practical implications.[111] Those were the questions Keynes turned to in the second volume of the *Treatise*.

A Constitutional Monarch?

As Keynes explained in the second volume, inquiring into the proper management of money entailed first of all reckoning with the role of credit creation by banks in a modern economy. Keynes highlighted the underlying political stakes deftly by staging a standoff between, on the one hand, the great army of heretics and money cranks whose extraordinary enthusiasm inversely mapped onto their influence, and, on the other hand, the complacent club of self-satisfied bankers. Keynes introduced the monetary heretics approvingly:

> Why then, he [the monetary heretic] asks, if the banks can create credit, should they refuse any reasonable request for it? And why should they charge a fee for what costs them little or nothing? Our

troubles seem to him to arise because the banks have monopolised this power of creating credit in order to enable them, by artificially restricting its supply, to charge a price for it and thus realise a profit. For why, if they possess this magical power, are they so stingy?[112]

The traditional reply of the bankers to this charge, Keynes concluded, was "singularly unconvincing."[113] As much as bankers might try to suggest to the outside world that their lending depended upon the amount of deposits in their own vaults or at least the amount of gold in the vaults of the central bank, even they ultimately could not deny that they could and did in fact *create* credit. But if the bankers had managed to secure a "monopoly of magic," was it any wonder that they exercised their powers sparingly in order to raise the price of magic?[114] After all, "if bakers were a close corporation who could make bread from stones, it does not follow that they would reduce the price of the loaf to the cost of a quartern of stones. Where magic is at work, the public do not get the full benefit unless it is nationalised."[115] Faced with the obvious shortcomings of the existing monopoly of credit magic, Keynes frankly admitted his own sympathy with the heretical demand.

Yet, while he agreed with the heretics in aligning credit creation with social justice, Keynes insisted that control over credit and investment could be achieved without nationalization.[116] Instead, he placed his hope in a reformed central bank steering investment and providing the right amount of credit to "keep to the middle path of continuous health."[117] If the revision of the concept of money meant that the money rate of interest was now endogenous to the operation of the financial system itself, Keynes nonetheless moved central banks center stage because it was ultimately the central bank that functioned as "the conductor of the orchestra" by setting the tempo of credit creation across the banking system.[118] A reformed central bank would be able to adjust the creation of credit so as to meet all genuine, noninflationary demands for working capital.[119] In order to control the credit cycle, and consequently the rate of investment, Keynes proposed two main tools: changes in the short-term discount rate (which was directly subject to "the will and *fiat* of the central authority") and open-market operations.[120] Where the former set the pace, the latter was able to adjust the structure of rates available in the market, including the long-term rate. Jointly used, these two tools together allowed central banks to control "not merely the volume of credit but the rate of investment, the level of prices and in the long run the level of incomes."[121] Underlying the proper management of money was thus an entwined technical and political question about how to establish "unchallengeable central-ised control" over the level and rate of investment in order to deploy it to achieve a more efficient and more just allocation of credit.[122]

Although Keynes rejected demands for the nationalization of the bank-ing system, his quest for centralized control over credit creation did imply putting the existing monetary system on a new constitutional footing. Instead of either faith in the natural order of value that gold represented or complacency toward the inequities and inefficiencies of unguided pri-vate credit creation, Keynes called for credit to be subjected to deliberate control. Ideally, as he had argued in the *Tract on Monetary Reform*, this would have meant doing away with the arbitrary and destabilizing restric-tions of gold all together. If that turned out to be impossible for the time being, Keynes suggested submitting money instead to a process of secu-larization and constitutionalization. As he put the demand poetically in the second volume of the *Treatise on Money*, gold had to brought from the heavens down to earth. "Thus gold, originally stationed in heaven with his consort silver, as Sun and Moon, having first doffed his sacred attributes and come to earth as an autocrat, may next descend to the sober status of a constitutional king with a Cabinet of banks; and it may never be neces-sary to proclaim a republic."[123] Where Proudhon had called in 1848 for the republicanization of credit in the form of a People's Bank, Keynes sketched instead a distinctly British path of political reform in which gradual con-cessions would turn money from a divine despot into a constitutional monarch, subjected to Parliament and "shorn of his ancient despotic pow-ers."[124] To make money subject to deliberate control meant for Keynes developing a kind of contained constitutional politics based on expertise.

This was an evocative way of framing his proposal. In the *Tract on Monetary Reform*, Keynes had still sought to distance the problem of deliberate control over money from the revolutionary change he associ-ated with "the Constitution." As he had explained there: "We can no lon-ger afford to leave [the standard of value] in the category of which the distinguishing characteristics are possessed, in different degrees, by the weather, the birth rate, and the Constitution—matters which are settled by natural causes, or are the resultant of the separate action of many indi-viduals acting independently, or require a revolution to change them."[125] Unlike the weather, the value of money was not natural. Unlike the birth rate, it was not the spontaneous result of many individual actions. But nei-ther was money a constitutional question that could be changed only with a revolution. Instead, money would have to be managed.[126] And while such a reform meant subjecting money to deliberate control, it also meant blocking it off from revolutionary politics. Indeed, the very point of exercising deliberate control over money was to forestall revolution.[127] The general strike of 1926 after Churchill's decision to restore gold convertibility at the old rate had been ominous for precisely this reason.

But if monetary reform was meant to forestall revolution, constitutional change also provided an analogue. Keynes's discussion of turning modern money into a constitutional monarch recalled Walter Bagehot's seminal Victorian analysis of the British constitution. While today mostly remembered as a theorist of central banking and the influential third editor of *The Economist*, Bagehot's account of the Bank of England in *Lombard Street* (1873) consciously mirrored his earlier analysis of the English constitution.[128] In Bagehot's telling, both the English constitution and the Bank of England relied on a fundamental illusion. Both cultivated a highly visible and dignified exterior that was meant to project grandeur and instill faith, while behind the facade a small committee governed from the dark without being exposed to external pressures and demands. Banking was for Bagehot, as Alexander Zevin has succinctly put it, "the mirror image of politics."[129] Just as understanding the British constitution meant looking beyond the monarchy to see the workings of Parliament coordinated by the cabinet, so in the realm of money one had to look beyond the glitter of gold to see the orchestra of private banks, extending credit and taking deposits, with the Bank of England acting as conductor. The outward appearance of the currency was from this perspective a powerful illusion from which everyone was said to benefit but that nonetheless ultimately relied on deception to work. In the 1870s Bagehot had insisted that one of the political implications of this analysis was that attempts to nationalize the Bank of England along French lines, or to fundamentally reorder the English money market, were as futile as they were dangerous.[130] Credit, like loyalty in government, was too delicate to survive such a revolution. Change, if indeed it was necessary, had to come gradually.[131]

Keynes consciously echoed this analysis, even where he advocated for change. His aspiration to give gold "the sober status of a constitutional king with a Cabinet of banks" implicitly invoked Bagehot's analysis in advocating for a distinctly British constitutionalization of money.[132] The Reform Acts had between 1867 and, most recently, 1928 gradually extended the suffrage and in doing so altered the dynamics of the unwritten British constitution. These were, in effect, successful efforts at keeping revolution and more radical change at bay. For Keynes a gradual reform of the monetary constitution could have similarly far-reaching effects. Money was ultimately tethered to the public good and its legitimacy was tied up with that of the state, but it nonetheless had to be shielded from direct democratic politics, nationalization, or indeed revolutionary change. Ideally, money would be governed by an institution that was public in its spirit and exposed to public opinion, and yet removed from immediate electoral politics by at least one degree.[133] As he put the finishing touches on the *Treatise* in the fall of 1930, Keynes could not have known that less than a year later Britain would go off gold and thereby throw open the door to more radical forms of monetary experimentation.

The End of Gold

When Britain suddenly abandoned gold in September 1931, Keynes looked prescient. For years he had been one of the most prominent and persistent voices calling for Britain to leave the interwar gold exchange standard during the Great Depression, even though he had largely failed to find a receptive audience. Mere days after Britain went off gold in September 1931, he consequently decided to assemble a selection of his writings from the previous twelve years as *Essays in Persuasion*. Keynes cast himself in the book as having stood on the margins as a maverick, before suddenly finding that almost every single one of his seemingly eccentric positions appeared to have been vindicated.[134] To entitle the collection *Essays in Persuasion* was thus always an ironic choice.[135] As Keynes himself pointed out, his arguments had by and large failed to persuade his contemporaries. Assembled for the reader, he joked, were thus "the croakings of a Cassandra who could never influence the course of events in time."[136]

The British abandonment of gold promised in this context a conscious break with the immediate past of a gold exchange standard that had become an unbearable burden. It also constituted, in its own way, a return to the Suspension Period during the Napoleonic Wars a century before. But if many in 1931 looked back to 1797, more than a few also pointed to the post-Napoleonic restoration of gold in 1821. Indeed, the general election that followed little more than one month after suspension in the fall of 1931 was fought exclusively over the currency issue and won by the Conservatives on the basis of a promise to restore gold. Labour, which had refused to commit to restoration, lost 215 of its 267 seats.[137] Democratic politics could produce surprising results in the realm of money.

For Keynes, by contrast, the end of gold was the leap into the future he had longed for. The appropriate response to the end of gold hinged on his larger vision of a new liberalism that would no longer define itself simply as the guardian of laissez-faire but advance a broader conception of human flourishing. And as he had insisted for years, any such attempt to formulate a new liberal response to economic questions in turn required a fundamental rethinking of the international system. After all, already in *The Economic Consequences of the Peace*, Keynes had emphasized the mutually constraining bind between international politics and domestic economic life, as well as the domestic difficulties of international economic coordination and compromise.[138] In his critique of the Versailles Peace Treaty he had not only argued against ruinous French and British demands for German reparations but also set out an argument for an imaginative political stroke in the form of intergovernmental debt forgiveness. Such an intervention in turn required, and itself further channeled, a broader change in opinions and attitudes toward the future of international relations.[139] Debt diplomacy was from this perspective not only essential to prevent a return of global war but could even serve as the foundation for new institutions of international economic governance through which the politics of the world economy could be managed.[140] Economic reform and international politics were for Keynes never far apart.

Many interpretations of Keynes have pinpointed his concerns primarily in the realm of domestic political economy; this is Keynes as the father of the "Keynesian" revolution in national macroeconomics and the postwar welfare state. Some have even detected echoes of economic nationalism in Keynes's theories. Fichte and Keynes rub shoulders, for example, as fellow economic nationalists in Michael Heilperin's classic study.[141] Recent readers of Fichte have similarly suggested an analogy between his proposal to close the commercial state and Keynes's consideration of self-sufficiency during the early 1930s.[142] As we saw in the third chapter, Fichte's sketch had emerged out of an earlier moment of monetary experimentation and the benefits of Fichtean monetary autonomy would not have failed to attract Keynes. And yet to reduce Keynes's position to a quest for national economic-policy autonomy misses a crucial dimension. What these interpretations elide is his emphasis on the importance of international coordination and his striving for a better system of international monetary management than those provided either by the gold exchange standard or freely floating exchange rates. Keynes—and Fichte, in his own way—emphasized national autonomy only as one piece of a broader internationalist program. Indeed, both sought to disentangle political internationalism from certain aspects of economic cosmopolitanism by articulating the ways in which international economic competition (in Fichte's case) and international financial flows (in Keynes's case) introduced conflicts and obstacles that made international peace and cooperation less likely.

The high point of Keynes's insistence on domestic autonomy came in the wake of the liberating British escape from the gold standard in 1931 and the discussions that followed on whether America should follow suit. What now mattered more than anything else was to avert being merely helplessly dragged along by the burden of the past. A Burkean appeal to political expediency converged on this point with Keynes's attempt to effect reform without revolution.[143] This sentiment found its clearest expression in a lecture on "National Self-Sufficiency" given on April 19, 1933, that marks the extreme end of Keynes's skepticism about the possibility of peaceful economic internationalism and his insistence on national policy experimentation.[144] It is worth remembering in this context that the lecture was given in Dublin in the midst of an intense trade war between Britain and Ireland.[145] "It is my central contention," Keynes exclaimed in the lecture, that "there is no prospect for the next generation of a uniformity of economic system throughout the world, such as existed, broadly speaking, during the nineteenth century; that we all need to be as free as possible of interference from economic changes elsewhere, in order to make our own favourite experiments towards the ideal social Republic of the future."[146] Self-sufficiency would free economic policy from previous international constraints and open up new possibilities of political and economic experimentation. Along these lines, in the Dublin lecture he repudiated any association of economic internationalism with peace. Instead, he suggested provocatively, greater economic isolation between countries might serve the cause of peace better than economic internationalism had done.[147]

But even the Dublin lecture was not simply an embrace of nationalism for its own sake; it was instead a call for bold experimentation. Indeed, Keynes ended by hinting at a subversion of his own argument. The enemy was not free coordination, he thought, but mindless uniformity. Experimentation, he explained, required unrestricted and remorseless self-criticism, not blithe conformity. Where criticism of economic policy was lacking—as it was in Stalin's Soviet Union, where "the bleat of propaganda bores even the birds and the beasts of the field into stupefaction"—true experimentation was impossible.[148] Faced with the prospect of doctrinalism without self-critique, Keynes admitted that his allegiance would revert to the old liberalism that had at least made possible the intellectual space for subversive thinking that his generation prided itself on. Keynes's campaign against the gold standard and his flirtations with national self-sufficiency showed him most explicitly focused on domestic policy autonomy. But even in the Dublin lecture demonstrates that this focus was embedded in a broader vision of monetary internationalism. The end of gold, opening up new possibilities for deliberate monetary policy as it did, never meant simply letting currencies float and turning one's back on the international realm. Rather, it was a question of finding ways to allow for stabilized exchange rates whose parity could nonetheless be adjusted through politics as necessary. The choices on offer during the 1930s were far from appealing and they only affirmed Keynes's open-minded embrace of experimentation and an interventionist search for an actual solution. Leaving the old system behind was merely the opening move in the construction of a new international monetary system that ideally would neither require domestic sacrifices nor give rise to competitive international behavior. Abandoning gold was not an end in itself.

Having established the need for the state to control the rate of investment in the *Treatise on Money*, in the closing chapters of the second volume Keynes turned to the international realm.[149] Indeed, from 1926 on all of Keynes's drafts for what would become the *Treatise* had culminated in reflections on the need for "international money" and the complexities of governing it.[150] In the concluding chapters of the *Treatise*, Keynes's discussion of "ideal money" seamlessly merged into a call to establish a global central bank of central banks that would engage in the "supernational management" of the monetary affairs of the world.[151] "The ideal arrangement," he wrote, "would surely be to set up a supernational bank to which the central banks of the world would stand in much the same relation as their own member banks stand to them."[152] The recently founded Bank for International Settlements in Basel, despite its obvious shortcomings, was a promising sign in this light.[153]

When Keynes subsequently sketched proposals for a new currency union during the 1930s, critics initially seemed confused and speculated about a reversal of his position.[154] Did the arch-critic of the interwar gold standard now favor its resurrection under new auspices? Keynes responded by insisting on a deeper continuity in his thought. Taking a swipe at those who had accused him before of having changed his mind in other contexts, he savored the moment: "Since there are people who deem it creditable if one does not change one's mind, I should like to get what *kudos* I can from not having done so on this occasion."[155] All his proposals since 1923, he explained, had been in perfect agreement with each other, even if their emphasis had changed. There was neither inconsistency nor an "evolution" of his ideas, as *The Economist* had speculated. Instead, as Keynes pointed out, while he had criticized gold as an overly rigid standard, in all his proposals he had at the same time looked for a stable international standard.[156] Moreover, as much as he had famously denounced the gold standard as a "barbarous relic," he had always been perfectly content to acknowledge that, for better or worse, it was backed by "a vast body of tradition and prestige." Fitted into a framework of managed money, gold could well continue its symbolic or conventional value. But this required placing the monetary order onto new political footings. "Such transformations," he added, "are a regular feature of those constitutional changes which are effected without a revolution."[157]

In a sign of the changing times, Keynes now came under fire not for his earlier dismissal of the gold standard but instead for placing limits on national policy autonomy and sovereignty.[158] Ever since, interpreters have sought to detect an order of preference between his different proposals. Was self-sufficiency perhaps a second-best option in case the international reflationary proposal failed?[159] Did they perhaps show Keynes in two different modes of thought, patriotic political thinker in one context and cool-headed economist in another? Keynes responded that he had been pursuing both lines of thought in parallel for many years and that his domestic and international proposals, for that very reason, were meant to "assist and supplement one another."[160] The Holy Grail was thus a system that could somehow reconcile the domestic benefits of monetary autonomy with the international coordination achieved by fixed but adjustable exchange rates: in other words, a system that could square domestic social and economic experimentation with peace and international cooperation.

As Keynes highlighted, the tension between the respective imperatives of domestic monetary autonomy and international economic integration was real and could easily entangle participants in a seemingly inescapable dilemma.[161] But there were clear and attainable ways to combine the coordinating power of stable exchange rates with their adjustability that could allow for the policy autonomy necessary to provide monetary liquidity and avoid unemployment.[162] But ensuring real monetary autonomy in a world of international trade would require new supernational institutions. Far from monetary autonomy and international monetary coordination being in tragic tension, the two made each other necessary. As we will see below, reconciling international trade with monetary autonomy ultimately required a global reserve currency that would have to be managed supernationally. Far from implying a turn away from internationalism, Keynes's critique of the interwar gold exchange standard was instead always a quest for a different kind of internationalism and with it a different form of globality that would not be characterized by uniformity but instead allow for greater policy experimentation.

Socializing Investment

Today, Keynes's *General Theory* (1936) has not only become the founding text of national macroeconomics, it is also often read as marking his turn away from monetary policy toward fiscal policy.[163] While Keynes came to grant fiscal policy a greater role than he had envisaged earlier, his fundamental point concerned instead how the two would be wielded together to steer investment. The insight here was less a revelation that activist policy could stimulate the economy; even the orthodoxy accepted as much, at least in the short run. Where Keynes differed was in his insistence that worries about activist policy imperiling the exchange rate were misplaced.[164] But this point directly tied domestic policy considerations once more to questions of international monetary coordination. As Keynes explained in chapter 23 on mercantilism in the *General Theory*, the overarching concern was how to achieve domestic reform in a way that would relieve pressures of external competition, while setting up new forms of international coordination that would remove the perceived obstacle of having to refrain from stimulus for fear of the exchange rate.

While it thus ultimately mattered little whether demand stimulus would come via monetary or fiscal policy, Keynes added a crucial qualification. Already in the *Treatise on Money* he had set out a comprehensive doctrine of how a central bank could manage the level of investment both through interest-rate policy as well as through open-market operations.[165] None of this changed. But by the mid-1930s Keynes had come to be frustrated by the slow speed of recovery led by monetary policy alone. After all, already in 1932 the Bank rate had been cut from 6 to 2 percent, where it would remain for two decades—barring a brief spike at the onset of World War II. But the effects had been disappointingly slow.[166] Keynes came to add to his analysis in this context an awareness of the conditions under which central bankers could end up "pushing on a string," as monetary economists like to put it in using a metaphor often attributed to Keynes.[167] The wonderful image Keynes himself used in an open letter to President Roosevelt in January 1934 was that of "trying to get fat by buying a larger belt."[168]

As he argued in the *General Theory*, hoping that output would rise simply as a result of increasing the quantity of money failed to take into account the way in which money could lie idle because banks and companies failed to put it to productive use. Under such circumstances something beyond a further change in the interest rate would be required; namely, a more direct management of the level of investment and the volume of expenditure.[169] This technical observation went hand in hand with a more political one. Keynes's experience of having served on the Macmillan Committee between 1929 and 1932 had made him even more suspicious than before of the inherent conservatism of central bankers. Seeing one representative of the Bank of England after another flat-out deny that the Bank had the kinds of powers Keynes and all close observers knew it had seems to have shaken his faith in the possibility that the Bank could ever be reformed or take on broader responsibilities of steering investment.[170] To Keynes's frustration, the central bankers seemed to be claiming that there was little they could do to affect credit and that, in any case, there was always exactly the right amount of credit in the economy.[171]

Becoming aware of the limits of monetary policy did not, however, relegate money to the margins. On the contrary, Keynes had arrived at the insights of the *General Theory* when he came to realize the full implications of his revisionist account of money in the *Treatise*. As he explained it in a short essay from 1933 entitled "The Monetary Theory of Production," much existing economics had hitherto conceived of money as a mere "neutral link between transactions in real things and real assets."[172] As he had shown in the *Treatise*, this was clearly an inadequate conception of money. But it was also an inadequate image of the economy. The goal was now instead to articulate an account of a truly monetary economy "in which money plays a part of its own and affects motives and decisions and is, in short, one of the operative factors in the situation, so that the course of events cannot be predicted, either in the long period or in the short, without a knowledge of the behaviour of money between the first state and the last."[173] Not only was money not neutral, but only with such a monetary theory of production at hand could economics begin to solve the problem of economic crises.[174]

As Keynes put it in retrospect in a letter in which he charted his own intellectual development, the most important change on the way to the *General Theory* had been his jettisoning of the theory of demand and supply for output as a whole.[175] It had been this sudden and overwhelming realization that allowed him to see that the existing theory of employment depended on monetary assumptions that were no longer tenable. In the preface to the *General Theory*, Keynes consequently explained that the book shared more with its predecessor than was apparent at first sight. What might appear to the reader as a change of mind was instead a logical evolution in a line of thought Keynes had been pursuing for many years.[176] Moreover, it was not his theory of money that had once more changed—Keynes stood by the *Treatise* in this regard—but merely the way in which that theory affected the entire general theory of supply and demand.[177] The goal now was to push back against the idea of a pure monetary theory that was somehow separate from production and toward a monetary theory of production. This did not mean that the call for the active management of money somehow disappeared. Rather, it was placed in the context of a broader theory of production that gave rise to a more comprehensive policy reversal of which active monetary policy was only one plank and which indeed began to question the strict delineation between monetary policy and fiscal policy.[178] In the *General Theory* Keynes consequently took a broader perspective as to what kind of state interventions it would take, depending on the circumstances, to move an economy out of unemployment and toward full employment. Monetary policy was still in many ways the preferred tool of economic management during normal periods, but it was no longer sufficient on its own.[179] What mattered ultimately was the ability to govern the level of investment more directly. Cooperation with private initiative would be helpful for this, but in the end only a "somewhat comprehensive socialisation of investment" would be able to secure full employment.[180]

While such central controls would necessarily involve an extension of the traditional functions of government, Keynes stressed once more that this was emphatically not a proposal for state socialism, which would nationalize the economic life of the community. Instead, the socialization of investment appeared precisely as a tool to forestall a broader socialization of the means of production or indeed the socialization of wage setting. Keynes had long felt deeply conflicted about flexible, neoclassical wage policy. On the one hand, he was convinced that freedom of occupational choice and variation in wages were essential to liberal economies.[181] To set wages centrally amounted in effect to planning. At the same time, he had become convinced that oscillating real wages constituted both a serious inefficiency as well as a violation of fundamental principles of social justice, including the fair sharing of burdens in periods of economic adjustment. A reduction in real wages, he explained in the *General Theory* in rehashing his arguments against Churchill's policy in 1925, would inevitably occur in a haphazard and irregular way, "justifiable on no criterion of social justice, . . . where those in the weakest bargaining position will suffer relatively to the rest."[182] To control the level of investment through monetary and fiscal policy offered the prospect of avoiding the injustice of wage adjustments without abolishing liberal wage contracting. The liberal state had to learn how to govern the economy, but it would do so indirectly through the steering powers of monetary and fiscal policy on the overall level of investment.[183]

In the concluding chapter of the *General Theory*, Keynes presented the result of this intervention in two radically different ways. From one perspective, he explained, the whole proposal was exceedingly conservative. Far from ushering in an economic revolution or nationalizing the means of production, the state would merely create the preconditions necessary for the classical theory and liberal society to come into its own again.[184] From another perspective, however, the changes promised a far more radical outcome that, Keynes hoped, had the power to alter the very nature of capitalism. By socializing investment and bringing down the rate of interest, the state would be able to essentially eliminate the scarcity value of capital. This would famously amount to nothing less than "the euthanasia of the rentier and, consequently, the euthanasia of the cumulative oppressive power of the capitalist to exploit the scarcity-value of capital."[185] Leaving behind the scarcity of capital could moreover be achieved in a slow and gradualist fashion by continuously driving down the return to capital.[186]

The Eutopia of Global Monetary Reform

Public control over not just the rate of interest but also the level of investment spoke at the same time to the international task the *General Theory* was meant to accomplish. As we have seen, Keynes's quest for domestic policy autonomy was always embedded in a broader consideration of the international dimension of the problem. We can reconstruct his vision of how the domestic socialization of investment would have to be brought into harmony with international trade by turning to his proposal for an International Clearing Union, which he began to sketch during the early 1940s as part of initial efforts at postwar planning.

Above all, Keynes aimed at avoiding or at least containing competitive international behavior both in the economic and the political realm. As he had argued since the 1920s, the gold standard had not only demanded economic sacrifices that had become so odious as to be considered indefensible in a democratic polity, but gold had also been unable to live up to its internationalist promises. Far from serving international cooperation and peace, it had set countries against one another. As Keynes polemicized in his chapter on mercantilism in the *General Theory*, "Never in history was there a method devised of such efficacy for setting each country's advantage at variance with its neighbours' as the international gold (or, formerly, silver) standard."[187] Unlike in the 1933 Dublin lecture when he had flirted with self-sufficiency, Keynes now set out to diagnose and prevent protectionism and mercantilist trade war. Whereas in Dublin he had urged experimentation precisely because he could not yet detect a clear path out of the economic and political impasse of the Great Depression and the crises of the interwar years in general, in the *General Theory* he proudly announced that he had discovered the policies necessary to reconcile national with international well-being.[188]

The closing chapters of the *General Theory* thus suggested one way to reconcile the seemingly contradictory forces of policy autonomy and international coordination. Were all countries to pursue his policies simultaneously, Keynes explained, the result would be to restore economic health both nationally and internationally, whether measured in terms of domestic employment or the volume of international trade.[189] To make the point, Keynes turned to seventeenth-century mercantilism. The mercantilists had been right to be concerned about imbalances of trade, he argued, albeit for the wrong reasons. Neoclassical economics had dismissed such concerns as mere short-run phenomena of adjustment, but the mercantilists' anxiety had captured "an element of scientific truth."[190] In a society in which neither the rate of interest nor the level of investment was under public authority, the government was right to preoccupy itself with the balance of foreign trade. Achieving a favorable balance of trade was the only direct tool at its disposal for increasing foreign investment in the form of an influx of precious metals and for reducing the domestic rate of interest, thereby inducing more domestic investment.[191]

This did not mean that Keynes came out as a defender of mercantilism, but he nonetheless reframed it as an intelligible response to a set of external constraints. Rather than joining the chorus of the 1930s that pitched the wisdom of free trade against the follies of neo-mercantilist protectionism, Keynes sought to explain mercantilism (and with it neo-mercantilism). The ultimate point was to remove the external obstacles that had produced the mercantilists' response. If the mercantilists' answer of protectionism was wrong, it was not because their analysis had been faulty. "The mercantilists perceived the existence of the problem," Keynes observed, "without being able to push their analysis to the point of solving it."[192] In Keynes's retelling of the history of mercantilism, Locke acquired a pivotal role. He stood, as Keynes put it, "with one foot in the mercantilist world and with one foot in the classical world."[193] Locke's reasoning was still steeped in the distinctions and aims of mercantilism even while his observations spilled beyond it. While Locke never fused these into a genuine synthesis, he had opposed attempts to fix a maximum rate of interest and was "perhaps" the first to express in abstract terms a relation between the rate of interest and the quantity of money. Locke stood thus on the threshold of the emergence of modern classical economic wisdom which Keynes sought to overturn.

If the mercantilists had not been fools but victims of their external circumstances, the same was true for the neo-mercantilists. As Keynes stressed, gold-standard thinking itself had bred neo-mercantilist jealousies by making "domestic prosperity directly dependent on a competitive pursuit of markets and a competitive appetite for the precious metals."[194] The right response to the protectionism of the 1930s was thus not to return to the gold standard once more, which would only reimpose the same golden fetters of a jealous appetite for precious metal. Instead, international cooperation and free trade would be best restored by allowing for domestic recovery rather than forestalling it. Setting interest rates and managing a national investment program with an eye toward achieving domestic full employment was "twice blessed in the sense that it helps ourselves and our neighbours at the same time."[195] Keynes's theory opened up the possibility of a new economic internationalism that was no longer the odious beggar-thy-neighbor internationalism of the gold standard but one that reconciled national demands with international benefits. This was no longer a proposal to close the commercial state for all trade, along Fichte's lines, but instead a tantalizing vow to make good on international trade's original promise of fair exchange and peaceful commerce.

The one element of the solution that Keynes bracketed in the *General Theory* was the problem of what monetary unit would come to serve as the international numeraire in this context. Keynes had already flagged the problem in the second volume of the *Treatise*. In a world of n trading states, each with its own fiat currency, one of the currencies will come to have two distinct roles (often in contradiction to each other), one as national currency and one as international unit of account. To avoid such a source of imbalance and instability, and to introduce a tool for possible adjustments, it would be necessary to establish an international reserve currency that was distinct from the existing currencies.[196] In the Clearing Union Proposal that Keynes came to develop during the 1940s, he sketched in detail what a global reserve currency might look like that would be able to reconcile domestic monetary autonomy and international monetary coordination by providing a tool of adjustment.[197] Under the gold standard, Keynes pointed out, adjustment had been asymmetric: *compulsory* for the debtor and *voluntary* for the creditor.[198] In a just and stable international monetary order, he insisted, adjustment had to be shared. The Clearing Union had to include provisions that would guard against the exploitation of borrower countries, not merely against the exposure of creditor countries.[199] Keynes's overriding goal was now to find an institutional equivalent that could also force surplus nations to recycle their trade surpluses. Crucially, he recognized that these were not merely technical economic questions but required a distinct politics of monetary politicization and depoliticization.

In his proposal, Keynes consequently pointed to on the need for subtle institutional ways to allow for the occasional intrusion of politics into the management of the economy if necessary. If this seemed to invoke a state of exception, Keynes proposed at the same time (pace Carl Schmitt) to regulate such states of exceptional politics within a framework of metarules that differed from those rules prevailing under normal circumstances. Violations by excess creditor or debtor countries would initially trigger punitive payments according to given rules, but these could be escalated and politicized if necessary.[200] Most importantly, the desire to depoliticize would have to be in good faith and could not afford to lose sight of the politics necessary to achieve fair depoliticization. Even in distancing economic life from politics, Keynes stressed the need for tools of governing capable of upholding the depoliticization or adjusting it politically if it threatened to become noxious. Remarkably, such a system, built on a new global reserve currency, was meant to denaturalize and thus politicize the global monetary system while at the same time functioning itself as a depoliticization engine that would provide technical and legal channels for readjustment instead of overt political standoffs. As such, his proposal coupled demands for international disarmament with a wholesale institutionalization of financial discipline, symmetrically imposed not merely against debtor countries but also, crucially, net-creditor countries running current-account surpluses.

Playing on Thomas More's original pun, Keynes insisted that his vision was not a non-place, *u-topia*, but a good place, *eu-topia*, that was practically feasible.[201] While arguing that his proposal was not impractical, Keynes conceded that "it assumes a higher degree of understanding, of the spirit of bold innovation, and of international cooperation and trust than it is safe or reasonable to assume."[202] But then, it was precisely the "complete break with the past" brought about by the war that "offers us an opportunity."[203] In his earliest sketches Keynes had straightforwardly built on his suggestion from the *Treatise* by basing the new international financial architecture unabashedly around a global central bank, a kind of supercharged Bank for International Settlements, acting in strict analogy to its domestic equivalents. But in preparation for the negotiations with the Americans, several members of the Treasury team urged Keynes to drop anything that could possibly smack of "supranational government."[204] As a result, in the different versions of his proposal Keynes seemed to run two parallel arguments. On the one hand, he insisted that monetary sovereignty would continue to rest with the member states and that it would not impose greater duties or infringements on sovereignty than existing treaties. But he added at the same time at several points subtle hints that the Clearing Union might nonetheless contain the seeds of a supranational organization that would eventually come to exceed the original treaty-like setup and include some elements of a genuine supranational "constitution" and a "constitutionalization of treaties."[205]

Keynes had many ideas of what to call the new international currency his Clearing Union would be based on: "Unitas," "Demos," and "Victor" were all possibilities. Somewhat dissatisfied with them, though, he asked the public to send in their own suggestions. A colorful palette emerged: "Bit," "Fint," "Proudof," "Poundol," "Dolphin," as well as Keynes's favorite, "Orb."[206] In the end, "Bancor"—a play on "bank gold"—prevailed. The idea of an international currency stirred up global excitement but was also immediately dismissed as far-fetched. Indeed, for Harry White and many of the Americans working on postwar economic planning, it was far from obvious that the new financial architecture would do entirely away with gold. Gold was not only, according White, "the best medium of international exchange yet devised" but 90 percent of it was now, fortuitously, sitting in American bank vaults.[207] As a result of these differences both the US and Britain were desperate to keep their competing plans secret.[208] But after parts of the American scheme were leaked to the press in April 1943, there was little choice other than to take the initiative and both the British and American proposals were presented to the public.[209]

Keynes seized the opportunity to launch a campaign of public education. For his maiden speech to the House of Lords in May 1943, he consequently chose to focus on the International Clearing Union. "The economic structure of the post-war world cannot be built in secret," he declared.[210] The rough outlines of negotiations had been revealed to the public and they immediately triggered a rush of skepticism, in particular in the US.[211] Not least because of the resulting public scrutiny, White frequently and intentionally sought to make the terms as complicated and convoluted as possible in the hope of disguising the real workings of the plan from the other signatory countries, not to mention Congress. Keynes saw through White's tactic of confusion but this did not stop him from regularly erupting in frustration at the endless legal twists he encountered in White's plan: "Having put these lunatic robes on his Frankenstein he then proceeds at various stages to introduce jokers, which might actually cause the scheme to work out in practice in a way exactly the opposite of what it appears to be on the surface."[212] American legalese became one of Keynes's favorite bugbears at Bretton Woods. As he quipped at the otherwise amiable closing dinner of the conference, when the *Mayflower* sailed from Plymouth, it must have been filled with lawyers.[213]

As it was, Keynes's initial optimism about the feasibility of his proposal underestimated the opposition to his constitutional vision of a rule-bound international reserve currency that would discipline not only weak, peripheral countries but also the rising net-creditor superpower—the United States. Unsurprisingly, the US thought very little of being bound by its indebted ally, a rapidly declining European imperial power that refused to see its diminished world political standing for what it was. Despite the shared drafting process, Bretton Woods reflected this rapidly changing power constellation. Instead of pivoting around a new international currency, Bretton Woods emerged as a US-centered system based on the dollar, which was in turn based on gold, while the adjustment procedures explicitly favored net-creditor countries.[214] Though disappointed by his failure to convince the Americans to base the system on a new international currency, Keynes was at the same time adamant that the proposal on the table was in no way a reversal back to the gold standard but instead a significant step forward. "If I have any authority to pronounce on what is and what is not the essence and meaning of a gold standard, I should say that this plan is the exact opposite of it."[215] As Treasury Secretary Henry Morgenthau put it, unlike the ambiguous dollar diplomacy of the interwar years, the new international monetary institutions of Bretton Woods would be "instrumentalities of sovereign governments and not of private financial interests."[216]

Even if Bretton Woods was a step forward and not a new gold standard, the contours of Britain's humiliating treatment at the hands of its American creditor were becoming harder and harder to ignore. By September 1944 Keynes openly expressed doubts as to whether Britain should ratify the Bretton Woods Agreement, in particular if the Americans were to cut off Britain's desperately needed lend-lease financing. Perhaps, he hoped tentatively, the agreed-upon "post-war transitional period" before the system became operational might go on indefinitely.[217] Most immediately, this sentiment derived from Britain's rapidly weakening bargaining position and the lack of any American inhibitions at taking advantage of its indebted ally. These American humiliations at the same time undermined the depoliticized nature of Keynes's vision for the postwar world. When it became clear that America had gotten its way and that the International Monetary Fund and the World Bank would not be based in London (or even New York) but instead in Washington, Keynes immediately worried that the Fund would become overly politicized as a tool of American hegemony. This anxiety about politicization also expressed itself concerning the Fund's internal workings. Where Keynes had originally envisioned a lean provider of credit tied to a tight set of rules and mechanisms, White had in mind a technocratic powerhouse providing all-round expertise. Where Keynes envisaged around thirty technicians supervising the semi-automatic mechanics of the Fund, White saw a staff of several hundred economists.[218]

In his surprisingly dark closing speech at the inaugural meeting of the Governors of the Fund and the Bank in Savannah in March 1946, Keynes even wondered whether the twins "Master Fund and Miss Bank" might not in the end be cursed. "You two brats shall grow up politicians; your every thought and act shall have an *arrière-pensée*; everything you determine shall not be for its own sake or on its own merits but because of something else."[219] If that were indeed the case, Keynes concluded, it would probably be best for the twins—Fund and Bank—to "fall into an eternal slumber, never to waken or be heard of again in the courts and markets of Mankind."[220]

Conclusion

More than anyone else during the interwar years, Keynes insisted with great verve and eloquence on the need to bring money under deliberate and legitimate control. The naturalistic illusion of gold had for too long disguised the systemic manner in which the monetary standard distributed economic burdens of adjustment unfairly, both domestically and internationally, while at the same time preventing governments from adequately responding to crises. Removing money from this quasi-theological realm meant subjecting it to standards of rationalization, justification, and expertise that would radically extend the realm of economic policy in pursuit of social justice to include monetary matters. This was the argument Keynes first set out in his *Tract on Monetary Reform* (1923). While

initially disregarded as Britain returned to gold in 1925, its main principles have since come to be widely accepted as the basis for central banking all around the world. In calling for a reconceptualization of the state's
economic responsibilities in the monetary realm, Keynes echoed Fichte's
earlier argument and language. It was necessary, Keynes explained, to
effect a "transition from economic anarchy to a regime which deliberately
aims at controlling and directing economic forces in the interests of social
justice and social stability."[221] It was furthermore no accident that the
opening stage of this political struggle would revolve around a new political understanding of monetary policy.[222]

In the two-volume *Treatise on Money* (1930) Keynes radicalized this
account of monetary policy by fundamentally rethinking the nature of
money itself, now stressing both the chartalist dimension of modern
money as well as the importance of bank credit as part of the monetary
system. As Keynes recognized, this posed immediate questions of both
domestic and international governance, including the peculiar political
status of the central bank, its relationship to its member banks, and the
relationships among different central banks. Just as the domestic provision of bank credit required centralized coordination in the form of a
central bank, so a kind of international central bank—a bank of banks—
would be necessary to manage money internationally. In 1936 the *General
Theory* further deepened the repercussions of this revisionist understanding of money by extending it to the rest of the productive realm, in the
process inverting the existing theory of production as a special case to
be actively brought about rather than to be taken for granted. Monetary
policy and an appreciation for the constitutional quality of the monetary
system did not disappear from these considerations, but they were now
tied to a supplementary role for fiscal policy as well as a comprehensive
call for the socialization of the level of investment with the ultimate goal
of reducing the return on rentier capital to zero.

Despite his critique of the gold standard and his pathbreaking articulation of national macroeconomic policy during the 1930s, Keynes nonetheless shared a keen sense of economic internationalism as well as an
appreciation of the liberal desirability of economic depoliticization. Even
where he sought to recover the lost need to manage money by placing it
anew on a constitutional footing, he remained at the same time acutely
attuned to the challenges that democratic politics could pose for monetary
and fiscal steering, which after all relied on expertise over opinion. Keynes
was keenly aware of both sides of the argument: of the vision of money
as a political institution whose naturalistic pretentions had to be stripped

away in the search for political justification, and of Lockean arguments insisting on the need to remove money from direct political interference. In order to reconcile the insights of these seemingly incompatible positions, Keynes proposed a distinct kind of constitutionalization of money, both domestically and internationally.

In his attention to the hybrid nature of money, suspended between politics and economics, between state and banks, between national autonomy and international cooperation, Keynes provided a conceptual tool kit for a constitutional theory of money that takes those mutual dependencies into account. Instead of having to choose between the politicization or depoliticization of money, Keynes's call for the constitutionalization of currency takes us to the limits of a liberal politics of depoliticization that seeks to neutralize economic relations yet hopes to do so in the service of social justice and with possible political safety valves built in. Like the enshrining of certain framing principles in constitutional law, depoliticization meant in this context the freezing of certain foundational political compromises.

This was different from naturalization in leaving no doubt that the underlying institution was a political one that would have to be measured by standards of social justice. But it meant, conversely, that there was nothing per se wrong with monetary depoliticization, particularly if such depoliticization allowed for the superior management of money. Indeed, if the principles thus enshrined were just and left enough room for discretion, monetary depoliticization would occur in a way that reflected the reciprocally shared burden of the founding compromise. His critique of the interwar gold standard was not born from a desire to democratize monetary policy or a rejection of economic depoliticization. Instead, it derived from a critique of the gold standard as a fundamentally flawed attempt at neutralization by naturalization that was both unfair in violating basic principles of social justice and profoundly counterproductive in sowing instability by insisting on stability. The problem was not depoliticization per se but that the interwar gold standard led to a gradual piling up of imbalances while its naturalization of money removed any room for discretionary action or public debate in response.

This approach to the politics of depoliticization allowed for economic neutralization as long as its terms were fair and did not exclude the possibility of politics as a necessary corrective.[223] And yet, as Keynes himself knew, this stress on the need for domestic and international technocratic expertise potentially left his argument ill at ease with democratic politics. It seems fair to say that Keynes never quite reconciled these two aspects of his thought: on the one hand, his call for exercising deliberate control over monetary and fiscal aggregates in order to submit economic life to general welfare, social justice, and democracy; on the other hand, his related insistence on the need for technocratic governance, with its somewhat antidemocratic suspicions and epistemic demands. To stress this tension between democratic politics and economic governance also helps to deepen our understanding of Keynes's ambivalent relation to monetary depoliticization.

Where Fichte embraced national fiat money in a repudiation of a Lockean (or indeed Kantian) appreciation for the internationalist universalism of precious metals, Keynes rejected the need to make such a choice. Instead, for him the domestic problem of employment and policy autonomy could be solved only through a new international monetary constitution in the form of an International Clearing Union. Domestic autonomy and internationalist coordination were not opposed to each other, let alone mutually exclusive, but instead depended on one another. Indeed, ensuring real monetary autonomy in a world of international trade would precisely require a global reserve currency that would have to be managed supranationally. In his plans for an International Clearing Union, Keynes complemented his earlier emphasis on autonomy with an attempt to salvage international trade and cooperation through a combination of appropriate domestic economic policies and an international monetary regime that could avoid mutually destructive behavior. In mediating between Fichte's proposal of a closed commercial state and Locke's depoliticization of money, Keynes's proposal sought to square the circle of monetary management by simultaneously solving the domestic problem of investment and the international problem of trade imbalances. Rather than a shift from economic nationalism to monetary internationalism, the *General Theory* and the Clearing Union together represented the fruits of a longstanding preoccupation with what it would be mean to constitutionalize money on new terms both domestically and internationally.

Looking toward the postwar period, this leaves us with the overarching observation that the postwar world—conventionally, and misleadingly, labeled "Keynesian"—fell in crucial respects short of Keynes's own vision. Put simply, Keynes was no "Keynesian." Instead of postwar Keynesianism's narrow reliance on fiscal fine-tuning along national lines embedded in the Bretton Woods system, Keynes himself had had in mind both a much more radical conception of money and monetary management as well as an awareness of the international implications of his argument that would have called for an International Clearing Union and an international reserve currency.

The postwar system that eventually emerged out of Bretton Woods failed to address Keynes's two most fundamental concerns. First, where he had insisted on the need for a clearing union based on a new international reserve currency, the Bretton Woods agreement instead tied member currencies to the US dollar, which was in turn linked to gold. Second, rather than distributing the burdens of adjustment equally to debtor and creditor countries, the Bretton Woods system reverted to the old asymmetric convention of imposing the entire burden of adjustment on debtor countries. It took until 1958 for the Bretton Woods system to become functional. Already during its first decade of operation, it quickly became hampered by a set of internal contradictions. The introduction in the late 1960s of a new international reserve currency in the form of so-called Special Drawing Rights to supplement member countries' official reserves failed to turn the tide. Instead, in August 1971 the US shocked its allies by unilaterally withdrawing from the system it had itself helped to devise. The Bretton Woods framework gradually collapsed over the subsequent months and years. This did not mean that all its institutional embodiments simply disappeared. Instead, the International Monetary Fund, the World Bank, and not least the supremacy of the US dollar survived into a new age of capital mobility and floating exchange rates. To this day, we live in the overgrown ruins of Bretton Woods. Keynes's original proposal meanwhile remains unrealized.

CHAPTER SIX

Silent Revolution

THE POLITICAL THEORY OF MONEY
AFTER BRETTON WOODS

The virtue of the market is that it disperses responsibility.[1]

—DANIEL BELL, 1976

ON DECEMBER 11, 1974, a cold winter morning in Sweden, Friedrich August Hayek stepped up to the lectern at the Stockholm School of Economics to deliver his lecture for the Nobel Memorial Prize in Economic Sciences he had been awarded the previous night. As Hayek announced in his opening lines, the chief practical problem across the Western world in 1974 was the experience of inflation.[2] This had made his choice of topic easy, indeed almost inevitable. The problem of inflation, Hayek exhorted, threatened Western civilization at its very foundation. "Economists are at this moment called upon," he explained, "to say how to extricate the free world from the serious threat of accelerating inflation." But they were failing. As a profession, "we have made a mess of things." Blaming inflation on the epistemological hubris of Keynesian national welfarism, Hayek instead presented an image of liberalism built on the hardy rock of "sound money."

As Hayek had already explained in *The Road to Serfdom* (1944)—a book that Keynes had read approvingly on his way to Bretton Woods— money "is one of the greatest instruments of freedom ever invented by man."[3] The "monetary framework," Hayek had similarly stressed in *The Constitution of Liberty* (1960), was critical for any liberal constitutional system.[4] The doctrine of sound money, Hayek insisted, had been central to the development of classical liberalism and the experience of inflation challenged its very possibility.

This declared centrality of price stability to political liberalism may come as a surprise to much of contemporary political theory. Conservative and libertarian critics of the postwar consensus had always been highly attuned to the politics of sound money and Hayek himself was deeply shaped by the monetary instability of the interwar period. Postwar liberal political philosophy, by contrast, not only accepted the postwar settlement of Bretton Woods but quickly came to take it for granted. The political problem of money seemed to have been solved. When the political philosopher John Rawls set out in the course of the 1950s and 1960s to develop a theory of justice, monetary politics featured at most obliquely on the margins. Instead, in focusing on the underlying principles of justice, Rawls agnostically abstracted away from institutional questions of monetary policy and central banks.[5]

More surprisingly, while the collapse of Bretton Woods in the early 1970s initially led to a renaissance of monetary thought, it ultimately did not translate into a resurgence of the political theory of money. On the contrary, by the 1980s money appeared once more as merely an economic tool. Communitarian critics of Rawls, from Michael Walzer to Michael Sandel, came to rest their contextualist accounts of political justice on a separation of the political from the economic realm that left little room for a hybrid institution like money.[6] The critical theorist Jürgen Habermas meanwhile reduced money in his mature social theory to a "norm-free steering medium" that merely functions as a "de-linguistified" medium of exchange.[7] By the late 1980s, when the Marxist philosopher G. A. Cohen reflected on the "currency of egalitarian justice," currency had become a pure metaphor entirely removed from the politics of money itself.[8]

This reduction of money to a seemingly straightforward economic institution—its political character ignored—echoed the treatment of money in conventional economics, but it stands in striking contrast to the political debates over the role of money we have already encountered in this book. As we saw in the previous chapters, at least since the introduction of coinage into the ancient Mediterranean world, discussions of the politics of money were a staple of Western political thought. If one aim of my genealogy has been to recover the forgotten conceptual resources inherent in that lost conversation, I have also been interested in reconstructing a genealogy of the arguments that, while coming from within this tradition, ended up contributing to the gradual eclipse of money as a subject of political thought. As I argued in the second chapter on Locke, one part of the contemporary invisibility of money in political thought has to do with the way in which modernity meant a reframing of the politics of money within the new parameters of a politics of monetary depoliticization that sought to remove money from political meddling. But the invisibility also derives, as we saw in the fourth chapter on Marx, from an analysis that took seriously money's new function as capital and pointed skeptically to the limits and indeed futility of monetary reform. While Locke and Marx themselves wrote extensively about the politics of money, both provided different reasons for considering money somehow beyond politics. Their arguments, and the long shadows extended by them, continue to cloud any attempt to reconceive of money as a malleable political institution in its own right.

But this can only capture part of the reason for the striking absence of money in much of contemporary political theory after Bretton Woods. Instead, as I argue in this chapter, a further reason can be traced back to a more specific and altogether more recent root, namely the Great Inflation of the 1970s that had also motivated Hayek's Nobel remarks. Only by recognizing how political theory itself has been shaped by the 1970s and 1980s, including the international politics of money after Bretton Woods, can we begin to understand its peculiar blind spot concerning the democratic politics of money. If the 1970s were a period of rupture, nowhere was this more the case than in monetary matters. The collapse of the Bretton Woods system after 1971 meant nothing less than a revolution in the modern monetary constitution. For the first time, outside of war conditions, money became fully untethered from gold or silver all around the world. States were forced to experiment with what it might mean to exercise "control" over their currencies. The most immediate result was that the question of money became as politically salient in the 1970s as perhaps at any other time before.

At first sight, contemporary political theorists' disinterest in and disavowal of the politics of money becomes all the more peculiar when seen in the context of the radical monetary change of the 1970s. How are we to square the reinvigorated political centrality of money with its subsequent neglect in political theory? The first clue to solving this puzzle lies in the burst of inflation that went hand in hand with the end of the Bretton Woods system. The Great Inflation of the 1970s was the highest ever experienced outside wartime or postwar conditions in more than two centuries of modern economic history.[9] Domestically, inflation and strikes led to intense polarization in economic relations, while internationally politics came to the fore in the world economy through the Organization of Arab Petroleum Exporting Countries (OPEC) and demands by the New International Economic Order (NIEO) to restructure international economic relations. In response to the inflationary politicization of the economy, states embarked on a systematic quest to

close down the political possibilities of fiat money and consciously depoliticized money on new terms.

In the course of the 1980s the inflationary threat was met with a concerted disinflationary push. A new politics of disinflationism oversaw the
institutionalization of novel modes of economic discipline based on a de-
democratization of money. We can detect the force of this most recent
politics of monetary depoliticization in the constrained monetary imagination of contemporary political theory. The neglect of the politics of
money by political philosophers after Bretton Woods is no historical coincidence; it reflects the violent repression of the specter of inflation. The
political theory of money was eclipsed not despite but in response to the
overt politicization of money during the 1970s. The contemporary neglect
of money by political theorists is then not ironic but symptomatic.

It was the new politics of monetary depoliticization in the name of
combating inflation that allowed political theorists—from Jürgen Habermas to Michael Walzer—to remove money once more from politics conceptually, thereby unwittingly immunizing the new monetary constitution against critique. Political theorists did, of course, develop powerful
critiques of the corrupting effects of commodification during this time
period. But this defensive posture has an unacknowledged implicit flip
side. In focusing on the role of money as a tool of commodification against
which emancipatory politics could at best be defended, political theorists
often inadvertently accepted the dubious premise that money is merely
economic in the first place. Crucially, this was not simply a conservative
turn or a rapprochement with neoliberalism; it reflected also in its own
way the long shadow cast by Locke's and Marx's critique of the malleable
politics of money. Today, democratic theory advances creative proposals for the institutional redesign of representative institutions, it pushes
back against the intrusion of wealth into the democratic process, and it
even points to the lack of democracy in the workplace, but these probing
questions are rarely extended to the central banks that oversee the monetary economy and manage the interactions between the financial system
and the democratic state. Understanding and escaping this self-imposed
silencing requires coming to terms with the trauma of the Great Inflation.

Out of Bretton Woods

During the postwar decades it was easy to take for granted the complex
international and domestic political settlement of the Bretton Woods system. Even where it allowed for adjustments, Bretton Woods imposed strict

constraints on domestic monetary policy.[10] There was some room for maneuver since international capital mobility was explicitly restricted— one of the few areas in which Keynes's argument prevailed—but monetary policy had nowhere near the same political significance as it has today.[11] More often than not, the heavily constrained quality of monetary policy at home and the seemingly stable nature of the international monetary system abroad appeared to render the politics of money an increasingly irrelevant sideshow. Soon the politics of money became almost invisible. Unprecedented increases in affluence across the entire Global North meanwhile instilled an almost natural expectation of rapid and evenly dispersed economic growth.[12] Across the postwar social sciences there reigned a widely shared belief in the ready availability of economic growth at rates between 5 and 10 percent. This was the era John Kenneth Galbraith memorably described in *The Affluent Society* (1958).[13] The problem was no longer scarcity, with its fixation on productive efficiency and fierce distributional struggles, but instead how society could best reap the rewards of unprecedented affluence.

It was this confident postwar context that formed the background to John Rawls's search for a theory of justice as fairness. Both the broad plausibility of Rawls's theory and in particular the account of stability it presupposed depended on a specific postwar political economy of national welfarism embedded in a formalized international monetary system founded in Bretton Woods in 1944.[14] Philosophically, Rawls remained self-consciously agnostic about the precise institutional form by which his two principles of justice were to be satisfied.[15] This was the price of abstraction. Moreover, like much of postwar political philosophy, he leaned heavily on contemporary economics, and the account of money he encountered there would have only affirmed its essential invisibility.[16] The consequence of Rawls's deference to postwar economics and his embrace of philosophical abstraction was that money could be safely left undertheorized.[17] This sidestepping of monetary theory and the politics of money was institutionally rendered plausible by the way in which the Bretton Woods monetary order had come to be taken for granted. Rawls's philosophical framing relied in this sense implicitly on the political and monetary conditions of statist welfarism and economic growth within the Bretton Woods system—while at the same time obscuring the political nature of these preconditions as they had emerged out of the domestic and international political struggles of the interwar years and World War II.

By the 1960s, cracks had begun to appear both in the supposedly self-perpetuating wealth-generation machine of the postwar state and the monetary framework that underpinned it. The Bretton Woods system, only fully operational by 1958, was already experiencing the strains of its contradictions. Keynes, who had died at the age of sixty-two in May 1946, had predicted these tensions from the outset and sought to circumvent them in his own rejected proposal. He would not have been surprised by the way in which the system, once operational, quickly failed even on its own terms. The belated attempt by the International Monetary Fund (IMF) to introduce a substitute international reserve currency in the form of Special Drawing Rights (SDRs) in 1969, a sad substitute for Keynes's original Bancor, could not prevent the system's contradictions from building up. For the US in particular, the pressure was growing. In 1971 the US trade account turned negative for the first time in the twentieth century.[18] President Richard Nixon, eager to take an aggressive stance on domestic stimulus (he regarded inaction by the Federal Reserve in 1960 as having cost him his first presidential bid against John F. Kennedy), surprised his Western allies by unilaterally closing the gold window.[19]

On August 15, 1971, Nixon announced that the US would suspend the dollar's convertibility into gold that had been at the heart of the Bretton Woods system. Struggling to finance the Vietnam War while acting as the anchor of the international monetary system, the Nixon administration sought to provide an ebullient vision of unilateral leadership to displace any perception of sacrificial hegemony.[20] As Nixon's treasury secretary John Connally famously quipped to the rest of the world, "The dollar might be our currency, but it is your problem."[21] In the hope of strengthening his reelection campaign, Nixon ushered in a monetary revolution. As the US withdrew its support, Bretton Woods gradually collapsed. By 1973 most countries had given up their currency peg to the US dollar after going through a phase of pronounced crises as their commitment to the dollar was repeatedly tested at great cost. The remnant ruins of Bretton Woods, in the form of the IMF and the World Bank, meanwhile clung to life. The sudden end of the Bretton Woods system also left its ironic mark on political philosophy. The collapse of the certainties of the postwar economic order coincided precisely with the publication of Rawls's magnum opus. A mere six months after *A Theory of Justice* appeared in early 1971, the world's monetary constitution had been altered. In a constellation that would not have failed to amuse Hegel, the moment in which thought captured reality coincided with that reality vanishing.[22]

The world meanwhile slid further into crisis. Whereas average annual GDP growth between 1950 and 1973 had consistently approximated 5 percent across Western Europe and the United States, growth came to an abrupt halt in the early 1970s. By 1974 industrialized economies grew a mere 1 percent; in 1975 they contracted.[23] Unemployment, virtually unheard of during the 1960s, was back. At the same time, inflation reached levels not witnessed during peacetime since the interwar years. By 1974 prices were rising 10 percent or more per year with few exceptions; in Britain, inflation reached 25 percent; in India, 30 percent; in Chile, it took on hyperinflationary levels.[24] For eight consecutive years from 1973 to 1981 inflation was, according to US opinion polls, the single most important problem facing the country.[25] As one analyst of American public opinion summarized in 1979, "For the public today, inflation has the kind of dominance that no other issue has had since World War II."[26] A political rhetoric of military metaphors took such analogies to heart. When President Ford declared inflation "our public enemy number one" in 1974, he compared it to a "well-armed wartime enemy."[27] Such analogies, fueled by crisis, only further stoked the underlying sentiment of desperation. At the same time as inflation eroded the natural appearance of economic relations, the world economy underwent its own process of politicization. In reaction to the Yom Kippur War, OPEC imposed an oil embargo in October 1973 that triggered the first oil-price shock. For the first time in the modern history of the West an essential raw material had entirely escaped its control. Alongside the OPEC embargo, a broad coalition of recently decolonized developing countries from the Global South formulated their own vision of a New International Economic Order (NIEO) of radical debt relief and a reshaping of global economic relations that was formally adopted by the United Nations General Assembly in May 1974.[28]

The Contradictions of Crisis Capitalism

The politicization of economic demands through the monetary upheavals following the end of Bretton Woods tore down the apolitical, technocratic facade of the advanced capitalist economy. The state's interventions, previously obscured by their very success and by invocations of technical expertise, became increasingly visible and thereby demystified. If the invisible hand of the market had in the postwar period been replaced by what Albert Hirschman dubbed the hiding hand of the state, the fumbling fingers of technocracy had now been revealed as all too clumsy.[29] As the German critical theorist Jürgen Habermas recognized in *Legitimation Crisis* (1973), the demystification brought about by this new visibility of interference would inevitably burden the technocratic state with additional demands for legitimating its interventionist policies and the

distributive outcomes they produced.[30] The demand for public justification of state actions easily bred legitimation crises, as economic relations
became openly repoliticized under the crisis conditions of the 1970s. In
times of economic crisis it was no longer possible to conceal the functional
relations between the state and the capitalist economy; technocratic fine-
tuning not only failed to achieve the intended result but produced yet further unintended consequences. As President Jimmy Carter had to admit
in 1978 when forced to address the economic turmoil, "I do not have all
the answers. Nobody does."[31] State intervention in the economy became
impossible to hide because it had ceased to work.

In its analysis of the resulting political pressures, Habermas's crisis theory converged, remarkably, with conservative anxieties about democratic
ungovernability. As the infamous 1975 report of the Trilateral Commission concluded, "The demands on democratic governments grow, while
the capacity of democratic government stagnates. This, it would appear,
is the central dilemma of the governability of democracy which has mani-
fested itself in Europe, North American, and Japan in the 1970s."[32] While
these worries concerning the compatibility of capitalism with the democratic welfare state were widely shared, policy recommendations differed
dramatically. One of the most probing accounts was that set out by the
American sociologist Daniel Bell in *The Cultural Contradictions of Capitalism* (1976).[33] In the postwar period, Bell explained, economic growth
had become a "secular religion" that provided industrial societies with a
potent "political solvent."[34] The availability of widely dispersed affluence
could for a while disguise the fact that more and more economic outcomes
were directly affected by the administrative welfare state. As Bell put it,
"We have begun to center the crucial decisions about the economy and
the society in the political cockpit, rather than in the diffused, aggregated
market."[35] While growth had helped to stabilize and legitimate technocratic economic government during the postwar period, the experience of
economic crisis and inflation during the 1970s meant that governmental
interventions and distributive political decisions had become increasingly
"visible" and thereby contestable. "In effect," Bell explained,

> decision-making has become "politicalized" and subject to all the multi-
> ple direct pressures of political decision making.... When one "burdens"
> the polity with more and more political issues, when housing, health, edu-
> cation, and the like become politicalized, strains are compounded.... In
> the coming years there will be more and more group conflicts in the
> society.[36]

In the face of a faltering technocratic ability to produce prosperity, citizens no longer directed their frustrations about hardship at the anonymous naturalized market but at the administrative state that had failed them. Now they knew whom to blame.

As Bell pointed out, the inflation of the 1970s had revealed a potent combination of rising expectations and democratic politics that had come to bind states, preventing them from either reducing governmental expenditure or cutting wages by way of "traditional modes of restraint or 'discipline' (in the archaic use of the term)."[37] Inflation appeared in this light as the price a polity had to pay for social peace. Bell and others concluded that it was unlikely that any democratic state could abolish inflation without disastrous political consequences. The only way out of the dilemma without recourse to a class war, according to Bell, was for governments to deploy strong wage and price controls as well as intervene directly in the capital markets.[38] These interventions would inevitably be based on contentious distributive judgments certain to provoke resentment from the respective losers, not to mention their lobby groups. The political system would struggle under the weight of these conflicting demands. But if this prediction of politically challenging distributive decisions was dire, Bell was adamant that there was no way around it. Democratic capitalist politics after the postwar boom was now stuck in "a peculiar contradiction."[39]

The only possible solution, Bell argued, consisted in squarely confronting the impasse as a supremely political problem. Difficult distributive decisions could avoid jeopardizing the legitimacy of the state only if they were accompanied by the formulation of a public political philosophy that accepted the economy as a politically contested arena to be publicly managed (he dubbed this "the public household"). This would mean developing widely accepted public norms of how to fairly share economic pain without stirring up resentment against the political system.[40] Bell agreed at this point with Habermas ("the leading Marxist scholar today," Bell thought) that legitimacy was the core concept to be addressed since it "goes to the root values of a society."[41]

If Bell and Habermas agreed about the pressures of legitimation, neither envisaged the concerted disinflation that was to come during the 1980s. But their analysis had in fact correctly highlighted all the elements that motivated the neoliberal turn toward a new politics of depoliticization. As Bell put it, where the administrative state concentrates decisions, makes the consequences visible, and exposes the legitimacy of the state, "the virtue of the market," conversely, "is that it disperses responsibility for decisions and effects."[42] This did not mean that the market removed power. As the

American political scientist Charles Lindblom showed in *Politics and Market* (an unlikely *New York Times* bestseller in 1977), it was misleading to disassociate markets from power and coercion.[43] Instead, what Bell had in mind was the market's ability to disperse responsibility by dispersing the *appearance* of power and coercion. This did not mean that Bell endorsed a turn to the market. But he was only too aware of its political attraction.

Habermas found himself in a similar position. Though he insisted that any return to the unregulated market of liberal capitalism was a fantasy, by the late 1970s he had grown more and more skeptical about the feasibility and desirability of economic democratization. "I wonder," Habermas reflected in 1978 in an interview with the Italian political philosopher Angelo Bolaffi, "if we should not preserve part of today's complexity within the economic system, limiting the discursive formation of the collective will precisely to the decisive and central structures of political power: that is, apart from the labour process as such, to the few but continuously made fundamental decisions which will determine the overall structure of social production and, naturally, of distribution."[44] This was an empirical question, he emphasized, that could not be answered abstractly but only through "experimental practice."[45] Speaking at the annual meeting of the German Political Science Association in Duisburg in 1975, Habermas had tentatively suggested one such experimental solution to the political dilemma of crisis capitalism. While citizens held the state responsible for economic crises and expected it to resolve them, the late-capitalist state could not simply deploy raw power to push through decisions without endangering its legitimacy. Instead, it could only "manipulate the decisions of others" while seemingly leaving their private autonomy untouched. "Indirect control is the answer to the dilemma," Habermas concluded.[46] To avoid a further escalation of legitimation crisis, economic control was necessary, but such control could not be exercised directly. Instead, it had to take the form of "indirect inducements" that rendered the state's guiding hand invisible again—at least for those willing to suspend disbelief.[47] What was required was a magician's sleight of hand that could once more make the state's hiding hand disappear.

As Habermas spoke in Duisburg, an altogether different Frankfurt School had arrived at a remarkably similar conclusion. Ever since the suspension of the dollar peg in March 1973, the central bankers at the Bundesbank in Frankfurt had been busy developing just such indirect steering by stealth. The float of the Deutschmark had liberated their hands, previously tied by the Bretton Woods system. Now West Germany was free to use the indirect forces of monetary steering to embark on its disinflationary monetarist *Sonderweg*. When the Bundesbank launched this grab for power by introducing its new policy of monetary targeting, it did so in a self-conscious attempt at disavowing its political nature. The words it employed in this context still echo down to our present: "There is no alternative," the Bundesbank declared in its 1974 Annual Report.[48]

Soon, the West German ordoliberal monetary experiment of reining in inflation through harsh policies of indirect steering attracted attention abroad. In particular, French president Valéry Giscard d'Estaing and his prime minister Raymond Barre made no secret of their admiration for the West German depoliticization of the economy and hoped to import some of its benefits in the form of a joint monetary system.[49] Michel Foucault's decision to dedicate a large part of his 1979 lecture course at the Collège de France to exploring the nature of German ordoliberalism has sometimes been seen as quixotic or, more recently, prophetic.[50] In fact, it could have scarcely been more topical. At least since 1976 much of Parisian punditry had been obsessively following West German economic policy and by the end of the decade, French political discourse was saturated with references to ordoliberalism and its emphasis on a strong, guiding role for the state in structuring a free-market economy. Drawing a suggestive arc to Fichte and his theory of politicized fiat money, Foucault explained that the West German state had inverted Fichte's proposal. "In contemporary Germany," he summarized pointedly,

> we have what we can say is a radically economic state, taking the word
> "radically" in the strict sense, that is to say, its root is precisely eco-
> nomic. As you know, Fichte—and this is generally all that is known
> about Fichte—spoke of a closed commercial state. I will have to come
> back to this a bit later. I will just say, making a somewhat artificial sym-
> metry, that we have here the opposite of a closed commercial state. We
> have a state-forming commercial opening. Is this the first example in
> history of a radically economic state?[51]

West Germany was peculiar in being perhaps the only state whose currency had preceded its own founding.[52] This had been a telling first sign of things to come. By the mid-1970s the Bundesbank had taken the lead in the international conquest of inflation and the associated depoliticization of money.[53]

Two Utopias

While inflation sent the Bundesbank searching for a new kind of technocratic steering, the inflationary repoliticization of money stirred up the political imagination of both the left and the right. Hayek had not been the sole recipient of the Nobel Prize in Economics in 1974. Instead, the Swedish Academy of Sciences jointly awarded the prize (and the prize money of 550,000 Swedish krona) to Hayek and the Swedish economist Gunnar Myrdal for their "pioneering work in the theory of money" as well as their analyses of the interdependence of economic and social phenomena.[54] Two radically divergent visions of money were on offer.

When giving his own Nobel Lecture, Myrdal agreed with Hayek about the problem of inflation, the pressing global situation of crisis, and indeed the constraints of national welfarism.[55] But instead of veering away from welfarism toward a world of liberalized global capital, Myrdal proposed an internationalization of the postwar welfare state.[56] Such an internationalization of the achievements of the welfare state was, by Myrdal's account, a necessary outcome of decolonization and the profound challenge it posed to the unequal welfarist settlement of the postwar world. As he reminded his audience in Stockholm, "The underdeveloped countries are therefore now proclaiming the necessity of not only increased aid but fundamental changes of international economic relations. By their majority votes they can in the United Nations carry resolutions like the Declaration on the Establishment of a New International Economic Order."[57] In aligning himself with the demands of the NIEO, which had successfully passed its UN resolution earlier the same year in May 1974, Myrdal insisted that "what the poor masses need is not a little money [but] fundamental changes in the conditions under which they are living and working." What he saw as the perilous state of the world—and here Myrdal was thinking as much of persistent famine as of inflation—posed a fundamental moral problem that required a comprehensive political reform of the international economic and monetary system.

If Hayek agreed in principle with the dire need for radical reform, the reforms he had in mind pulled in a rather different direction. Spurred on by the recurring bouts of inflation during the 1970s and utilizing the prestige of the Nobel Prize, Hayek updated his earlier monetary writings with startlingly radicalized conclusions. Before the 1970s Hayek had largely conceded the need for some kind of government monopoly over monetary policy. In the background of his theoretical debate with Keynes in the 1930s, the dispute had not been over whether central banks should exist but what their appropriate role ought to be. Nor did Hayek disagree with Keynes concerning the importance of price stability, though Hayek gave this a distinct twist. According to Hayek, the primary function of the price system was to act as a mechanism for communicating information. A stable monetary system was hence imperative not just for economic reasons but for the very functioning of society.[58]

The proper functioning of the price mechanism required an appropriate legal and monetary system, something that, Hayek had conceded in *The Road to Serfdom*, could never be adequately provided by private enterprise.[59] Instead this was a political task. It was the government that had to set up laws and provide stable money "to provide a favorable framework for individual decisions."[60] Given the vast power that derived from the management of the currency, he explained, it was only natural to question whether governments were entitled to control monetary policy. "Why, it is asked, should we not rely on the spontaneous forces of the market to supply whatever is needed for a satisfactory medium of exchange as we do in most other respects?" Though sympathetic toward such proposals, by 1960 Hayek still cautioned against them as politically impracticable and, even if practicable, "probably . . . undesirable," all consequences considered. As Hayek had to admit, historical developments had created conditions that made necessary at least some deliberate control of the interacting money and credit systems.[61] Keynes's interwar demand for governments to exercise deliberate control over the currency had become an inescapable fact. As Hayek added, granting this did not entail embracing the state's monetary monopoly for good but was instead merely a temporary truce.[62] The politicization of money during the inflationary 1970s suddenly gave this wager new urgency and momentum, ultimately altering Hayek's assessment.

Addressing a London-based free-market think tank in 1975, Hayek exhorted his audience that unemployment should not be blamed on capitalism but on "governments denying enterprise the right to produce good money."[63] Economic crisis and inflation were a result of "the exclusion of the most important regulator of the market mechanism, money, from itself being regulated by the market process."[64] The lecture was immediately expanded into a short pamphlet entitled *The Denationalization of Money*, which entered wide circulation on the back of Hayek's Nobel fame. The time had now come, Hayek declared, to eliminate the government monopoly over money and fully privatize its issuance. No government with direct control over money could ever be trusted not to abuse it. In inverting Polanyi's argument, Hayek concluded that "the past instability of the market economy is the consequence of the exclusion of the most important regulator of the market mechanism, money, from itself being regulated by the market process."[65] Hayek blamed the inflationary malaise on Keynesian welfarism specifically, but his critique now extended to all political control over money.[66] Money, he insisted, was simply too dangerous an instrument to be left to the state and the "fortuitous expediency" of politicians or indeed economists. "Our only hope for a stable money," he exclaimed in consciously echoing Locke's original intervention, "is indeed now to find a way to protect money from politics."[67]

But if Hayek portrayed his solution as a turn away from politics, he was at the same time clear that it originated itself in a particular vision of politics, albeit of a very different kind. He insisted that his nostalgia for the gold standard was not borne out of some confused economic doctrine that gold somehow directly determined the value of money, but instead arose from a political argument. What gold had provided, and what was now so sorely lacking, was "discipline."[68] As a tool of depoliticization, gold had naturalized economic sacrifices that would otherwise have been visible as conscious political decisions. Hayek explicitly linked this line of thought to classical liberalism and credited both Locke and Smith for it. As his epigraph for *The Denationalization of Money* he chose a passage from the *Wealth of Nations* in which Smith echoed Locke in lamenting the widespread injustice of debasement.[69] Hayek now grasped for anything that could once more enforce sacrifice and discipline—with the regrettably necessary result of unemployment. He couched the alternative in apocalyptic terms; left unchecked, he fulminated, inflation would "lead to the destruction of our civilization."[70] Depriving governments of their monopolistic control of money was the only "possible escape from the fate which threatens us."[71] To be sure, privatizing money was only one part of a far-reaching reform of political institutions, including a proposal to raise the voting age for a second legislative chamber to forty-five.[72] But, Hayek declared in a fever pitch, it was an essential part "if we are to escape the nightmare of increasingly totalitarian powers."[73]

{⚔️}

In 1980, as Hayek was on the lecture circuit spreading his gospel of a world of private monies, an altogether different coalition had gathered in the Tanzanian city of Arusha. Instigated by the Tanzanian president Julius Nyerere and the Jamaican prime minister Michael Manley, the South-North Conference on "The International Monetary System and the New International Order" met in the Arusha International Conference Center from June 30 to July 3, 1980 to discuss the future of the international monetary system.[74] While the NIEO had burst onto the international scene six years earlier in the immediate wake of the collapse of the Bretton Woods system, it had in many ways still been an outgrowth of the anticolonial commodity-trade struggles of the 1950s and 1960s.[75] Though it made references to the need for monetary reform, these were fleeting.

By the end of the 1970s, however, the monetary dimension of postcolonial political struggle had fully asserted itself internationally. While the experience of peacetime inflation had traumatized most OECD countries, the Global South had experienced the worst impacts; in fact, hard-hit Jamaica and Tanzania had just gotten a first bitter taste of the IMF's "structural adjustment" policies.

Within sight of Mount Kilimanjaro, the Arusha conference was meant both as an expression of solidarity and a call for a UN conference on international monetary reform.[76] Confronted with the technocratic imperatives of the IMF, the participants pointed instead to the inescapable politics of money. "Those who wield power control money. Those who manage and control money wield power. An international monetary system is both a function and an instrument of prevailing power structures."[77] The stabilizing elements of the Bretton Woods order may have collapsed in the course of the 1970s but the governing boards of the IMF and the World Bank continued to reflect the power balances of an international order in which the majority of Third World countries had not yet existed. Although the Third World counted close to one hundred countries that included more than two-thirds of the world's population, its cumulative voting share at the IMF amounted to no more than 35 percent and thus less than the 40 percent of the five leading industrial powers alone.

Even worse, in the course of the 1970s, as the United States abandoned the embedded multilateralism of the postwar period for unilateralism, the IMF had become more beholden to the G7 than ever before. As the Third World countries had declared the previous fall in Jamaica, "The IMF, acting on behalf of the major industrialized capitalist countries, has assumed a growing role as a financial and economic policeman in Third World countries."[78] In addition to the previous political imbalances of the Bretton Woods system, during the 1970s a new tendency had "emerged for the Fund to exercise a major influence on the process of internal decision-making in a number of the Third World countries."[79] The collapse of the Bretton Woods system, imperfect as it had been, had left behind an ad hoc "non-system" that combined an evasion of responsibilities with heightened opportunism.[80] The postwar dollar had already been both the domestic currency of the United States as well as the international currency of choice for reserves and shadow banking.[81] But the collapse of Bretton Woods lifted most obligations previously associated with this "exorbitant privilege."[82] Given the increasingly destabilizing effect of largely unregulated flows of so-called Eurodollars under conditions of floating exchange rates and increasing capital mobility, the dollar's impact on the rest of the world was deeper and more unpredictable.[83]

Amid this uncertainty of the post–Bretton Woods moment, the Arusha Initiative's emphasis on the international monetary system's burden of hierarchical imbalances was a powerful attempt to insist on money's political nature by countering claims to neutral technical expertise asserted by the Fund's money doctors. The IMF may have claimed a neutral, objective, scientific stance but all scholarly evidence, including the Fund's own internal documentation (which Nyerere leaked to the international press), pointed the other way.[84] The Fund was, in fact, deeply ideological in the way it framed underdevelopment as a lack of private markets but systematically applied double standards in ignoring similar market controls in "developed" countries. In reducing the international politics of money to seemingly scientific theories of underdevelopment and domestic structural reforms, the IMF was a depoliticization machine.[85] Its denial of the political nature of money was, ultimately, proof of its political agenda. This is what I have in mind when speaking of the politics of depoliticization throughout this book. As the Arusha Initiative perceptively declared, in denying the politics of money the IMF "has proved to be a basically political institution."[86]

Instead of the IMF's recommendation of domestic adjustment, the Arusha Initiative called for a wholesale, democratic reform of the international monetary constitution. This meant that money had to "be demystified and exposed to public debate and scrutiny."[87] The necessary political decisions would have to be taken "by governments acting in a collective and democratic manner."[88] This was bold but as the Arusha Initiative explained, unlike the redistributive confrontation of the NIEO, global monetary reform was not a zero-sum game. After all, South and North both had an interest in creating a truly stable international monetary system that would be better equipped to address the issue of inflation. The Arusha Initiative ended in this spirit by stressing the common interest in a "universal and democratic monetary system."[89] The Global North's abrogation of political agency in international monetary matters had become a source of embarrassment to human rationality and ingenuity. If the Arusha Initiative thus converged with Hayek in detecting political forces behind the ad hoc international monetary order of the 1970s, their respective conceptions and assessments of the politics of money could hardly have diverged more strongly. Where Hayek saw states abusing their monetary monopoly to create inflation, the signatories in Arusha saw developed countries cynically bending the post–Bretton Woods monetary order to their will while denying any political agency. Hayek's call for the removal of money from politics found its exact counterpart in the Arusha Initiative's attempt to raise an awareness of money's political purpose.[90]

The Politics of Disinflation

In the end, both Hayek's vision of competing private currencies and the Arusha vision of a postcolonial international monetary constitution were disappointed. But it was nonetheless Hayek who had the last laugh. What won the day was a continuation of the ad hoc system of floating fiat currencies, now ruled in a seemingly depoliticized manner by experts in formally independent central banks. This was a surprise for Hayek who had declared the democratic state incapable of reining in inflation. And yet it unexpectedly approximated his goal of enforcing economic discipline in a depoliticized manner. States were left nominally in control of currencies but they explicitly abrogated many of their prior political responsibilities. Hayek's vision was further vindicated in the unprecedented sums of global private money—money that was created by commercial banks and often denominated in US dollars but beyond the direct reach of governments—that began to circulate around the world as capital controls were lifted. Financial deregulation meanwhile opened the taps of consumer credit that would muffle the immediate pain imposed by the new system of economic discipline.[91]

By the late 1970s the spirit of Hayek's arguments, if not his specific proposal, quite unexpectedly resonated with a wider circle of policymakers.[92] Though the disinflationary push would later come to be associated with Paul Volcker and the political patronage of Reagan and Thatcher, it was in fact the Carter administration that began to sound the theme and that appointed Volcker to chair the Federal Reserve in 1979.[93] Alfred Kahn, Carter's key adviser on inflation who had previously overseen the deregulation of the American airline industry as chairman of the US Council on Wage and Price Stability, captured the Hayekian longing for economic discipline when asking rhetorically: "Can a democracy discipline itself? What is it that creates this sense of helplessness? It's clearly something that has to do with the lack of social discipline."[94] Hayek's radical proposal for the full privatization of money required a leap of faith too great even for many of his closest sympathizers. But in an age of deepening inflation anxiety the search for discipline changed the terms of debate and legitimated a new politics of anti-inflationism. Hayek was, in retrospect, in the intellectual vanguard of an army of theorists and policymakers who remade the monetary order. Full denationalization was a step too far, but why not tie monetary policy to fixed and unalterable rules?[95] Why not allow for more private credit money? Milton Friedman proved to be the ideal salesman for a political program that packaged economic liberalization with a hawkish, monetarist anti-inflationism.[96] After a decade of cease-less mobilization, by the end of the 1970s Friedman could announce that "the tide is turning."[97] Ushered in under Carter, but subsequently exem-plified by Reagan and Thatcher, political leadership came to be redefined in terms of anti-inflation politics. It may have been centrist and social democratic governments that initiated this turn in the late 1970s, but ulti-mately it was conservative moral and political entrepreneurs who could more credibly inhabit the role of anti-inflation hawk and, with the help of swarms of social scientists and policy advisers, rationalize the new logic of discipline.[98]

With the successful assertion of a newly depoliticized appearance of money since the early 1980s, Myrdal's call for a welfare world and the pleas of developing countries for international monetary reform fell on deaf ears and faded from view.[99] The new international monetary order instead took the Arusha Initiative's insistence on money's political nature but derived from it Hayek's objectives of discipline and price stability. The age of floating national fiat currencies unexpectedly produced a new poli-tics of monetary depoliticization. To Hayek's surprise, the lesson of the 1970s thus illustrated the unexpected way in which a "reflexive modernity" could end up defining itself by foreclosing its own agency.[100] For better or worse, democracies turned out to be remarkably able and willing to bind themselves. If the collapse of Bretton Woods had revealed money as an object of political will and imagination, one expression of that monetary politics consisted in the disavowal of its democratic potential.

The indirect but no less violent control over the economy through dis-inflationary "depoliticized" monetary policy emerged as an extraordinarily effective tool of discipline. The Canadian scholar of public policy Alasdair Roberts has described these changes toward a new logic of discipline since the early 1980s as nothing less than a "quiet revolution."[101] Since the 1980s the Federal Reserve has gone to extraordinary lengths so as not to appear deliberately in control of monetary policy—and therefore not politically responsible for it. During this period the Fed developed numer-ous technical but also rhetorical tools to be able to raise interest rates without being blamed for doing so.[102] If tight monetary policy meant putting people out of work and causing economic harm, it was better not to be seen doing so intentionally. Initially, this involved the pretense of following certain fixed monetarist rules to control the money supply in order to justify sharp increases in interest rates that undercut inflationary expectations but also deliberately increased unemployment.[103] The move toward depoliticization thus came in part out of policymakers' desire to avoid taking responsibility for making distributive decisions. Central bankers shielded from the political process would by contrast be free to steer without having to bear the burden of democratic justification for the distributive consequences of their actions. At other times, central banks actively encouraged elected politicians to come to their help. When a newly elected President Reagan crushed an air traffic controllers' strike in August 1981 during his first summer in office by summarily firing more than eleven thousand federal workers with devastating symbolic force, Paul Volcker nodded in grateful approval from the Federal Reserve.[104]

As the political possibilities of fiat money were closed down, the appearance of money was consciously depoliticized on new terms. Made nominally independent of the political process by governments, central banks embraced a shifting mix of monetarism, nondiscretionary rules, and "market-led" monetary policy. Governments now self-consciously constrained themselves in their ability and willingness to politicize economic conflicts. What followed was nothing less than a radical transformation of the state. If monetary policy now presented itself as apolitical for reasons of legitimacy, this also meant that central banks were no longer obliged to take economic justice or distributive concerns into account. With democracies' reach into economic policy thus curtailed, political parties were left to compete over the unenviable prize of "ruling the void."[105]

Demonetizing Political Theory

The depoliticization of money during the 1980s and 1990s also left its imprint in political theory albeit in the form of a subsequent neglect of the politics of money. Where the politics of inflation had dominated the immediate post–Bretton Woods years during the 1970s, the new politics of depoliticization sought to present money once more as a purely economic medium best left to technocratic rule. Somewhat surprisingly, political theory seemingly accepted this reframing and the politics of money subsequently disappeared from political theory's field of vision. How can we explain this silence?

To begin with, initially at least, political theorists on the left widely underestimated the politics of disinflation with incredulity and complacency. Habermas, for example, still dismissed in 1979 any talk of "rolling back the welfare state" as empty reactionary chatter. It was impossible to take seriously, he explained, the grandiose pronouncements by neoconservatives about a monetarist revolution or the empty posturing of the anti–welfare state prophets. No responsible politician would intentionally cause unemployment by single-mindedly pursuing a course of disinflation at the enormous economic and, presumably, political costs that could risk the very legitimacy of government.[106] The American political theorist Michael Walzer similarly confidently declared in 1980 that what was most striking about contemporary politics was that there was "so little opposition to the welfare state as a whole. There is no serious revolutionary program for dismantling it or for replacing it with some radically different institutional arrangement."[107] This was, of course, not entirely accurate. There were plenty of voices clamoring for an end to welfare. Habermas and Walzer were nonetheless right that the state's interference in the economy was essential and ineliminable. What they overlooked was that there were numerous concrete proposals circulating for how state interference could be deployed in the service of economic discipline rather than welfare. According to this neoliberal logic, politics had to step in to better protect the market against democratic politics. What both Habermas and Walzer failed to appreciate was the way in which steering could be decoupled from democratic politics to become once more hidden behind a facade of technocratic rhetoric, but now in the service of discipline.

Even where they failed to see the contours of the new age of discipline, Habermas and others had in fact clearly perceived the political dilemma faced by the administrative welfare state. As we saw above, Habermas, like Bell, had perceptively identified the pressures of legitimacy confronting economic policy, in effect trapping the administrative state.[108] On the one hand, the political system was required for economic governance. On the other, the issues involved were so politically salient and divisive that they threatened to overload the political system's legitimacy. Crucially, monetary policymakers confronted a particularly acute version of this dilemma.[109] What Bell and Habermas underestimated then was the extent to which a new politics of disinflation could be derived from these pressures. They misjudged, in other words, the neoliberal and neoconservative capacity to set forth an alternative path out of the legitimacy impasse of welfare capitalism by systematically redrawing the boundary between economics and politics.[110] If visible intervention in the economy imposed strains on the political system, a politics of economic de-democratization was a conceivable and intelligible response. Ironically, what proved Habermas's and Bell's predictions wrong then was not mis-diagnosis but a failure to take their own analysis to its logical conclusion.

The neoliberal great transformation is from this perspective best understood as the outcome of a political experiment to evade the dilemma of legitimation.[111] The question that emerged for policymakers after the repoliticization of economic relations during the 1970s was how to guide market outcomes while avoiding responsibility for lackluster economic performance and divisive distributive decisions. Initially, policymakers had sought to deregulate markets in the 1970s in the hope of disciplining the proliferating demands that reached the state from below. But these hopes were frustrated. "Paradoxically," as the sociologist Greta Krippner has observed, "the market was not the strict disciplinarian imagined by neoliberal visionaries, operating with the blunt force of unforgiving nature, but a surprisingly lax master."[112] Instead, market discipline had to be deliberately enforced in the form of monetary policy whose political discretion had at the same time to be hidden and shielded from demo-cratic politics. Just as in Polanyi's paradox of laissez-faire having been planned, the discipline of monetarist market forces had to be artificially created by the invisible hand of the state, especially the central bank.[113]

The disappearance of money from political theory shadowed this new politics of monetary depoliticization. Where Habermas and Walzer had during the 1970s extensively commented on the politics of inflation, by the end of the 1980s money appeared in their respective conceptual frameworks as somehow removed from democratic politics. Two related strands converged to produce this result: a tacit withdrawal from attempts to democratize the capitalist economy, and the long shadow of Marx's cri-tique of the politics of money. Both Walzer and Habermas tacitly shared the sense that the repoliticization of the economy during the 1970s had been an inflationary dead end. We already saw the way in which Haber-mas had grown increasingly skeptical about the desirability of a politicized economy, not least because of the inflationary demands on legitimation this would imply. Walzer underwent a similar development. During the 1970s his participatory conception of democracy still included the demand that democratic control must include the economy in its ambit.[114] This was reflected in his detailed engagement with the politics of inflation, wage bargaining, and the welfare state in his political essays during the 1970s.[115]

But by the end of the 1970s Walzer had developed serious doubts about the possibility, let alone desirability, of such democratic control over the economy. He gradually came to affirm an analysis of a strained political-economic system that shared key aspects with Habermas's diagnosis of a crisis of legitimation.[116] As Walzer explained in 1978, "Deference and indoctrination are failing, and the result is a steady rise in the demands made by workers on the capitalist economy. These demands shake stability even though the unions that press them cannot yet challenge the power of capital."[117] The result was an overburdened political system. This meant, on the one hand, that a political program of collective self-restraint became both more necessary and politically harder to achieve. But it also meant that government was increasingly constrained in extending its support. "Businessmen," Walzer summarized laconically in reviewing Lindblom's *Politics and Markets* in 1978, "need, it turns out, an enormous amount of cosseting from the political authorities, and relatively minor successes for democratic movements may deprive them of what they need. Then they won't invest, they won't expand, they won't innovate. The result (Britain may be an example) is an economic slowdown that threatens the stability of the liberal market regime."[118]

Any state attempting to impose even minor democratic demands on the economy was in other words vulnerable to an investment strike. Where Lindblom had still thought it possible (and necessary) to devise constitutional arrangements for democratic decision-making in the economic realm, by the early 1980s many political theorists—including Walzer—had grown decidedly skeptical about the feasibility of such democratic extensions into the economy. Behind the turn away from economic democracy loomed the specter of inflation. Others, by contrast, were alarmed by this tacit shift. Brian Barry, for example, described the clamoring over inflation as little more than a ploy to put democracy in its place. "The beauty of inflation," he explained, "is that it can be used as a rallying cry to sweep up people who might otherwise be chary of plans to cripple the ability of governments to make economic policy."[119] Libertarians had long sought to bind the hands of the state but failed to get democratic approval for such plans. Now the "anti-inflationary hysteria" offered them a golden opportunity to realize their plans.[120] But it was far from clear that one had to choose between democracy and inflation. And even if that was the choice and if inflation was the price democracies had to pay for social struggle, was it so obvious that it was democracy that would have to give way? In the end, Barry's awareness of the politics of disinflation was drowned out. While liberal political theory remained committed to ambitious programs of redistribution, attempts to democratize economic relations themselves faded away. The missing political theory of money was from this perspective not just the unwitting victim of such a withdrawal from the economy but the price that had to be paid.

At this point the first strand of disenchantment with economic democracy combines with a second strand that reflects Marx's influence. Habermas and Walzer did not come to question economic democracy because they agreed with the neoconservative critiques of the welfare state but because they wondered whether Marx had not been right all along in pointing to the limits of imposing justice on capitalist economic relations. Taking the welfare state for granted while having grown skeptical about the democratization of the economy, by the early 1980s Habermas placed money rigidly in the economic realm and thus beyond democratic politics. While the economy had previously lingered in his thought somewhat ambiguously between steering and a semblance of depoliticization, Habermas now reduced money to a "de-linguistified" (*entsprachlicht*) steering medium that lacked normativity.[121] Instead of distinguishing between economy and state or, with Polanyi, between market and society, Habermas instead opposed a rich lifeworld to an administrative-economic system with money firmly rooted in the latter. Where communication characterized the former, the latter was a cold machine of instrumental reason alone. The "depoliticized" economy, Habermas explained, owed "its emergence to a new mechanism, the steering medium of money. This medium is specifically tailored to the economic function of society as a whole, a function relinquished by the state."[122] Habermas consequently drew a strict opposition between emancipatory politics and money.[123]

This was not meant as a concession to neoliberalism but instead also reflected the long shadow of Marx. While the monetization of social relations might offer itself as a tempting relief mechanism, this came with an inevitable experience of loss. For Habermas, this "colonization of the lifeworld" thesis was an attempt to translate Georg Lukács's account of reification (*Verdinglichung*) into his own social theory of communicative action.[124] The politics of money was one unwitting victim of this move. Reduced to instrumental rationality and reification, there was little room for money as a malleable institution in its own right. Where he had previously spoken of the necessity for the mere semblance of depoliticization, Habermas now seemingly took the depoliticization of money at face value and turned it into a fundamental building block of his social theory. It is helpful to contrast Habermas's depoliticized treatment of money with the more ambivalent role he granted law. Law, he explained in *Between Facts and Norms* (1992), was always more than instrumental reason and functioned instead as a "hinge" between system and lifeworld.[125] But the same did not apply to money. Like pure administrative power, money lacked communicative reason and instead operated "behind the backs" of participants.[126] While rejecting such reductionism for legal discourse, Habermas defined money by cutting it off from genuine intersubjectivity and thus normativity. Where law possessed a "peculiar dual position and mediating function," money was unambiguously beyond emancipatory politics.[127] The possibility that money could also have a malleable political dimension determined by political struggles was thereby ruled out.

During the early 1980s Walzer similarly came to reconceive of the relation of the economy as separate from democratic politics.[128] Like Habermas, it was a curious mixture of Marx and the actual depoliticization of disinflation that drove this reframing. In *Spheres of Justice* (1983) Walzer now argued that goods should be distributed in accordance with their social meaning and the principles that flow from that meaning. Social goods belonged to distinct distributive spheres that differed across both societies and time. Only empirical investigations could ascertain the boundaries between these spheres.[129] This contextualist separation of social justice into distinct spheres, which marked Walzer's transition from a local-participatory form of democratic socialism to a local-participatory form of communitarian liberalism, had direct implications for the politics of money. First and foremost, it meant that money had a proper sphere of its own, namely the economy, and that it could and should be contained in this proper sphere. This implied both that politics had to be protected from the power of money but also, on the flip side, that money had to be protected from state power. Walzer noted that he found inspiration for his first point—that there are things money cannot buy—in Marx's early critique of the commodification of love in the *Paris Manuscripts*. But where Marx had rejected the separation of politics from economics, Walzer's new liberalism on the contrary strove "to endorse and extend it [the separation], to enlist liberal artfulness in the service of socialism."[130] What mattered was simply getting the lines right. The politics of money became in the process at best unintelligible, at worst an illegitimate infringement of the boundaries Walzer drew between his spheres of justice. While this framing of separation aligns with appealing critiques of corruption and commodification, its rarely considered implication is that an articulation of the politics of money was ruled out. Where economic sociologists, such as in particular Viviana Zelizer, have tirelessly drawn attention to the malleability and pluralism of money, Walzer instead reduced money to a perfectly fungible and purely economic means of exchange.[131]

If it was the shadow of Marx—and to a lesser extent Locke—that hung over the resulting invisibility of the politics of money, what rendered this invisibility plausible was the actually occurring politics of monetary depoliticization of the disinflationary squeeze. Almost despite themselves, Habermas and Walzer inadvertently partook in the depoliticization of the economy.[132] The apparent depoliticization of money and the resulting mirage of disentanglement between politics and economics now made plausible again accounts of justice that, as in Walzer's case, rigorously separated between an economic sphere and a political one, or social theories that, as in Habermas's case, sharply distinguished between a normative realm of speech and the norm-free steering medium of money. Where the contestations and politicizations of monetary relations during the 1970s had served as a reminder of their political nature, the anti-inflationary turn of the 1980s rendered plausible once more the idea that money was a mere tool of economic functioning. Its contested political foundations had become once more invisible.

Conclusion

Liberalism's latent inclination to conceive of economic relations outside of politics, as well as its attendant anxieties about the moral and civic disruption of money, have long tended to marginalize and partially obscure arguments about the political nature of money. If the art of separation, as Walzer laid it out in a classic essay in the early 1980s, was a core characteristic of liberalism, the politics of money was always going to be a likely victim.[133] But the politics of monetary depoliticization since the early 1980s decisively strengthened this tendency by rendering a conceptually disentangled account of politics and economics once more plausible as a depiction of capitalist appearances. This was the context in which political theory turned away from the hybrid politics of money toward accounts of commodification (or the "colonization of the lifeworld," in Habermas's words) that were now recast as infractions of the separation between depoliticized money and politics. The idea that money could itself be a political tool for justice was increasingly alien to this line of thought.

If the eventual effects of the new politics of disinflation were difficult to imagine at the time, it would be wrong to make the opposite mistake today and conclude that they were structurally inevitable. Instead, as the German sociologist Ulrich Beck has perceptively put it, "not the failures of politics but its *successes* have led to the loss of state intervention power

and to the delocalization of politics."[134] It was a specific *politics* of depoliticization that instituted policies designed to give the appearance of a
spontaneous, depoliticized economic realm and that ended up heavily cur-
tailing the ability of states to intervene in economic relations. If the state
was previously constrained by having to satisfy multiplying demands of
legitimacy, the escape from the impasse of legitimacy has not freed up economic policy but chained it to a different master. Where the 1970s had been
characterized by anxieties over ungovernability, by the 1990s the political
bonds of legitimacy had been replaced by the fetters of investor "credibility."
But these chains, and the bond vigilantes enforcing them, were not originally imposed against the state. They were the tools of discipline that had
been deliberately unleashed by central-bank politics.

What this points to is the devastatingly effective politics of the "anti-
Keynesian" revolution of the 1970s, which not only paved the way to disinflationary discipline but also effectively buried Keynes, at least until the
global financial crisis of 2008. Hayek, like many others, blamed the Great
Inflation of the 1970s after all on Keynes's hubris. But Keynes had precisely
warned against both the contradictions of the Bretton Woods system and
the instabilities of freely floating currencies. Keynes's more radical options
for how to reconcile democracy with modern money were never tried. At
the very moment in which Keynes was once more as relevant as ever,
namely the crisis of the 1970s, it became crucial to forestall this option by
tainting his entire monetary theory with the failure of the postwar model.
Attacking Keynes on the level of economic theory accompanied the new
politics of monetary depoliticization, which proved that the discretionary
powers of central banks could be used as much to maintain and raise the
value of capital—thus artificially reimposing scarcity and discipline—as
they could have been used to erode it along Keynes's lines.[135]

Despite their many constraints, central banks have discretionary powers that can be used for vastly different political projects. They are able to
conjure bond vigilantes or neutralize them—as has effectively happened
during the COVID-19 crisis. Today markets in government debt across
the Global North are no longer the playthings of bond investors exercising pressure but instead once more firmly in the grip of central banks.[136]
This has not only economic repercussions but also speaks to the very
possibility of maintaining a space for democratic politics without the
intimidation and threats of bond markets. But if the ability of the state
to interfere with economic matters was never in question, what social and
political theorists—such as Bell, Habermas, and Walzer—underestimated
was the ease with which democratic states willingly abandoned their

responsibilities in the economic realm. Rather than being politically punished for having to make difficult distributive choices, politicians much rather pretended to be powerless.

This raises once more the paradox of excessive democratic self-binding. To be sure, the politicians of disinflation and discipline were quick to point to the state's seemingly shrinking power in the face of globalization. But there are good reasons not to take such claims at face value. The fact that the political importance of monetary policy has only grown as the state has tied its hands illustrates this tension powerfully. During the 2008 financial crisis and the global COVID shutdown, the same voices that previously painted the state as increasingly constrained and powerless suddenly counted on the ability of states to intervene in economic relations.[137] They were not disappointed. Many of the fetters that keep the state and central banks in check are not so much externally imposed but reflect instead attempts at democratic self-binding. This means that the depoliticization of money is a mirage that results from a sleight of hand. It is never the case that money ceases to be political but merely that it is removed from democratic politics.

It is worth recalling in this context that the reason so few could envisage during the 1970s that inflation would trigger a wholesale political revolution was not because they viewed money as somehow beyond politics, but precisely because they appreciated it as a supremely political question: they were only too aware of the enormous political strife it embodied. Our ability to forget about the politics of money is no less striking than the failure, back in the 1970s, to anticipate the transformation that lay ahead. We tend to lose sight of how miraculous the successful de-democratization of money would have appeared to most observers in the 1970s. Instead, the anti-inflationary politics of depoliticization has reshaped our political imagination so comprehensively as to become itself almost invisible.

{⚓W⚓}

This was, arguably, the scenario closest to the original hopes of the benefactor of the Nobel Memorial Prize in Economic Sciences that Myrdal and Hayek had received in 1974. As is well-known, unlike the other Nobel Prizes, the prize in economics was not endowed by Alfred Nobel but established only in 1969. Less well-known is that it was created by the Swedish central bank (the Sveriges Riksbank) and that the donation reflected the Riksbank's own quest to acquire greater independence from political oversight and democratic accountability.[138] In the context of disputes over political interference, the Swedish central bank began to claim a mantle of scientific credibility that could appear to transcend politics. The invention and endowment of the Nobel Memorial Prize in Economic Sciences was a direct outgrowth of this attempt to render invisible the political dimension of money while validating the apolitical appearance of the Riksbank's monetary policy. Indeed, even the prize money attached to the award was the product of the Riksbank refusing to hand over its profits to the Treasury.[139] Central banks' budgets (for research, for example) tend not to come from taxes but are instead simply created by the central banks themselves. These are—admittedly limited but still very real—"fiscal" operations in which money is spent without having been taxed.

Myrdal and Hayek were somewhat aware of the peculiarly political act the prize constituted and both were uneasy about it, albeit for tellingly different reasons. In his Banquet speech the night before his lecture, Hayek even counseled the queen and king of Sweden against awarding the very prize he had just received. A Nobel Prize in economics, Hayek feared, risked conferring on an individual "an authority which in economics no man ought to possess."[140] Ironically, this cautionary warning applied to Hayek perhaps more than anyone else. As his biographer chronicles, in one single swoop the prize effectively brought Hayek back from obscurity and paved his path to global authority.[141] Myrdal agreed with Hayek's conclusion, albeit for different reasons. Since economics was not a natural but a social science, Myrdal explained, a prestigious award such as the Nobel Prize inevitably constituted a political act plotted under "draconian rules of secrecy" by the Swedish Academy of Science. Bringing up his own prize, Myrdal admitted that "as I have now come to see the problem of whether there should be a Nobel Prize in economic science—in former times rightly called 'political economy'—I should have declined to receive it."[142] Unfortunately, the message informing him of the prize had reached him very early in the morning in New York and he was caught off guard.

As the politics of monetary depoliticization gathered pace and eventually hit its triumphalist stride after the end of the Cold War, it began to consolidate its narrative of neutrality and inevitability. This meant first and foremost insulating economic decisions against the democratic pressures of distributive legitimacy. Nowhere was this more true than for monetary policymaking.[143] Independent central banks credibly committed to inflation targeting were expected to maintain a "Goldilocks" economy that would provide both low inflation and growth of employment. The de-democratization of money was seen to have broken the previous trade-off between inflation and growth. According to the narrative of the Great

Moderation, financial liberalization and deregulation would meanwhile offer a way out of the distributive legitimacy dilemma of the 1970s and the pressures created by stagnant wages.

As the financial crisis of 2008 revealed, this optimistic triumphalism proved premature. Inflation targeting was perfectly compatible with enormous asset-price inflation and a buildup of financial bubbles. Financialization proved ultimately unable to hide the gradual erosion of economic gains for all but the top percentiles of the wealth distribution over the past three decades. In calm times it had been possible to reduce money to a seemingly neutral means of economic exchange. During the financial crisis it became exponentially harder to disguise the formative nature of fiat money and the political choices inherent in it. Central banks were revealed as agents with vast discretion in a system that was supposed to be without alternatives. As the veil fell, money emerged once more as a construct of our collective imagination, after all *not* immune to questions of justice and justification.

Democratic money is bad money.

—RUDI DORNBUSCH[1]

We refuse to believe that the bank of justice is bankrupt.

—MARTIN LUTHER KING JR.[2]

THREE DAYS HAD PASSED since Lehman Brothers had disappeared into the vortex. On Thursday, September 18, 2008, at 11 a.m., Treasury Secretary and former CEO of Goldman Sachs, Hank Paulson gave members of Congress a stark warning: $5.5 trillion in wealth would disappear within the next three hours unless the government took immediate action.[3] The world economy, he added casually, would otherwise likely collapse within twenty-four hours. Federal Reserve Chairman Ben Bernanke, who only days earlier had helped to push Lehman toward bankruptcy, underscored the message. "If we don't do this," he warned, "we may not have an economy on Monday."[4]

Paulson and Bernanke got what they asked for, and the euphemistically labeled Troubled Asset Relief Program (TARP) inaugurated a series of bailouts unprecedented in the history of capitalism. Where the original bill promised the purchase of toxic assets from a broad range of economic agents, including homeowners, within days Paulson and Bernanke ditched the clause and instead injected billions of dollars in capital directly into struggling banks. TARP's $700 billion were shortly followed by the Federal Reserve creating trillions of dollars in order to purchase troubled assets directly from banks and corporations. The Fed meanwhile extended unlimited swap lines to a select group of central banks around the world so that these too could inject dollars into their own banks.[5]

It is tempting in retrospect to see in TARP the moment at which the sovereign state snatched back control over the financial and monetary system. After all, the bailout revealed that the financialized economy was ultimately dependent on the ability of the American state to create dollars. But in his seminal account of the financial crisis, the economic historian Adam Tooze flips this around. Instead of an autonomous sovereign state taking charge of a crisis, those enacting the bailouts came from the very same Wall Street-to-Washington networks as those sitting on the other side of the table as recipients.[6] If this was an act of sovereignty, who precisely was sovereign—the American people or Wall Street? Whose interest did the state pursue? In its quest to restore faith and confidence in the financial system, even the most benign elements of the American state found themselves hostage to the "finance franchise."[7]

One of the architects of the bailouts candidly summarized the resulting logic. In order to ensure that banks accepted capital injections, the terms had to be excessively attractive, not punitive. "This had to be the opposite of the 'Sopranos' or the 'Godfather'—not an attempt to intimidate banks," he explained, "but instead a deal so attractive that banks would be unwise to refuse it."[8] Given the chance to offload their own troubled past, banks were quickly able to generate profits again. But as asset prices soared and funding costs dropped, these same banks foreclosed on mortgages on a scale not seen before, particularly in Black and Hispanic neighborhoods across the US, where record numbers of homeowners were forced into foreclosure.[9] The inequality of the bailouts spurred on the Occupy Wall Street movement, and the fallout of the crisis has rippled through the entire American and international political landscape over the subsequent decade.[10] As Treasury Secretary Timothy Geithner put it retrospectively, "We saved the economy but we lost the country doing it."[11] Despite its sober acknowledgment of the political costs, this was meant as a self-congratulatory declaration. After all: "We saved the economy!" Implicit in this defense was the comparison to Europe. Underwriting the profitability of banks—what Geithner memorably described as "foaming the runway"— seemed still preferable to failing to do so and ending up with credit cratering, millions unemployed, and a "sovereign" debt crisis. Blank-check bailouts or an entire generation lost to youth unemployment. Those were seemingly the only two grim options on this account. But what is perhaps most telling in this framing is the extent of impoverishment of the political imagination that it reflects. Among policymakers at least, the inverted relation of power between banks and the state has become entirely taken for granted.

The monetary tools first trialed in the financial crisis have since become part of the tool kit of contemporary central banks. They were quickly reactivated in the spring of 2020 in response to COVID-19. In March 2020 the Federal Reserve immediately cut interest rates to zero and announced that it would buy $700 billion in US government debt.[12] As de facto central bank to the world, the Fed once more used swap lines to make dollars available to chosen allies—this time especially to Asian economies. Central banks asserted their role as liquidity providers of last resort and often market makers of first resort, including now in markets for sovereign debt. According to the International Monetary Fund, three-quarters of all government debt issued in 2020 was bought by central banks themselves.[13] Central banks around the world today actively manage the long-term interest rates of government debt. The Bank of Japan—a pioneer in these matters—has formally committed to ensuring that the interest the government has to pay on its ten-year bonds remain at zero. The magic money tree, or so it seems, does exist after all.

And yet, while central banks appear more pervasive and powerful than ever, they are in a peculiar bind. Despite their active bond buying, the direct financing of government deficits remains an unspeakable taboo. Indeed, as central bankers themselves are only too keen to stress, even when they buy government bonds what drives their actions is not the goal of aiding the public weal but to keep financial markets liquid. The powers of central banks largely work through the private banking system, which is only too aware of its own structural importance. The generous treatment of banks during the financial crisis was not merely a favor, though it was that too. Rather, what allows banks to live by a different set of rules from the rest of society is the privilege that derives from being the exclusive purveyor of credit in the economy. In the private-public partnership by which the state delegates the provision of a crucial public good—money— to private agents, the people ended up as hostages to the agents it itself once empowered. The result has been a perverse situation of central-bank supremacy in order to provide financial liquidity for banks rather than in the service of broad-based credit provision and a more egalitarian financial citizenship.

Both in 2008 and 2020, there was of course much debate concerning who stood to benefit from the monetary interventions in the economy. But behind the high distributive stakes lurks an even more fundamental set of questions: Who gets to decide who creates money? Where should money power reside in our constitutions? Is a more democratic money possible? In moments of crisis, interventions in the economy become visible for everyone to see. In the realm of modern money, however, they are not one-off emergency measures but a constant feature of our entire monetary system. Global finance desperately needs the state to provide liquidity and safe assets. And yet this does not seem to give the state the upper hand, because the state in turn depends on banks to provide credit.

{⁕⁕⁕}

This book began with the lamentation that our current political language for articulating the politics of money—its democratic possibilities, but also its oligarchic limitations—remains impoverished and inadequate. My guiding premise was that the competing and complementary conceptions of the political theory of money put forward by Aristotle, John Locke, Johann Gottlieb Fichte, Karl Marx, and John Maynard Keynes can provide us with much-needed conceptual clarity. They can enrich our democratic vocabulary by placing money alongside law and speech as a tool of power but also recognition and reciprocity. They can also improve our understanding of our own often contradictory monetary imagination, torn between echoes of the past. By recovering a layered set of debates across the history of political thought in a variety of political contexts, I sketched a topographical map of the politics of money and the layers in which it accumulated and solidified.

In beginning my journey in the most remote layer in Athens, I issued a reminder about the political hopes once placed in political currency, even if these seem now further removed than ever. Few today, if anyone, would recognize in modern money a tool of equality and reciprocity. From this perspective, Aristotle's ambivalent account foreshadowed tragedy. And yet, recovering the political aspirations once placed in money helps to account for the latent possibilities inherent in it and the way in which it can never be fully removed from the quest for justice. If Aristotle grounded my genealogical inquiry, my discussion of the modern political theory of money was bookended by John Locke and John Maynard Keynes respectively. Locke's foundational move of a new politics of monetary depoliticization sought to constrain discretionary meddling with the standard of value. Turned into a mantra of "sound money" and divorced from Locke's own more political argument, Lockeanism became the orthodoxy of modern times that misleadingly framed money as removed from politics. Fichte, Proudhon, Marx, and Keynes all offered overlapping and divergent critiques of this predicament that continue to echo through to us today. Where Fichte embraced the tantalizing possibilities of national fiat money in an economy isolated from world trade, others—not least Proudhon—offered a vision of egalitarian monetary reform that would republicanize credit. Marx, by contrast, critically vindicated orthodoxy by tying money indissolubly to capital in order to overcome it. Keynes navigated all of these strands and saw their attractions and pitfalls perhaps more clearly than anyone else. He can serve in this context not just as a contributor to the political theory of money but also as a guide to mapping its underlying choices. The challenges Fichte, Proudhon, Marx, and Keynes posed have still not been answered. Today, the orthodoxy of neutral money is discredited but it is far from clear what could possibly replace it.

Following past thinkers yet deeper into the past is not meant to produce a catalog of answers. The fundamental point is not to "mine" the history of political thought in order to pit various thinkers against one another. Instead, the purpose of my excavation is not so much extractive—in the sense of a petroleum geologist—but a genuinely geological inquiry in the hope of providing a better understanding of the ground we stand on, whether consciously or not, and the intellectual resources that are available to us. Global capital and the interdependent politics of money engulf all countries around the world today. The canon of Western political and economic thought out of which the concept of modern money as credit and capital emerged remains indispensable for understanding the global politics of money, even where it is obviously insufficient on its own.[14] But becoming aware of the episodic and layered character of political thinking about money also has the ability to change the way we understand the nature of that tradition itself. The different moments and contributions to the political theory of money not only rest on one another but also condition each other. This is not, then, a story of heroes and villains—disappointingly so perhaps. Instead, my hope is that our journey through the sedimented geological strata of the history of political reflection on money can help us to understand ourselves and our political struggles by providing a better language to capture the politics of money, including its promises and limitations. To appreciate the opportunity and challenges of the current moment, it is worth making explicit the prolonged monetary crisis from within which this book itself is written.

As I mentioned at the outset, I myself write from within a moment of crisis that has been aptly described as a monetary interregnum. In the typology offered by Eric Helleiner, a scholar of the international political economy of money, we can distinguish between different stages of monetary change. In this sequence, interregnum is the period after a legitimacy crisis had led to a breakdown of the old order but before a new "constitutive phase"—a moment of founding—can emerge.[15] Where the interregnum is pregnant with ideas, the constitutive phase gives birth to a new monetary order. As we continue to linger in the interregnum, the future of money remains profoundly uncertain. This can produce an overburdening sense of helplessness and even cynicism. And yet this condition of uncertainty and flux also offers an opportunity to set out the contours of any future monetary constitution by formulating the basic demands it must address and by shaping the political coalitions necessary to ensure it does so.

Crucially, as we have seen throughout, the seeming depoliticization of money is better understood as a de-democratization. It is itself a political move in an ongoing struggle over the status of money. Appreciation of this sleight of hand clears the way for a more comprehensive democratic debate about the status of money power in our constitutions. Money is never beyond politics. Instead, the real question is what kind of politics ought to shape it. My genealogy of the political theory of money and its excavation of unfamiliar ideas from the political realm of money allow, I hope, for an improved articulation of fundamental democratic demands concerning the future of money, but also for an appreciation of the difficulties inherent in doing so. The resulting debates will center on what structures we may want to raise on the ground we stand on, and in these closing pages I want to turn to some of the possible implications of my genealogy of the political theory of money.

The Future of Money

Money is today overwhelmingly issued by private banks. It is also, for related reasons, relentlessly global and seemingly beyond the state. And yet modern money continues to be shot through with power and hierarchy. Where the Bretton Woods system had formally elevated the US dollar to a special status, the dollar remains today in effect a global currency but now founded on the dense private networks of financial markets.[16] This produces a peculiar situation, namely, that one country's central bank, the Federal Reserve, has become the world's de facto central bank. As one European central banker put it memorably during the financial crisis, "In a way, we became the thirteenth Federal Reserve district."[17] Others were not so lucky. This system can easily seem unassailable. Even crises only seem to entrench its power structures and deepen existing hierarchies. But the domestic and international legitimacy of this system of international monetary hierarchy is brittle. It is held together not by a coherent internal logic but, for the time being, by a lack of plausible alternatives.

The world is in desperate need of a new global monetary constitution and a monetary system that is more democratic in its governance. Digital-payments systems and cryptocurrencies flaunt in this light the promise of a new global money, indeed a decentralized democratization of entrenched money power. The reality is starkly different. It is important here to distinguish between cryptocurrencies and the digital-payment projects of fintech firms and global internet platforms. Cryptocurrencies promise a future of global money not just beyond the state and beyond banks, but also most fundamentally beyond trust since all information is stored in a decentralized public ledger while cryptography ensures the uniqueness of each entry. Technology is meant to overcome the fragility of human relations. This is deeply deceptive. Existing cryptocurrencies are money in name only. Their wild price fluctuations, intentional inefficiencies, and environmental impact render them uniquely unfit to serve as currency. Instead, they are first and foremost speculative assets that peddle a misleading pretense. The idea of decentralized money beyond trust and power is a dangerous delusion—a counterfeit of democratic money. Even worse, like the deception of depoliticized money, it disguises who actually stands to benefit and who calls the shots. By contrast, attempts by global internet platforms—most prominently Facebook—to create their own digital currency are an entirely different matter. Facebook's Libra project (since rebranded as Diem) does not promise a decentralized future of monetary democracy and instead touts the benefits of fiat money with the convenience of an app. This project and others like it are based on so-called stable coins that are themselves backed by baskets of fiat money. But this promise of convenience is little more than a well-disguised grab for the privatization of money that essentially free rides on the state's support. This touches on fundamental questions concerning the status of money as a public good, on which more in a moment. If then not the fiction of trustless cryptocurrencies or Facebook's dystopian vision of a private global currency, what can a more democratic global money look like that takes seriously its own status as a public good?

There has been a flurry of proposals for international monetary reform, a new Bretton Woods conference, a revival of Keynes's original plan, and a genuine international reserve currency to replace the dollar.[18] But what are the chances that a genuinely democratic global monetary conference could take up the challenge of formulating a new monetary constitution and a new global reserve currency? The prospects of anything resembling Keynes's proposal taking shape anytime soon are sadly less than slim and certainly slimmer than the odds of Facebook's Libra/Diem succeeding. After all, even the Bretton Woods compromise—itself already based on a repudiation of Keynes's original plan—emerged among the victorious powers in the context of global war. Its internationalism was from the outset shaped by the power dynamics of the mid-century in which the United States claimed the right to project its emergent hegemony onto the world of money. So evident are these power dynamics that one has to ask why Bretton Woods continues to circulate as a totem for "international cooperation."[19] Given Keynes's failure in Bretton Woods, given the failure of the Bretton Woods system itself during the 1970s, and given the unlikely prospect of a new democratic global monetary constitution anytime soon, we seem to be cast back onto the Marxian paradigm, firmly in the grip of capital.

And yet, as Marx's contemporary Walter Bagehot already observed in the 1860s, money cannot manage itself.[20] As much as capital might appear to turn money into a rigid crystal, the modern monetary system is structurally dependent on the state and its actions. In moments of crisis this dependence becomes most explicitly visible, but it is a permanent feature of modern money, and one that provides an opening toward reforming it.

Democratic Money

Despite the proliferation of capital, the politics of money is inescapable. What can be lost, however, is sight of the ways in which we can shape money. Even if such attempts face serious obstacles and inevitably fall short of transcending capital, we can assert public control over money as an essential institutions of collective self-rule. Money as "political currency" is a constitutive element of democratic political communities, yet its continued ability to play that role is not a given; it requires ongoing political struggle. As Christine Desan puts it, "Recognizing money as public credit installs a particular challenge at the heart of democratic governance in a monetary world."[21] Though we may ultimately decide to delegate certain money powers to public agencies and private actors, we have to begin from the premise that money is a public good whose provision needs to live up to standards of social justice.

There is a growing recognition, including among former central bankers themselves, that the current monetary system no longer serves the interest of those it ought to serve. Equally, many monetary policymakers have acknowledged that there is an urgent need to address underlying questions of legitimacy, equality, and fairness.[22] Even those who hope to defend the broad outlines of the current system stress that central bankers' attempt to sidestep questions of democratic legitimacy by reciting the mantra of apolitical neutrality has by now backfired.[23] Our democratic polities are caught in a paradoxical impasse. Financial capitalism and liberal democracy turn out to hinge ever more on the decisions of central banks, but such interventions, however necessary, unravel the thin thread of their own legitimacy. Recognition of the distributive—and indeed fiscal—effects of monetary policy prompts further calls for democratic accountability, to which central bankers respond by doubling down on market neutrality. An insistence on apolitical aloofness itself fuels the very politicization of monetary policy that it seeks to avoid.[24] The increasing insulation of monetary policy from democratic politics, then, has incurred political costs because political disagreement is displaced, critique silenced, and legitimation hollowed out.[25] The solution, it would seem, is to push for the greater democratization of money power. But what would this actually mean? Before we can have any hope of answering this question, the first task must be to see the problem more clearly, to pose the underlying democratic questions more precisely, and to develop a richer conceptual vocabulary for articulating the underlying political stakes. Let me suggest three possible angles for how political theory can contribute to this effort.

A first perspective offered by political theory directs our attention to underlying questions of privatization. Any inquiry into the possibility of more democratic money has to start from the twin observations that we live in an age of central-bank capitalism and that our money today is to an overwhelming extent issued by private banks. Central banks orchestrate the credit creation of banks because it is through banks that credit arrives in the economy. Banks in turn wield money power, but they remain ultimately backed by the state and dependent on central banks. From one perspective this means that "the ascendancy of finance" has fundamentally altered the locus of sovereignty in our polities.[26] Modern money is a public good whose provision has been handed over to the private sector. But why should we accept this delegation as an inevitable feature of modernity?

The private provision of the public good of money calls for much more scrutiny and, fortunately, political theorists have far more resources at their disposal for this purpose than they themselves might realize. There is a rich literature on how to democratize access to public goods, and political theorists have recently turned their attention to powerful critical dissections of "the privatized state."[27] The delegation of credit creation to private agents is perhaps the original instance of privatization. The attempt to issue private forms of money and to further privatize existing monies can in this sense be reframed as a troubling example of "private government."[28] If money is not just a neutral convenience of commerce but a public good as well as—at least aspirationally—a political institution of self-rule, critiques of privatization can help us to interrogate the privileges of private banks in democracies as well as conceptualize contemporary struggles over the status of cryptocurrency and the prospect of international monetary reform. In developing conceptual tools for assessing the legitimacy of privatization, for checking the exercise of private economic power, and for determining which areas of our collective lives should be beyond private control, political theorists have at their disposal a catalog of arguments that remain to be deployed to tame and harness money power.

The arguments political theorists have developed against private power caution in this light against the further privatization of money by global banks, tech platforms, or indeed private cryptocurrencies, as well as against countries adopting monetary standards that are entirely beyond their control, a phenomenon known as "dollarization."[29] In order to prevent a slide into digital feudalism in which tech platforms function as private governments able to issue their own parallel scrip money, we need to include questions of money power in any critique of privatization and private economic power. These struggles matter crucially for reasons of democratic legitimacy. But they also have vast economic repercussions that feed into contemporary patterns of inequality. The hierarchical logic of private credit creation has far-reaching effects and, as an entire generation of scholars have since pointed out, it has been one of the key drivers of ever-widening wealth disparities in the US, often along racial lines.[30] As a study by the Federal Reserve Bank of Boston found already before the pandemic, the median net worth of an African American household in Boston is eight dollars.[31] This was not a typo, the *Boston Globe* had to add when reporting on the finding.[32] Addressing the racial wealth gap at its root would mean tackling the way in which the current monetary system, tied to private credit creation and a perfunctory housing market, actively deepens existing inequalities and undermines financial citizenship.

A second critical reassessment has in this context drawn on the conceptual tools of political theory to spell out the obligations that arise from the privatized provision of credit in democracies. The legal scholar Mehrsa Baradaran has, for example, reframed the relation between banks and the state as a social contract of sorts.[33] Although this is an admittedly unusual use of the concept, as a metaphor it succeeds in capturing an important element of reciprocity that has been lost. The delegation of powers of money creation to banks was meant to provide mutual benefits to the public and to banks, but these now accrue in a decidedly lopsided manner. This alone recalls the societal obligations and responsibilities that come attached to the privilege of credit creation. As such, the reference to a social contract constitutes a powerful reminder that banks are unlike other corporations and that money is more than a commodity. The plausibility of a social contract with banks, indeed the very image of the state and banks meeting one another at eye level, serves at the same time as an indication of how distorted the relationship has become. It bears emphasizing that only one of the two parties—the state—has the coercive means to hold banks accountable in ways that have not been used of late.

On one level this points to tougher and better banking regulation that would reassert the terms of delegation in order to force banks to live up to the promised public benefits. This would also entail forcing shadow banks into the light by insisting they rise to the same obligations and expectations. And yet, reasserting any kind of social contract between banks and the state through tougher regulation seems both unlikely politically and insufficient for democratizing credit. As Baradaran herself stresses, we will instead likely need some kind of alternative means of provisioning the public with credit and banking services. One promising proposal envisages in this context a revival of postal banking.[34] Others have started to think openly about ways to make the benefits of money creation more equally available as part of a new conception of financial citizenship and a democratic redesign of the central bank's balance sheet.[35] This could entail, for example, granting accounts at the Federal Reserve ("FedAccounts") to everyone, not just to banks as is currently the case.[36] Apart from its immediate effect on democratizing access to banking services, potentially including credit, this would have the additional benefit of rendering the state less dependent on the goodwill of banks to achieve its monetary goals. Central banks could directly deposit money into citizens' accounts held at a public institution. Credit would flow irrespectively of the profit calculations of banks. As a result, the state would be able to gradually free itself from its condition of dependence on private banks. This matters all the more in light of the impasse whereby currently any state hoping to deploy its powers of regulatory punishment to force banks to live up to their social obligations is vulnerable to the credible threat that doing so might cripple the economy. Without some form of public provision of credit we are all hostage to this blackmail.

A final, complementary vantage point takes seriously the pivotal role of central banks in contemporary capitalism. If political theorists have recently creatively turned their attention again to what it would mean to democratize capitalism, central banks would appear to be prime sites for such attempts. After all, they are already public institutions situated at the very heart of financial capitalism. We have long been familiar with calls to treat sites of production as fundamentally political and to democratize the relations of power that structure them. Not only should the same political logic apply to the production of credit as well, but the democratization of credit holds arguably even greater promise than those workplace strategies since today the balance of power between capital and labor has decisively tilted toward the former. Central banks and financial regulators emerge in this picture as essential sites of political contestation in contemporary capitalism. Although both are of course severely constrained in their actions, they nonetheless wield vast powers on which financial markets utterly depend. We find ourselves firmly in the grip of capital, yet it turns out that finance requires the state at least as much as—and arguably more than—the state requires finance.[37]

Learning how to exploit this structural dependence requires joining those scholars who have started to explore the contemporary meaning of democracy in capitalist institutions and extending that democratic quest from corporations to central banks. Instead of falling back on dated conceptions of central-bank independence, the political theory of money should embolden us to conduct more creative discussions of novel institutional setups. Most fundamentally, this would imply embracing the possibility that central banks can become laboratories of "open democracy."[38] If our primary concern is the division of powers, why not set up a distinct democratic body to direct monetary affairs? Such a body could be partially elected but it could also draw on other innovative institutional solutions that political theorists have explored for nonelective representation— from sortition to mixed deliberative councils.[39] If our concern is with more democratic decisions, why not organize central banks more democratically internally? For example, we could ensure that various segments of society—not least labor alongside capital—are equally represented. It would be perfectly possible, for example, to have a central bank operate internally on more democratic principles, be it those of "open democracy" or simply a more representative decision-making body, while nonetheless shielding that more democratic body against the whims of public opinion or the will of the executive.[40] Instead of responding to the democratic shortcomings of central banks by simply yoking them to political systems that have themselves serious democratic deficits (a likely recipe for disaster), we can democratize central banks while shielding them against undue influence. Rather than remaining stuck in stale debates about central-bank independence, the more fundamental constitutional question would be how we can make central banks more democratic internally and at once more independent, by redefining independence as not against democracy but rather against the executive and financial markets.

These three vantage points do not offer us easy answers, nor are they beyond reproach, and they are certainly not meant to somehow end the conversation. Instead, they serve as illustrations of the ways in which political theorists can open up unfamiliar vistas of the politics of money and enrich the language in which the underlying political stakes will have to be debated. I invite others to join me in this quest.

Democratizing money would mean in this light extending languages that are familiar in other political domains, as well as developing new languages that would allow for a more serious and precise consideration of the democratic legitimacy of monetary politics. The main obstacle here is not simply the seemingly technical nature of monetary policy or its heavy epistemic burden but rather an institutionalized linguistic obfuscation that arises from a perceived tension between genuine open-ended democratic debate and the objectives of monetary policy rooted in "credibility." Central bankers have long prided themselves on their elaborate silence. "Never explain, never apologize" was the infamous mantra of the British central banker Montagu Norman during the interwar years. As former Federal Reserve chairman Alan Greenspan quipped, "Since becoming a central banker, I have learned to mumble with great incoherence."[41] Until 2011 the Federal Reserve did not even hold regular press conferences. Today, by contrast, central bankers champion transparency. But their understanding of communication is drawn from the realm of public relations, not democratic deliberation. The prime constituency of central banks' monetary-policy decisions consists after all to an overwhelming extent not of the citizenry but the financial markets. As a protester named Josephine Witt declared at a European Central Bank press conference on Greece in 2015, "A press conference is not enough to call it 'democracy.'"[42]

To articulate a more democratic vision of how money power might be deployed and rendered accountable, that power must first be rendered visible. This will mean developing a better public understanding of how money works, but that in turn requires a richer normative and political vocabulary concerning the powers of making money and how they form part of our political systems. Our language shapes our political choices and constrains what we even perceive as choices. Political theorists have much to contribute here by approaching money more creatively in analogy to law and civic speech. An improved public understanding of the power of money, its political possibilities, and how these are currently unfulfilled can point to new avenues for democratizing money and safeguard against attempts to further privatize it. This is all the more the case because debating money—its history and politics—has a peculiarly self-reflexive quality. For better or worse, our very thoughts about money and the expectations we place in it have themselves the power to potentially change money. This is not just because they feed back into different forms of political action (though that too) but because money in the sense of credit is itself made up of expectations and beliefs. Money is above all an institution of our collective imagination and our collective trust in the fictive institutions it creates.

Faced with the provocation of the fictitious nature of money, it is tempting to be suspicious of its Faustian character. Faced with the overpowering yet fragile politics of money outlined here, it is tempting to seek to avoid, repress, or delimit its political character. Calls for rooting money again in some precious commodity or an unalterable algorithm removed from human control are understandable responses to these anxieties. But this impulse should make us pause. Our political world is full of fictions. The modern state is after all "a fictitious body."[43] Despite being rooted in our collective imagination, that fiction is no less real. It gives rise to embodied institutions and material forces that shape our lives. Contrary to Jeremy Bentham's prediction, the season of fiction is not over.[44] Rather than turning our back on either the state or modern money simply because both ultimately originate in complex collective fictions, our task must be to improve those fictions and make them more inhabitable. Any hope for democratizing the financialized state will require better collective fictions than those that currently rule us despite having been authored by us.

Nor should we be tempted into abandoning politics simply because its demands seem to be too onerous and its promises too tentative. Money is too important to be left solely to economists and central bankers, let alone bankers. Appreciating that money is a collective fiction, then, does not have to incapacitate us or render us cynical. Instead, it can point us to the possibilities of shaping money according to our political values, not least by better aligning it with our democratic expectations. It is precisely money's unique reliance on the forces of the imagination that also renders it a malleable political institution. For better or worse, thanks to its self-confirming nature the politics of money is singularly unpredictable. Instead of being dazzled or frightened by the fictional character of money, we can and should embrace its underdetermined political possibilities and hold the institutions that govern it to standards of justification and justice.

In order to strengthen our ability to subject money power to democratic scrutiny, we need to make that power first visible and then articulate how it currently falls short of its own democratic possibilities. In order to turn a defensive moralistic critique of commodification into a positive program of democratic contestation of money power, we need to attend to the precise moments in which money becomes a bond of domination and ceases to be the currency of politics. As a first step this means cultivating a richer democratic language better capable of capturing the political theory of money.

A NOTE ON THE COVER AND FRONTISPIECE

OTIS KAYE, *HEART OF THE MATTER* (1963)

I HAVE LEARNED a great deal from many different disciplines and literatures in the course of exploring the political theory of money. I have tried to
capture these debts as best as possible in the notes and acknowledgments.
But there is one perspective that became important for me and that is
nonetheless insufficiently reflected there. Grappling with the paradoxical
possibilities and limitations of money as a social and political institution,
I was repeatedly struck by the ability of visual art to express these peculiar
qualities of money with great eloquence and wit. Otis Kaye's *Heart of the
Matter* (1963)—the painting on this book's cover—is a prime illustration.

Employing techniques of layering and optical illusions, Kaye's painting
traces money's broken promises and disruptive deceptiveness. Reflecting
on the acquisition of Rembrandt's *Aristotle with a Bust of Homer* (1653)
by the New York Metropolitan Museum of Art in 1961 for what was at the
time the highest amount ever paid for a painting ($2.3 million, or around
$21 million in today's money), Kaye places money in multiple temporali-
ties that stretch from Aristotle to the Dutch Golden Age to the uneven
affluence of postwar America. The painting's illusory play with texture
and depth immediately drew me in when I first saw it by chance. The
juxtaposition of Dutch golden chains in thick oil colors next to neat stacks
of seemingly printed dollar bills was jarring. Disentangling the painting's
strata of meaning and decoding its array of symbols requires time. What
emerges is a witty commentary on the sublime nature of modern money
and its peculiarly layered history.

Kaye (1885–1974) only painted for himself and friends, and he gave
Heart of the Matter originally to friends as a wedding gift. Part of this
refusal of the commercial realm of art seems to have been a conscious
critique, but it also reflected the legally precarious status of his paintings of banknotes. In 1909, Congress had passed a law that prohibited

any facsimiles of currency. This effectively rendered *trompe-l'œil* paintings of paper money—once a wildly popular genre in nineteenth-century American art—illegal for much of Kaye's lifetime. Undeterred, or perhaps attracted by the illicit genre, Kaye dedicated himself to producing some of the finest depictions of currency, usually embedded in cryptic commentaries about the social meaning of money and art. As far as I know, Kaye never exhibited or sold any of his paintings during his lifetime. It was only after his death in 1974, just as money was fully decoupled from metal, that Kaye's paintings themselves slowly started to sell at auctions at previously unimaginable prices.

The Art Institute of Chicago received *Heart of the Matter* as an anonymous gift in 2015. I am grateful to the Art Institute for permission to reproduce the painting on the cover. For more on Kaye's paintings, see *Otis Kaye: Money, Mystery, and Mastery*, ed. James M. Bradburne and Geraldine Banks, with an essay by Mark D. Mitchell (New Britain, CT: New Britain Museum of American Art, 2014).

ACKNOWLEDGMENTS

IN WRITING THIS BOOK I have accumulated many debts. I will do my best to name those to whom they're owed. While I can never repay them adequately for their help, support, and friendship, it gives me great pleasure to acknowledge my debts to them. This may seem a convenient loophole in the currency of acknowledgments. But I take solace in the thought that instead of expunging these debts, I can continue to circulate them as credit myself.

I am grateful to my many teachers along the way. I was exceedingly lucky in the inspiring and wise advisers and friends I found during graduate school at Yale where this book began life as a dissertation. They gave me the space to find my voice and pushed my thinking further than I could have possibly gone alone. Seyla Benhabib's challenging questions and perceptive suggestions guided the project from the outset. She modeled the pleasures of thinking and created an extraordinary community of comradery and collegiality. Adam Tooze was my interlocutor from my first day on campus in New Haven and he encouraged me to reimagine the tasks of political theory and to bring together my seemingly disparate interests in political theory, history, and economics. I am deeply grateful to count him as a mentor, colleague, and friend. Without the wisdom (and humor) of Karuna Mantena I would not have been able to make it through graduate school. Bryan Garsten always posed the most probing questions that helped me to see the large in the small and the small in the large. Ian Shapiro supported me throughout my time at Yale and encouraged me in my unconventional explorations of political economy. As an external reader, Hélène Landemore brought a fresh perspective to the project and I have been thinking about her questions ever since.

Many friends and colleagues from graduate school sustained me throughout the early phase of writing of this book. I would not have been able to complete the project without them. Thanks to Grey Anderson, Martin Baesler, Aner Barzilay, Umur Basdas, Alyssa Battistoni, Jonny Bunning, Carmen Dege, Blake Emerson, Lucas Entel, Ted Fertik, David Froomkin, Adom Getachew, Devin Goure, Philipp Hacker, Anna Jurkevics, Jeremy Kessler, Mordechai Levy-Eichel, Paul Linden-Retek, Nicolas Medina Mora, Darren Nah, Shmulik Nili, Travis Pantin, Hari Ramesh, Tim Shenk, Wolfgang Silbermann, Anurag Sinha, Brandon Terry, Eduardo Vivanco, Patrick Waldron, Mike Weaver, and Robin Winkler.

This book would not be the same—perhaps not exist—were it not for the Society of Fellows at Princeton. I would like to express my deepest thanks to Susan Stewart, Mary Harper, Michael Gordin, Beate Witzler, and Rhea Dexter, as well as to the faculty fellows who made our Friday seminars unforgettable, my colleagues from the Humanities Sequence, and in particular Benjamin Morrison with whom I was fortunate enough to take two classes to Greece (trips that turned into eye-opening archaeological adventures thanks to Aristotle Koskinas). The Society of Fellows is an extraordinary garden of intellectual life, but it also became a place of close friendship. I would like to thank Monica Huerta, Nijah Cunningham, Alessandro Giammei, and Maria Paula Saffon Sanin, as well as Chloë Kitzinger, Natalie Prizel, Bernadette Perez, Justin Perez, Johan Samsing, and Ava Shirazi. At Princeton's Department of Politics, Charles Beitz, Shuk Ying Chan, Greg Conti, Desmond Jaghmohan, Dongxian Jiang, Steven Kelts, Melissa Lane, Steven Macedo, Jan-Werner Müller, Alan Patten, Philip Pettit, Lucia Rafanelli, Annie Stilz, Johan Trovik, and Ian Walling became valued conversation partners about the project but also about political theory more broadly. As friends and writing partners, Desmond Jaghmohan and Steven Kelts read my original book proposal and several drafts of much else. The Society also sponsored and organized an exhilarating manuscript workshop that was essential for my revisions. In addition to the invaluable Princeton participants I would like to thank Alex Gourevitch and Carolyn Biltoft for reading the manuscript so closely and for providing me with extensive comments that helped me to see the book with new eyes.

More people than I can possibly remember read various parts of the book or material related to it. I have learned an enormous amount from their comments and suggestions. I would like to thank Martin Baesler, Lawrie Balfour, Eric Beerbohm, Teresa Bejan, Benjamin Braun, Peter Breiner, Richard Bourke, Angus Burgin, Daniela Cammack, Samuel Chambers, Christine Desan, Peter Dietsch, Alexander Douglas, Leah Downey, John Dunn, Andrew Edwards, Izhak Englard, Jill Frank, Kinch Hoekstra, Graham Hubbs, Nicolas Jabko, Duncan Kelly, Martijn Konings, Andrew March, John Marshall, James Ashley Morrison, Isaac Nakhimovsky, Eric Nelson, Martin O'Neill, William Rassieur, Jonny Thakkar, Richard Tuck, Mara van der Lugt, Jens van 't Klooster, Sitta von Reden, Patrick Weil, and Sam Zeitlin. The ideas in this book have benefited from comments and questions at a number of different workshops and conferences: the Yale Political Theory workshop, the Political Theory Workshop at Freiburg University, the "Money as a Democratic Medium" conference at Harvard Law School organized by Christine Desan (who has been a source of inspiration and support throughout), the Seminar in Political and Moral Thought at

Johns Hopkins University, the Political Theory workshop at SUNY Albany, the PPE Society Conference in New Orleans, and a Leverhulme Workshop on Justice and Monetary Policy organized my Martin O'Neill at the University of York. While I was finishing the book, I benefited enormously from our discussions in the "Democratic Politics of Central Banking" workshop series supported by Brown University's Rhodes Center. I am grateful to my two co-conveners, Mark Blyth and Leah Downey, and our extraordinary fellow participants for forming Zoom salon that has actually created an ongoing conversation across disciplines and time zones.

At a crucial moment of revision, just before the pandemic struck in February 2020, I was fortunate to be invited to present parts of the manuscript at the Kadish Workshop in Law, Philosophy, and Political Theory at UC Berkeley Law School. Many thanks to Joshua Cohen and Jonathan Gould for the stimulating day discussion and comments. During my visit to Berkeley, David Grewal, who had accompanied and shaped the project from the very beginning at Yale, generously read the entire manuscript once more and provided me with extensive comments that were unmatched in their incisiveness. I am deeply grateful to him and Daniela Cammack for their friendship. Our many conversations and walks, first in East Rock Park and then in the Berkeley hills, first set me on this path and then continued to nourish me during the subsequent year of lockdown.

Finishing this project at Georgetown has been richly rewarding. My political theory colleagues—Shannon Stimson, Richard Boyd, Joshua Cherniss, Mark Fisher, Terrence Johnson, and Joshua Mitchell—remind me every day how lucky I am to count them as readers, interlocutors, and colleagues. I would also like to thank Richard Boyd, Tom Kerch, and the Tocqueville Forum for inviting me to co-organize a conference on "Burke, Keynes, and the Political Economy of Time" that helped me to close this project and see where I am headed next. My intellectual debt to Georgetown extends far beyond the confines of our subfield and I have benefited from conversations with and advice from my colleagues Tony Arend, Lise Howard, Diana Kapiszewski, Charles King, Eric Langenbacher, Jamie Martin, Kate McNamara, Abe Newman, Dan Nexon, Terry Pinkard, Adam Rothman, Joseph Sassoon, George Shambaugh, and Olúfẹ́mi Táíwò. I would also like to thank Carole Sargent for her extraordinary writing group and the solidarity she crafts there. Finally, I am grateful to the students at Princeton and Georgetown whose dedication and enthusiasm have energized me and reminded me for whom I am writing. I learned at least as much from them as they learned from me.

My editor Rob Tempio enthusiastically supported the project from the outset and has been a constant source of wisdom and advice. No author can dream of a better editor. At the press, Mark Bellis, Chloe Coy, Matt Rohal, and the rest of the team seamlessly shepherded the book through production and publication. James Ashton and David Hornik provided excellent copyediting. I am grateful to David Luljak for the superb index. At Georgetown, Soumil Dhayagude, Felicia Miller, and Sam Walton provided outstanding research assistance and editorial help. Thank you above all to the two readers for Princeton University Press for their generously thoughtful comments, incisive questions, and constructive suggestions that helped me to clarify the arguments and sharpen my intervention. A version of chapter 1 appeared as "Between Justice and Accumulation: Aristotle on Currency and Reciprocity," *Political Theory* 47, no. 3 (2019): 363–90; material from chapter 2 appeared as "John Locke and the Politics of Monetary Depoliticization," *Modern Intellectual History* 17, no. 1 (March 2020): 1–28. I am grateful to the journals for allowing me to publish revised and expanded versions of this work. For financial support during graduate school I am grateful to Yale University's Department of Political Science and the Macmillan Center's European Studies Council, which provided grants for research for this book. A visiting fellowship at the Institute for Human Sciences (IWM) in Vienna provided me with a wonderful writing environment at a critical stage. I thank the librarians and staff at the John Maynard Keynes Papers at King's College, Cambridge, the Lovelace Collection at Oxford's Bodleian Library, the Bank of England Archive, Yale Manuscripts & Archives, and the Library of Congress. I am furthermore indebted to Iman Javadi for his insights based on cataloging Keynes's rare-books library at King's, as well as to Sabrina Sondhi of Columbia Law School's Arthur W. Diamond Law Library who made available to me some additional Keynes materials. In the final stage of completing the book, I benefited from the generosity and wisdom of several friends and colleagues who agreed to reread various parts, often more than once. I am deeply grateful for all their time and counsel. Many thanks to Seyla Benhabib, Mark Fisher, Katrina Forrester, Jamie Martin, Kate McNamara, Matthew Specter, Shannon Stimson, and Adam Tooze.

This book is dedicated to my wife Priya Rajana who enriches my life in a million ways and who made completing the book a joy. She helped me see the bigger picture and always reminded of what matters, both in the manuscript and in particular beyond it. Whenever I disappeared into the book, she also distracted our troublesome puppy Bella (who more than once tried to chew her way through the Marx chapter). I am deeply grateful to Priya for all her love, support, and encouragement. But above all I dedicate this book to her as a small token of my love for her.

Preface

1. John Maynard Keynes, *The General Theory of Employment, Interest and Money*, in *The Collected Writings of John Maynard Keynes*, vol. 7, ed. Austin Robinson and Donald Moggridge (Cambridge: Cambridge University Press, 2013), 294.

2. John Maynard Keynes, *A Tract on Monetary Reform* (London: Macmillan, 1923).

3. John Maynard Keynes to Lydia Lopokova, January 18, 1924, as quoted in Robert Skidelsky, *John Maynard Keynes: The Economist as Savior, 1920–1937* (London: Macmillan & Co, 1992), 175.

4. Written perhaps by Aristotle himself; more likely by one of his students. Ps.-Aristotle, *The Athenian Constitution*, trans. H. Rackham, Loeb Classical Library (Cambridge, MA: Harvard University Press, 1935). See also P. J. Rhodes, *A Commentary on the Athenaion Politeia*, rev. ed. (Oxford: Clarendon Press, 1993).

5. John Maynard Keynes, "Note on the Monetary Reform of Solon," in *The Collected Writings of John Maynard Keynes*, vol. 28 *(Social, Political and Literary Writings)*, ed. Elizabeth Johnson and Donald Moggridge (Cambridge: Cambridge University Press, 1982), 226. In August 1920 Keynes had first compiled notes on Solon. John Maynard Keynes Papers, Archives Centre, King's College, Cambridge, TM/3/1.

6. Karl Marx, *Das Kapital: Kritik der politischen Ökonomie*, Erster Band [1867], *Marx-Engels Gesamtausgabe* (MEGA²), II.6, 69–113; Karl Marx, *Capital: A Critique of Political Economy*, vol. 1, trans. Ben Fowkes (London: Penguin, 1976), 125–77.

7. Reinhart Koselleck, *Sediments of Time: On Possible Histories*, trans. Sean Franzel and Stefan-Ludwig Hoffmann (Stanford, CA: Stanford University Press, 2018), 3–9.

8. J.G.A. Pocock, *Virtue, Commerce and History: Essays on Political Thought and History, Chiefly in the Eighteenth Century* (Cambridge: Cambridge University Press, 1985), 108.

9. Reinhart Koselleck, "Some Questions Regarding the Conceptual History of 'Crisis' [1986]," trans. Todd Presner, in *The Practice of Conceptual History: Timing History, Spacing Concepts* (Stanford, CA: Stanford University Press, 2004), 236–47; see also Reinhart Koselleck, *Futures Past: On the Semantics of Historical Time*, trans. and ed. Keith Tribe (Cambridge, MA: MIT Press, 1985).

10. Joseph Vogl, *The Ascendancy of Finance*, trans. Simon Garnett (Cambridge, UK: Polity, 2017), vi. As already perceptively observed (and exploited) by none other than Milton Friedman. See Milton Friedman, "Preface, 1982," in *Capitalism and Freedom* (Chicago: University of Chicago Press, 1982), xiv.

11. Rainer Forst, *The Right to Justification: Elements of a Constructivist Theory of Justice*, trans. Jeffrey Flynn (New York: Columbia University Press, 2011).

12. These have recently been partially revived in calls for workplace democracy and critiques of economic domination as "private government." See Elizabeth

Anderson, *Private Government: How Employers Rule Our Lives (and Why We Don't Talk about It)* (Princeton, NJ: Princeton University Press, 2017); as well as Hélène Landemore and Isabelle Ferreras, "In Defense of Workplace Democracy: Towards a Justification of the Firm-State Analogy," *Political Theory* 44, no. 1 (2016): 53–81.

Introduction

1. Walter Bagehot, *Lombard Street: A Description of the Money Market* (London: Henry S. King, 1873), 20.

2. Hanna Fenichel Pitkin, *The Attack of the Blob: Hannah Arendt's Concept of the Social* (Chicago: University of Chicago Press, 1998), 3.

3. As Tooze puts it, "No doubt all commodities have politics. But money and credit and the structure of finance piled on them are constituted by political power, social convention and law in a way that sneakers, smartphones and barrels of oil are not." Adam Tooze, *Crashed: How a Decade of Financial Crises Changed the World* (New York: Viking, 2018), 10.

4. Adam Tooze, "Chartbook Newsletter #15: Talking (and Reading) about Bitcoin," March 2021, https://adamtooze.substack.com/p/chartbook-newsletter-15. For the notion of a monetary interregnum, see Eric Helleiner, "A Bretton Woods Moment? The 2007–2008 Crisis and the Future of Global Finance," *International Affairs* 86, no. 3 (May 2010): 619–36.

5. By "linguistic impasse" I do not simply mean that we lack the right technical terms; instead, I have a more democratic obstacle in mind. We continue to labor under the burden of a prior theoretical and political impoverishment of our political language concerning monetary power, rule, and justice.

6. As cited in Ann Pettifor, *The Production of Money: How to Break the Power of Banks* (London and New York: Verso, 2017), 16.

7. To be sure, most states still issue their own currency but money has at the same time become profoundly deterritorialized, not least through the unmatched significance of the dollar far beyond the US itself. Claus Zimmermann, "The Concept of Monetary Sovereignty Revisited," *European Journal of International Law* 24, no. 3 (2013): 799–800; Benjamin J. Cohen, "The New Geography of Money," in *Global Monetary Governance* (London: Routledge, 2008), 207–24.

8. Since the abolition of capital controls in the 1980s, capital is moreover able to crisscross the globe beyond the reach of states. Rawi Abdelal, *Capital Rules: The Construction of Global Finance* (Cambridge, MA: Harvard University Press, 2007). Even more, banks are able to create credit money outside of that currency's jurisdiction, for example in the form of so-called "Eurodollars." One can draw here a further distinction between bank money and shadow money. Hyman P. Minsky, "The Evolution of Financial Institutions and the Performance of the Economy," *Journal of Economic Issues* 20, no. 2 (1986): 345–53, at 352; Daniela Gabor and Jakob Vestergaard, "Towards a Theory of Shadow Money," Institute for New Economic Thinking, April 2016, https://www.ineteconomics.org/perspectives/blog/towards-a-theory-of-shadow-money.

9. More precisely, the state remains the only entity able to provide risk-free assets and enforce the convertibility of debt claims. Katharina Pistor, "Moneys' Legal Hierarchies," in Lisa Herzog, ed., *Just Financial Markets?* (Oxford: Oxford University

Press, 2017), 185–204. To use Hyman Minsky's terminology, the state is the only entity able to manipulate its own "survival constraint." Hyman P. Minsky, *Stabilizing an Unstable Economy* [1986] (New York: McGraw-Hill Education, 2008), 336.

10. Adam Tooze, *Shutdown: How Covid Shook the World's Economy* (New York: Viking, 2021).

11. Antonio Gramsci, *Prison Notebooks*, ed. and trans. Joseph A Buttigieg, 3 vols. (New York: Columbia University Press, 1992–2007), 2:33.

12. For an analysis of our international monetary interregnum as a Hirschmanian moment of "productive incoherence," see Ilene Grabel, *When Things Don't Fall Apart: Global Financial Governance and Developmental Finance in an Age of Productive Incoherence* (Cambridge, MA: MIT Press, 2017).

13. See, for example, the widely used Gregory Mankiw, *Macroeconomics*, 7th ed. (New York: Worth, 2009), 80–83.

14. As Paul Samuelson put it in his postwar economics textbook: "Even in the most advanced industrial economies, if we strip exchange down to its barest essentials and peel off the obscuring layer of money, we find that trade between individuals or nations largely boils down to barter." Paul Samuelson, *Principles of Economics*, 9th ed. (New York: McGraw-Hill, 1973), 55. For a close analysis of the "neutrality" of money in neoclassical economics, see Christine Desan, "The Key to Value: The Debate over Commensurability in Neoclassical and Credit Approaches to Money," *Law and Contemporary Problems* 83, no. 2 (2020): 1–22.

15. Over the past decade a lively set of revisionist literatures has upended the study of money. For an excellent general introduction to this new literature, see Felix Martin, *Money: The Unauthorized Biography* (London: Bodley Head, 2014). For an overview of recent work by economic sociologists and anthropologists, see Nina Bandelj, Frederick F. Wherry, and Viviana A. Zelizer, eds., *Money Talks: Explaining How Money Really Works* (Princeton, NJ: Princeton University Press, 2017); as well as Keith Hart and Horacio Ortiz, "The Anthropology of Money and Finance," *Annual Review of Anthropology* 43, no. 1 (2014): 465–82.

16. David Graeber, *Debt: The First 5,000 Years* (New York: Melville House, 2011), 21–41.

17. Toby Green, *A Fistful of Shells: West Africa from the Rise of the Slave Trade to the Age of Revolution* (Chicago: University of Chicago Press, 2019).

18. John Maynard Keynes, *The Economic Journal* (September 1914), in *The Collected Writings of John Maynard Keynes*, vol. 11 (*Economic Articles and Correspondence: Academic*), ed. Donald Moggridge (Cambridge: Cambridge University Press, 1983), 403.

19. For the best analysis of money as transferable debt, see Geoffrey Ingham, *The Nature of Money* (Cambridge, UK: Polity, 2004), 107–51; and for a concise summary, Geoffrey Ingham, "The Nature of Money," *Economic Sociology* 5, no. 2 (2004): 18–28, at 25. In her work on American colonial legal history, Christine Desan has similarly shown the ways in which money precedes markets. Christine Desan, "The Market as a Matter of Money: Denaturalizing Economic Currency in American Constitutional History," *Law & Social Inquiry* 30, no. 1 (Winter 2005): 1–60.

20. This is the language used in Stephanie Kelton, *The Deficit Myth: Modern Monetary Theory and the Birth of the People's Economy* (New York: Public Affairs, 2020), 26. There are numerous examples of this "just so" narrative, especially in

MMT-inspired economics textbooks. See, for example, L. Randall Wray, *Modern Money Theory: A Primer on Macroeconomics for Sovereign Monetary Systems*, 2nd ed. (Basingstoke, UK: Palgrave Macmillan, 2015), 49; L. Randall Wray, *Understanding Modern Money: The Key to Full Employment and Price Stability* (Cheltenham, UK: Edward Elgar, 2006), 40. Sometimes this tax-money story is referred to as "Danegeld" in reference to the extractive claims imposed by Anglo-Saxon leaders to buy off Danish attacks late in the tenth century. See M. K. Lawson, "Danegeld and Heregeld Once More," *English Historical Review* 105, no. 417 (October 1990): 951–61.

21. Jamie Merchant, "The Money Theory of the State: Reflections on Modern Monetary Theory," *The Brooklyn Rail* (2021), https://brooklynrail.org/2021/02/field-notes/The-Money-Theory-of-the-State-Reflections-on-Modern-Monetary-Theory.

22. The monetary standard constitutes in this sense a powerful illustration of what David Grewal has described as "the use of sovereignty to command and reengineer the relations of sociability on behalf of a democratic polity." David Singh Grewal, *Network Power: The Social Dynamics of Globalization* (New Haven, CT: Yale University Press, 2008), 103.

23. Michel Aglietta and André Orléan, *La monnaie entre violence et confiance* (Paris: Odile Jacob, 2002); see also Michel Aglietta and André Orléan, *La violence de la monnaie* (Paris: Presses universitaires de France, 1982).

24. Ingham, *Nature of Money*, 12, 33, 128; Pistor, "Moneys' Legal Hierarchies."

25. Max Weber, *Economy and Society*, trans. Keith Tribe (Cambridge, MA: Harvard University Press, 2019), ch. 2, par. 32, 284–86; Max Weber, *Wirtschaft und Gesellschaft: Grundriss der Sozialökonomik. III. Abteilung* (Tübingen: J.C.B. Mohr, 1922), ch. 2, par. 32, 97–8.

26. For an argument that locates central banks in a republican constitutional tradition of the division of powers and legitimate delegation to administrative agencies, see Paul Tucker, *Unelected Power: The Quest for Legitimacy in Central Banking and the Regulatory State* (Princeton, NJ: Princeton University Press, 2018).

27. Christine Desan, *Making Money: Coin, Currency, and the Coming of Capitalism* (Oxford: Oxford University Press, 2015); but also see Katharina Pistor, *The Code of Capital: How the Law Creates Wealth and Inequality* (Princeton, NJ: Princeton University Press, 2019), 77–107; and for two overviews, Jamee K. Moudud, "Analyzing the Constitutional Theory of Money: Governance, Power, and Instability," *Leiden Journal of International Law* 31, no. 2 (June 2018), 289–313; and Andrew David Edwards, "The American Revolution and Christine Desan's New History of Money," *Law & Social Inquiry* 42, no. 1 (Winter 2017): 252–78.

28. While I will hence at times speak of money when making a general point, I use "political currency" in its more specific sense whenever the distinction between political currency and money matters. While political currency is thus money, not all monies qualify as political currency. This is the case conceptually as well as historically.

29. Kathleen R. McNamara, "Consensus and Constraint: Ideas and Capital Mobility in European Monetary Integration," *Journal of Common Market Studies* 37, no. 3 (September 1999): 455–76; Jonathan Kirshner, "The Study of Money," *World Politics* 52, no. 3 (April 2000): 407–36; Jeffry A. Frieden, *Currency Politics: The Political Economy of Exchange Rate Policy* (Princeton, NJ: Princeton University Press, 2015); Juliet Johnson, *Priests of Prosperity: How Central Bankers Transformed the*

Postcommunist World (Ithaca, NY: Cornell University Press, 2016); Jacqueline Best, "Rethinking Central Bank Accountability in Uncertain Times," *Ethics and International Affairs* 30, no. 2 (Summer 2016): 215–32; Eric Helleiner, "The Macro-Social Meaning of Money: From Territorial Currencies to Global Money," in Nina Bandelj, Frederick F. Wherry, and Viviana A. Zelizer, eds., *Money Talks: Explaining How Money Really Works* (Princeton, NJ: Princeton University Press, 2017), 145–58.

30. There is now a small but growing literature concerning the normative, and in particular redistributive, questions surrounding "unconventional" monetary policy such as quantitative easing. See, for example, Peter Dietsch, "Normative Dimensions of Central Banking: How the Guardians of Financial Markets Affect Justice," in Lisa Herzog, ed., *Just Financial Markets* (Oxford: Oxford University Press, 2017); Peter Dietsch, Francois Claveau, and Clement Fontan, *Do Central Banks Serve the People?* (Cambridge, UK: Polity, 2018); Jens van 't Klooster, "Central Banking in Rawls's Property-Owning Democracy," *Political Theory* 47, no. 5 (2019): 674–98. For an excellent recent article that touches on credit and the architecture of the monetary system itself, see Peter Dietsch, "Money Creation, Debt, and Justice," *Politics, Philosophy & Economics* 20, no. 2 (2021): 151–79.

31. Such relations do not have to entail democratic equality, though for democracies the maintenance of such civic relations is all the more important. Even hierarchical political communities stand in need of rendering their citizens sufficiently commensurable, to use Aristotle's terminology. Citizenship defines at the same time the boundaries of the political. A hierarchical community in which members do not see each other as fellow citizens ceases to be a "political" community in a meaningful sense.

32. As Jonathan Kirshner puts it, "Even if all the passengers on an otherwise sound plane don't think it will take off, it will. But if just enough of the holders of a given currency don't think an otherwise sound monetary reform makes sense, it won't fly. Ideas about money management, then, have a distinct and profound influence in the world of money, regardless of whether or not those ideas are right or wrong." Jonathan Kirshner, "Money Is Politics," *Review of International Political Economy* 10, no. 4 (2003): 645–660, at 645. On the relation between economic interests and ideas associated with the politics of money, see Kathleen R. McNamara, *The Currency of Ideas: Monetary Politics in the European Union* (Ithaca, NY: Cornell University Press, 1998); and Mark Blyth, "The Political Power of Financial Ideas," in Jonathan Kirshner, ed., *Monetary Orders: Ambiguous Economics, Ubiquitous Politics* (Ithaca, NY: Cornell University Press, 2003), 239–59.

33. I am here reminded of Hirschman's table of seemingly competing but actually complementary accounts of market society. Albert O. Hirschman, "Rival Interpretations of Market Society: Civilizing, Destructive, or Feeble," *Journal of Economic Literature* 20 (December 1982): 1463–84, at 1468. As Hirschman put it, "It is conceivable that, even at one and the same point in space and time, a simple thesis holds only a portion of the full truth and needs to be complemented by one or several of the others, however incompatible they may look at first sight" (1482)

34. Schumpeter deployed this bifurcation to structure the discussion of money in his (never completed) *History of Economic Analysis*, in many ways primarily a history of monetary theories. Joseph A. Schumpeter, *History of Economic Analysis*

[1955] (London: Routledge, 2006). Ingham follows Schumpeter in this regard, even where he does so to defend a credit theory of money by defining money, with Keynes, as providing an abstract unit of account for debt claims. Ingham, *Nature of Money*, 6. Skidelsky similarly structures his recent account through the opposition between credit and commodity theories of money. Robert Skidelsky, *Money and Government: The Past and Future of Economics* (New Haven, CT: Yale University Press, 2018).

35. Or a representation thereof (say, a promissory note that is convertible into gold). Ingham, "Nature of Money," 21.

36. Alfred Mitchell-Innes, "What Is Money?," *Banking Law Journal* (May 1913): 377–408; Alfred Mitchell-Innes, "The Credit Theory of Money," *Banking Law Journal* (January 1914): 151–68.

37. Samuel A. Chambers, *Money Has No Value* (Berlin: De Gruyter, forthcoming).

38. Schumpeter, *History of Economic Analysis*, 58–67. Ingham too, unfortunately, follows Schumpeter in referring to an Aristotelian commodity conception of money. Ingham, *Nature of Money*, 10.

39. Remarkably, a roughly similar chronology holds for the almost parallel invention of coinage in India and China. David Schaps, "The Invention of Coinage in Lydia, in India, and in China," *Bulletin du Cercle d'Etudes Numismatiques* 44, no. 1–2 (2007): 281–322.

40. Aristotle, *Politics* 1257a33–42.

41. Aristotle, *Politics* 1257b10–11.

42. For the broader significance of the introduction of coinage, see Richard Seaford, *Money and the Early Greek Mind: Homer, Philosophy, Tragedy* (Cambridge: Cambridge University Press, 2004); Sitta von Reden, *Exchange in Ancient Greece* (London: Duckworth, 1995); Leslie Kurke, *Coins, Bodies, Games, and Gold: The Politics of Meaning in Archaic Greece* (Princeton, NJ: Princeton University Press, 1999); David Schaps, *The Invention of Coinage and the Monetization of Ancient Greece* (Ann Arbor: University of Michigan Press, 2004).

43. David Fox and Wolfgang Ernst, eds., *Money in the Western Legal Tradition: Middle Ages to Bretton Woods* (Oxford: Oxford University Press, 2016); Odd Inge Langholm, *Wealth and Money in the Aristotelian Tradition: A Study in Scholastic Economic Sources* (Bergen: Universitetsforlaget, 1983); and Joel Kaye, *Economy and Nature in the Fourteenth Century* (Cambridge: Cambridge University Press, 1998). Aristotelian monetary nominalism also left a strong imprint in Islamic political thought. See, for example, Nasir al-Din Tusi, *The Nasirean Ethics*, trans. G. M. Wickens (London: George Allen & Unwin, 1964), 97–98, 157, 191.

44. Thomas Aquinas, *Commentary on the* Nicomachean Ethics, vol. 1, bk. 5, lecture 9, par. 982.

45. Langholm, *Wealth and Money*, 10–20; André Lapidus, "Metal, Money, and the Prince: John Buridan and Nicholas Oresme after Thomas Aquinas," *History of Political Economy* 29, no. 1 (1997): 21–53, at 27; Wittreck helpfully points out that one influential Thomist claim—namely the prince's power to fix a *valor impositus*—derives in fact from a pseudograph written by Ptolemy of Lucca (*De Regno*, book 2, ch. 13). Fabian Wittreck, "Money in Medieval Philosophy," in David Fox and Wolfgang Ernst, eds., *Money in the Western Legal Tradition: Middle Ages to Bretton Woods* (Oxford: Oxford University Press, 2016), 53–70, at 60–61.

46. Nicole Oresme, *The "De moneta" of Nicholas Oresme and English Mint Documents*, trans. Charles Johnson (London: Thomas Nelson and Sons, 1956), 13. Oresme explicitly lamented the great waves of debasements and currency depreciations that "have lately been seen to occur in the realm of France" (30). The classic account is Carlo M. Cipolla, "Currency Depreciation in Medieval Europe," *Economic History Review* 15, no. 3 (1963): 413–22.

47. For a recent reading of Oresme's argument as an early account of popular sovereignty, see Adam Woodhouse, "'Who Owns the Money?': Currency, Property, and Popular Sovereignty in Nicole Oresme's *De moneta*," *Speculum* 92, no. 1 (January 2017): 85–116, at 89.

48. Jean Bodin, *Les six livres de la Republique* (Paris: Iacques du Puys, 1577), bk. 1, ch. 10, 177; Jean Bodin, *On Sovereignty: Four Chapters from the Six Books of the Commonwealth* (Cambridge: Cambridge University Press, 1992), bk. 1, ch. 10, 78. Thomas Hobbes similarly recognized "the Power to coyn Mony" in *Leviathan* as a sovereign prerogative. Thomas Hobbes, *Leviathan* (Cambridge: Cambridge University Press, 1991), ch. 18, section 16, 127. On whether this prerogative could be delegated or transferred, see Jean Barbeyrac's note in his translation of Hugo Grotius, *The Rights of War and Peace* [1625], ed. Richard Tuck, 3 vols. (Indianapolis: Liberty Fund, 2005), bk. 2, ch. 4, section 13, 502n1.

49. See Jean Bodin, *Réponse au paradoxe de M. de Malestroict touchant l'enchérissement de toutes choses, et le moyen d'y remédier* (Paris, 1568), as well as Jean Bodin, *Discours de Jean Bodin, sur le Rehaussement et diminution des monnoyes, tant d'or que d'argent, & le moyen d'y remedier: & responce aux Paradoxes de Monsieur de Malestroict* (Paris, 1578); and Jean Bodin, *Les Paradoxes du seigneur de Malestroit* (Lyon, 1578). See also Bodin, *Les six livres de la Republique*, bk. 6, ch. 3, 696; Jean Bodin, *Six Bookes of a Commonweale*, ed. Kenneth Douglas McRae (Cambridge, MA: Harvard University Press, 1962), bk. 6, ch. 3, 687–700. Modernized spelling of the translation. I have in this context enormously benefited from Daniel Lee, *The Right of Sovereignty: Jean Bodin on the Sovereign State and the Law of Nations* (Oxford: Oxford University Press, 2021).

50. Indeed, in sixteenth-century France a sizable share of the money in circulation appears to have been of Spanish coinage. Jotham Parsons, *Making Money in Sixteenth-Century France: Currency, Culture, and the State* (Ithaca, NY: Cornell University Press, 2014). I owe this observation to Andrew Sartori.

51. For an overview, see Frederic Chapin Lane and Reinhold C. Mueller, *Money and Banking in Medieval and Renaissance Venice*, vol. 1 (Baltimore: Johns Hopkins University Press, 1985).

52. Peter Spufford, *Money and Its Use in Medieval Europe* (Cambridge: Cambridge University Press, 1988); Fernand Braudel and Frank Spooner, "Prices in Europe from 1450 to 1750," in *The Cambridge Economic History of Europe from the Decline of the Roman Empire*, ed. E. E. Rich and C. H. Wilson (Cambridge: Cambridge University Press, 1967), 374–486; Craig Muldrew, *The Economy of Obligation: The Culture of Credit and Social Relations in Early Modern England* (New York: St. Martin's, 1998).

53. On the history of promissory notes, see Francesca Trivellato, *The Promise and Peril of Credit: What a Forgotten Legend about Jews and Finance Tells Us about the Making of European Commercial Society* (Princeton, NJ: Princeton University Press,

2019). On the earlier uses of bills of exchange, see Peter Spufford, *Handbook of Medieval Exchange* (London: Royal Historical Society, 1986).

54. See in particular Desan's extensive discussion of *The Case of Mixed Money* (1695) as the high watermark of monetary nominalism. Desan, *Making Money*, 266–74. For the case, see Gilbert v. Brett ("The Case of Mixt Monies"), in *Cobbett's Complete Collection of State Trials*, vol. 2 (London: Hansard, 1809), 113–30; for a reading that stresses the influence of the sixteenth-century French jurist Carolus Molinaeu on the decision, see David Fox, "The Case of Mixt Monies," in Fox and Ernst, *Money in the Western Legal Tradition*, 224–43.

55. Ingham, *Nature of Money*, 134–51; Ingham, "Nature of Money," 26. In Keith Hart's terminology, this meant that money's two sides merged: state power (heads) and private calculation (tails) became two sides of the same coin. Keith Hart, "Heads or Tails? Two Sides of the Coin," *Man* 21, no. 4 (December 1986): 637–56.

56. For Desan, the distinctive quality of capitalism lies precisely in this privatization of modern money. Desan, *Making Money*, 434.

57. As I explain in the epilogue, I explicitly include cryptocurrencies in this claim.

58. Pistor, "Moneys' Legal Hierarchies," 185.

59. Desan, *Making Money*, 2, 5, 295–329.

60. The new system emerged, as Desan observed, "by happenstance, improvisation, and some shrewd calculation." Desan, "Key to Value," 19.

61. John Locke, *Second Treatise*, in *Two Treatises of Government* (Cambridge: Cambridge University Press, 1988), par. 41. Jeremy Waldron had described the passage once as "one of the worst arguments in the Second Treatise." Jeremy Waldron, *God, Locke, and Equality: Christian Foundations in Locke's Political Thought* (Cambridge: Cambridge University Press, 2002), 176.

62. Douglass C. North and Barry R. Weingast, "Constitutions and Commitment: The Evolution of Institutions Governing Public Choice in Seventeenth-Century England," *Journal of Economic History* 49, no. 4 (December 1989): 808–32; Margaret Levi, *Of Rule and Revenue* (Berkeley: University of California Press, 1988); David Stasavage, "Credible Commitment in Early Modern Europe: North and Weingast Revisited," *Journal of Law, Economics, and Organization* 18, no. 1 (2002): 155–86.

63. Johann Gottlieb Fichte, *Der Geschloßne Handelsstaat: Ein Philosophischer Entwurf als Anlage zur Rechtslehre, und Probe einer künftig zu liefernden Politik* (Tübingen: J. G. Cotta, 1800). Reprinted in *Gesamtausgabe der Bayerischen Akademie der Wissenschaften*, ed. Hans Gliwitzky and Reinhart Lauth, I.7 (Stuttgart-Bad Cannstatt: Frommann, 1988), 37–141. Translated as Johann Gottlieb Fichte, *The Closed Commercial State*, trans. Anthony Curtis Adler (Albany: SUNY Press, 2012). See chapter 3 below.

64. Isaac Nakhimovsky, *The Closed Commercial State: Perpetual Peace and Commercial Society from Rousseau to Fichte* (Princeton, NJ: Princeton University Press, 2011).

65. Pierre-Joseph Proudhon, *Système des contradictions économiques, ou, Philosophie de la misère*, 2 vols. (Paris: Chez Guillaumin et cie, 1846); Pierre-Joseph Proudhon, *Property Is Theft! A Pierre-Joseph Proudhon Anthology*, ed. Iain McKay (Oakland, CA: AK Press, 2011), 167–256.

66. Karl Marx and Friedrich Engels, *The Communist Manifesto*, with an introduction by Gareth Stedman Jones (London: Penguin, 2002), 243.

67. Karl Marx, *La misère de la philosophie* (Paris: A. Frank and Brussels: C. G. Vogler, 1847); Karl Marx, *The Poverty of Philosophy*, in *Marx and Engels Collected Works* (hereafter MECW), vol. 6 (London: Lawrence & Wishart, 1987), 257–417; as well as Karl Marx, *Zur Kritik der politischen Ökonomie* [1859], *Marx-Engels Gesamtausgabe* (hereafter MEGA²), II.2, 95–245; Karl Marx, *A Contribution to the Critique of Political Economy* [1859], MECW 29, 257–417. See chapter 4 below.

68. Marx to Friedrich Adolph Sorge, dated September 1, 1870, MECW 44, 57–58. As quoted in William Clare Roberts, *Marx's Inferno: The Political Theory of Capital* (Princeton, NJ: Princeton University Press, 2017), 74n75.

69. Karl Marx, *Das Kapital: Kritik der politischen Ökonomie*, Dritter Band [1894], MEGA² II.15; Karl Marx, *Capital: A Critique of Political Economy*, vol. 3, trans. David Fernbach (London: Penguin, 1981).

70. Marx, *Capital*, vol. 1, ch. 1 (MEGA² II.6, 85; Penguin 144).

71. Karl Polanyi, *The Great Transformation: The Political and Economic Origins of Our Time*, 2nd ed. (Boston: Beacon, 2001), 72–6.

72. Marx, *Capital*, vol. 1, ch. 3 (MEGA² II.5, 59; II.6, 121; Penguin 188).

73. Christine Desan, "The Constitutional Approach to Money: Monetary Design and the Production of the Modern World," in Nina Bandelj, Frederick F. Wherry, and Viviana A. Zelizer, eds., *Money Talks: Explaining How Money Really Works* (Princeton, NJ: Princeton University Press, 2017), 109–30.

74. After all, in Hobbes's language the social contract is strictly speaking not a contract at all but a covenant: not a one-off exchange but a mutual exchange of pledges that extends into the future and has to be continuously realized.

75. Rebecca L. Spang, *Stuff and Money in the Time of the French Revolution* (Cambridge, MA: Harvard University Press, 2015), 272.

76. During the 1970s the West German Bundesbank actively cultivated the specter of Weimar's hyperinflation, deliberately reviving popular memories of 1923. Peter A. Johnson, *The Government of Money: Monetarism in Germany and the United States* (Ithaca, NY: Cornell University Press, 1998), 199.

77. Danielle Allen notes in this context the centrality of reciprocal sacrifice and the fair sharing of economic burdens in democratic societies. Danielle Allen, *Talking to Strangers: Anxieties of Citizenship since Brown v. Board of Education* (Chicago: University of Chicago Press, 2004), 28–29.

78. I am on this point indebted to conversations with my colleague Kate McNamara. See in particular Kathleen R. McNamara, "Rational Fictions: Central Bank Independence and the Social Logic of Delegation," *West European Politics* 25, no. 1 (January 2002): 47–76. Two texts that have helped me in their own ways to think through the meaning of "depoliticization" have been James Ferguson, *The Anti-Politics Machine: "Development," Depoliticization, and Bureaucratic Power in Lesotho* (Minneapolis: University of Minnesota Press, 1994) and Martti Koskenniemi, *From Apology to Utopia: The Structure of International Legal Argument*, reissue with a new epilogue (Cambridge: Cambridge University Press, 2006). For the recent literature on depoliticization, see Paul Fawcett, Matthew Flinders, Colin Hay, and Matthew Woods, eds., *Anti-Politics, Depoliticization, and Governance* (Oxford: Oxford University Press, 2017).

79. On the metaphor of "encasement" to describe the shielding of the market (and money) against the threat of democracy, see Quinn Slobodian, *Globalists: The End of*

Empire and the Birth of Neoliberalism (Cambridge, MA: Harvard University Press, 2018), 5–16, esp. 13.

80. Rudi Dornbusch, *Keys to Prosperity: Free Markets, Sound Money, and a Bit of Luck* (Cambridge, MA: MIT Press, 2000), 15. A variation of the quote in another essay by Dornbusch is cited in Tooze, *Shutdown*, 15. See also Jacqueline Best, "Technocratic Exceptionalism: Monetary Policy and the Fear of Democracy," *International Political Sociology* 12, no. 4 (2018): 328–45.

81. On the notion of "antipolitics" as the evasion of democratic politics in the context of the environment, see Jedediah Purdy, *After Nature: A Politics for the Anthropocene* (Cambridge, MA: Harvard University Press, 2015), 21–45.

82. Democracies might, of course, decide to remove certain options from the table of electoral politics but that is itself a political decision that needs to be democratically justified.

83. To adapt an observation coined for quantification by Nikolas Rose in "Governing by Numbers: Figuring Out Democracy," *Accounting, Organizations and Society* 16, no. 7 (1991): 673–92.

84. Samuel Moyn, *Not Enough: Human Rights in an Unequal World* (Cambridge, MA: Harvard University Press, 2018); Katrina Forrester, *In the Shadow of Justice: Postwar Liberalism and the Remaking of Political Philosophy* (Princeton, NJ: Princeton University Press, 2019).

85. Alasdair Roberts, *The Logic of Discipline: Global Capitalism and the Architecture of Government* (Oxford: Oxford University Press, 2010); Greta Krippner, *Capitalizing on Crisis: The Political Origins of the Rise of Finance* (Cambridge, MA: Harvard University Press, 2011).

86. Michael J. Sandel, *What Money Can't Buy: The Moral Limits of Markets* (New York: Farrar, Straus & Giroux, 2012); Debra Satz, *Why Some Things Should Not Be for Sale: The Moral Limits of Markets* (Oxford: Oxford University Press, 2010).

87. Tellingly, the one concept never interrogated or investigated in Sandel's *What Money Can't Buy* is money itself.

88. Jens van 't Klooster and Clément Fontan, "The Myth of Market Neutrality: A Comparative Study of the European Central Bank's and the Swiss National Bank's Corporate Security Purchases," *New Political Economy* 25, no. 6 (2020): 865–79.

89. Bruce G. Carruthers and Sarah Babb, "The Color of Money and the Nature of Value: Greenbacks and Gold in Postbellum America," *American Journal of Sociology* 101, no. 6 (May 1996): 1556–91; Martijn Konings, *The Emotional Logic of Capitalism* (Stanford, CA: Stanford University Press, 2015), 7.

Chapter 1. The Political Institution of Currency

1. Jean-Jacques Rousseau, *Émile ou De l'éducation* [1762], in *Oeuvres complètes*, tome 4 (Paris: Bibliothèque de la Pléiade, 1969), 461; Jean-Jacques Rousseau, *Emile: Or, on Education*, trans. Allan Bloom (New York: Basic Books, 1979), 189.

2. Josiah Ober, *Democracy and Knowledge: Innovation and Learning in Classical Athens* (Princeton, NJ: Princeton University Press, 2008), 227–9.

3. Ober, *Democracy and Knowledge*, 229.

4. In the language of New Institutional Economics, coinage lowered transaction costs. Josiah Ober, *The Rise and Fall of Classical Greece* (Princeton, NJ: Princeton

University Press, 2015), 12; Alain Bresson, *The Making of the Ancient Greek Economy* (Princeton, NJ: Princeton University Press, 2016), 271.

5. Bresson gives an estimate of 650–625 BCE for the Lydian invention of coinage. Bresson, *Ancient Greek Economy*, 264. These first Lydian coins were made from electrum, a naturally occurring amalgam of gold and silver that made it difficult to tell the proportion of the two metals. See Robert W. Wallace, "The Origin of Electrum Coinage," *American Journal of Archaeology* 91, no. 3 (July 1987): 385–97

6. Herodotus, *The Histories*, trans. Andrea Purvis (New York: Anchor Books, 2007), 19–32 [bk. 1, pars. 30–56].

7. Of the 1,035 poleis catalogued by Hansen and Nielsen, a mint and coinage is attested for 444. Mogens Herman Hansen and Thomas Nielsen, *An Inventory of Archaic and Classical Poleis* (Oxford: Oxford University Press, 2005), 148. The number of discovered coinage hoards from the fifth and fourth centuries BCE is more than twice those from earlier centuries—and their content more than triples. Ober, *Rise and Fall*, 39, 83.

8. Bresson, *Ancient Greek Economy*, 269.

9. Andrew Meadows and Kirsty Shipton, eds., *Money and Its Uses in the Ancient Greek World* (Oxford: Oxford University Press, 2001).

10. Moses Finley, *The Ancient Economy* (Berkeley: University of California Press, 1999).

11. Sitta von Reden, *Exchange in Ancient Greece* (London: Duckworth, 1995); Sitta von Reden, "Money, Law, and Exchange: Coinage in the Greek Polis," *Journal of Hellenic Studies* 117 (1997): 154–76; Leslie Kurke, *Coins, Bodies, Games, and Gold: The Politics of Meaning in Archaic Greece* (Princeton, NJ: Princeton University Press, 1999); David Schaps, *The Invention of Coinage and the Monetization of Ancient Greece* (Ann Arbor: University of Michigan Press, 2004); Richard Seaford, *Reciprocity and Ritual: Homer and Tragedy in the Developing City-State* (Oxford: Oxford University Press, 1994); Richard Seaford, *Money and the Early Greek Mind* (Cambridge: Cambridge University Press, 2004); Bresson, *Ancient Greek Economy*.

12. For a concise overview of the Greek "birth of politics," see Melissa Lane, *The Birth of Politics: Eight Greek and Roman Political Ideas and Why They Matter* (Princeton, NJ: Princeton University Press, 2015).

13. Already Benjamin remarked on ancient coins as one of the very few items produced on a mass scale. Walter Benjamin, *The Work of Art in the Age of Its Technological Reproducibility* [1928] (Cambridge, MA: The Belknap Press of Harvard University Press, 2008), 27, 142.

14. Benedict Anderson, *Imagined Communities: Reflections on the Origin and Spread of Nationalism* (London and New York: Verso, 1983).

15. I am indebted here to Sitta von Reden's powerful reframing of ancient coinage as part of a broader set of "transactional orders." von Reden, *Exchange in Ancient Greece*, 175.

16. Seaford, *Reciprocity and Ritual*, 191–206; Seaford, *Money and the Early Greek Mind*, 175–89, 292–317.

17. The term "agora" derives itself after all from the Greek word for speaking in public (*agoreuō*).

18. Bresson, *Ancient Greek Economy*, 268.

19. *Nicomachean Ethics* 1132b33.

20. Aristotle, *Politics* 1261a30–32.

21. Danielle Allen, *Talking to Strangers: Anxieties of Citizenship since Brown v. Board of Education* (Chicago: University of Chicago Press, 2004); Jill Frank, *A Democracy of Distinction: Aristotle and the Work of Politics* (Chicago: University of Chicago Press, 2005); Gabriel Danzig, "The Political Character of Aristotelian Reciprocity," *Classical Philology* 95, no. 4 (2000): 399–424; Kazutaka Inamura, "The Role of Reciprocity in Aristotle's Theory of Political Economy," *History of Political Thought* 17, no. 4 (Winter 2011): 565–87.

22. Notable exceptions include Ann Ward, *Contemplating Friendship in Aristotle's Ethics* (Albany: SUNY Press, 2016), 67–82; Michael D. Chan, *Aristotle and Hamilton on Commerce and Statesmanship* (Columbia: University of Missouri Press, 2006), 36–43; and Frank, *Democracy of Distinction*, 65–69, 86–91. None of these, however, is primarily interested in *nomisma*.

23. Desmond McNeill, "Alternative Interpretations of Aristotle on Exchange and Reciprocity," *Public Affairs Quarterly* 4, no. 1 (1990): 55–68. For a more subtle engagement, see David Singh Grewal, "The Political Theology of Laissez-Faire: From Philia to Self-Love in Commercial Society," *Political Theology* 17, no. 5 (2016): 417–33, at 424.

24. As a reminder I have left "*nomisma*" at times untranslated. Where translated, I render it as "currency" to preserve its conventional character. Translations rely on Terrence Irwin for the *Nicomachean Ethics* (hereafter *NE*) and on C.D.C. Reeve's new translation for the *Politics* (hereafter *Pol*). I have noted where I have adapted their translations.

25. Hannah Arendt, *The Human Condition* (Chicago: University of Chicago Press, 1958), 28–37. For two divergent challenges, see Martha Nussbaum, "Aristotelian Social Democracy," in R. Bruce Douglass, Gerald M. Mara, and Henry S. Richardson, eds., *Liberalism and the Good* (London: Routledge, 1990), 203–52; and Judith Swanson and David Corbin, *Public and Private in Aristotle's Politics* (Ithaca, NY: Cornell University Press, 1992).

26. *Pol* 1261a13–19.

27. Marcel Hénaff, *The Price of Truth: Gift, Money, and Philosophy* (Stanford, CA: Stanford University Press, 2010), 80.

28. Fully reconciling the two passages would require a more extensive account of Aristotelian desire and of the metaphysics of *nomisma* as an institution that is conventional yet linked to natural use.

29. I here build on Todd Mei's account of ethical deliberation in "use" (himself building on Frank) by applying it to *nomisma*. Todd S. Mei, "The Preeminence of Use: Reevaluating the Relation between Use and Exchange in Aristotle's Economic Thought," *Journal of the History of Philosophy* 47, no. 4 (October 2009): 523–48.

30. For an important corrective, see David Singh Grewal, *The Invention of the Economy* (Cambridge, MA: Harvard University Press, forthcoming).

31. Most English editions of Aristotle tend to translate two distinct Greek terms as "money": *chrēmata*, which meant material wealth in general, including nonmonetary wealth; and *nomisma*, which indicated a specific conception of currency issued by the polis, as exemplified in the then relatively new invention of coinage.

32. von Reden, *Exchange in Ancient Greece*, 189n22. See also Robert C. Bartlett and Susan D. Collins, *Aristotle's Nicomachean Ethics* (Chicago: University of Chicago Press, 2011), 100n25.

33. For example: "Truly she [Athena] was bringing together a scattered army, inspiring them with *nomisma*." Alcaeus fr. 382 L–P. As quoted in Seaford, *Money and the Early Greek Mind*, 142–43, on whose detailed discussion I draw here.

34. Aeschylus, *Seven against Thebes,* line 269. In the *Oresteia*, the *ololugē* is a frequent feature that changes its meaning over the course of the trilogy from the celebration of victory and sacrifice to the cry of the Furies. Suzanne Saïd, "Aeschylean Tragedy," in Justina Gregory, ed., *A Companion to Greek Tragedy* (Oxford: Blackwell, 2005), 215–32, at 229.

35. Euripides, *The Bacchae*, 689; Euripides, *Herakleidai*, 777–83.

36. Laura McClure, *Spoken like a Woman: Speech and Gender in Athenian Drama* (Princeton, NJ: Princeton University Press, 1999), 52–54, 76–80, 110; Joan Breton Connelly, *The Parthenon Enigma* (New York: Knopf, 2014), 268; Herodotus, *Histories*, 359 [bk. 4, par. 189].

37. Seaford, *Money and the Early Greek Mind*, 143. Seaford also suggestively links this sense of collective confidence to the gold-tasseled, sacrificial shield or animal skin (*aegis*) carried by Athena into battle. (143n109).

38. In Athens, the image that combined all these elements of coinage, sacrifice, and ululation was that of owls. Athenian *tetradrachm* coins were known as "little owls" (*glaux*) since they depicted an owl on the obverse. But owls were also closely associated with Athena, seen as harbingers of death, and the sound of owls was linked to ululation, which itself provided the root for the Latin word for owl: *ulula*. Connelly, *Parthenon Enigma*, 285.

39. von Reden, *Exchange in Ancient Greece*, 190n.

40. Aristophanes, *Clouds*, lines 247–48. See also von Reden, *Exchange in Ancient Greece*, 145n54.

41. Diogenes Laertius, "Diogenes," in *Lives of Eminent Philosophers*, vol. 2 (Cambridge, MA: Harvard University Press), 23–83; Malcolm Schofield, *Saving the City: Philosopher-Kings and Other Classical Paradigms* (London: Routledge, 1999), 58.

42. von Reden, *Exchange in Ancient Greece*, 128.

43. *Pol* 1271a15–17.

44. When speaking of "political justice" I refer to Aristotle's conception of what is just by convention (*to politikon dikaion*) as opposed to either the character trait of righteousness (*dikaiosynē*) or the concept of natural justice. See Daniela Cammack, "Plato and Athenian Justice," *History of Political Thought* 36, no. 4 (Winter 2015): 611–42.

45. *Pol* 1257a31–33; 1257b1–5.

46. Joseph A. Schumpeter, *History of Economic Analysis* [1955] (London: Routledge, 2006), 59–60.

47. *Pol* 1257b5–7.

48. *Pol* 1257b10–11.

49. *Pol* 1257a28–31.

50. From *Pol* 1256b28 until 1258a8, *oikonomikē* and *chrēmatistikē* are in this regard used in distinct senses as mutually exclusive (with *ktētikē* serving as the general term). In 1258a8, however, *chrēmatistikē* is suddenly once more used as the general term. See von Reden, *Exchange in Ancient Greece*, 174–75, 189n31. By contrast, in other instances Aristotle often names the genus after its most developed species (such as most famously *politeia*). See Kevin M. Cherry, "The Problem of Polity," *Journal of Politics* 71, no. 4 (2009): 1406–21.

51. von Reden, *Exchange in Ancient Greece*, 175.

52. Karl Polanyi, *The Great Transformation: The Political and Economic Origins of Our Time*, 2ⁿᵈ ed. (Boston: Beacon, 2001), 56; Karl Polanyi, "Aristotle Discovers the Economy," in Karl Polanyi, Conrad M. Arensberg, and Harry W. Pearson, eds., *Trade and Market in the Early Empires: Economies in History and Theory* (Glencoe, IL: Free Press, 1957), 66.

53. Polanyi, *Great Transformation*, 56.

54. *Pol* 1258a7.

55. Plato, *Laws*, 870a.

56. Plato, *Republic*, 416e–417a.

57. Plato, *Republic*, 371b. "We will need a market-place [*agora*] then, and currency [*nomisma*] as a token [*sumbolon*] for exchange will be the result of this." On Plato's ambivalence, see also Seaford, *Money and the Early Greek Mind*, 250. As Schindler has pointed out perceptively, "When Socrates introduced money in the ideal city, it was precisely as a token, as a 'symbol' of exchange, and thus as something that has its reality in allowing the transition from one real good to another." D. C. Schindler, "Why Socrates Didn't Charge: Plato and the Metaphysics of Money," *Communio: International Catholic Review* 36, no. 3 (Fall 2009): 394–426, at 402–3.

58. Solon, "Fragment 4," in *Greek Elegy and Iambus* (Cambridge, MA: Loeb Classical Library, 1982), 118; Seaford, *Money and the Early Greek Mind*, 206; von Reden, *Exchange in Ancient Greece*, 182.

59. *NE* 1119b26–27.

60. Jonny Thakkar, *Plato as Critical Theorist* (Cambridge, MA: Harvard University Press, 2018), 294–96; Jonny Thakkar, "Moneymakers and Craftsmen," *European Journal of Philosophy* 24, no. 4 (December 2016): 735–59, at 745–50.

61. Frank, *Democracy of Distinction*, 66. Frank is careful to highlight that this does not mean money is treated in an unequivocally derogatory manner but that it contains a certain "liberatory dimension" (68).

62. *NE* 1130b32–33.

63. See, for example, John Burnet, *The Ethics of Aristotle* (London: Methuen, 1900), 203.

64. Leo Strauss, *History of Political Philosophy* (Chicago: University of Chicago Press, 1987), 128.

65. Lindsay Judson, "Aristotle on Fair Exchange," in C.C.W. Taylor, ed., *Oxford Studies in Ancient Philosophy*, vol. 15 (Oxford: Clarendon Press, 1997), 147–75.

66. Terence Irwin, *Aristotle's First Principles* (Oxford: Oxford University Press, 1988), 625; Charles Young, "Aristotle's Justice," in Richard Kraut, ed., *The Blackwell Guide to Aristotle's Nicomachean Ethics* (Oxford: Wiley-Blackwell, 2006), 179–97, at 187. See also Scott Meikle, *Aristotle's Economic Thought* (New York: Oxford University Press, 1995).

67. The discussion of reciprocity tellingly concludes with the statement that "we have now said what it is that is unjust and just" (*NE* 1133b30).

68. *NE* 1132b21–22.

69. Theodore Scaltsas, "Reciprocal Justice in Aristotle's Nicomachean Ethics," *Archiv für Geschichte der Philosophie* 77, no. 3 (1995): 248–62.

70. Thucydides, *History of the Peloponnesian War*, 3.61, 6.35.

71. *NE* 1132b34.

72. Indeed, Henry Billingsley, the sixteenth-century Lord Mayor of London and first translator of Euclid into English in 1570, appears to have coined the term "reciprocall" in his translation. Nicholas J. Theocarakis, *"Antipeponthos* and Reciprocity: The Concept of Equivalent Exchange from Aristotle to Turgot," *International Review of Economics* 55, no. 1 (2008): 29–44, at 33.

73. For a prior interpretation along these lines, see D. G. Ritchie, "Aristotle's Subdivisions of Particular Justice," *Classical Review* 8, no. 5 (May 1894): 185–92.

74. I thus follow Frank in considering distributive and corrective justice as instantiations of reciprocal justice. Frank, *Democracy of Distinction*, 82.

75. *NE* 1132b33–34. Irwin translation adapted.

76. As Finley noted, when Aristotle discusses reciprocity he does not use any of the conventional Greek terms for trade—as he does elsewhere—but instead speaks abstractly of mutual exchanges (*allaxis*) and agreements (*synallagma*). Moses Finley, "Aristotle and Economic Analysis," *Past and Present* 47, no. 1 (May 1970): 3–25, at 14.

77. See in particular Allen, *Talking to Strangers*; Frank, *Democracy of Distinction*; and Susan D. Collins, "Moral Virtue and the Limits of the Political Community in Aristotle's *Nicomachean Ethics," American Journal of Political Science* 48, no. 1 (January 2004): 47–61.

78. Frank, *Democracy of Distinction*, 82, 99.

79. Allen, *Talking to Strangers*, 135.

80. As Frank puts it, "The equality characteristic of reciprocal justice is one that accommodates, indeed, that depends on, differences." Frank, *Democracy of Distinction*, 88.

81. *NE* 1134a26–28; as well as *NE* 1134b10–15.

82. *NE* 1134b14.

83. Danielle Allen, *The World of Prometheus: The Politics of Punishing in Democratic Athens* (Princeton, NJ: Princeton University Press, 2000), 286.

84. *NE* 1131a29.

85. Aristotle, *Topics*, 186a6.

86. Aristotle, *Poetics*, 1457b1–25; see also *Rhetoric*, 1405a, 1410b–1411a.

87. Aristotle, *Historia Animalium*, 486b21.

88. *NE* 1133a27–29. Irwin translates *alētheia* as "in reality," Rackham as "in the strict sense." I have instead preferred the more literal "in truth." I translate *chreia* as "use" or "need" to reflect that it is not a quality of the parties of exchange but describes the relation between thing and person.

89. *NE* 1133a21–23.

90. *NE* 1133a30. Syntax slightly altered from Irwin.

91. *NE* 1133b19–21.

92. *NE* 1133b16–19.

93. Bresson, *Ancient Greek Economy*, 268.

94. Gregory Vlastos, "Justice and Equality," in Jeremy Waldron, ed., *Theories of Right* (Oxford: Oxford University Press, 1984), 41–77, at 42.

95. *NE* 1133b30–34. As Ann Ward has put it, monetary reciprocity specifies Aristotle's concept of equality when dealing with particular justice. Ann Ward, "Justice as Economics in Aristotle's *Nicomachean Ethics," Canadian Political Science Review*

4, no. 1 (2010): 1–11, at 10; Ward, *Contemplating Friendship*, 67–82; Collins, "Moral Virtue," 55.

96. *NE* 1131a13–14. Irwin here translates *meson* as "intermediate." I have preferred "mean" since it replicates the double meaning of "measure" and "intermediate."

97. Meikle, *Aristotle's Economic Thought*, 135–46. Meikle, following Marx, reads Aristotle's concepts of use and exchange as mapping onto the modern distinction between use and exchange value. For a critique of Meikle's position, see Mei, "Preeminence of Use," 534–36.

98. *NE* 1131a21; Collins, "Moral Virtue," 55.

99. *NE* 1131a24–29; 1135a1–6.

100. *Pol* 1275a3–5.

101. *NE* 1155a23–26. See also Schofield, *Saving the City*, 72–87.

102. *NE* 1163b34–1164a2.

103. Robert L. Gallagher, "Incommensurability in Aristotle's Theory of Reciprocal Justice," *British Journal for the History of Philosophy* 20, no. 4 (2012): 667–701.

104. Aristotle, *Eudemian Ethics*, 1242b18–21.

105. Frank, *Democracy of Distinction*, 98.

106. *Pol* 1281a40-b10. Ober has suggested that Athenian collective meals consisted mainly of contributions in kind. Josiah Ober, "Democracy's Wisdom: An Aristotelian Middle Way for Collective Judgment," *American Political Science Review* 107, no. 1 (February 2013): 104–22, at 111n16. There is, however, much literary and epigraphic evidence to suggest that at least the large-scale festivals crucially depended on monetary contributions. See Vincent J. Rosivach, *The System of Public Sacrifice in Fourth-Century Athens* (Atlanta: Scholars Press, 1994), 96; Richard Seaford, "Money and Tragedy," in W. V. Harris, ed., *The Monetary Systems of the Greeks and Romans* (Oxford: Oxford University Press, 2008), 51–53; Daniela Cammack, "Aristotle on the Virtue of the Multitude," *Political Theory* 41, no. 2 (2013): 175–202, at 183.

107. See the perceptive commentary on this point in Allen, *World of Prometheus*, 225.

108. Ps.-Aristotle, *The Constitution of the Athenians* 27.2, 41.3.

109. *Pol* 1317b33–35; see also *NE* 1134b8.

110. Aristophanes, *The Knights*, line 255. One *drachma*—meaning roughly "handful"—consisted of six *obols* since this was as many as the hand could grasp. See Plutarch, *The Life of Lysander*, section 17.

111. Kurke, *Coins, Bodies, Games, and Gold*, 46–47.

112. Kurke, *Coins, Bodies, Games, and Gold*, 47.

113. Paul Millett, *Lending and Borrowing in Ancient Athens* (Cambridge: Cambridge University Press, 1991). For other ancient democracies, see Eric W. Robinson, *Democracy beyond Athens* (Cambridge: Cambridge University Press, 2011), 102, 119, 157.

114. Ward, "Justice as Economics," 10; see also Ann Ward, "Friendship and Politics in Aristotle's *Nicomachean Ethics*," *European Journal of Political Theory* 10, no. 4 (2011): 443–62, at 451.

115. Currency allowed in this sense "for a greater dimension of belonging-together (*koinōnia*) of the *polis*." Mei, "Preeminence of Use," 525–56.

116. *Pol* 1332b26–27.

117. As Ward has put it, "Although the political community may initially come into being to satisfy the mutual needs of its members, the satisfaction of need facilitated through monetary exchange is not enough to maintain unity, but friendship is needed in addition." Ward, "Justice as Economics," 10.

118. *NE* 1155a22–29.

119. Ward, *Contemplating Friendship*, 82.

120. Arlene Saxonhouse highlights the gendered dynamics of this shift from masculine virility—be it martial or acquisitive—to feminine virtues of restraint. Arlene Saxonhouse, "Aristotle: Defective Males, Hierarchy and the Limits of Politics," in Mary L. Shanley and Carole Pateman, eds., *Feminist Interpretations and Political Theory* (Cambridge, UK: Polity, 1991), 50.

121. As Michael Chan has pointed out, the inclusion of the commercial hub of Carthage alongside Crete and Sparta is striking and surprising. Chan, *Aristotle and Hamilton*, 36–43.

122. *Pol* 1289a3–7.

123. *Pol* 1253a13–18.

124. Seaford has most forcefully linked ancient money to tragedy. Richard Seaford, "Monetisation, Ritual, and the Genesis of Tragedy," in Dimitrios Yatromanolakis and Panagiotis Roilos, eds., *Greek Ritual Poetics* (Cambridge, MA: Harvard University Press, 2004), 71–93; Seaford, *Money and the Early Greek Mind*, 197.

125. Michel Foucault, *Lectures on the Will to Know: Lectures at the Collège de France, 1970–1971*, trans. Graham Burchell (New York: Palgrave Macmillan, 2013), 133–65.

126. Foucault, *Lectures on the Will to Know*, 141.

127. Foucault, *Lectures on the Will to Know*, 143; Michel Aglietta and André Orléan, *La monnaie entre violence et confiance* (Paris: Odile Jacob, 2002).

128. Foucault, *Lectures on the Will to Know*, 140.

129. Sophocles, *Antigone*, lines 295–301. Karl Marx, *Das Kapital*, Erster Band, *Marx-Engels Gesamtausgabe* (MEGA²), II.6, 154; Karl Marx, *Capital*, vol. 1, trans. Ben Fowkes (London: Penguin, 1976), 230.

130. Millett, *Lending and Borrowing*, 7.

131. Aeschylus, *Eumenides*, lines 1011, 319.

132. See also von Reden, *Exchange in Ancient Greece*, 220; as well as David Luban, "Some Greek Trials," in *Legal Modernism: Law, Meaning, and Violence* (Ann Arbor: Michigan University Press, 1994), 283–334, at 321.

133. Aeschylus, *Eumenides*, line 1028. See also Patchen Markell, *Bound by Recognition* (Princeton, NJ: Princeton University Press, 2003), 79–80, 192.

134. Aeschylus, *Agamemnon*, line 437.

135. For René Girard, for example, it was precisely boundless "mimetic desire" that turned money into an essentially self-defeating institution. René Girard, *Violence and the Sacred* (Baltimore: Johns Hopkins University Press, 1977), 39–67. In their influential account of money as ambivalently suspended between trust and violence, Aglietta and Orléan (*La monnaie entre violence et confiance*) invoke Girard yet historicize monetary desire as a feature of capitalism, not a constant fact of society.

136. *Pol* 1321b6–13. Tellingly, when the Athenian visitor in Plato's *Laws* emphasizes the political importance of market stewards, he plays on the shared linguistic origin of currency (*nomisma*) and regulations (*nomima*) (916d–918a).

137. *Pol* 1321b15.

138. Melissa Lane, "Introduction," in Jonathan Barnes, ed., *Aristotle's Politics* (Princeton, NJ: Princeton University Press, 2016), xiv.

139. *Pol* 1257b24.

140. *Pol* 1257b15–18.

141. Plato, *Apology*, 19e–20c.

142. Plato, *Republic*, 416e–417a, 422d.

143. Malcolm Schofield has described the abolition of money as a core aspect of "the mainstream of all Greek utopian thinking." Schofield, *Saving the City*, 58.

144. Thomas More, *Utopia* [1516], ed. George M. Logan and Robert M. Adams (Cambridge: Cambridge University Press, 2002), 105.

145. More, *Utopia*, 37.

146. Fredric Jameson, *Archaeologies of the Future: The Desire Called Utopia and Other Science Fictions* (London and New York: Verso, 2005), 20, 229.

147. Plato, *Republic*, 416e–417a. "We will tell them that they [the guardians] always have gold and silver [*khrusion kai argurion*] of a divine sort in their souls as a gift from the gods and so have no further need of human gold [*tou anthrōpeiou*]. . . . For them alone among the city's population, it is unlawful to touch or handle gold or silver [*khrusou kai argurou*]."

148. Without the historical background of ancient Greek coinage, the central role currency (*nomisma*) plays in Aristotelian reciprocity and political justice is easily missed. While overly narrow readings of reciprocity have tended to restrict Aristotelian reciprocity to retribution, gift exchange, or commercial exchange, overly broad readings of his critique of wealth accumulation have tended to extend the critique to all forms of monetary exchange. Aristotle's discussion of currency complicates these readings of reciprocity and wealth accumulation by regarding currency as an essential, if self-defeating political institution.

149. Odd Inge Langholm, *Wealth and Money in the Aristotelian Tradition: A Study in Scholastic Economic Sources* (Bergen: Universitetsforlaget, 1983); Joel Kaye, *Economy and Nature in the Fourteenth Century: Money, Market Exchange, and the Emergence of Scientific Thought* (Cambridge: Cambridge University Press, 1998); Christine Desan, *Making Money: Coin, Currency, and the Coming of Capitalism* (Oxford: Oxford University Press, 2015), 266–74; Diana Wood, *Medieval Economic Thought* (Cambridge: Cambridge University Press, 2002), 69–88.

150. Thomas Aquinas, *Commentary on the* Nicomachean Ethics, vol. 1, bk. 5, lecture 9, par. 982.

151. Nicole Oresme, *The "De moneta" of Nicholas Oresme and English Mint Documents*, trans. Charles Johnson (London: Thomas Nelson and Sons, 1956); see also the excellent Adam Woodhouse, "'Who Owns the Money?': Currency, Property, and Popular Sovereignty in Nicole Oresme's *De moneta*," *Speculum* 92, no. 1 (January 2017): 85–116.

152. See, for example, Pufendorf's invocation of book 1 of the *Politics* (1257a32–41) alongside the *Ethics*. Samuel Pufendorf, *De Jure Naturae et Gentium Libri Octo* (Oxford: Carnegie Classics of International Law Series, 1934), 5.1.11, 468; Samuel Pufendorf, *De Jure Naturae et Gentium: Of the Law of Nature and Nations*, with an introduction by W. Simmons, trans. C. H. Oldfather and W. A. Oldfather, 2 vols. (Oxford: Carnegie Classics of International Law Series, 1934), 5.1.12, 690–91.

153. Jean-Jacques Rousseau, "Discours sur les sciences et les arts," in *Oeuvres complètes*, tome 3 (Paris: Bibliothèque de la Pléiade, 1964), 20; Jean-Jacques Rousseau, "Discourse on the Sciences and Arts," in *The Discourses and Other Early Political Writings*, ed. and trans. Victor Gourevitch (Cambridge: Cambridge University Press, 1997), 19.

154. Jean-Jacques Rousseau, "Du contrat social," in *Oeuvres complètes*, tome 3 (Paris: Bibliothèque de la Pléiade, 1964), 429; Jean-Jacques Rousseau, *The Social Contract and Other Later Political Writings*, ed. and trans. Victor Gourevitch (Cambridge: Cambridge University Press, 1997), 113.

155. Rousseau, *Émile*, 461; Rousseau, *Emile*, 189.

156. Rousseau, *Émile*, 462; Rousseau, *Emile*, 189.

157. Albert O. Hirschman, *The Passions and the Interests: Political Arguments for Capitalism before Its Triumph* (Princeton, NJ: Princeton University Press, 1977), 131.

158. Hirschman, *Passions and the Interests*, 131.

Chapter 2. The Modern Depoliticization of Money

1. William Molyneux to John Locke, June 6, 1696, in John Locke, *The Correspondence of John Locke*, ed. E. S. de Beer, 8 vols. (Oxford: Clarendon Press, 1979–1989), vol. 5, letter no. 2100, 653. All dates in this chapter are Old Style dates. I break with early modern English practice only in assuming the New Year begins on January 1, not March 25. Most notably, this affects the dating of several texts published between January 1 and March 24.

2. For the argument of 1688 as the first modern revolution, see Steven Pincus, *1688: The First Modern Revolution* (New Haven, CT: Yale University Press, 2009).

3. Ludovic Desmedt, "Les fondements monétaires de la 'révolution financière' anglaise: Le tournant de 1696," in Bruno Théret, ed., *La monnaie dévoilée par ses crises* (Paris: Éditions de l'EHESS, 2007), 311–38, at 325; Kepa Ormazabal, "Lowndes and Locke on the Value of Money," *History of Political Economy* 44, no. 1 (2012), 157–80, at 158; Patrick Hyde Kelly, "General Introduction," in John Locke, *Locke on Money*, ed. Patrick Hyde Kelly, Clarendon Edition of the Works of John Locke (Oxford: Clarendon Press, 1991), 116.

4. Pincus, *1688*, 438, 608n3.

5. John Locke to William Molyneux, March 30, 1696, in Locke, *Correspondence*, vol. 5, letter no. 2059, 594. Pincus (*1688*, 438) also cites the letter but attributes it to Molyneux. To render legible Locke's preoccupation with linguistic unreliability and variability (on which more below), I have chosen to preserve the seventeenth-century spelling, capitalization, and punctuation where possible.

6. For the historiography of the Coinage Crisis, see Albert Feavearyear, *The Pound Sterling: A History of English Money* (Oxford: Oxford University Press, 1931); Peter Laslett, "John Locke, the Great Recoinage and the Board of Trade," *William and Mary Quarterly*, Third Series, 14, no. 3 (July 1957): 370–402; J. Keith Horsefield, *British Monetary Experiments, 1650–1710* (Cambridge, MA: Harvard University Press, 1960); Ming-Hsun Li, *The Great Recoinage of 1696 to 1699* (London: Weidenfeld & Nicholson, 1963); P.G.M. Dickson, *The Financial Revolution in England: A Study in the Development of Public Credit, 1688–1756* (London: Macmillan, 1967). See also Mara Caden's work on recoinage and its effects for Britain and its empire

in the early eighteenth century. Mara Caden, *Mint Conditions: The Politics and Geography of Money in Britain and Its Empire, 1690–1730* (PhD diss., Yale University, 2017).

7. John Locke, *An Essay Concerning Humane Understanding, in Four Books* (London: T. Basset, 1690 [1689]); John Locke [anon.], *Some Thoughts Concerning Education* (London: A. & J. Churchill, 1693). The latter was initially also published anonymously but carried Locke's name by the third edition two years later.

8. John Locke [anon.], *Short Observations on a Printed Paper. Intituled, For Encouraging the Coining Silver Money in England, and after for keeping it here* (London, 1695). Reprinted as "Short Observations on a Printed Paper," in Locke, *Locke on Money*, 2:345–59; John Freke and Edward Clarke to Locke, February 28, 1695, in Locke, *Correspondence*, vol. 5, letter no. 1853, 278; Roger Woolhouse, *Locke: A Biography* (Cambridge: Cambridge University Press, 2007), 322, 355.

9. John Locke, "Propositions sent to the Lord Justices," in Locke, *Locke on Money*, 2:374–80. At this point Locke was still moving outside the public eye. He was giving expert advice and writing pamphlets—all the while pleading with his correspondents to keep his name out of it. "But, pray, whatever use you make of it, conceal my name." Locke to William Molyneux, November 20, 1695, in Locke, *Correspondence*, vol. 5, letter no. 1966, 464.

10. John Locke, *Further Considerations Concerning Raising the Value of Money: Wherein Mr. Lowndes's Argument for it in his late Report concerning An Essay for the Amendment of the Silver Coins, are particularly Examined* (London: A. & J. Churchill, 1695). The book was published on December 27, 1695; a second, corrected edition appeared on January 9, 1696. The book was dedicated to Sir John Somers MP. Later in 1696, Locke added the two previous anonymous pamphlets from 1691 and earlier in 1695 and published the volume as *Several papers relating to money, interest and trade, &c. Writ upon several occasions, and published at different times. By John Locke Esq* (London: A. & J. Churchill, 1696). In a recently resurfaced manuscript memoir, one of Locke's closest acquaintances, James Tyrrell (1642–1719), claims that Locke's "book on Money" was "a copy of another." Felix Waldmann, "John Locke as a Reader of Thomas Hobbes's *Leviathan*: A New Manuscript," *Journal of Modern History* 93, no. 2 (June 2021): 245–82, at 258. Tyrrell referred to Thomas Mun's *Discourse of Trade* (1621) in this context.

11. As discussed below, while Locke's insistence on a recoinage without devaluation succeeded, its procedural implementation deviated in a number of ways from his advice. While Locke had recommended a swift demonetization of the old coins, the actual Recoinage proceeded gradually over a prolonged time period. Furthermore, where Locke had insisted on payment at the old coins' reduced metal weight, during the Recoinage holders of clipped coins were compensated. See also Thomas J. Sargent and François R. Velde, *The Big Problem of Small Change* (Princeton, NJ: Princeton University Press, 2002), ch. 19.

12. Two excellent, and rather distinct, recent exceptions are Douglas John Casson, *Liberating Judgment: Fanatics, Skeptics, and John Locke's Politics of Probability* (Princeton, NJ: Princeton University Press, 2011) and Daniel Carey, "John Locke's Philosophy of Money," in Daniel Carey, ed., *Money and Political Economy in the Enlightenment* (Oxford: Oxford University Press, 2014), 57–81.

13. As Mark Goldie has noted, "The greatest impact exerted by Locke on the everyday lives of his contemporaries arose from his advice during the Coinage Crisis." Mark Goldie, "Coinage and Commerce, 1695–1696," in *John Locke: Selected Correspondence from the Clarendon Edition by E. S. de Beer*, ed. Mark Goldie (Oxford: Oxford University Press, 2002), 213.

14. Locke's monetary thought thus constitutes an intriguing exception to Duncan Bell's otherwise apt observation that Locke's *political* thought largely failed to excite before its mid-twentieth-century liberal refashioning. See Duncan Bell, "What Is Liberalism?," *Political Theory* 42, no. 6 (2014): 682–715.

15. As the historian Albert Feavearyear summarized in 1931, Locke's monetary opinion "has been looked back to ever since as a sterling example to be kept in mind at any time when there may be a temptation to alter the standard of the Mint." Feavearyear, *The Pound Sterling*, 135.

16. Lord King, *The Life and Letters of John Locke, with extracts from his correspondence, journals and common-place books* (London: Henry Colburn, 1829), 240–45.

17. Thomas Babington Macaulay, *The History of England from the Accession of James the Second* [1849–55], vol. 2 (London: Longmans, Green, 1871), 547.

18. Karl Marx, *Das Kapital*, Erster Band, *Marx-Engels Gesamtausgabe* (hereafter MEGA²), II.6, 70n4; Karl Marx, *Capital*, vol. 1, trans. Ben Fowkes (London: Penguin, 1976), 126n4. Below I will first provide page references to the MEGA² edition of *Capital*, followed by page references to the Penguin translation.

19. By 1824, in its twelfth edition, the fourth volume contained first the three coinage essays and only then the *Two Treatises*. John Locke, *Works of John Locke in Nine Volumes*, 12th ed. (London: Rivington, 1824).

20. Joyce Oldham Appleby, "Locke, Liberalism and the Natural Law of Money," *Past & Present* 71, no. 1 (May 1976): 43–69; reprinted in Joyce Appleby, *Liberalism and Republicanism in the Historical Imagination* (Cambridge: Cambridge University Press, 1992), 58–89.

21. Joyce Oldham Appleby, *Economic Thought and Ideology in Seventeenth-Century England* (Princeton, NJ: Princeton University Press, 1978), 203.

22. Appleby, "Locke, Liberalism, and the Natural Law of Money," 73.

23. I here drew on a more recent literature on Locke's coinage writings that has effectively questioned Appleby's account of monetary naturalization while shifting attention to the neglected linguistic and epistemological premises of Locke's position. For a powerful critique of Appleby's reading, see Daniel Carey, "John Locke, Money, and Credit," in Daniel Carey and Christopher J. Finlay, eds., *The Empire of Credit: The Financial Revolution in the British Atlantic World, 1688–1815* (Dublin: Irish Academic Press, 2011), 25–51. On money and Locke's philosophy of language, see Constantine George Caffentzis, *Clipped Coins, Abused Words, and Civil Government: John Locke's Philosophy of Money* (New York: Autonomedia, 1989/1990); Hannah Dawson, *Locke, Language and Early-Modern Philosophy* (Cambridge: Cambridge University Press, 2007); Daniel Carey, "John Locke's Philosophy of Money," in Daniel Carey, ed., *Money and Political Economy in the Enlightenment* (Oxford: Oxford University Press, 2014), 57–81; Daniel Carey, "Locke's Species: Money and Philosophy in the 1690s," *Annals of Science* 70, no. 3 (2013): 357–80; Douglas John Casson, "John Locke, Clipped Coins, and the Unstable Currency of Public Reason," *Etica & Politica* 18, no. 2 (2016): 153–80.

24. John O'Brien, "John Locke, Desire, and the Epistemology of Money," *British Journal for the History of Philosophy* 15, no. 4 (2007): 685–708, at 686.

25. In his introduction to Locke's monetary writings Patrick Hyde Kelly remarks, without further elaboration, that "there would seem to be a large debt to Aristotle." Kelly, "General Introduction," 98. Making a more specific claim, James Tully has argued that "Locke explains the introduction of money in the traditional, Aristotelian manner." James Tully, *A Discourse on Property: John Locke and His Adversaries* (Cambridge: Cambridge University Press, 1980), 147. Marx referenced Locke in the opening pages of *Kapital*—quoting from Locke's *Some Considerations on the Consequences of the Lowering of Interest* (1691)—for having retained an Aristotelian distinction between natural use value and conventional monetary value. Marx, *Capital*, vol. 1, ch. 1 (MEGA^2 II.5, 45n4; II.6, 70n4; Penguin 126n4).

26. To render Locke's preoccupation with linguistic unreliability and variability legible, I have chosen to preserve the seventeenth-century spelling, capitalization, and punctuation where possible.

27. In shielding money from political meddling, Locke's theory of money was nonetheless never intended to remove currency completely from the realm of politics. While I here emphasize Locke's intention to disentangle money from political interference, Lee Ward has recently pushed a similar framing in the opposite direction by arguing that Locke in fact meant to encourage new forms of political deliberation on currency based on prudential judgments, including in relation to distributive justice. Lee Ward, "Trust and Distributive Justice in John Locke's Politics of Money," *Review of Politics* 83, no. 4 (2021): 510–32.

28. Karl Polanyi, *The Great Transformation: The Political and Economic Origins of Our Time* [1944] (Boston: Beacon, 2001), 147. As Appleby herself noted, "By insisting that gold and silver alone were money, Locke not only dismissed the power of civil authority to create value, he also avoided consideration of that value which came from utility and which fluctuated with demand." Appleby, "Locke, Liberalism, and the Natural Law of Money," 66–67.

29. My argument of modern money's depoliticization mirrors in this regard Christine Desan's account of the privatization of money creation during the seventeenth century. Christine Desan, *Making Money: Coin, Currency, and the Coming of Capitalism* (Oxford: Oxford University Press, 2015).

30. Desmedt, "Les fondements monétaires," 325; Carey, "Locke's Philosophy of Money," 58; Nicholas Mayhew, *Sterling: The Rise and Fall of a Currency* (London: Allen Lane, 1999), 97.

31. The new milled coins were resistant to clipping thanks to their edges being inscribed with a motto (*decus et tutamen*, "an ornament and a safeguard") taken from Virgil's *Aeneid* (book 5, line 262) that can still be found on one-pound coins to this day.

32. Locke himself adamantly refused to accept clipped coins, rejecting them as not "the lawfull coin" of England. Locke, *Correspondence*, vol. 5, letter no. 1908, 381.

33. Dwyryd Jones goes as far as describing clipping as a "lucky circumstance" and "salvation that allowed England to hang on for longer than it otherwise would have been able to." Dwyryd W. Jones, *War and Economy: In the Age of William III and Marlborough* (Oxford: Basil Blackwell, 1988), 247–48.

34. Macaulay, *History of England*, 2:545.

35. Pincus, *1688*, 438, 608n3.

36. John Evelyn, *Numismata: A Discourse of Medals, Antient and Modern* (London: Benjmin Tooke, 1697), 221–23.

37. John Childs, *The Nine Years' War and the British Army, 1688-1697* (Manchester: Manchester University Press, 1991), 26.

38. On the history of standing armies, see John Childs, "The Military Revolution I: The Transition to Modern Warfare," in Charles Townshend, ed., *The Oxford History of Modern War*, new updated ed. (Oxford: Oxford University Press, 2005), 20–39.

39. Childs, "Military Revolution," 30.

40. Childs, *Nine Years' War*, 1. See also H. V. Bowen, *War and British Society 1688-1815* (Cambridge: Cambridge University Press, 1998), as well as the excellent Jones, *War and Economy*.

41. Kelly, "Introduction," 39.

42. Bowen, *War and British Society*, 13; Jones, *War and Economy*, 19.

43. As Childs puts it starkly, "William could not acquire enough hard cash to pay his British troops and the foreign contingents funded by the English Treasury, nor could he meet the demands of the various bread, waggon and forage contractors." Childs, *Nine Years' War*, 305–6.

44. Childs, *Nine Years' War*, 268–69.

45. Childs, *Nine Years' War*, 297; Li, *Great Recoinage*, 58. See also Thomas Levenson, *Newton and the Counterfeiter* (London: Faber & Faber, 2010), 115.

46. "The King's Speech reported [November 26, 1695]," in *Journal of the House of Commons*, vol. 11, 339. As partially quoted in Levenson, *Newton and the Counterfeiter*, 116.

47. "The King's Speech," 339.

48. "The King's Speech," 339.

49. For a discussion of the different factions concerning the timing of recoinage, see Li, *Great Recoinage*, 65.

50. William Lowndes, *A Report Containing an Essay for the Amendment of the Silver Coins* (London: Charles Bill, 1695).

51. Desan, *Making Money*, 267–74. While Lowndes was right that raising the coin had been a widespread policy for hundreds of years across all of Europe, the English standard (as well as, interestingly, the Dutch one) had not been raised for decades, though at least in the English case largely because of political weakness and instability. Fernand Braudel, *Civilization and Capitalism*, vol. 1 (Berkeley: University of California Press, 1992), 458.

52. Lowndes, *Report*, 56.

53. In March 1695 this would have meant a devaluation of around 9 percent, but as the gap between the price of silver and the nominal value of coins widened the adjustment necessary to restore parity rose with it. By September 1695 Lowndes recommended a nominal raise of 20 percent. Lowndes, *Report*, 123; Carey, "Locke's Philosophy of Money," 58.

54. Locke, *Further Considerations*.

55. Pincus, *1688*, 460; Carey, "John Locke, Money, and Credit," 45.

56. Nicholas Barbon, *A Discourse Concerning Coining the New Money Lighter. in answer to Mr. Lock's Considerations about raising the value of money* (London: Richard Chiswell, 1696), 1.

57. Barbon, *Discourse Concerning Coining*, 96.

58. Barbon, *Discourse Concerning Coining*, 92.

59. Abbott Payson Usher, "Introduction," in Usher, ed., *Two Manuscripts by Charles Davenant* (Baltimore: Johns Hopkins University Press, 1942), vi.

60. Charles Davenant, "A Memorial Concerning the Coyn of England, November 1695," in Usher, *Two Manuscripts*, 5–63, at 8. See Thomas Hobbes, *Leviathan*, ch. 24, section 11.

61. Christopher Wren, "Proposal," in Li, *Great Recoinage*, 183–94, at 183. As Wren put it, "The Spoyl of the Coyn is but a consequence of the Over balance of Trade."

62. Charles Davenant, "A memoriall concerning Creditt [1696]," in Usher, *Two Manuscripts*, 67–108. Crucially, however, Davenant embraced the possibilities of credit money more fully than Locke ever did. See Carey, "John Locke, Money, and Credit," 42–44; Li, *Great Recoinage*, 63.

63. Isaac Newton, "Concerning the Amendment of English Coins," in Li, *Great Recoinage*, 217–23.

64. Newton, "Amendment of English Coins," 217.

65. Newton, "Amendment of English Coins," 222.

66. A collection of the monetary views of Locke's contemporaries can be found as an appendix to Li, *Great Recoinage*, 182–239. See also John Ramsay McCulloch, ed., *A Select Collection of scarce and valuable Tracts on Money* (London: Printed for the Political Economy Club, 1856).

67. Locke's library included five works by Petty, and in his papers can be found two further unpublished papers by him. Kelly, "General Introduction," 97.

68. *Sir William Petty his Quantulumcunque concerning money to the Lord Marquess of Halyfax, anno 1682* (London: A. and J. Churchill, 1695). Reprinted as William Petty, "Quantulumcunque concerning Money," in *The Economic Writings of William Petty*, ed. Charles Henry Hull, vol. 2 (Cambridge: Cambridge University Press, 1899), 437–48.

69. Petty, "Quantulumcunque concerning Money," 440. Question 14 equally resembled Locke's position: "Why hath Money been raised, or retrencht, or imbased by many wise States, and so often? Answ. When any State doth these things, they are like Bankrupt Merchants" (443).

70. For Locke's library, see John Harrison and Peter Laslett, *The Library of John Locke*, 2nd ed. (Oxford: Clarendon Press, 1971), 207; as well as Felix Waldmann, "The Library of John Locke: Additions, Corrigenda, and a Conspectus of Pressmarks," *Bodleian Library Record* 26 (2013): 36–58.

71. Li, *Great Recoinage*, 81–82.

72. Li, *Great Recoinage*, 82. On broader debates about the role of rent through the lens of "agrarian capitalism" during the closing decades of the seventeenth century, see David McNally, *Political Economy and the Rise of Capitalism: A Reinterpretation* (Berkeley: University of California Press, 1988), 22–84.

73. John Locke, "Some of the Consequences that are likely to follow upon lessening of interest to 4 per cent," in Locke, *Locke on Money*, 1:167–202. The text is based on Lovelace MS. e8, a draft manuscript dated 1668 that was first published in 1963.

74. Josiah Child, *Brief Observations Concerning Trade and Interest of Money* (London: Elizabeth Calvert and Henry Mortlock, 1668). For Locke's engagement with

Child, see Maurice Cranston, *John Locke: A Biography* (London: Longmans, Green, 1957), 118; as well as Kelly, "General Introduction," 9.

75. Locke, "Some of the Consequences," 202.

76. Locke, "Some of the Consequences," 172.

77. John Locke, "Second Tract," in *Political Essays*, ed. Mark Goldie (Cambridge: Cambridge University Press, 1997), 56–57.

78. On the sovereign right of coinage, see also Hugo Grotius, *The Rights of War and Peace* [1625], ed. Richard Tuck, 3 vols. (Indianapolis: Liberty Fund, 2005), bk. 2, ch. 4, section 13, 502.

79. Locke, "Some of the Consequences," 195.

80. Kelly, "General Introduction," 5. Locke's involvement in Carolina reached from constitutional and monetary concerns of the highest order all the way to detailed plans for viticulture. Eventually, Locke took over much of the administration of Carolina and was appointed, briefly, to the Council of Trade and Foreign Plantations. David Armitage, "John Locke, Carolina, and the Two Treatises of Government," *Political Theory* 32, no. 5 (2004): 602–27; John Locke, "The Fundamental Constitutions of Carolina," in *Political Essays*, ed. Mark Goldie (Cambridge: Cambridge University Press, 1997), 160–81.

81. For the dating of Locke's encounter with Pufendorf, see John Marshall, *John Locke: Resistance, Religion and Responsibility* (Cambridge: Cambridge University Press, 1994), 203. When later asked to compile a reading list on politics and the origin of society, Locke placed Pufendorf's *De Jure* on top of his list of recommended books. Locke, *Political Essays*, 377. In *Some Thoughts concerning Education* (§186), he similarly singled out Pufendorf.

82. Samuel Pufendorf, *De Jure Naturae et Gentium Libri Octo* (Londini Scanorum [Lund, Sweden]: Junghans, 1672).

83. To summarize his conclusions for teaching in the universities, Pufendorf reduced *De Jure* to a brief teaching compendium, *De Officio Hominis & Civis Juxta Legem Naturalem*. Samuel Pufendorf, *On the Duty of Man and Citizen according to Natural Law* [1673], ed. James Tully, trans. Michael Silverstone (Cambridge: Cambridge University Press, 1991), bk. 1, ch. 14, 96. In the process, Pufendorf elided an extensive history of money that had taken up much of book 5 of *De Jure* and which I discuss below.

84. Where ordinary value (*pretio vulgare*) referred in Pufendorf's account to things or actions that actually "afford service and pleasure to men," eminent value (*pretio eminens*) was linked to "money and whatever serves in its place [*numo, & quicquid eius vicem gerit*] . . . to furnish a common standard for their measurement." Samuel Pufendorf, *De Jure Naturae et Gentium Libri Octo* (Oxford: Carnegie Classics of International Law Series, 1934), 5.1.3–11, 458–67; Samuel Pufendorf, *De Jure Naturae et Gentium: Of the Law of Nature and Nations*, with an introduction by W. Simmons, trans. C. H. Oldfather and W. A. Oldfather, 2 vols. (Oxford: Carnegie Classics of International Law Series, 1934), 5.1.12, 676–89.

85. Pufendorf, *De Jure Naturae et Gentium*, 5.1.11, 467; Pufendorf, *Of the Law of Nature and Nations*, 5.1.11, 690.

86. Pufendorf, *De Jure Naturae et Gentium*, 5.1.12, 468; Pufendorf, *Of the Law of Nature and Nations*, 5.1.12, 690. Pufendorf's emphasis.

87. Pufendorf reproduced the passage in full. Pufendorf, *De Jure Naturae et Gentium*, 5.1.11, 468; Pufendorf, *Of the Law of Nature and Nations*, 5.1.12, 690–91.

88. Pufendorf in fact merged two passages into one. Pufendorf, *De Jure Naturae et Gentium*, 5.1.12, 468; Pufendorf, *Of the Law of Nature and Nations*, 5.1.12, 691. Besides the passages from the *Nicomachean Ethics* and the *Politics*, Pufendorf also reproduced two short lines from Aristotle's *Magna Moralia* and the *Rhetoric*, respectively. Pufendorf, *De Jure Naturae et Gentium*, 5.1.12, 468; Pufendorf, *Of the Law of Nature and Nations*, 5.1.12, 690.

89. Pufendorf, *De Jure Naturae et Gentium*, 5.1.12, 468; Pufendorf, *Of the Law of Nature and Nations*, 5.1.12, 690.

90. Pufendorf, *De Jure Naturae et Gentium*, 5.1.13, 469; Pufendorf, *Of the Law of Nature and Nations*, 5.1.13, 691.

91. Pufendorf, *De Jure Naturae et Gentium*, 469; Pufendorf, *Of the Law of Nature and Nations*, 5.1.13, 692; also Pufendorf, *On the Duty of Man and Citizen*, 1.14.8, 96.

92. Grotius had made a similar point but in more general terms when he denied that money simply derived its value from its metal content but instead defined it as the capacity of offering comparison in stable value. The difference from Locke is subtle but substantive. Grotius, *Rights of War and Peace*, bk. 2, ch. 12, section 17, 751.

93. Pufendorf, *De Jure Naturae et Gentium*, 5.1.14, 470; Pufendorf, *Of the Law of Nature and Nations*, 5.1.14, 693–94. Pufendorf's emphasis on foreign trade also points toward his influential attempt to carve out a space for commercial sociability before and alongside the state. On the significance of Pufendorf's defense of commercial, prepolitical sociability, see Istvan Hont, "The Language of Sociability and Commerce: Samuel Pufendorf and the Theoretical Foundations of the 'Four Stages' Theory," in *Jealousy of Trade: International Competition and the Nation-State in Historical Perspective* (Cambridge, MA: Harvard University Press, 2005), 159–84; as well as Istvan Hont, "Introduction," in *Jealousy of Trade*, 37–41. Where Hont discerned a pragmatic utilitarianism on Pufendorf's part, Richard Tuck stresses a theologically inflected assertion of natural sociability. See Richard Tuck, *The Rights of War and Peace: Political Thought and the International Order from Grotius to Kant* (Oxford: Oxford University Press, 1999), 140–65, esp. 141–42.

94. Pufendorf, *De Jure Naturae et Gentium*, 4.4.4, 366; Pufendorf, *Of the Law of Nature and Nations*, 4.4.4. 537. On Pufendorf's (as well as Grotius's) allowance of either express or tacit consent, see also David Singh Grewal, *The Invention of the Economy* (Cambridge, MA: Harvard University Press, forthcoming). As Tuck, Tully, and Hont have shown, despite relying heavily on Pufendorf in the *Second Treatise* Locke at the same time advanced a subtle critique of Pufendorf's argument concerning property and, relatedly, the role of consent, money, and property in prepolitical society. Tuck has, for example, stressed Locke's denial of prior Native American rights to land ownership. Tuck, *Rights of War and Peace*, 167–81; Tully, *Discourse on Property*, 98; Istvan Hont and Michael Ignatieff, "Needs and Justice in the Wealth of Nations: An Introductory Essay," in *Wealth and Virtue: The Shaping of Political Economy in the Scottish Enlightenment* (Cambridge: Cambridge University Press, 1983), 39; Armitage, "John Locke, Carolina, and the Two Treatises of Government," 606.

95. John Locke, *Second Treatise*, in *Two Treatises of Government* (Cambridge: Cambridge University Press, 1988), par. 34.

96. Locke, *Second Treatise*, par. 45.

97. Istvan Hont, *Politics in Commercial Society: Jean-Jacques Rousseau and Adam Smith* (Cambridge, MA: Harvard University Press, 2015), 67. See also Istvan Hont, "Adam Smith's History of Laws and Government as Political Theory," in Richard Bourke and Raymond Geuss, eds., *Political Judgement: Essays for John Dunn* (Cambridge: Cambridge University Press, 2009), 131–71, at 143–44; esp. 144n46.

98. Onur Ulas Ince, "Enclosing in God's Name, Accumulating for Mankind: Money, Morality, and Accumulation in John Locke's Theory of Property," *Review of Politics* 73, no. 1 (2011): 29–54. The theological ambivalence of this productive deceit can be detected in Locke's tone when discussing the seductive power of money in his educational writings. Locke admonished parents, for example, to delay contact with money for as long as possible and to avoid monetary rewards. Locke [anon.], *Some Thoughts Concerning Education*, 51–52.

99. Tuck, *Rights of War and Peace*, 167–81, esp. 175 where the point is made succinctly in passing; Tully, *Discourse on Property*, 98; and Hont and Ignatieff, "Needs and Justice," 39.

100. Locke, *Second Treatise*, par. 36.

101. Locke, *Second Treatise*, par. 49. On this, see also James Tully, "Aboriginal Property and Western Theory: Recovering a Middle Ground," *Social Philosophy and Policy* 11, no. 2 (July 1994): 153–80; and Onur Ulas Ince, *Colonial Capitalism and the Dilemmas of Liberalism* (Oxford: Oxford University Press, 2018), 38–73.

102. Richard Tuck, in particular, has emphasized the novelty of this argument. Tuck, *Rights of War and Peace*, 175. Already Jean Barbeyrac perceived this to be the truly novel and provocative feature of the fifth chapter of the *Second Treatise*. Samuel Pufendorf, *Le droit de la nature et des gens*, trans. and annotated by Jean Barbeyrac, 2 vols., 4th ed. (1732) [first ed. 1706], 4.4.3.n4, 4.4.4.n2, 4.4.9.n2, 4.6.2.n1.

103. Locke, *Second Treatise*, par. 35.

104. Barbara Arneil, *John Locke and America: The Defence of English Colonialism* (Oxford: Oxford University Press, 1996), 145.

105. Jeremy Waldron, for example, has described the passage as "one of the worst arguments in the Second Treatise." Jeremy Waldron, *God, Locke, Equality* (Cambridge: Cambridge University Press, 2002), 176–77. See also Ince, *Colonial Capitalism*, 57–60.

106. Locke, *Second Treatise*, par. 50.

107. Locke, *Second Treatise*, par. 46.

108. Locke, *Second Treatise*, par. 184.

109. Locke, "Propositions sent to the Lords Justices," 374.

110. For this link between Locke's philosophies of money and his account of language in the *Essay Concerning Human Understanding*, I here draw on the work of Caffentzis, *Clipped Coins*, 77–123; and Carey, "Locke's Philosophy of Money," 74–81. Both insist, rightly I think, on crucial parallels between Locke's discussion of language and money, though I diverge from them in the way I reconstruct Locke's drawing of a disanalogy between metal money and words.

111. Steven Forde, *Locke, Science, and Politics* (Cambridge: Cambridge University Press, 2013).

112. Locke, *Essay Concerning Human Understanding*, 3.9.7.

113. Locke, *Essay Concerning Human Understanding*, 3.10.12.

114. Hannah Dawson, "Locke on Language in (Civil) Society," *History of Political Thought* 26, no. 3 (Autumn 2005): 397–425, at 402; see also Dawson, *Locke, Language and Early-Modern Philosophy*, 286–89.

115. Locke, *Essay Concerning Human Understanding*, 3.11.8–9.

116. Locke, *Essay Concerning Human Understanding*, 3.11.11.

117. Locke, *Essay Concerning Human Understanding*, 3.9.8.

118. Locke, *Essay Concerning Human Understanding*, 3.5.8.

119. Locke, *Essay Concerning Human Understanding*, 3.5.8.

120. Locke, *Essay Concerning Human Understanding*, 3.1.1. This foreshadows my discussion of trust below. See also 3.10.13: ". . . language, which was given us for the improvement of knowledge and bond of society."

121. John Locke, *A Letter Concerning Toleration: Latin and English Texts Revised and Edited with Variants and an Introduction*, ed. Mario Montuori (The Hague: Martinus Nijhoff, 1963), 134.

122. Dawson has referred to this as "the doubly contractual nature of language." Dawson, *Locke, Language and Early-Modern Philosophy*, 277; however, whereas Dawson analogizes this contractual nature to a compact, I believe language in Locke's account is better captured by the tacit notion of "consent" than by formal contractual requirements. Language and money are based on consent, government on compact. Dawson, "Locke on Language in (Civil) Society," 403–8.

123. See in particular Locke, *Essay Concerning Human Understanding*, 3.10.13, 3.11.8–12. Hence my choice of preserving the seventeenth-century spelling conventions in this chapter's quotations.

124. Dawson, *Locke, Language and Early-Modern Philosophy*, 289.

125. Locke, *Essay Concerning Human Understanding*, 3.5.3.

126. Locke, *Essay Concerning Human Understanding*, 3.9.11. Similarly in the next chapter where Locke contrasts mixed modes with substances, citing the example of gold (3.10.19).

127. Caffentzis, *Clipped Coins*, 78.

128. Dawson, *Locke, Language and Early-Modern Philosophy*, 289. The opacity of language and its constitutive reliance on the precarious semantic malleability of mixed modes could at best be contained by clarity and consistency. Locke, *Essay Concerning Human Understanding*, 3.9.8 and 3.11.8–9.

129. Locke, "Some of the Consequences," 172–73.

130. Fool's gold could now be revealed as such in the laboratories that both Locke and Newton operated. William R. Newman, *Atoms and Alchemy: Chymistry and the Experimental Origins of the Scientific Revolution* (Chicago: University of Chicago Press, 2006); Peter R. Anstey, *John Locke and Natural Philosophy* (Oxford: Oxford University Press, 2011), 176–77.

131. In speaking of "the mint of knowledge," Bacon explained that "words are the tokens current and accepted for conceits, as moneys are for values, and . . . it is fit men be not ignorant that moneys may be of another kind than gold and silver." Francis Bacon, "The Advancement of Learning," in *The Oxford Francis Bacon*, vol. 4, ed. Michael Kiernan (Oxford: Oxford University Press, 2000), 91. Hobbes meanwhile compared linguistic reasoning to the use of counters on counting tables (whose value derived from their position) and contrasted these with money (whose

value was affixed by authority): "For words are wise men's counters, they do but reckon by them: but they are the money of fools, that value them by the authority of an Aristotle, a Cicero, or a Thomas, or any other doctor whatsoever, if but a man." Thomas Hobbes, *Leviathan* (Cambridge: Cambridge University Press, 1991), ch. 4, section 13.

132. Sextus Empiricus's aphorism ran as follows: "In a state where a certain kind of money is locally current, whoever employs it may conduct every kind of business there without let or hindrance, while the man who does not accept this, but mints some new variety and wishes to use it as money, is a fool; so also in life, he who is unwilling to follow the kind of speech which is customarily employed, as he would use the current money, but coins a new language for himself, is not far from being a mad man." Sextus Empiricus, *Against the Mathematicians*, book 1, ch. x. As quoted in Pufendorf, *De Jure Naturae et Gentium Libri Octo*, 4.1.6, 466. Hannah Dawson also partially quotes the line from Basil Kennet's translation but fails to mention that Pufendorf is here quoting Sextus Empiricus. Dawson, *Locke, Language and Early-Modern Philosophy*, 157.

133. The second part of Pufendorf's argument is remarkably reminiscent of Wittgenstein's private-language argument.

134. Locke, *Essay Concerning Human Understanding*, 3.10.2.

135. John Locke, *Some Considerations of the Consequences of the Lowering of Interest and Raising the Value of Money. In a Letter to a Member of Parliament* (London: A. & J. Churchill, 1692); reprinted as John Locke, "Some Considerations," *Locke on Money*, 1:203–342.

136. Locke, "Some Considerations," 213.

137. Locke, "Some Considerations," 214.

138. Locke, "Further Considerations," 416.

139. All creditors, Locke explained, would be "defrauded" by 20 percent of their loans. This was particularly tragic for those who had entrusted their savings to the postrevolutionary Whig state, for example by investing in the Million Lottery. Locke, "Further Considerations," 417. That recoinage at the old rate would at the same time violate the property of *debtors* who had contracted their debt in clipped coins was initially not mentioned by Locke, though he added a minor concession in later printings. Locke, "Further Considerations," 477.

140. Feavearyear, *The Pound Sterling*, 124.

141. Locke's pamphlet was "mightyly Commended at Courtt." Martha Lockhart to Locke, January 4, 1696. Cited in Kelly, "General Introduction," 37.

142. Newton was promoted from Warden to Master of the Mint in 1700, a post he held until the end of his life in 1727. For an account of the importance of capital punishment in defending the post-Recoinage monetary system, see Carl Wennerlind, *Casualties of Credit: The English Financial Revolution, 1620–1720* (Cambridge, MA: Harvard University Press, 2011), 123–57. On Newton's initially reluctant but then meticulously earnest and devastatingly effective pursuit of counterfeiters, see Levenson, *Newton and the Counterfeiter*, 107–44.

143. Carey, "Locke's Philosophy of Money," 57n3.

144. Reading Locke on coinage, Schumpeter remarked that a "sorry picture unfolds itself before the eyes." Joseph A. Schumpeter, *History of Economic Analysis*, ed. Elizabeth Boody Schumpeter (New York: Oxford University Press, 1954), 117.

Sargent and Velde declare Locke's monetary advice an "embarrassment" to the discipline of economics. Sargent and Velde, *The Big Problem of Small Change*, 288.

145. The standard view, with deep roots in British Whig historiography, has by contrast long been that his recommendations were straightforwardly "adopted as government policy." J. R. Milton, "Locke's Life and Times," in Vere Chappell, ed., *The Cambridge Companion to Locke* (Cambridge: Cambridge University Press, 1994), 5–25, at 20–21.

146. Jones, *War and Economy*, 245.

147. As quoted in Jones, *War and Economy*, 246.

148. Childs, *Nine Years' War*, 306.

149. Li, *Great Recoinage*, 67.

150. Laslett, "John Locke, the Great Recoinage and the Board of Trade," 370–402.

151. Locke, "Further Considerations," 415. Locke employed an almost identical phrasing in Locke, "Propositions sent to the Lord Justices," 375.

152. Locke, "Some Considerations," 213, 231, 336; Locke, "Further Considerations," 418, 463–67; Locke [anon.], "Short Observations on a Printed Paper," 357; as well as John Locke, "A Paper given to Sir William Trumbull which was written at his request, September 1695," in *Locke on Money*, 2:365–73, at 368; and Locke, "Propositions sent to the Lord Justices," 376–77.

153. Locke, "Some Considerations," 213. The circulation of clipped coins had to be stopped, Locke wrote, "or else we are undon." He added, "Its continuance will unevitably ruin the nation." Locke to Cornelius Lyde, April 24, 1696, in Locke, *Correspondence*, vol. 5, letter no. 2072, 616.

154. John Dunn, "Trust," in *The History of Political Theory and Other Essays* (Cambridge: Cambridge University Press, 1995), 91–99; John Dunn, *Locke: A Very Short Introduction* (Oxford: Oxford University Press, 2003), 64. On the broader significance of trust, see also John Dunn, "Toleration, Trust and the Travails of Living Together Globally," in Laszlo Kontler and Mark Somos, eds., *Trust and Happiness in the History of European Political Thought* (Leiden: Brill, 2017), 19–32, at 30–32.

155. "That Men should keep the Compacts, is certainly a great and undeniable Rule of Morality." Locke, *Essay Concerning Human Understanding*, 1.3.5.

156. Locke, *Second Treatise*, par. 128.

157. Thomas Hobbes, *De Cive: The Latin Version*, ed. Howard Warrender (Oxford: Clarendon Press, 1983), 8.3, 161: "pactum autem nisi fide habita nullum est."

158. John Locke, *Essays on the Law of Nature: The Latin Text with a Translation, Introduction and Notes*, ed. Wolfgang von Leyden (Oxford: Clarendon Press, 1954), 118–19; Locke, *Letter Concerning Toleration*, 92. Locke thus reinterpreted the concept of the *vinculum* of the Church in terms of civic trust. See Teresa Bejan, *Mere Civility: Disagreement and the Limits of Toleration* (Cambridge, MA: Harvard University Press, 2017), 112–43; Teresa Bejan, "John Locke on Toleration, (In)civility, and the Quest for Concord," *History of Political Thought* 37, no. 3 (2016): 556–87. This meant in turn that the untrustworthy had to be excluded from religious toleration. In particular, according to Locke, atheists posed a profound danger. See Locke, *Letter Concerning Toleration*, 52–53.

159. Locke, *Letter Concerning Toleration*, 12.

160. Locke, "Some Considerations," 329.

161. Locke, "Further Considerations," 415.

162. Locke, "Some Considerations," 312.

163. Crawford Brough Macpherson, *The Political Theory of Possessive Individualism: Hobbes to Locke* (Oxford: Oxford University Press, 1964), 206.

164. Desan, *Making Money*, 345, 73. Felix Martin has similarly credited—or rather, charged—Locke with having effected "a complete reversal of perspective" that single-handedly displaced more than a millennium of monetary wisdom. Felix Martin, *Money: The Unauthorised Biography* (London: Bodley Head, 2014), 129–30. For a different but related account of the impact of Locke's thinking on property, see Andrew Sartori, *Liberalism in Empire: An Alternative History* (Berkeley: University of California Press, 2014), 7–11.

165. For a reading of Locke's grappling with money as a "social form" that was not itself the product of political authority, see Andrew Sartori, "Silver and the Social in Locke's Monetary Thought," *Journal of Modern History* 93, no. 3 (September 2021): 501–32.

166. If, as Duncan Bell has pointed out, Locke's political thought was largely met with "omission, disavowal, and scorn" before the twentieth century, Locke's political theory of money was by contrast influentially received and widely praised. Bell, "What Is Liberalism?," 697.

167. Macaulay, *History of England*, 2:547.

168. On the emergence of public debt as the crucible of eighteenth-century political thought, see Michael Sonenscher, *Before the Deluge: Public Debt, Inequality, and the Intellectual Origins of the French Revolution* (Princeton, NJ: Princeton University Press, 2007), 1–21.

169. This ambivalence toward credit is well captured by his attitude toward the Bank of England. When the Bank was founded in 1694, Locke's response betrayed a characteristic double play. While he became one of its founding investors in June 1694 by investing £500, he refused to lend the Bank his voice. *Bank of England Archive*, 10A20/1.

170. James Hodges to Locke, February 8, 1697, in Locke, *Correspondence*, vol. 5, letter 2194.

171. Locke, "Further Considerations," 403–4.

172. Adam Smith, "Early Draft of the Wealth of Nations," in *Lectures on Jurisprudence*, ed. R. L. Meek, D. D. Raphael, and P. G. Stein (Oxford: Oxford University Press, 1978), 502 [LJ(B)242], 101 [LJ(A)81]; Adam Smith, *An Inquiry into the Nature and Causes of the Wealth of Nations*, ed. R. H. Campbell and A. S. Skinner (Oxford: Oxford University Press, 1976), 43–44 [I.iv.11] and 929–32 [V.iii.59–64].

173. Smith, "Early Draft of the Wealth of Nations," 370 [LJ(A)vi, 106].

Chapter 3. The Monetary Social Contract

1. Johann Wolfgang von Goethe to Thomas Carlyle, July 20, 1827, in Johann Wolfgang von Goethe, *Goethes Briefe. Band 4: Briefe der Jahre 1821–1832*, ed. Karl Robert Mandelkow (Hamburg: Christian Wegner, 1962), 236.

2. Edmund Burke to French Laurence, March 1, 1797, in Edmund Burke, *The Correspondence of Edmund Burke, vol. 9, May 1796–July 1797*, ed. R. B. McDowell (Cambridge and Chicago: Cambridge University Press and University of Chicago Press, 1970), 264.

3. F. P. Lock, *Edmund Burke, Volume II, 1784–1797* (Oxford: Clarendon Press, 2006), 577.

4. Richard Bourke, *Empire and Revolution: The Political Life of Edmund Burke* (Princeton, NJ: Princeton University Press, 2015), 908.

5. *The Morning Chronicle* (London), February 27, 1797, 1.

6. Since Sir Isaac Newton (then Master of the Mint) fixed in 1717 the price of gold to silver at a slightly overvalued rate of £4.25 per ounce of silver, Britain had slid from an official bimetallic standard toward a de facto reliance on gold.

7. Barry Eichengreen and Marc Flandreau, eds., *The Gold Standard in Theory and History* (London: Routledge, 1997).

8. Eckart Förster, *The Twenty-Five Years of Philosophy: A Systematic Reconstruction*, trans. Brady Bowman (Cambridge, MA: Harvard University Press, 2012).

9. Throughout this chapter I have benefited from conversations with Isaac Nakhimovsky and in particular his excellent reconstruction of Fichte's political thought, on which I build here by highlighting its monetary underpinnings and implications. See in particular Isaac Nakhimovsky, *The Closed Commercial State: Perpetual Peace and Commercial Society from Rousseau to Fichte* (Princeton, NJ: Princeton University Press, 2011) and Isaac Nakhimovsky, Béla Kapossy, and Richard Whatmore, "Introduction," in Isaac Nakhimovsky, Béla Kapossy, and Richard Whatmore, eds., *Commerce and Perpetual Peace in Enlightenment Thought* (Cambridge: Cambridge University Press, 2017), 1–19.

10. Michael Sonenscher, *Before the Deluge: Public Debt, Inequality, and the Intellectual Origins of the French Revolution* (Princeton, NJ: Princeton University Press, 2007); Michael Sonenscher, "The Nation's Debt and the Birth of the Modern Republic," *History of Political Thought* 18, nos. 1–2 (Spring and Summer 1997): 64–103 and 267–325.

11. Nathan Sussman and Yishay Yafeh, "Institutional Reforms, Financial Development and Sovereign Debt: Britain 1690–1790," *Journal of Economic History* 66, no. 4 (December 2006): 906–35.

12. Carl Wennerlind, *Casualties of Credit: The English Financial Revolution, 1620–1720* (Cambridge, MA: Harvard University Press, 2011), 197–234.

13. Jean-Jacques Rousseau, "Considerations on the Government of Poland," in *The Social Contract and Other Later Political Writings* (Cambridge: Cambridge University Press, 1997), 225.

14. David Hume, "Essay of Public Credit [1752]," in *Political Essays*, ed. Knud Haakonssen (Cambridge: Cambridge University Press, 1994), 166–79. Where Pocock read Hume's antipathy toward public credit as born out of a concern for the self-generating instability of commercial society, Hont has argued that Hume's ambivalence derived neither from within commercial society nor from the fictional qualities of credit but merely from its malicious use in pursuit of international power politics. J.G.A. Pocock, "Hume and the American Revolution: The Dying Thoughts of a North Briton," in *Virtue, Commerce and History: Essays on Political Thought and History, Chiefly in the Eighteenth Century* (Cambridge: Cambridge University Press, 1985), 125–41; Istvan Hont, "The Rhapsody of Public Debt: David Hume and Voluntary State Bankruptcy," in *Jealousy of Trade* (Cambridge, MA: Harvard University Press, 2005), 325–53. See also Carl Wennerlind and Margaret Schabas, *A Philosopher's Economist:*

Hume and the Rise of Capitalism (Chicago: University of Chicago Press, 2020), 196–204.

15. For a reading of Burke's aesthetic theory of the sublime in relation to the contemporary discourses of debt, see Peter De Bolla, "The Discourse of Debt," in *The Sublime: A Reader in British Eighteenth-Century Aesthetic Theory* (Cambridge: Cambridge University Press, 1996), 103–40.

16. J.G.A. Pocock, *Virtue, Commerce and History: Essays on Political Thought and History, Chiefly in the Eighteenth Century* (Cambridge: Cambridge University Press, 1985), 108, as well as 113.

17. Pocock, *Virtue, Commerce and History*, 98.

18. See also Reinhart Koselleck, "Modernity and the Planes of Historicity," *Economy and Society* 10, no. 2 (1981): 166–83, at 170; Martijn Konings, *Capital and Time: For a New Critique of Neoliberal Reason* (Stanford, CA: Stanford University Press, 2018), 71–72.

19. Richard Tuck, *The Sleeping Sovereign: The Invention of Modern Democracy* (Cambridge: Cambridge University Press, 2016), 79–80, 258, 263. On the craze for constitutions, see Linda Colley, *The Gun, the Ship, and the Pen: Warfare, Constitutions, and the Making of the Modern World* (New York: Liveright, 2021).

20. For an earlier if less systematic argument along these lines, see Louis-Sébastien Mercier (known by contemporaries for his obsessive devotion to Rousseau as "le singe de Jean-Jacques"), who had argued that only Rousseau's "severe morality" had prevented him from developing a monetary theory and a more optimistic assessment of the possibilities of public credit. Louis-Sébastien Mercier, *De Jean-Jacques Rousseau, considéré comme l'un des premiers auteurs de la révolution* (Paris: Buisson, 1791), 79–81. Further discussed in Michael Sonenscher, *Sans-Culottes: An Eighteenth-Century Emblem in the French Revolution* (Princeton, NJ: Princeton University Press, 2008), 110–33, at 129; as well as Evelyn L. Forget, *The Social Economics of Jean-Baptiste Say: Markets and Virtue* (London: Routledge, 1999), 188.

21. Edmund Burke, "Reflections on the Revolution in France," in *The Writings and Speeches of Edmund Burke*, vol. 8, *The French Revolution, 1790–1794*, ed. L. G. Mitchell and William B. Todd (Oxford: Clarendon Press, 1989). For an important revisionist account of the assignats, see Rebecca L. Spang, *Stuff and Money in the Time of the French Revolution* (Cambridge, MA: Harvard University Press, 2015).

22. J.G.A. Pocock, "Introduction," in Edmund Burke, *Reflections on the Revolution in France*, ed. J.G.A. Pocock (Indianapolis: Hackett, 1987), xxxiv. See also Sunil M. Agnani, *Hating Empire Properly: The Two Indies and the Limits of Enlightenment Anticolonialism* (New York: Fordham University Press, 2013).

23. Pocock, "Introduction," xxii. See also Karl Polanyi, *The Great Transformation: The Political and Economic Origins of Our Time*, 2nd ed., with a new introduction by Fred Block and a foreword by Joseph E. Stiglitz (Boston: Beacon, 2001), 235.

24. Pocock, "Introduction," xxxiii.

25. Edmund Burke to Florimond-Claude, Comte de Mercy-Argenteau, c. August 6, 1793. Burke, *Correspondence*, 389.

26. As Rebecca Spang has shown, the French delegates would have been surprised by this assessment. They had precisely been at pains to avoid giving this impression and the proposal to issue assignats eventually won their approval because it promised

to raise funds while protecting the sanctity of private property. Spang, *Stuff and Money*, 58, 64, 73.

27. Burke to Florimond-Claude, Comte de Mercy-Argenteau, c. August 6, 1793. Burke, *Correspondence*, 388. As Burke quipped in drawing an analogy between country and coin, "I am not willing to receive [this new-coined France] in currency in place of the old Louis d'or." Edmund Burke, "Fourth Letter on a Regicide Peace [1795]," in *The Writings and Speeches of Edmund Burke*, vol. 9, *The Revolutionary War, 1794–1797*, ed. R. B. McDowell and William B. Todd (Oxford: Clarendon Press, 1991), 51.

28. Burke, "First Letter on a Regicide Peace [1796]," in *The Writings and Speeches of Edmund Burke*, vol. 9, *The Revolutionary War, 1794–1797*, ed. R. B. McDowell and William B. Todd (Oxford: Clarendon Press, 1991), 241. David Bromwich has described the letter as the "most condensed" to have ever flowed from Burke's pen. David Bromwich, "Burke on Anti-Revolutionary War, 1795–1797," paper presented at the CHESS Workshop, Yale University, January 23, 2015, 18.

29. Burke, "Reflections on the Revolution in France," 238, as well as 204.

30. Burke, "Reflections on the Revolution in France," 238.

31. Burke, "Reflections on the Revolution in France," 203.

32. Burke, "First Letter on a Regicide Peace [1796]," 230.

33. See also Gregory M. Collins, *Commerce and Manners in Edmund Burke's Political Economy* (Cambridge: Cambridge University Press, 2020), 428–29.

34. Burke, "Reflections on the Revolution in France," 203–4.

35. Burke, "Reflections on the Revolution in France," 89–90. See also Patrick Brantlinger, *Fictions of State: Culture and Credit in Britain, 1694–1994* (Ithaca, NY: Cornell University Press, 1996), 105.

36. Burke to Florimond-Claude, Comte de Mercy-Argenteau, c. August 6, 1793. Burke, *Correspondence*, 389.

37. Burke, "Reflections on the Revolution in France," 166.

38. Burke, "Reflections on the Revolution in France," 167.

39. Immanuel Kant, *Metaphysische Anfangsgründe der Rechtslehre* (Königsberg: Friedrich Nicolovius, 1797).

40. Immanuel Kant, *Metaphysik der Sitten*, vol. 12, Werkausgabe: Schriften zur Anthropologie, Geschichtsphilosophie, Politik und Pädagogik (Frankfurt am Main: Suhrkamp, 2000), 400–404; Immanuel Kant, *Metaphysics of Morals* (Cambridge: Cambridge University Press, 1991), 104–6.

41. Kant, *Metaphysik der Sitten*, 401; Kant, *Metaphysics of Morals*, 104. The table of rights, listed in §31, presented a "dogmatic division of all rights acquirable through contracts."

42. Kant, *Metaphysik der Sitten*, 401; Kant, *Metaphysics of Morals*, 104.

43. Kant, *Metaphysik der Sitten*, 401; Kant, *Metaphysics of Morals*, 104.

44. Kant, *Metaphysik der Sitten*, 401; Kant, *Metaphysics of Morals*, 104.

45. Christian Garve's German translation of the *Wealth of Nations* based on the fourth English edition had appeared in two volumes in 1794 as Adam Smith, *Untersuchungen über die Natur und die Ursachen des Nationalreichtums*, trans. Christian Garve (Breslau: Wilhelm Gottlieb Korn, 1794). On the "tremendous synergy" (Hont) between Smith's writings and Kant's work of the 1790s, see Istvan Hont, "Adam Smith's History of Laws and Government as Political Theory," in Richard Bourke,

Raymond Geuss, and John Dunn, eds., *Political Judgement: Essays for John Dunn* (Cambridge: Cambridge University Press, 2009), 169.

46. Kant, *Metaphysik der Sitten*, 402; Kant, *Metaphysics of Morals*, 106.

47. Adam Smith, *An Inquiry into the Nature and Causes of the Wealth of Nations*, ed. R. H. Campbell and A. S. Skinner, 2 vols., Glasgow Edition of the Works and Correspondence (Oxford: Clarendon Press, 1976), book 1, ch. iv, 11, 44. Scholars continue to debate Smith's ambivalent attitude toward paper money. In the *Contribution to the Critique of Political Economy* (1859), Marx judged Smith's views on "credit money" (*Kreditgeld*) to be "original and profound." Karl Marx, *Zur Kritik der politischen Ökonomie* [1859], *Marx-Engels Gesamtausgabe* (MEGA²) II.2, 95–245, at 228; Marx, *A Contribution to the Critique of Political Economy* [1859], in *Marx and Engels Collected Works* (MECW), vol. 29 (London: Lawrence & Wishart, 1987), 257–417, at 399. Smith's (already somewhat hesitant) faith in paper notes appears, however, to have been seriously undermined by the 1772 Scottish banking crisis, which delayed publication of *The Wealth of Nations* by several years and led him to rewrite large sections on money. While in his Glasgow lectures on jurisprudence of the 1760s Smith had praised the contribution of banks and paper credit in expanding commerce (LJ [B], 246–50), in *The Wealth of Nations* (1776) after the spectacular failure of the Ayr Bank in 1772 Smith described paper money more ambivalently as a useful "waggonway through the air" that rested, however, "upon Daedalian wings" (WN II.ii.86) On the delay in publication due to the Scottish banking crisis, see Ian Simpson Ross, *The Life of Adam Smith* (Oxford: Oxford University Press, 1995), 260. Istvan Hont, in particular, has stressed Smith's advocacy of paper money. Istvan Hont, *Jealousy of Trade: International Competition and the Nation-State in Historical Perspective* (Cambridge, MA: Harvard University Press, 2005), 306. See also Sydney Checkland, "Adam Smith and the Bankers," in Andrew Skinner and Thomas Wilson, eds., *Essays on Adam Smith* (Oxford: Clarendon Press, 1975); James Gherity, "The Evolution of Adam Smith's Theory of Banking," *History of Political Economy* 26, no. 3 (1994), 423–41; and Carl C. Wennerlind, "The Humean Paternity to Adam Smith's Theory of Money," *History of Economic Ideas* 8, no. 1 (2000): 77–97.

48. Kant, *Metaphysik der Sitten*, 401–2; Kant, *Metaphysics of Morals*, 104–5.

49. Kant, *Metaphysik der Sitten*, 401–2; Kant, *Metaphysics of Morals*, 104–5.

50. It was arguably this insistence on form that explains why Kant included the money excursus right after the metaphysical table of contracts.

51. Kant, *Metaphysik der Sitten*, 402; Kant, *Metaphysics of Morals*, 106.

52. Kant, *Metaphysik der Sitten*, 400; Kant, *Metaphysics of Morals*, 104.

53. Kant, *Metaphysik der Sitten*, 401–2; Kant, *Metaphysics of Morals*, 104–5.

54. Immanuel Kant, *Zum Ewigen Frieden*, vol. 11, Werkausgabe: Schriften zur Anthropologie, Geschichtsphilosophie, Politik und Pädagogik (Frankfurt am Main: Suhrkamp, 2000), 368; Immanuel Kant, "Toward Perpetual Peace," in *"Toward Perpetual Peace" and Other Writings on Politics, Peace, and History*, ed. Pauline Kleingeld (New Haven, CT: Yale University Press, 2006), 92. See Sankar Muthu, "Conquest, Commerce, and Cosmopolitanism in Enlightenment Political Thought," in Sankar Muthu, ed., *Empire and Modern Political Thought* (Cambridge: Cambridge University Press, 2012), 222.

55. On the broader eighteenth-century context and responses to Hume's jealousy of trade argument, see Hont, *Jealousy of Trade*.

56. Kant, *Zum Ewigen Frieden*, 345; Kant, "Toward Perpetual Peace," 69.

57. Kant, *Zum Ewigen Frieden*, 345; Kant, "Toward Perpetual Peace," 69. For a brief discussion, see Peter Niesen, "Restorative Justice in International and Cosmopolitan Law," in Katrin Flikschuh and Lea Ypi, eds., *Kant and Colonialism: Historical and Critical Perspectives* (Oxford: Oxford University Press, 2014), 185.

58. Kant, *Zum Ewigen Frieden*, 345; Kant, "Toward Perpetual Peace," 69.

59. Kant, *Zum Ewigen Frieden*, 345; Kant, "Toward Perpetual Peace," 69. Note at the same time that Kant had also conceded that civic protection in a modern commercial republic may itself require some type of economic safety in the form of economic assistance for hardship as well as possible restrictions on certain kinds of trade. Immanuel Kant, "On the Common Saying: This May Be True in Theory, but It Does Not Hold in Practice [1793]," in *Political Writings*, ed. H. Reiss (Cambridge: Cambridge University Press, 1970), 80n. On this, and its link to Fichte, see Hont, "Adam Smith's History," 170.

60. Christine Desan, *Making Money: Coin, Currency, and the Coming of Capitalism* (Oxford: Oxford University Press, 2015), 360–403.

61. What made the events of 1797 moreover distinct for a European audience was that unlike in previous experiments with paper money, such as during the American War of Independence, this time it was the imperial metropole itself that had suspended gold. For an initial overview of American revolutionary money, see the classic chapter in John Kenneth Galbraith, *Money: Whence It Came, Where It Went* (Boston: Houghton Mifflin, 1975), 67–77; for a discussion in light of the recent revisionist historiography of how Americans "made" money, see Christine Desan, "From Blood to Profit: Making Money in the Practice and Imagery of Early America," *Journal of Policy History* 20, no. 1 (2008): 26–46; as well as Andrew Edwards, "The American Revolution and Christine Desan's New History of Money," *Law and Social Inquiry* 43, no. 1 (Winter 2017): 252–78; for the postrevolutionary debate over paper money, see Michael J. Klarman, *The Framers' Coup: The Making of the United States Constitution* (Oxford: Oxford University Press, 2016), 84–85, 162, 375; on American monetary debates more broadly, see Jeffrey Sklansky, *Sovereign of the Market: The Money Question in Early America* (Chicago: University of Chicago Press, 2017).

62. Polanyi interestingly attributed the initial confusion of the weekend to the mistaken cognitive separation of markets from politics characteristic of market society. Polanyi, *The Great Transformation*, 204.

63. Apart from great care not to overissue new notes, the other main reason prices did not move much initially was because the government quickly moved to impose new taxes, such as the first income tax in 1799. On the history of taxation since 1799, see Martin Daunton, *Trusting Leviathan: The Politics of Taxation in Britain, 1799–1914* (Cambridge: Cambridge University Press, 2007).

64. For John Law's paper-money experiment, see James Buchan, *John Law: A Scottish Adventurer of the Eighteenth Century* (London: MacLehose, 2018); as well as Arnaud Orain, *La politique du merveilleux: Une autre histoire du Système de Law (1695–1795)* (Paris: Fayard, 2018).

65. Ian Haywood, *Romanticism and Caricature* (Cambridge: Cambridge University Press, 2013).

66. On the consequent violence, see Wennerlind, *Casualties of Credit*, 123–60. Forgery could equally be used as a tool of war. At least since 1793 William Pitt had

encouraged French royalist émigrés in England to forge assignats for export to France, a form of economic warfare already well tried during the American War of Independence.

67. Kant's famous essay on truth and lying appeared in the *Berlinische Blätter* in September 1797 and was immediately the focus of an intense debate around questions of "truth and truthfulness." Immanuel Kant, "Über ein vermeintes Recht aus Menschenliebe zu lügen," *Berlinische Blätter*, no. 1 (1797); Anon., "Über Wahrheit und Wahrhaftigkeit [Antwort auf Kant]," *Berlinische Blätter*, no. 2 (1797). This was moreover not only the golden age of monetary counterfeit and caricature but also of literary forgeries.

68. See Esther Chadwick, "Bewick's 'Little Whimsies': Printmaking, Paper Money and Currency Radicalism in Early Nineteenth-Century Britain," *Art History* 41, no. 1 (February 2018): 42–71; as well as Haywood, *Romanticism and Caricature*, 41.

69. Edmund Burke, "Extracts from Mr. Burke's Table-Talk at Crewe Hall, written down by Mrs. Crewe," *Miscellanies of the Philobiblon Society* 7 (1862–63): 4.

70. Burke, "Extracts," 4.

71. Burke to George Canning, March 1, 1797. Burke, *Correspondence*, vol. 9, 268. See also Burke, *Correspondence*, vol. 9, 268n3.

72. Burke to George Canning, 1 March 1797. Burke, *Correspondence*, vol. 9, 269.

73. Burke to George Canning, 1 March 1797. Burke, *Correspondence*, vol. 9, 269.

74. In this sense Burke was closer to Richard Price's observation that money owed "its currency to opinion" than he could admit in the *Reflections*. Richard Price, "Observations on the Nature of Civil Liberty, the Principles of Government, and the Justice and Policy of the War with America [1776]," in *Political Writings*, ed. D. O. Thomas (Cambridge: Cambridge University Press, 1991), 58.

75. See also Uday S. Mehta, "Edmund Burke on Empire, Self-Understanding, and Sympathy," in Sankar Muthu, ed., *Empire and Modern Political Thought* (Cambridge: Cambridge University Press, 2012), 174n39.

76. "Publick credit, that great but ambiguous principle, . . . had it's [sic] origin, and was cradled, I may say, in bankruptcy and beggary." Burke, "First Letter on a Regicide Peace [1796]," 230.

77. Again, for a corrective to Burke's assessment of the French delegates' intentions, see Spang, *Stuff and Money*, 57–96.

78. Burke to George Canning, 1 March 1797. Burke, *Correspondence*, vol. 9, 269.

79. Burke to French Laurence, 5 March 1797. Burke, *Correspondence*, vol. 9, 271.

80. The Letter appeared only on November 13, 1797, after Burke's death. Lock, *Burke, Vol. II*, 561. See Bromwich, "Burke on Anti-Revolutionary War."

81. Burke, "Third Letter on a Regicide Peace [1797]," in *The Writings and Speeches of Edmund Burke*, vol. 9, *The Revolutionary War, 1794-1797*, ed. R. B. McDowell and William B. Todd (Oxford: Clarendon Press, 1991), 346–47.

82. Burke, "Third Letter on a Regicide Peace [1797]," 346–47.

83. Burke to William Windham, 30 March 1797. Burke, *Correspondence*, vol. 9, 299; as well as 271–72.

84. Lock, *Burke, Vol. II*, 570.

85. Over the next two decades, from 1797 until 1819, prices rose overall by around 80 percent, an annualized rate of less than 4 percent. This was enough to shake contemporaries, especially since the annual fluctuations were often far larger. But in light

of the enormous military struggle against the French, it is hard not to see it as a relatively modest annualized rate. François Crouzet, "Politics and Banking in Revolutionary and Napoleonic France," in Richard Sylla, Richard Tilly, and Gabriel Tortella, eds., *The State, the Financial System and Economic Modernization* (Cambridge: Cambridge University Press, 1999), 47.

86. The most important English contribution to the debate as it unfolded in London was undoubtedly Henry Thornton's *An Enquiry into the Nature and Effects of the Paper Credit of Great Britain* (London: M. P., 1802), republished as Henry Thornton, *An Enquiry into the Nature and Effects of the Paper Credit of Great Britain*, ed. and with an introduction by F. A. Hayek (London: George Allen & Unwin, 1939). See also Francis Horner, "Review of Henry Thornton: 'Inquiry into the Nature and Effects of the Paper Credit of Great Britain,'" *Edinburgh Review* (October 1802), Art. XXV, 172–201.

87. Besides the *Neue Berlinische Monatsschrift* some of the other main German-speaking journals covering the monetary events in England and France were *Minerva*, *Der neue Teutsche Merkur, London und Paris*, as well as Friedrich Gentz's *Historisches Journal* (1799–1800). Indeed, *London und Paris* was the only contemporary journal anywhere in Europe, including Britain, to provide running commentary based on James Gillray's caricatures covering the events. See Christiane Banerji and Diana Donald, *Gillray Observed: The Earliest Account of His Caricatures in "London und Paris"* (Cambridge: Cambridge University Press, 2009).

88. Johann Gottlieb Fichte, *Der Geschloßne Handelsstaat: Ein Philosophischer Entwurf als Anlage zur Rechtslehre, und Probe einer künftig zu liefernden Politik* (Tübingen: J. G. Cotta, 1800). Reprinted as Johann Gottlieb Fichte, "*Der Geschloßne Handelsstaat*," in *Gesamtausgabe der Bayerischen Akademie der Wissenschaften*, ed. Hans Gliwitzky and Reinhart Lauth, I.7 (Stuttgart-Bad Cannstatt: Frommann, 1988), 37–141. The text has been translated as Johann Gottlieb Fichte, *The Closed Commercial State*, trans. Anthony Curtis Adler (Albany: SUNY Press, 2012). When citing from the *Commercial State* below, I first give page numbers to the *Gesamtausgabe* and then to the English translation. Unless otherwise noted I rely on Adler's translation, though I have adapted it where necessary and also consulted Nakhimovsky's rendering where available.

89. Nakhimovsky, *Closed Commercial State*; as well as the brief comment emphasizing Kant's influence in Hont, "Adam Smith's History," 170. See also Andreas Verzar, *Das autonome Subjekt und der Vernunftstaat: Eine systematisch-historische Untersuchung zu Fichtes "Geschlossenem Handelsstaat" von 1800* (Bonn: Bouvier, 1979).

90. See Nakhimovsky, *Closed Commercial State*, 105, 124. Nakhimovsky rightly notes that Fichte's proposal rested in particular on his "radical vision of the transformative potential of a paper-money system." As Fichte himself clarified, it would nonetheless be a mistake to read his proposal as simply derived from a certain theory of money; the causality ran in both directions. Fichte, *Closed Commercial State*, 107; Fichte, *Geschloßne Handelsstaat*, 86.

91. Nakhimovsky, *Closed Commercial State*, 113–14.

92. Prussian financial backwardness could appear from this perspective as an unexpected advantage. Nakhimovsky, *Closed Commercial State*, 105, 119, 124; see also Sonenscher, *Before the Deluge*, 251. For the link between Prussia and Mirabeau

detailed by Nakhimovsky, see François Honoré-Gabriel de Riquetti, Count de Mirabeau, *Lettre remise a Frederic-Guillaume II* (Berlin, 1787), 275; Mirabeau to Calonne, November 7, 1786, and December 16, 1786, in Mirabeau, *Histoire secrète de la cour de Berlin* (London: Paterson, 1789), vol. 2, 19–20 (letter 44) and 165–67 (letter 56).

93. Fichte, *Geschloßne Handelsstaat*, 125–26; Fichte, *Closed Commercial State*, 180–81. Fichte's argument was thus a simultaneous embrace and radicalization of the monetary ideas behind the British suspension of gold, embracing fiat money but pointing critically toward the unique position of the British Empire (soon cut off from much European trade because of Napoleon's blockade).

94. Fichte to Cotta, August 16, 1800, in Johann Gottlieb Fichte, *Gesamtausgabe der Bayerischen Akademie der Wissenschaften* III.4 (Stuttgart-Bad Cannstatt: Frommann, 1973), 285–26. Also quoted in Nakhimovsky, *Closed Commercial State*, 103.

95. Fichte to Friedrich Schlegel, August 16, 1800, in Fichte, *Gesamtausgabe der Bayerischen Akademie der Wissenschaften* III.4, 284.

96. Johann Gottlieb Fichte, "Grundlage des Naturrechts nach Principien der Wissenschaftslehre (1796)," in *Gesamtausgabe der Bayerischen Akademie der Wissenschaften* I.3 (Stuttgart-Bad Cannstatt: Frommann, 1962), 313–460; Johann Gottlieb Fichte, *Foundations of Natural Right: According to the Principles of the Wissenschaftslehre*, ed. Frederick Neuhouser, trans. Michael Baur (Cambridge: Cambridge University Press, 2000), 1–164. See also Nakhimovsky, *Closed Commercial State*, 38–41, as well as Ulrich Thiele, *Distributive Gerechtigkeit und demokratischer Staat: Fichtes Rechtslehre von 1796 zwischen vorkantischem und kantischem Naturrecht* (Berlin: Duncker & Humblot, 2002).

97. Johann Gottlieb Fichte, "Grundlage des Naturrechts nach Principien der Wissenschaftslehre, Zweiter Theil oder Angewandtes Naturrecht (1797)," in *Gesamtausgabe der Bayerischen Akademie der Wissenschaften* I.4 (Stuttgart-Bad Cannstatt: Frommann, 1970), 5–165; Fichte, *Foundations of Natural Right*, 165–265.

98. Fichte, "Angewandtes Naturrecht," 16; Fichte, *Foundations of Natural Right*, 178. Translation adapted.

99. Fichte, "Angewandtes Naturrecht," 42; Fichte, *Foundations of Natural Right*, 208.

100. Fichte, "Angewandtes Naturrecht," 43; Fichte, *Foundations of Natural Right*, 209.

101. Johann Gottlieb Fichte, "Über StaatsWirthschaft," in *Gesamtausgabe der Bayerischen Akademie der Wissenschaften* II.6 (Stuttgart-Bad Cannstatt: Frommann, 1962), 4–9. On the dating, see also Reinhard Lauth and Hans Gliwitzky, "Vorwort," in *Gesamtausgabe der Bayerischen Akademie der Wissenschaften* II.6 (Stuttgart-Bad Cannstatt: Frommann, 1983), 3.

102. Fichte, "Über StaatsWirthschaft," 6.

103. Fichte, "Über StaatsWirthschaft," 8.

104. Fichte, "Über StaatsWirthschaft," 7.

105. Fichte, "Über StaatsWirthschaft," 9.

106. Fichte, "Angewandtes Naturrecht," 43; Fichte, *Foundations of Natural Right*, 209.

107. As readers of Fichte have pointed out, this echoed similar proposals put forward by Babeuf in 1795 before the Conspiracy of the Equals. David James, *Fichte's*

Social and Political Philosophy: Property and Virtue (Cambridge: Cambridge University Press, 2011), 79; R. B. Rose, *Gracchus Babeuf: The First Revolutionary Communist* (Stanford, CA: Stanford University Press, 1978), 50. Already Marianne Weber had linked Fichte's economic proposals to Babeuf's. Marianne Weber, *Fichtes Sozialismus und sein Verhältnis zur Marx'schen Doktrin* (Tübingen: J.C.B. Mohr, 1900), 18.

108. Fichte, *Geschloßne Handelsstaat*, 122; Fichte, *Closed Commercial State*, 79. Fichte's emphasis.

109. Johann Gottlieb Fichte, "System der Rechtslehre (1812)," in *Gesamtausgabe der Bayerischen Akademie der Wissenschaften* II.13 (Stuttgart-Bad Cannstatt: Frommann, 1962), 197–293, at 249.

110. Fichte, *Geschloßne Handelsstaat*, 126; Fichte, *Closed Commercial State*, 83. See also Nakhimovsky, *Closed Commercial State*, 107–8. Already in part 2 of his *Foundations of Natural Right,* Fichte had argued that "the very concept of money implies that the substance of the money, as such, is completely useless to human beings. The value of this substance must be based simply on general opinion and agreement [*allgemeine Meinung und Übereinkunft*]. Each person must merely know that every other person will recognize it as the equivalent of the corresponding portion of what is marketable within the state." Fichte, "Angewandtes Naturrecht," 42; Fichte, *Foundations of Natural Right*, 208.

111. Fichte, *Geschloßne Handelsstaat*, 173; Fichte, *Closed Commercial State*, 120.

112. Fichte, *Geschloßne Handelsstaat*, 176; Fichte, *Closed Commercial State*, 123. Cf. Nakhimovsky, *Closed Commercial State*, 106.

113. Fichte, *Geschloßne Handelsstaat*, 174–75; Fichte, *Closed Commercial State*, 121–24.

114. Fichte, *Geschloßne Handelsstaat*, 122; Fichte, *Closed Commercial State*, 78–79. See also Nakhimovsky, *Closed Commercial State*, 106. As mentioned above, Fichte had made the same point already in his *Foundations of Natural Right* (1797) and would reiterate them in his "System der Rechtslehre (1812)." See Fichte, "Angewandtes Naturrecht," 42; Fichte, *Foundations of Natural Right*, 208; as well as Fichte, "System der Rechtslehre (1812)," 249.

115. Fichte would himself experience the vulnerability of paper to counterfeiting when his publisher's fears about illegal reprints of *The Closed Commercial State* were realized in 1801 with the appearance of an unlicensed reprint in Vienna as Johann Gottlieb Fichte, *Der Geschlossne Handelsstaat* (Vienna: Doll, 1801). See Reinhard Lauth and Hans Gliwitzky, "Vorwort," in *Gesamtausgabe der Bayerischen Akademie der Wissenschaften* I.7 (Stuttgart-Bad Cannstatt: Frommann, 1962), 3–36, at 8.

116. Fichte, *Geschloßne Handelsstaat*, 122; Fichte, *Closed Commercial State*, 175. See also 125; 82.

117. Fichte, *Geschloßne Handelsstaat*, 96; Fichte, *Closed Commercial State*, 143.

118. Adler similarly suggests that the reference is meant to be to book 1, ch. 5 and bk. 2, ch. 2 of *The Wealth of Nations*. Anthony Curtis Adler, "Translator's Notes," in J. G. Fichte, *The Closed Commercial State*, trans. and with an interpretative essay by Anthony Curtis Adler (Albany: SUNY Press, 2012), 214.

119. Fichte, *Geschloßne Handelsstaat*, 96; Fichte, *Closed Commercial State*, 143.

120. Fichte, *Geschloßne Handelsstaat*, 121; Fichte, *Closed Commercial State*, 175. See also Nakhimovsky, *Closed Commercial State*, 106–7.

121. Thomas Hobbes, *The Elements of Law: Natural & Politic,* ed. Ferdinand Tönnies (Cambridge: Cambridge University Press, 1928), part 2, ch. 29, par. 8. Hobbes took a keen interest in the logic of currencies, weights, and measures, which he saw as prime illustrations of the kind of covenant based on mutual acknowledgment that was to found the commonwealth by institution.

122. Fichte, *Geschloßne Handelsstaat,* 79; Fichte, *Closed Commercial State,* 123. Fichte affirmed this analysis of money in Fichte, "System der Rechtslehre (1812)," 197–293. For the sections on money, see 249–58, esp. "Grunderfordernisse des Geldes." Cf. also Johann Gottlieb Fichte, "Kommentar zum *Handbuch der Staatswirthschaft* von Theodor Schmalz," in *Gesamtausgabe der Bayerischen Akademie der Wissenschaften* II.13 (Stuttgart-Bad Cannstatt: Frommann, 2002), 7–10; and Fichte, "Abhandlung über Pfandbriefe und das Finanzsystem usw. Finanzbetrachtungen," in *Gesamtausgabe der Bayerischen Akademie der Wissenschaften* II.13 (Stuttgart-Bad Cannstatt: Frommann, 2002), 11–34.

123. See also Anthony Curtis Adler, "Interpretative Essay: Fichte's Monetary History" in Johann Gottlieb Fichte, *The Closed Commercial State* (Albany: SUNY Press, 2012), 1–71, at 58.

124. Fichte, *Geschloßne Handelsstaat,* 96–97; Fichte, *Closed Commercial State,* 144.

125. Adler has described this process as akin to a transubstantiation. Adler, "Interpretative Essay," 66.

126. Fichte, *Geschloßne Handelsstaat,* 81; Fichte, *Closed Commercial State,* 124.

127. John Maynard Keynes, *A Tract on Monetary Reform* (London: Macmillan, 1923).

128. Fichte, *Geschloßne Handelsstaat,* 127; Fichte, *Closed Commercial State,* 181.

129. Fichte, *Geschloßne Handelsstaat,* 123; Fichte, *Closed Commercial State,* 175.

130. Fichte, *Geschloßne Handelsstaat,* 122; Fichte, *Closed Commercial State,* 174.

131. Nakhimovsky, *Closed Commercial State,* 115. As Fichte insisted in his lectures on the "System der Rechtslehre": "Ich sage auf dieses alles: der Staat den wir bis jezt beschrieben haben, kann dies nicht wollen; er würde dadurch sich selbst vernichten: die Ordnung aufheben, u. sich alle die Noth der Unordnung auf den Hals ziehen." Fichte, "System der Rechtslehre (1812)," 250.

132. Fichte, *Geschloßne Handelsstaat,* 127; Fichte, *Closed Commercial State,* 182.

133. Fichte, *Geschloßne Handelsstaat,* 57–58; Fichte, *Closed Commercial State,* 96.

134. Fichte, *Geschloßne Handelsstaat,* 95; Fichte, *Closed Commercial State,* 141.

135. Fichte, *Geschloßne Handelsstaat,* 91; Fichte, *Closed Commercial State,* 135. On the invention of a "history of the present" around 1800, see Iwan-Michelangelo D'Aprile, *Die Erfindung der Zeitgeschichte: Geschichtsschreibung und Journalismus zwischen Aufklärung und Vormärz* (Berlin: Akademie Verlag, 2013); for the temporalization of philosophy, see Jürgen Habermas, "Conceptions of Modernity: A Look Back at Two Traditions," in *The Postnational Constellation: Political Essays,* trans., ed., with an introduction by Max Pensky (Cambridge, MA: MIT Press, 2001), 130–56, at 132.

136. Fichte, *Geschloßne Handelsstaat,* 139; Fichte, *Closed Commercial State,* 195. As quoted in Adler, "Interpretative Essay," 66–67.

137. David Ricardo, *The Works and Correspondence of David Ricardo,* vol. 4, *Pamphlets 1815–1823* (Cambridge: Cambridge University Press, 1951). On Ricardo, see

Murray Milgate and Shannon C. Stimson, *Ricardian Politics* (Princeton, NJ: Princeton University Press, 1992).

138. Galbraith, *Money*, 36.

139. Adam Müller, *Versuch einer neuen Theorie des Geldes* (Leipzig and Altenburg: Brockhaus, 1816).

140. Note, in particular, the paper-money scene in the second part of Goethe's *Faust*. Johann Wolfgang von Goethe, *Faust: Der Tragödie zweiter Theil* [1832] (Munich: C. H. Beck, 1986). See also Goethe's novella *Das Mährchen* (1795), in which a hand gets used as collateral in a debt trade. Instead of signing the debt note, the debtor has to dip his hand into a river. It subsequently turns black, begins to shrink, and becomes—so to speak—an invisible hand. On the monetary dimension of the novella, see Fritz Breithaupt, *Der Ich-Effekt des Geldes: Zur Geschichte einer Legitimationsfigur* (Frankfurt am Main: Fischer, 2008), 82.

141. Fichte, *Geschloßne Handelsstaat*, 83; Fichte, *Closed Commercial State*, 127. Another instance is Fichte's recurring pun on the homonyms of *die Waare* (commodity) and *das Wahre* (truth). Fichte, *Geschloßne Handelsstaat*, 125–26; Fichte, *Closed Commercial State*, 180–81. See also Marc Shell, *Money, Language, and Thought: Literary and Philosophic Economies from the Medieval to the Modern Era* (Baltimore: Johns Hopkins University Press, 1993), esp. ch. 5.

142. E. P. Thompson, *The Making of the English Working Class* [1963] (Toronto: Penguin, 1991), 669–99.

143. John Maynard Keynes, *The General Theory of Employment, Interest and Money*, in *The Collected Writings of John Maynard Keynes*, vol. 7, ed. Austin Robinson and Donald Moggridge (Cambridge: Cambridge University Press, 2013), 32.

144. This was the case even (or perhaps in particular) for some of the closest observers and participants, such as Ricardo himself. "During the late discussions on the bullion question," Ricardo explained, "it was most justly contended, that a currency, to be perfect, should be absolutely invariable in value." Ricardo, *Pamphlets 1815–1823*, 4:58. As Keynes later observed, this seemingly commonsense "sound money" position casually deleted both the political questions behind the currency and the immediate war context behind the suspension. "As a theoretical economist," Keynes summarized, Ricardo was "apt to be blind to what was happening under his nose—for example, the fact that the country was at war." Keynes, *General Theory*, 32.

145. Georg Wilhelm Friedrich Hegel, *Elements of the Philosophy of Right*, ed. Allen W. Wood (Cambridge: Cambridge University Press, 1991), §240. See on this, in passing, Christopher Brooke, "Population, Pauperism, and the Proletariat: Rousseau, Malthus, and the Origins of the Social Question," paper presented at the International Conference for the Study of Political Thought (CSPT) meeting "On the Economy," Yale University, May 8–9, 2015.

146. Hegel, *Elements of the Philosophy of Right*, §299. This echoed Pufendorf's earlier discussion. See David Singh Grewal, *The Invention of the Economy* (Cambridge, MA: Harvard University Press, forthcoming).

147. Benjamin Constant, "The Liberty of the Ancients Compared with that of the Moderns" [1819], in Benjamin Constant, *Political Writings*, ed. Biancamaria Fontana (Cambridge: Cambridge University Press, 1988), 309–28, at 325.

148. Constant, "Liberty of the Ancients," 325. Constant attributed these observations to the French political economist Charles Ganilh (1758–1836).

Chapter 4. Money as Capital

1. Karl Marx, *Zur Kritik der politischen Ökonomie [1859]*, in *Marx-Engels Gesamtausgabe* (hereafter MEGA²), II.2, 95–245, at 114; Marx, *A Contribution to the Critique of Political Economy*, in *Marx and Engels Collected Works* (hereafter MECW), vol. 29 (London: Lawrence & Wishart, 1987), 257–417, at 276.

2. Letter from Friedrich Engels to Karl Marx, after September 26, 1856, MEGA² III.8, 53. Also quoted in Francis Wheen, *Karl Marx: A Life* (New York: W. W. Norton, 2001), 222.

3. Karl Marx, "The Monetary Crisis in Europe" [October 3, 1856], MECW 15, 113–14. Cited in Gareth Stedman Jones, *Karl Marx: Greatness and Illusion* (Cambridge, MA: The Belknap Press of Harvard University Press, 2016), 352.

4. Already three years earlier, in the fall of 1853, Marx had been greatly animated by the onset of a small panic that had, however, quickly evaporated. Stedman Jones, *Marx*, 360. Karl Marx, "Panic on the London Stock Exchange—Strikes" [September 27, 1853], MECW 12, 334.

5. Stedman Jones, *Marx*, 352. On the crisis of 1847, see also Rudiger Dornbusch and Jacob Frenkel, "The Gold Standard and the Bank of England in the Crisis of 1847," in Michael D. Bordo and Anna J. Schwartz, eds., *A Retrospective on the Classical Gold Standard, 1821–1931* (Chicago: University of Chicago Press, 1984).

6. Charles P. Kindleberger and and Robert Z. Aliber, *Manias, Panics and Crashes: A History of Financial Crises*, 5th ed. (Basingstoke, UK: Palgrave Macmillan, 2005), 91. For a gripping account of the ship's last journey, see Gary Kinder, *Ship of Gold in the Deep Blue Sea: The History and Discovery of the World's Richest Shipwreck* (New York: Grove, 2009).

7. Kindleberger and Aliber, *Manias, Panics and Crashes*, 95.

8. Kindleberger and Aliber, *Manias, Panics and Crashes*, 95.

9. Kindleberger and Aliber, *Manias, Panics and Crashes*, 44.

10. Wheen, *Marx*, 225.

11. Engels to Marx, November 15, 1857, MEGA² III.8, 196. As quoted in Wheen, *Marx*, 225.

12. Engels to Marx, December 7, 1857, MEGA² III.8, 206. As quoted in Wheen, *Marx*, 225.

13. Engels to Marx, December 17, 1857, MEGA² III.8, 219.

14. Engels to Marx, November 15, 1857, MEGA² III.8, 196.

15. While Marx's *interest* in political economy dates back to the readings that immediately preceded the Paris Manuscripts in 1844, his project of a systematic *critique* of political economy can be dated to the early 1850s. Michael Heinrich, "Reconstruction or Deconstruction? Methodological Controversies about Value and Capital, and New Insights from the Critical Edition," in Riccardo Bellofiore and Roberto Fineschi, eds., *Re-Reading Marx: New Perspectives after the Critical Edition* (London: Palgrave Macmillan, 2008), 71–98, at 78–89; see also Stedman Jones, *Marx*, 375–79.

16. Marx to Ferdinand Lassalle, December 21, 1857, MEGA² III.8, 223–25. As quoted in Stedman Jones, *Marx*, 322.

17. Marx to Engels, December 18, 1857, MEGA² III.8, 221. As Marx frantically bragged to Engels, "I am working like mad all night and every night collating my economic studies, so that I at least get the outlines [*Grundrisse*] clear before the *déluge*."

Marx to Engels, December 8, 1857, MEGA² III.8, 210. See also Stedman Jones, *Marx*, 375; and Wheen, *Marx*, 227.

18. A selection of these pieces have been translated and published as Karl Marx, *Dispatches for the New York Tribune: Selected Journalism of Karl Marx* (London: Penguin Classics, 2008). A more complete collection is available in MECW 15.

19. We now understand this intellectual development better not least because of the recent availability as part of MEGA² of more of Marx's notebooks from both the early and late 1850s. In reconstructing his intellectual development, then, I rely both on his published writings for the *New-York Tribune* as well as on a set of notebooks on the crisis of 1857 that only recently have become available for the first time: Marx's Crisis Notebooks (the *Krisenhefte*) of the winter of 1857–58: *Exzerpte, Zeitungsausschnitte und Notizen zur Weltwirtschaftskrise (Krisenhefte): November 1857 bis Februar 1858 (Weltwirtschaftskrise von 1857)* (Berlin: De Gruyter, 2017).

20. Karl Marx, *La misère de la philosophie* (Paris: A. Frank and Brussels: C. G. Vogler, 1847); translated as Karl Marx, *The Poverty of Philosophy*, MECW 6, 104–212.

21. Karl Marx, *Zur Kritik der politischen Ökonomie* (Berlin: Franz Duncker, 1859). Reprinted as Marx, *Zur Kritik der politischen Ökonomie*, MEGA², II.2, 95–245; translated as Marx, *Contribution to the Critique of Political Economy*, MECW 29, 257–417. See also Maurice Dobb, "Introduction," in Karl Marx, *A Contribution to the Critique of Political Economy*, ed. with an introduction by Maurice Dobb (London: International Publishers, 1970), 15.

22. "In former modes of production . . . neither credit nor credit-money can develop greatly." Karl Marx, *Das Kapital*, Dritter Band [1894], MEGA² II.15, 511.

23. These range from Lenin to Luxemburg and from David Harvey to Christian Marazzi today. See, for example, the representative comment in Ivan Ascher, *Portfolio Society: On the Capitalist Mode of Prediction* (Cambridge, MA: MIT Press/Zone Books, 2016), 10.

24. Joseph A. Schumpeter, *History of Economic Analysis* (London: Routledge, 2006), 276, 668–71.

25. Geoffrey Ingham, *The Nature of Money* (Cambridge, UK: Polity, 2004), 61–63.

26. Ingham, *Nature of Money*, 61. André Orléan has posited a similarly orthodox reading of Marx's labor theory of value as grounding a concept of value "peculiar to exchangeable commodities." André Orléan, *The Empire of Value: A New Foundation for Economics* (Cambridge, MA: MIT Press, 2014), 12–14; as cited in Isabella M. Weber, "On the Necessity of Money in an Exchange-Constituted Economy: The Cases of Smith and Marx," *Cambridge Journal of Economics* 43, no. 6 (November 2019), 1459–83, at 1460. See also André Orléan, "Money: Instrument of Exchange or Social Institution of Value," in Jocelyn Pixley and G. C. Harcourt, eds., *Financial Crises and the Nature of Capitalist Money: Mutual Developments from the Work of Geoffrey Ingham* (Basingstoke, UK: Palgrave Macmillan, 2013).

27. William Clare Roberts, *Marx's Inferno: The Political Theory of Capital* (Princeton, NJ: Princeton University Press, 2017).

28. Roberts, *Marx's Inferno*, 74.

29. Marx to Friedrich Adolph Sorge, September 1, 1870, MECW 44, 57–58; *Marx-Engels Werke*, vol. 33, 140. As quoted in Roberts, *Marx's Inferno*, 74n75. Marx here lumped together Proudhon with Edward Kellogg's *New Monetary System* (New York: Kiggins, Tooker, 1861).

30. Walter Bagehot, *Lombard Street: A Description of the Money Market* (London: Henry S. King, 1873).

31. In France, the prominence of credit experiments as tools of political emancipation can be traced back to the French Revolution, in particular debates about the Caisse Lafarge and the assignats. See Rebecca L. Spang, *Stuff and Money in the Time of the French Revolution* (Cambridge, MA: Harvard University Press, 2015), 30–31. See also Rebecca Spang, "The Caisse Lafarge: Fraud, Financialization, and the French Revolution," paper presented at the Princeton University Eighteenth-Century Seminar, February 19, 2019.

32. In this section I have benefited enormously from William Clare Roberts's excellent situating of Marx's interest in "the money mystery" in relation to early French socialist debates. Roberts, *Marx's Inferno*, 70–78. Where Roberts juxtaposes Marx to Proudhon through the combined lens of the *Grundrisse*, the *Contribution to the Critique of Political Economy*, and *Capital*, I hope to account for this eventual juxtaposition by capturing Marx in transition. For this purpose I focus on two transitional phases, namely, Marx's Ricardian critique of Proudhon during the late 1840s and his subsequent pivot during the 1850s toward a critique of Proudhon based on the Banking School.

33. Stedman Jones, *Marx*, 396. See also Lorenz von Stein, *Der Socialismus und Communismus des heutigen Frankreichs: Ein Beitrag zur Zeitgeschichte* (Leipzig: Otto Wigand, 1842).

34. Pierre-Joseph Proudhon, "Qu'est-ce que la propriété? Ou Recherche sur le principe du Droit et du Gouvernement" [1840], in *Oeuvres complètes*, vol. 1 (Bruxelles: Lacroix, Verboeckhoven, & Cie, 1867), 1–226; Proudhon, "What Is Property?," in *Property Is Theft! A Pierre-Joseph Proudhon Anthology*, ed. Iain McKay (Oakland, CA: AK Press, 2011), 87–138.

35. Proudhon, *Système des contradictions économiques, ou, Philosophie de la misère*, 2 vols. (Paris: Chez Guillaumin et cie, 1846); *Proudhon Anthology*, 167–256. See especially vol. 2, chs. 2 (gold and silver) and 10 (metal).

36. Proudhon, *Système*, vol. 2, ch. 14, 526. As cited in George Woodcock, *Pierre-Joseph Proudhon: A Biography* (Montreal: Black Rose Books, 1987), 97.

37. Proudhon, *Système*, vol. 2, ch. 10, 118; *Proudhon Anthology*, 233.

38. Proudhon, *Système*, vol. 2, ch. 10, 118; *Proudhon Anthology*, 233.

39. Woodcock, *Proudhon*, 123.

40. Woodcock, *Proudhon*, 123.

41. Woodcock, *Proudhon*, 100.

42. Pierre-Joseph Proudhon, *Solution du problème social* [1848], in *Oeuvres complètes*, vol. 6, 112.

43. Woodcock, *Proudhon*, 122. The full title of the pamphlet was *The Organisation of Credit and Circulation and the Solution of the Social Problem without Taxation, Loans, Specie, Paper Money, Price Control, Levies, Bankruptcy, Agrarian Law, Poor Law, National Workshops, Association, Sharing or State Intervention, without Impediment to Commerce and Industry, and without Attacking Property*.

44. Proudhon, *Oeuvres complètes*, vol. 10:343–406. As quoted in Roberts, *Marx's Inferno*, 72. See also Olivier Chaïbi, *Proudhon et la Banque du peuple* (Paris: Connaissances et Savoirs, 2010); Rob Knowles, *Political Economy from Below: Economic Thought in Communitarian Anarchism, 1840–1914* (London: Routledge, 2004),

93–111; and Nigel Dodd, *The Social Life of Money* (Princeton, NJ: Princeton University Press, 2014), 351–55.

45. Woodcock, *Proudhon*, 144.

46. Woodcock, *Proudhon*, 146. See also Charles Anderson Dana, *Proudhon and His "Bank of the People"* (New York: Benjamin Tucker, 1896).

47. Woodcock, *Proudhon*, 144. Proudhon frequently linked the scarcity and perils of existing private credit to his own life story, chronicling how his farming father had lost all his land when the family mortgages had been foreclosed. "Perhaps if there had been a good rural credit institution I should have remained all my life a peasant and a conservative," Proudhon would joke later. Woodcock, *Proudhon*, 9.

48. See Alfredo Saad-Filho, "Labor, Money, and 'Labour-Money': A Review of Marx's Critique of John Gray's Monetary Analysis," *History of Political Economy* 25, no. 1 (1993): 65–84. Reprinted in Saad-Filho, *Value and Crisis: Essays on Labour, Money and Contemporary Capitalism* (Leiden: Brill, 2019), 67–83; and see Roberts, *Marx's Inferno*, 67, 72.

49. Roberts, *Marx's Inferno*, 72.

50. John Francis Bray, *Labour's Wrongs and Labour's Remedy; or, The Age of Might and the Age of Right* (London: Routledge, 1968), 136. As quoted in Roberts, *Marx's Inferno*, 72.

51. These notes are to be found in MEGA² IV.2, 428–70; MECW 3, 211–28. These notes were also later published separately under the misleading title *Auszüge aus James Mill*. I here draw on the discussion in Keith Tribe, *The Economy of the Word: Language, History, and Economics* (Oxford: Oxford University Press, 2014), 208. For a reading of these notes on Mill that explores the concept of alienation but largely sidesteps money, see David Leopold, *The Young Karl Marx: German Philosophy, Modern Politics, and Human Flourishing* (Cambridge: Cambridge University Press, 2007), 232–34.

52. Marx, "Exzerpte aus James Mill: Élémens d'économie politique," MEGA² IV.2, 447; MECW 3, 212. Tribe's translation corrected and adapted. Tribe speaks of the mediating activity "of" movement instead of mediating activity "or" movement.

53. Marx, "Exzerpte aus James Mill," MEGA² IV.2, 448; MECW 3, 212.

54. Roberts, *Marx's Inferno*, 72.

55. Marx, "Exzerpte aus James Mill," MEGA² IV.2, 450; MECW 3, 214.

56. Marx, "Exzerpte aus James Mill," MEGA² IV.2, 450; MECW 3, 214.

57. Marx, "Exzerpte aus James Mill," MEGA² IV.2, 450; MECW 3, 214.

58. Marx, "Exzerpte aus James Mill," MEGA² IV.2, 451; MECW 3, 215.

59. Marx, "Exzerpte aus James Mill," MEGA² IV.2, 449–50; MECW 3, 214.

60. Marx, "Exzerpte aus James Mill," MEGA² IV.2, 449–50; MECW 3, 214.

61. Marx, "Economic and Philosophical Manuscripts," MEGA² I.2, 323–438, at 286; MECW 3, 229–346, at 312.

62. Marx and Proudhon had inconclusively exchanged letters in May 1846 about a correspondence circle of European socialists. For an excellent account of Marx's encounter with Proudhon and his first steps toward a critique of the latter's doctrines, see Roberts, *Marx's Inferno*, 63–65.

63. Marx, *The Poverty of Philosophy*, MECW 6, 109. The MEGA² volume covering Marx and Engels's writing from January 1846 to February 1847 (MEGA² I.6) is still in process.

64. Marx, *Poverty of Philosophy*, MECW 6, 145.

65. Marx, *Poverty of Philosophy*, MECW 6, 150.

66. Marx, *Poverty of Philosophy*, MECW 6, 150.

67. Marx, *Poverty of Philosophy*, MECW 6, 150.

68. Marx, *Poverty of Philosophy*, MECW 6, 145.

69. Marx, *Poverty of Philosophy*, MECW 6, 144.

70. Marx, *Poverty of Philosophy*, MECW 6, 144.

71. Marx, *Poverty of Philosophy*, MECW 6, 147.

72. As quoted in Marx, *Poverty of Philosophy*, MECW 6, 147.

73. Marx, *Poverty of Philosophy*, MECW 6, 147.

74. Marx, *Poverty of Philosophy*, MECW 6, 147–48.

75. Marx, *Poverty of Philosophy*, MECW 6, 148.

76. Marx, *Poverty of Philosophy*, MECW 6, 148. All attempts to set up "equitable-labour-exchange bazaars" in London, Sheffield, Leeds, and other towns in England had unsurprisingly ended in scandalous failures. As Engels added in a note to the 1885 German edition of *The Poverty of Philosophy*, Proudhon's bank would come to be the most prominent example on this list of failures. Marx, *Poverty of Philosophy*, 58 (MECW 6, 144). Marx had in fact covered Proudhon's speech in the National Assembly on August 3, 1848 for the *Neue Rheinische Zeitung*. Karl Marx, "Proudhons Rede gegen Thiers" [August 5, 1848], MEGA² I.7, 492–95; MECW 7, 321–24.

77. Marx and Engels, *The Communist Manifesto*, with an introduction by Gareth Stedman Jones (London: Penguin, 2002), 243. See also Stedman Jones, *Marx*, 222.

78. Marx and Engels, "Demands of the Communist Party in Germany" [March 1848], MECW 7, 4.

79. Marx and Engels, "Demands of the Communist Party in Germany" [March 1848], MECW 7, 4. The later Cologne printing of the pamphlet replaced "government" with "revolution."

80. Karl Marx, "Thiers' Rede über eine allgemeine Hypothekenbank mit Zwangskurs" [October 14, 1848], MEGA² I.7; MECW 7, 467–71. See also Avner Cohen, "The Turning Point in Marx's Monetary Theory and Its Relation to His Political Positions," *Journal of the History of Economic Thought* 15, no. 2 (Fall 1993): 268–69.

81. Karl Marx, "Thiers' Rede" [October 14, 1848], MEGA² I.7; MECW 7, 470–71.

82. Tribe, *Economy of the Word*, 207; Roberts, *Marx's Inferno*, 63. See Marx, "Communism and the Augsburg Allgemeine" [October 16, 1842], MECW 1, 220; MEGA² I.1, 240.

83. See, for example, MEGA² IV.7; Cohen, "Marx's Monetary Theory," 269.

84. Marx to Engels, February 25, 1859, MEGA² III.9, 329.

85. Alex Callinicos, "Review of William Clare Roberts's *Marx's Inferno: The Political Theory of Capital*," *Review of Politics* 80, no. 3 (2018): 566; MEGA² IV.7, 316–28.

86. MEGA² II.4.2, 545.

87. The London Notebooks are twenty-four notebooks written between 1850 and 1853 that will form MEGA² IV.7–11. Already published are MEGA² IV.7–9. I am particularly interested in Notebook 5 from January 1851 (MEGA² IV.7, 345–466) and Notebook 7 from March 1851 (MEGA² IV.8, 227–34; MECW 10, 584–92). Cohen, "Marx's Monetary Theory," 269–72. See also Lucia Pradella, *Globalization and the Critique of Political Economy: New Insights from Marx's Writings* (London: Routledge, 2014), ch. 4.

88. See also Costas Lapavitsas, "The Banking School and the Monetary Thought of Karl Marx," *Cambridge Journal of Economics* 18, no. 5 (1994): 447–61.

89. Torrens, as quoted in John Stuart Mill, "The Currency Question," *Westminster Review* 41 (June 1844): 579. On the Currency School versus the Banking School, see also Robert Skidelsky, *Money and Government: The Past and Future of Economics* (New Haven, CT: Yale University Press, 2018), 49–50.

90. Mill, "Currency Question," 597.

91. Thomas Tooke, *History of Prices*, 6 vols. (London: Longman, 1838–57). The first two volumes appeared in 1838, the third in 1840, the fourth in 1848, and the fifth and sixth together in 1857, the year before Tooke's death.

92. Stedman Jones, *Marx*, 672n76.

93. "The Banking School," Perry Mehrling summarizes, "explained how what they called a 'currency of credit' was maintained as a close substitute of gold money by the 'reflux' of excess currency back to banks of issue in repayment of maturing bills of exchange." Perry Mehrling, "The Vision of Hyman P. Minsky," *Journal of Economic Behavior & Organization* 39, no. 2 (1999): 151.

94. See also Mill, "Currency Question," 578.

95. Tooke incorporated John Fullarton's conception of the "flux" and "reflux" of bullion (developed in his *The Regulation of Currencies* from 1844) into vol. 4 of the *History of Prices*. Tooke, *History of Prices*, vol. 4, 185. See Arie Arnon, *Thomas Tooke: Pioneer of Monetary Theory* (Cheltenham, UK: Edward Elgar, 1993), 135; and Suzanne de Brunhoff, *Marx on Money* (London and New York: Verso, 2015), 91–92.

96. Marx, "Reflection," MEGA² IV.8, 227–34; MECW 10, 584–92.

97. Marx, "Reflection," MEGA² IV.8, 227; MECW 10, 584.

98. Marx, "Reflection," MEGA² IV.8, 227, 230; MECW 10, 584, 588.

99. Marx, "Reflection," MEGA² IV.8, 230; MECW 10, 588. This also meant that "the convertibility of bank-notes into gold is in the end necessary, because the convertibility of commodities into money is necessary, in other words because commodities have exchange value, which necessarily has a *special* existence distinct from commodities, i.e. because in fact the system of private exchange prevails." Marx, "Reflection," MEGA² IV.8, 227; MECW 10, 587.

100. Marx to Engels, February 3, 1851, MECW 38, 273; MEGA² III.4, 24.

101. Engels to Marx, August 11, 1851, MECW 38, 421, 419; MEGA² III.4, 179.

102. Marx to Engels, February 3, 1851, MECW 38, 273; MEGA² III.4, 27.

103. Geoffrey Ingham, "Finance and Power," *New Left Review*, no. 109 (January–February 2018): 135.

104. Marx to Engels, February 3, 1851, MECW 38, 273; MEGA² III.4, 24.

105. Engels to Marx, August 11, 1851, MECW 38, 419; MEGA² III.4, 178.

106. Engels to Marx, August 11, 1851, MECW 38, 421; MEGA² III.4, 179.

107. Engels to Marx, August 11, 1851, MECW 38, 419; MEGA² III.4, 179.

108. Engels to Marx, August 11, 1851, MECW 38, 419; MEGA² III.4, 179.

109. Jonathan Sperber, *Karl Marx: A Nineteenth-Century Life* (New York: Liveright, 2013), 292; Karl Marx, "Die Klassenkämpfe in Frankreich 1848 bis 1850," January 1850, MEGA² I.10, 119–40.

110. Marx, "Revolution in China and in Europe," June 14, 1853, MEGA² I.12, 147–53, at 152.

111. He wrote his first article for the *Tribune* roughly a year later in August 1852, shortly after finishing the "Eighteenth Brumaire." Miles Taylor, "The English Face of Karl Marx," *Journal of Victorian Culture* 1, no. 2 (1996): 227–53, at 230.

112. Richard Kluger, *The Paper: The Life and Death of the New York Herald Tribune* (New York: Alfred A. Knopf, 1986), 17.

113. Taylor estimates that up to a hundred of Marx's articles, in particular on military matters, were likely written by Engels. Taylor, "English Face of Karl Marx," 231. Wheen counts five hundred articles submitted to the *Tribune* and estimates that Marx can take the credit for at least half. Wheen, *Marx*, 187. Marx frequently asked Engels for help with his articles, often citing illness or his research on political economy: "As to the *New York Tribune*, you've got to help me, now that I'm so busy with political economy. Write a series of articles on Germany, from 1848 onwards. Witty and uninhibited." Marx to Engels, August 14, 1851, MEGA² III.4, 183; MECW 38, 422.

114. Initially Marx wrote his articles in German and sent them to Engels to be translated. By the end of January 1853, he announced proudly that he had written his first draft in English with the help of a friend and a dictionary. Ironically, given the subject matter of transatlantic finance, the process of getting paid from New York for his columns was exceedingly complicated, lengthy, and expensive. Taylor, "English Face of Karl Marx," 231; Sperber, *Marx*, 302.

115. Karl Marx, "Der kommerzielle und finanzielle Zustand" [September 28, 1855], MEGA² I.14, 687; MECW 14, 534.

116. Karl Marx, "The French Crédit Mobilier I–III," *New-York Daily Tribune*, June–July 1856, MECW 15, 8–24.

117. Marx, *Zur Kritik der politischen Ökonomie*, MEGA² II.2, 102; Marx, *Contribution to the Critique of Political Economy*, MECW 29, 265. As Miles Taylor has pointed out, "Although he was always at pains to deny it, Marx's concerns in his *Tribune* journalism fed into much of his 'mature' work. In the *Grundrisse*, and later in *Das Kapital*, . . . the endless preoccupation with the currency and the nature of money, owed not a little to his immersion in the English radical and Tory press of the 1850s." Taylor, "English Face of Karl Marx," 247.

118. Karl Marx, "Der kommerzielle und finanzielle Zustand" [September 28, 1855], MEGA² I.14, 688; MECW 14, 535–36.

119. Karl Marx, "The French Crédit Mobilier [I]" [June 1856]; "The French Crédit Mobilier [II]" [June 24, 1856]; and "The French Crédit Mobilier [III]" [July 11, 1856].

120. Marx, "The French Crédit Mobilier [I]" [June 1856], MECW 15, 10.

121. Helen M. Davies, *Emile and Isaac Pereire: Bankers, Socialists and Sephardic Jews in Nineteenth-Century France* (Manchester: Manchester University Press, 2015).

122. As quoted in Marx, "The French Crédit Mobilier [III]" [July 11, 1856], MECW 15, 20.

123. Marx, "The French Crédit Mobilier [I]" [June 1856], MECW 15, 11.

124. Marx, "The French Crédit Mobilier [I]" [June 1856], MECW 15, 12.

125. Marx, "The Economic Crisis in Europe" [September 26, 1856], MECW 15, 110.

126. Marx, "The French Crédit Mobilier [II]" [June 24, 1856], MECW 15, 15.

127. Marx, "The Economic Crisis in France" [November 7, 1856], MECW 15, 130–35, at 134.

128. Marx, "The Economic Crisis in Europe" [September 26, 1856], MECW 15, 109–12, at 109.

129. Marx, "The French Crédit Mobilier [III]" [July 11, 1856], MECW 15, 19.

130. Marx, "The Economic Crisis in Europe" [September 26, 1856], MECW 15, 109.

131. Marx, "Monetary Crisis in Europe," 114; Stedman Jones, *Marx*, 352.

132. Marx, "The French Crédit Mobilier [II]" [June 24, 1856], MECW 15, 15.

133. Marx, "Monetary Crisis in Europe" [October 3, 1857], MECW 15, 115.

134. Marx, "Class Struggles in France, 1848–1850," MECW 10, 135, 510. As quoted in Cohen, "Marx's Monetary Theory," 275.

135. Karl Marx, "Zur Kritik der politischen Ökonomie: Urtext," MEGA² II.2, 23.

136. Marx, "The Monetary Crisis in Europe" [October 3, 1857], MECW 15, 113.

137. Marx, "The Causes of the Monetary Crisis in Europe" [October 27, 1856], MECW 15, 117–22, at 119.

138. Marx, "The European Crisis" [November 21, 1856], MECW 15, 136–38, at 136.

139. Marx, "The European Crisis" [November 21, 1856], MECW 15, 136–38, at 136.

140. Marx, "The Book of the Commercial Crisis," *Krisenhefte*, MEGA² I/32, Band 2, MEGA² IV.14, 484. On the *Krisenhefte* in MEGA², see also Carl-Erich Vollgraf, "Marx auf dem Trampelpfad: Zur Plantreue eines großen Sozialisten (1844–1862)," *Z. Zeitschrift Marxistische Erneuerung*, no. 111 (September 2017).

141. Hans Rosenberg, *Die Weltwirtschaftskrise von 1857–1859* (Stuttgart: Verlag von W. Kohlhammer, 1934), 136, as quoted in Kindleberger and Aliber, *Manias, Panics and Crashes*, 117. See also Sperber, *Marx*, 320.

142. Kindleberger and Aliber, *Manias, Panics and Crashes*, 44.

143. Kindleberger and Aliber, *Manias, Panics and Crashes*, 221. France had become, as Van Vleck put it in his classic study of the panic, "the center from which fluctuations in the economic cycle radiated." George W. Van Vleck, *The Panic of 1857: An Analytical Study* (New York: Columbia University Press, 1943), 42.

144. Dred Scott v. John F. A. Sandford, 60 U.S. (19 How.) 393 (1856).

145. Kindleberger and Aliber, *Manias, Panics and Crashes*, 185. Kindleberger stresses the failure of the New York banks to cooperate to halt the run.

146. Kindleberger and Aliber, *Manias, Panics and Crashes*, 116.

147. Karl Marx to Conrad Schramm, December 8, 1857, MEGA² III.8, 212–15. Also quoted in Sperber, *Marx*, 321.

148. Karl Marx, "The English Bank Act of 1844, August 28, 1858, MECW 16, 4. "Twice in ten years their expectation has been baffled, despite the extraordinary and unexpected aid afforded to the working of the act by the great gold discoveries."

149. Of the more than 1,500 excerpts and newspaper clippings in three crisis notebooks, almost half came from *The Economist*. See MEGA² IV/14: *Exzerpte, Zeitungsausschnitte und Notizen zur Weltwirtschaftskrise (Krisenhefte): November 1857 bis Februar 1858 (Weltwirtschaftskrise von 1857)* (Berlin: De Gruyter, 2017). The three crisis notebooks consist of 192 manuscript pages with excerpts, newspaper clippings, and notes from between November 1857 and February 1858.

150. Walter Bagehot, "The Monetary Crisis of 1857," *National Review*, January 1858; reprinted in Bagehot, *The Works and Life of Walter Bagehot*, ed. Mrs Russell Barrington (London: Longmans, Green, 1915), 2:326, 328. On Bagehot's monetary

views, see also Walter Bagehot, "The Credit Mobilier and Banking Companies in France," *National Review*, January 1858, reprinted in Bagehot, *Works and Life*, 2:328; as well as his very first published article in which the twenty-two-year old Bagehot engaged with James Wilson's *Capital, Currency, and Banking* (1847): Walter Bagehot, "The Currency Monopoly," *Prospective Review* (1848); reprinted in Bagehot, *Works and Life*, 8:146–87. See also Alexander Zevin, *Liberalism at Large: The World according to the Economist* (London and New York: Verso, 2019), 81.

151. Karl Marx, "The Crisis in Europe," written December 18, 1857, printed in the *New-York Tribune* on January 5, 1858, MECW 15, 410–12, at 411; partially reprinted in Marx, *Dispatches for the New York Tribune*, 198–200. See also Marx, "The Trade Crisis in England," *New-York Tribune*, December 15, 1857; Marx, "British Commerce and Finance," *New-York Tribune*, October 4, 1858; Taylor, "English Face of Karl Marx," 242.

152. Benjamin Disraeli on the Bank Issues Indemnity Bill, House of Commons, December 4, 1857. I here draw on the discussion in Taylor, "English Face of Karl Marx," 243.

153. Disraeli on the Bank Issues Indemnity Bill, House of Commons, December 4, 1857.

154. Taylor, "English Face of Karl Marx," 242.

155. Karl Marx, "Commercial Crises and Currency in Britain," written August 10, 1858, published in the *New-York Daily Tribune* on August 28, 1858, MECW 16, 8–12, at 8. Partially quoted in Stedman Jones, *Marx*, 356.

156. Marx, "Commercial Crises," 8. Partially quoted in Stedman Jones, *Marx*, 356.

157. Karl Marx, "Grundrisse der Kritik der politischen Ökonomie," in *Ökonomische Manuskripte 1857/58*, Teil 1 und 2, MEGA² II.1.1–2; Karl Marx, *Grundrisse: Foundations of the Critique of Political Economy*, trans. with a foreword by Martin Nicolaus (London: Penguin, 1993). See also Wheen, *Marx*, 229–30; Stedman Jones, *Marx*, 376–91. Below I will first provide page references to the MEGA² edition of the *Grundrisse*, followed by page references to the Penguin translation.

158. Marx, *Grundrisse* (MEGA² II.1.1, 57; Penguin 122).

159. Marx, *Grundrisse* (MEGA² II.1.1, 57; Penguin 123).

160. Marx, *Grundrisse* (MEGA² II.1.1, 57; Penguin 122).

161. Marx, *Zur Kritik der politischen Ökonomie*, MEGA² II.2, 228; Marx, *A Contribution to the Critique of Political Economy*, MECW 29, 399.

162. For a recent exception, see Samuel A. Chambers, *There's No Such Thing as "The Economy": Essays on Capitalist Value* (Santa Barbara, CA: Punctum Books, 2018).

163. Marx to Weydemeyer, February 1, 1859, MEGA² III.9, 295; MECW 40, 377–78. As partially quoted in Roberts, *Marx's Inferno*, 59.

164. In his correspondence Marx insisted that his decision "to hold back" the third chapter on capital was due to "*political* reasons." Marx to Weydemeyer, February 1, 1859; MEGA² III.9, 294.

165. Marx to Engels, January 21, 1859, MEGA² III.9, 278; Marx to Weydemeyer, February 1, 1859, MEGA² III.9, 295; MECW 40, 377–78. As partially quoted in Roberts, *Marx's Inferno*, 59.

166. Karl Marx, "Value, Price, and Profit," lecture series delivered to the First International Working Men's Association on June 20 and 27, London, 1865; reprinted

as Karl Marx, *Wage-Labour and Capital & Value, Price and Profit* (New York: International Publishers, 1976), 21.

167. Karl Marx, *Das Kapital: Kritik der politischen Ökonomie*, Erster Band, MEGA^2 II.6, 81; Karl Marx, *Capital: A Critique of Political Economy*, vol. 1, trans. Ben Fowkes (London: Penguin, 1976), 139. Below I will first provide page references to the MEGA^2 edition of *Capital*, followed by page references to the Penguin translation. "Genesis" is here not meant in the sense of historical origin; instead, Marx is interested in the nature of the money form under capitalism. See Heinrich, *Introduction*, 56. In what follows I will offer references both to the MEGA^2 volumes of the first and second German edition as well as to Ben Fowkes's 1976 Penguin translation.

168. Marx, *Capital*, vol. 1, preface to the first edition (MEGA^2 II.5, 11; II.6, 65; Penguin 89).

169. Hans-Georg Backhaus, *Dialektik der Wertform* (Freiburg: Ça ira, 1997); Michael Heinrich, *Die Wissenschaft vom Wert: Die Marxsche Kritik der politischen Ökonomie zwischen wissenschaftlicher Revolution und klassischer Tradition* (Münster: Westfälisches Dampfboot, 1999); Michael Heinrich, *Kritik der politischen Ökonomie: Eine Einführung* (Stuttgart: Schmetterling Verlag, 2004). Heinrich's influential introduction has been translated (by Alex Locascio) as *An Introduction to the Three Volumes of "Capital"* (New York: Monthly Press, 2012).

170. Samuel A. Chambers, "Marx's Unorthodox Account of Money," 2019, working paper on file with the author. As Chambers notes equally aptly, it has not helped that in the recent foundational debates about the nature of money among economic sociologists, Marx was represented by adherents of a rather orthodox labor theory of value that only seemed to confirm the old suspicion of Marx as a commodity theorist of money. For the so-called Zelitzer-Fine-Lapavitsas-Ingham debate, see Viviana Zelizer, "Fine Tuning the Zelizer View," *Economy and Society* 29, no. 3 (2000): 383–89; Ben Fine and Costas Lapavitsas, "Markets and Money in Social Science: What Role for Economics?," *Economy and Society* 29, no. 3 (2000), 507–29; Geoffrey Ingham, "Fundamentals of a Theory of Money: Untangling Fine, Lapavitsas and Zelizer," *Economy and Society* 30, no. 3 (2001): 304–23. Lapavitsas's articles on the topic have since been collected in *Marxist Monetary Theory: Collected Papers* (Leiden: Brill, 2016). Ingham elaborated on his position in his seminal *The Nature of Money* (Cambridge, UK: Polity, 2004).

171. For an illuminating commentary on this point, see Heinrich, *Introduction*, 56.

172. Marx, *Capital*, vol. 1, ch. 2 (MEGA^2 II.5, 54n35; II.6, 116n40; Penguin 181n4).

173. Marx, *Capital*, vol. 1, ch. 1 (MEGA^2 II.5, 54n35; II.6, 99–100; Penguin 161n26). The respective note in the first edition made the same point but lacked the image that Marx added to the second edition. See Marx, *Capital*, vol. 1, ch. 1 (MEGA^2 II.5, 40n23).

174. Marx, *Grundrisse* (MEGA^2 II.1.1, 61; Penguin 126).

175. Heinrich, *Introduction*, 57.

176. Marx, *Capital*, vol. 1, ch. 2 (MEGA^2 II.5, 53; II.6, 115; Penguin 180).

177. Heinrich, *Introduction*, 63.

178. Heinrich, *Introduction*, 65.

179. Heinrich, *Introduction*, 64. It is thus slightly misleading to say that money is on Marx's account a mere medium that transmits but does not create. Duncan Foley, "Introduction," in de Brunhoff, *Marx on Money*, viii.

180. Michael Heinrich, "Karl Marx's Monetary Theory of Value" (lecture, Franke Lectures in the Humanities, Macmillan Center, Yale University, October 28, 2020).

181. Marx, *Zur Kritik der politischen Ökonomie*, MEGA² II.2, 215; Marx, *Contribution to the Critique of Political Economy*, MECW 29, 387.

182. Marx, *Capital*, vol. 1, ch. 2 (MEGA² II.5, 57; II.6, 119; Penguin 184–85).

183. Marx, *Capital*, vol. 1, ch. 2 (MEGA² II.5, 57; II.6, 119; Penguin 185n10).

184. Marx, *Capital*, vol. 1, ch. 2 (MEGA² II.5, 57; II.6, 119; Penguin 184–85).

185. For an illuminating way to express how Marx's very framing of the question stands outside the distinction between credit and commodity theories of money, see Chambers, "Marx's Unorthodox Account," 2–3.

186. While Ingham is then right to observe that Marx is not a credit theorist, he is wrong to associate him with the commodity theory and the Currency School. Ingham, *Nature of Money*, 62.

187. Marx, *Capital*, vol. 1, ch. 2 (MEGA² II.5, 58; II.6, 120; Penguin 186). Adapted translation.

188. Marx, *Capital*, vol. 1, ch. 2 (MEGA² II.5, 57; II.6, 119; Penguin 184).

189. Roberts, *Marx's Inferno*, 76. Marx had summarized the point already memorably in the *Grundrisse*: "All commodities are perishable money; money is the imperishable commodity." Marx, *Grundrisse* (MEGA² II.1.1, 155; Penguin 149).

190. Marx, *Capital*, vol. 1, ch. 3 (MEGA² II.5, 59; II.6, 121; Penguin 188).

191. Marx, *Capital*, vol. 1, ch. 3 (MEGA² II.5, 59; II.6, 121; Penguin 188).

192. Moishe Postone, *Time, Labor, and Social Domination: A Reinterpretation of Marx's Critical Theory* (Cambridge: Cambridge University Press, 1993).

193. Marx, *Capital*, vol. 1, ch. 2 (II.6, 72; Penguin 128). Translation modified. The passage was added only to the second edition. For a discussion of the line, see also Dipesh Chakrabarty, *Provincializing Europe: Postcolonial Thought and Historical Difference* (Princeton, NJ: Princeton University Press, 2000), 53.

194. Heinrich, *Introduction*, 49, 64.

195. Marx, *Capital*, vol. 1, preface (MEGA² II.5, 14; II.6, 68; Penguin 93).

196. Marx, *Capital*, vol. 1, ch. 3 (MEGA² II.5, 89; II.6, 153; Penguin 229). See also Marx, *Capital*, vol. 1, ch. 2 (MEGA² II.5, 54; II.6, 116; Penguin 181). Marx at times paired the image of the crystal with that of value as gelatinized labor power: "As value, the linen consists only of labor and forms a transparent, crystalized gelatin [*Gallerte*]. In reality, however, the crystal is rather opaque." Marx, *Capital*, vol. 1, ch. 1 (MEGA² II.5, 30). Or as he put it in the second edition, value was "mere gelatin" (*bloße Gallerte*) of abstract labor. Marx, *Capital*, vol. 1, ch. 2 (II.6, 72; Penguin 128). Translation modified.

197. Marx, *Capital*, vol. 1, ch. 3 (MEGA² II.5, 59; II.6, 121; Penguin 188).

198. Heinrich, *Introduction*, 64.

199. Marx, *Capital*, vol. 1, ch. 2 (MEGA² II.6, 104; Penguin 165–66).

200. Marx speaks specifically of the "verrückte Form." Marx, *Capital*, vol. 1, ch. 1 (MEGA² II.5, 47; II.6, 106; Penguin 229).

201. It also explains why "anyone can use money as money without necessarily understanding what money is." Marx, *Theories of Surplus Value*, MECW, vol. 32, 348. As cited in Heinrich, *Introduction*, 77.

202. Christine Desan, *Making Money: Coin, Currency, and the Coming of Capitalism* (Oxford: Oxford University Press, 2015); Andrew David Edwards, "The American

Revolution and Christine Desan's New History of Money," *Law & Social Inquiry* 42, no. 1 (Winter 2017): 252–78.

203. Marx, *Grundrisse* (MEGA² II.1.1, 161; Penguin 239).

204. I am indebted to Alex Gourevitch for discussion of this point. See also, relatedly, Callinicos, "Review of *Marx's Inferno*," 564–88, at 566.

205. Marx, *Grundrisse* (MEGA² II.1.1, 144; Penguin 217).

206. See also Marx's related discussion of commodity fetishism in Marx, *Capital*, vol. 1 (MEGA² II.5, 50–59; II.6, 103–13; Penguin 163–77). For Marx's reference to an "objective" or "necessary illusion [*nothwendiger Schein*]," see *Grundrisse* (MEGA² II.1.2, 412; Penguin 509); for a further discussion, see Stedman Jones, *Marx*, 393.

207. Karl Marx, *Das Kapital: Kritik der politischen Ökonomie*, Erster Band, Dritte vermehrte Auflage (Hamburg: Otto Meisner, 1883); reprinted as MEGA² II.8.

208. In much of the secondary literature (including the annotations in the Penguin edition of volume 1 of *Capital*) one can find the mistaken claim that the note on "monetary crises" was added by Engels only in the third edition of *Capital*. But already the first and second editions, as well as the French edition, contained a note on monetary crises. What was changed in the third edition was the wording of the definition. Marx, *Capital*, vol. 1, ch. 1 (MEGA² II.5, 94; II.6, 159; II.8, 157; Penguin 236n50). See also Michael R. Krätke, "Das Marx-Engels-Problem," *Marx-Engels-Jahrbuch* (2006): 142–70, at 162.

209. The manuscript that came to form the basis for the third volume of *Capital* was written in 1864–65 but only published for the first time in its full unedited state in 1992 as MEGA², II/4.2. An English translation has since appeared as Fred Moseley, ed., *Marx's Economic Manuscript of 1864–1865* (Leiden: Brill, 2015).

210. Karl Marx, *Das Kapital: Kritik der politischen Ökonomie*, Dritter Band [1894], MEGA² II.15; Karl Marx, *Capital: A Critique of Political Economy*, vol. 3, trans. David Fernbach (London: Penguin, 1981).

211. The term Engels used to describe the fifth section was *Hauptschwierigkeit*. See Friedrich Engels, "Preface," in Marx, *Capital*, vol. 3 (MEGA² II.15, 8; Penguin 94).

212. Much investigative effort has since gone into retracing Engels's editorial work and comparing it to the unfinished state of Marx's manuscript that formed the basis for the volume. See Michael Heinrich, "Engels' Edition of the Third Volume of *Capital* and Marx's Original Manuscript," *Science & Society* 60, no. 4 (Winter 1996–97): 452–66; Fred Moseley, "Introduction," in Fred Moseley, ed., *Marx's Economic Manuscript of 1864–1865* (Leiden: Brill, 2015), 1–44.

213. Walter Bagehot, *Lombard Street: A Description of the Money Market* (London: Henry S. King, 1873); see also Bagehot, "Monetary Crisis," reprinted in Bagehot, *Works and Life*, 2:326–58.

214. On this point, see Heinrich, "Engels' Edition," 462.

215. Karl Marx, *Capital*, vol. 3, ch. 32 (MEGA² II.15, 511; Penguin, 649). Emphases in the original. See also Makoto Itoh and Costas Lapavitsas, *Political Economy of Money and Finance* (Basingstoke, UK: Palgrave Macmillan, 1999), 124; as well as Ramaa Vasudevan, "The Significance of Marx's Theory of Money," *Economic and Political Weekly* 52, no. 37 (September 2017): 70–82.

216. Marx, *Capital*, vol. 3, ch. 34 (MEGA² II.15, 539–57; Penguin 672–98).

217. Marx, "Value, Price, and Profit," 24.

218. Marx, *Capital*, vol. 1, ch. 3 (MEGA² II.5, 98; II.6, 165; Penguin 240–41).

219. Marx, *Capital*, vol. 1, ch. 3 (MEGA² II.5, 83; II.6, 147; Penguin 221–22).

220. Marx, *Capital*, vol. 1, ch. 3 (MEGA² II.5, 83; II.6, 147; Penguin 221–22).

221. Marx, *Capital*, vol. 1, ch. 1 (MEGA² II.6, 85; Penguin 144).

222. In Dipesh Chakrabarty's terminology, currency is thus an instance of "History 2" that cannot be fully subsumed by capital and does not fully disappear under capitalism. Chakrabarty, *Provincializing Europe*, 64–65.

223. In the manuscript draft from 1864–65 that would become volume 3 of *Capital*, Marx highlighted for example that it was evident that a temporary extension of credit could alleviate a credit panic, just as a further contraction of credit would worsen it. Karl Marx, *Capital*, vol. 3, ch. 32 (MEGA² II.15, 511; Penguin, 649). In her writings on Marx's theory of money, Susanne de Brunhoff tries to capture this subtlety by arguing that while it *seems* as if the supply of money is subject to state control, this is truly so only in extraordinary moments of crises. De Brunhoff, *Marx on Money*, 121.

224. See Geoffrey Ingham, "Finance and Power," *New Left Review*, no. 109 (January–February 2018): 135; as well as more broadly the concluding observations in Desan, *Making Money*.

225. Ralph Miliband, *The State in Capitalist Society* (New York: Basic Books, 1969); Nicos Poulantzas, *Political Power and Social Classes* (London: New Left Books, 1973). See also Clyde W. Barrow, *Toward a Critical Theory of States: The Poulantzas-Miliband Debate after Globalization* (Albany: SUNY Press, 2016).

226. Werner Bonefeld, "Money, Equality and Exploitation: An Interpretation of Marx's Treatment of Money," in Werner Bonefeld and John Holloway, eds., *Global Capital, National State and the Politics of Money* (London: Palgrave Macmillan, 1995), 196; as well as Werner Bonefeld, "Social Constitution and the Form of the Capitalist State," in Werner Bonefeld, ed., *Open Marxism 1. Dialectics and History* (London: Pluto, 1992), 93–132.

227. As Bonefeld puts it, the state is a political form through which the "social power of money" subsists but within which struggles are staged over the specific shape this power assumes. Bonefeld, "Money, Equality and Exploitation," 179.

228. Duncan Foley, "Preface," in de Brunhoff, *Marx on Money*, xi.

Chapter 5. Managing Modern Money

1. John Maynard Keynes in a letter to his mother, April 23, 1933, JMK Papers, King's College, Cambridge, PP/45/168/10/145. For the context, see Robert Skidelsky, *John Maynard Keynes: The Economist as Savior, 1920–1937* (London: Macmillan, 1992), 481.

2. John Maynard Keynes, "The 1931 Financial Crisis," ed. Donald Moggridge, in *The Collected Writings of John Maynard Keynes*, vol. 20 (*Activities 1929–1931: Rethinking Employment and Unemployment Policies*), ed. Elizabeth Johnson and Donald Moggridge (Cambridge: Cambridge University Press, 2013), 589. Whenever hereafter citing from Keynes's *Collected Writings*, I will refer to them as CW followed by the volume number.

3. D. E. Moggridge, *Maynard Keynes: An Economist's Biography* (London: Routledge, 1992), 518–19.

4. John Maynard Keynes, "An Economic Analysis of Unemployment," CW 13, 343. See also CW 20, 554–55, and Liaquat Ahamed, *Lords of Finance: The Bankers Who Broke the World* (London: Penguin, 2009), 4. As the governor of the Bank of England, Montagu Norman, echoed in a similarly worded note to his colleague at the Banque de France: "Unless drastic measures are taken to save it, the capitalist system throughout the civilized world will be wrecked within a year." Parts of the letter appeared in "Germany: Ein' Feste Burg," *Time*, July 27, 1931. As cited in Ahamed, *Lords of Finance*, 392.

5. One of those who lost their savings was a law professor named Carl Schmitt. Reinhard Mehring, *Carl Schmitt: A Biography*, trans. Daniel Steuer (Cambridge, UK: Polity, 2014), 230.

6. Exchanging letters with the prime minister, who had sought his council, Keynes warned that any additional cuts would amount to "a most gross perversion of social justice." Keynes to Ramsay MacDonald, August 5, 1931, CW 20, 590.

7. Keynes to Ramsay MacDonald, August 5, 1931, CW 20, 591–93. As Keynes put it a week later, "There will be a crisis within a month unless the most drastic and sensational action is taken." Keynes to Ramsay MacDonald, August 12, 1931, CW 20, 594.

8. Ahamed, *Lords of Finance*, 4–5.

9. For a detailed account of the events, see James Ashley Morrison, "Shocking Intellectual Austerity: The Role of Ideas in the Demise of the Gold Standard in Britain," *International Organization* 70, no. 1 (December 2016): 175–207.

10. The same day, Monday, September 21, Keynes was invited to join the Economic Advisory Council for a series of meetings on the new situation. Moggridge, *Keynes*, 527–28.

11. As quoted in Moggridge, *Keynes*, 527.

12. John Maynard Keynes, "The End of the Gold Standard" [September 27, 1931], CW 9, 245.

13. John Maynard Keynes, "Preface" [November 8, 1931], in *Essays in Persuasion*, CW 9, xix.

14. Tobias Straumann, *1931: Debt, Crisis, and the Rise of Hitler* (Oxford: Oxford University Press, 2019).

15. A.J.P. Taylor, *English History, 1914–1945* (Oxford: Oxford University Press, 1965), 297. Also paraphrased in Fred Hirsch, *Money International* (London: Penguin, 1969), 20.

16. Adam Tooze, *The Wages of Destruction: The Making and Breaking of the Nazi Economy* (London: Penguin, 2006), 20.

17. Kenneth Mouré, *The Gold Standard Illusion: France, the Bank of France, and the International Gold Standard, 1914–1939* (Oxford: Oxford University Press, 2002).

18. For the most influential articulation of this "Keynesian" framing, see Barry Eichengreen, *Golden Fetters: The Gold Standard and the Great Depression, 1919–1939* (Oxford: Oxford University Press, 1992).

19. Scholarship in international relations, international political economy, and international economic law has of course long recognized Keynes's "ambitious vision" (Ruggie) of a new internationalism. See, for example, most influentially, John Gerard Ruggie, "International Regimes, Transactions, and Change: Embedded Liberalism in the Postwar Economic Order," *International Organization* 36,

no. 2 (Spring 1982): 379–415. Despite numerous caveats, Ruggie nonetheless problematically presents Keynes's vision as largely synonymous with the postwar system of "embedded liberalism." But Keynes's proposal failed to prevail at Bretton Woods and it remains unrealized. The postwar system that emerged instead was arguably primarily one of American hegemony. For a thoughtful engagement with Keynes and international relations, see Donald John Markwell, *John Maynard Keynes and International Relations: Economic Paths to War and Peace* (Oxford: Oxford University Press, 2006).

20. See the section on "The End of Gold" below where I engage with Keynes's call for national self-sufficiency and how it fits into his larger internationalism.

21. According to the orthodox view, international stability and domestic autonomy were of course always closely entwined for an open economy that prized exchange-rate stability because of its benefits for domestic stability and predictability. See Jeffry A. Frieden, "Invested Interests: The Politics of National Economic Policies in a World of Global Finance," *International Organization* 45, no. 4 (Autumn 1991): 425–51. My point is that Keynes's rejection of orthodoxy did not in fact pit domestic autonomy against international cooperation but instead sought to supply a new template for how to integrate the two.

22. Keynes to Ramsay MacDonald, August 5, 1931, CW 20, 592. As Keynes put it immediately after the British exodus from gold, "There are a good many possible alternative schemes and I am not at the moment very clear in my own mind which I prefer." Keynes to Frederick Leith-Ross, October 14, 1931, CW 21, 2.

23. John Maynard Keynes, *The Economic Consequences of the Peace* (London: Macmillan, 1919), CW 2, 6.

24. Barry Eichengreen and Marc Flandreau, eds., *The Gold Standard in Theory and History* (London: Routledge, 1997), 5. China, Persia, and parts of Latin America remained by contrast on silver or bimetallic standards.

25. Keynes, *Economic Consequences*, CW 2, 1.

26. For the otherwise admiring essay on Burke, see John Maynard Keynes, "The Political Doctrine of Edmund Burke," JMK Papers, King's College, Cambridge, UA/20/3/1–89, at 28.

27. See also Keynes, "The End of Laissez-Faire" [1926], CW 9, 272–94.

28. His first substantive scholarly publication was an article on the relation between the Indian trade balance and inflation. John Maynard Keynes, "Recent Economic Events in India," *Economic Journal*, March 1909, CW 11, 1–22. See also Keynes's 1910 lectures on "Currency, Finance and the Level of Prices in India" at the London School of Economics, which formed the basis for his first book. CW 15, 65–84.

29. Keynes, "Recent Economic Events," CW 11, 1.

30. The system consisted of a rupee paper currency that was maintained at par with the gold standard through sterling reserves kept in London. Marcello De Cecco, *Money and Empire: The International Gold Standard, 1890–1914* (Totowa, NJ: Rowman & Littlefield, 1975).

31. Eric Hobsbawm, *Industry and Empire: The Birth of the Industrial Revolution* (London: New Press, 1999), 126–27. Also quoted in Anand D. Chandavarkar, *Keynes and India: A Study in Economics and Biography* (London: Macmillan, 1989), 3.

32. CW 15, 36. As quoted in Markwell, *Keynes and International Relations*, 20.

33. John Maynard Keynes, *Indian Currency and Finance* (London: Macmillan, 1913), CW 1. In the wake of the book's publication Keynes joined the Royal Commission on Indian Currency and Finance.

34. De Cecco, *Money and Empire*, 67–72.

35. For a critical rejoinder, see B. R. Ambedkar, *The Problem of the Rupee: Its Origin and Its Solution* (London: P. S. King & Son, 1923). On Ambedkar and Keynes, see Stefan Eich, "The Problem of the Rupee," in Anupama Rao and Shailaja Paik, eds., *The Cambridge Companion to Ambedkar* (Cambridge: Cambridge University Press, forthcoming).

36. John Maynard Keynes, *A Tract on Monetary Reform* (London: Macmillan, 1923), 2; CW 4, 1.

37. Karl Polanyi, *The Great Transformation: The Political and Economic Origins of Our Time*, 2nd ed., with a new introduction by Fred Block and a foreword by Joseph E. Stiglitz (Boston: Beacon, 2001), 25.

38. Adam Tooze, *The Deluge: The Great War and the Remaking of Global Order 1916–1931* (New York: Viking, 2014), 353–73.

39. Keynes, "Inflation (1919)," CW 9, 57–58, at 57.

40. Keynes, "Social Consequences of Changes in the Value of Money," CW 9, 75. As Keynes noted in a Treasury memo from February 1920, inflationism "will strike at the whole basis of contract, of security, and of the capitalist system generally." As cited in Allan H. Meltzer, *Keynes's Monetary Theory: A Different Interpretation* (Cambridge: Cambridge University Press, 1989), 46.

41. This was the title of a book proposal Keynes sketched during 1919–20. JMK Papers, King's College, Cambridge, EC/7/2/21; EC/7/2/32. John Maynard Keynes, *The Economic Consequences of the Peace* (London: Macmillan, 1919), CW 2, 148. On whether Lenin ever uttered the phrase, see Frank Whitson Fetter, "Lenin, Keynes and Inflation," *Economica* 44, no. 173 (February 1977): 77–80; and Michael White and Kurt Schuler, "Who Said 'Debauch the Currency': Keynes or Lenin?," *Journal of Economic Perspectives* 23, no. 2 (Spring 2009): 213–22.

42. John Maynard Keynes, "Lecture to the Institute of Bankers" [December 5, 1922], CW 19, 47. See also Keynes, *Tract on Monetary Reform*, CW 4, 36, 118, 122.

43. Mark Metzler, *Lever of Empire: The International Gold Standard and the Crisis of Liberalism in Prewar Japan* (Berkeley: University of California Press, 2006), 38.

44. Keynes, "Alternative Aims in Monetary Policy" [1923], CW 9, 181. See also Keynes, *Tract on Monetary Reform*, CW 4, 174–75; as well as Robert Skidelsky, "Keynes's Road to Bretton Woods," in Marc Flandreau, Carl-Ludwig Holtfrerich, and Harold James, eds., *International Financial History in the Twentieth Century: System and Anarchy* (Cambridge: Cambridge University Press, 2003), 136.

45. Keynes, *Tract on Monetary Reform*, CW 4.

46. While the old quantity equation had assumed that the velocity at which money circulates (what Keynes called the "volume of real balances") was constant, Keynes showed that the fluctuations were instead likely large and rapid.

47. Keynes, *Tract on Monetary Reform*, CW 4, 35.

48. Keynes, *Tract on Monetary Reform*, CW 4, 35.

49. Keynes, *Tract on Monetary Reform*, CW 4, 36. Original emphasis.

50. Keynes, *Tract on Monetary Reform*, CW 4, 56.

51. Keynes, *Tract on Monetary Reform*, CW 4, 56.

52. Keynes, "The End of Laissez-Faire" [1926], CW 9, 272–94.

53. Keynes, "Am I a Liberal?" [1925], CW 9, 305.

54. Keynes, "The End of Laissez-Faire" [1926], CW 9, 288.

55. Keynes, "The End of Laissez-Faire" [1926], CW 9, 288.

56. Keynes, "The End of Laissez-Faire" [1926], CW 9, 292.

57. As a result of this need for expertise, Keynes could easily come across as someone "ill at ease with democracy." Wayne Parsons, "Politics and Markets: Keynes and His Critics," in Terence Ball and Richard Bellamy, eds., *The Cambridge History of Twentieth-Century Political Thought* (Cambridge: Cambridge University Press, 2003), 50. In this regard he was always closer to the self-understanding of the Bank of England than he could possibly admit—though he did dedicate the *Tract on Monetary Reform* to the governors and court of the Bank. Keynes, *Tract on Monetary Reform*, CW 4, xv.

58. See, for example, Keynes's exchange with William Beveridge over the proposal to set up an Economic General Staff. Letter to the *Westminster Gazette* (July 17, 1926), CW 19, 567–58. See also Robert Skidelsky, "Keynes's Political Legacy," in Omar F. Hamouda and John N. Smithin, eds., *Keynes and Public Policy after Fifty Years* (Aldershot, UK: Edward Elgar, 1988), 19.

59. John Maynard Keynes, "Am I a Liberal?," part 1, *The Nation & Athenaeum*, August 8, 1925, 563–54; and part 2, August 15, 1925, 587–88. Tellingly, in the version reprinted in the 1931 edition of *Essays on Persuasion*, Keynes chose to excise this passage—leaving it unclear whether this reflected a change of mind or an awareness of the destructive public potential of the words themselves (or indeed both). Keynes, "Am I a Liberal?" [1925], CW 9, 295–96.

60. For a meticulous analysis of the decision to return to gold with regard to the complex role of ideas in international political economy, see James Ashley Morrison, *England's Cross of Gold: Keynes, Churchill, and the Governance of Economic Beliefs* (Ithaca, NY: Cornell University Press, 2021).

61. Belgium and France followed in 1926, Italy in 1927, and Japan in 1930. See Eichengreen, *Golden Fetters*, 153–221.

62. Churchill had in fact confronted his advisers with these arguments but was repeatedly reassured. The classic account is Donald Moggridge, *The Return to Gold, 1925: The Formulation of Economic Policy and Its Critics* (Cambridge: Cambridge University Press, 1969). This might still underestimate the extent to which both Churchill and Montagu Norman had in fact taken on board Keynes's critique even where they presented their policy simply as restoration. See Morrison, *England's Cross of Gold*, 175–76.

63. Much of the disagreement here turned on how much distance would have to be traversed. Where the Treasury expected no more than 5 percent, Keynes thought it was substantially more. Thanks to James Morrison for discussion on this point. See Morrison, *England's Cross of Gold*, 283; as well as Barry Eichengreen and Olivier Jeanne, "Currency Crisis and Unemployment," in Paul Krugman, ed., *Currency Crises* (Chicago: University of Chicago Press, 2000), 7–46, at 11.

64. Keynes, "The Economic Consequences of Mr. Churchill" [1925], CW 9, 211.

65. Keynes, "The Economic Consequences of Mr. Churchill" [1925], CW 9, 218.

66. Keynes, "The Economic Consequences of Mr. Churchill" [1925], CW 9, 218. Since I am here primarily interested in reconstructing Keynes's position, I remain agnostic about Churchill's actual motivations. There is some suggestion that Churchill precisely eyed restoration in order to address unemployment. See Morrison, *England's Cross of Gold*, 248–49.

67. Keynes exposed himself on this point, as indeed on others, to charges of hypocrisy. He had been only too happy to override and ridicule public opinion when it seemed to him to suggest economic folly, but he was happy to stir it when he hoped he could sway it in support of his own position.

68. Keynes, "The Economic Consequences of Mr. Churchill" [1925], CW 9, 215.

69. Keynes, "The Economic Consequences of Mr. Churchill" [1925], CW 9, 225.

70. Keynes, "The Economic Consequences of Mr. Churchill" [1925], CW 9, 229.

71. G. A. Phillips, *The General Strike: The Politics of Industrial Conflict* (London: Weidenfeld & Nicolson, 1976).

72. Morrison, *England's Cross of Gold*, 283. The claim seems to come from Churchill's principal private secretary at the time, James Grigg. See P. J. Grigg, *Prejudice and Judgment* (London: Jonathan Cape, 1948), 180.

73. See also the discussion in CW 13, 15.

74. This involved primarily a conception of the quantity equation based on "real balances," that is, balances, in hand or at the bank, measured in terms of purchasing power. Keynes, *Tract on Monetary Reform*, CW 4, 63n1, 67.

75. Concerning the external value of money, too, Keynes remained largely within conventional confines by basing the value of currencies on purchasing-power parity. Keynes, *Tract on Monetary Reform*, CW 4, 70–86.

76. Some of this material is reproduced in CW 28, 223–94.

77. CW 13, 41.

78. CW 13, 113–17.

79. John Maynard Keynes, *A Treatise on Money*, 2 vols. (London: Macmillan, 1930), CW 5 and 6. In the midst of completing the book, Keynes had also in 1929 been nominated to the Macmillan Committee on Finance and Industry, which provided him with insights and examples for the second volume on the applied theory of money.

80. Keynes, *Treatise on Money*, vol. 1, CW 5, 3.

81. Keynes, *Treatise on Money*, vol. 1, CW 5, 3.

82. CW 11, 403.

83. Geoffrey Ingham, *The Nature of Money* (Cambridge, UK: Polity, 2004), 34, 38–58.

84. Keynes, *Treatise on Money*, vol. 1, CW 5, 4.

85. Georg Friedrich Knapp, *Staatliche Theorie des Geldes* (Munich and Leipzig: Duncker & Humblot, 1905). Translated into English based on the fourth German edition, as *The State Theory of Money*, trans. H. M. Lucas and J. Bonar (London: Macmillan, 1924). The translation had been initiated by the Royal Economic Society of which Keynes was a member. See also the positive discussion of the German edition by one of its subsequent translators. James Bonar, "Knapp's Theory of Money," *Economic Journal* 32, no. 125 (March 1922): 39–47.

86. CW 11, 400–403. The reviewed book was Friedrich Bendixen's *Geld und Kapital* (Leipzig: Duncker & Humblot, 1912), which Keynes reviewed alongside Ludwig von Mises's *Theorie des Geldes und der Umlaufsmittel* (Munich: Duncker & Humblot,

1912). Keynes also added Knapp's *Staatliche Theorie des Geldes* as a reference work for his prewar lectures on the theory of money in Cambridge. CW 12, 726.

87. CW 11, 403.

88. CW 11, 412.

89. Knapp, *State Theory of Money*, 32, 38.

90. Knapp, *State Theory of Money*, 39. Astute observers immediately noticed the way in which Knapp collapsed a diverse set of theories of monetary nominalism into his own state theory at this point. See Joseph A. Schumpeter, "Das Sozialproduct und die Rechenpfennige: Glossen und Beiträge zur Geldtheorie von heute," *Archiv für Sozialwissenschaft und Sozialpolitik*, no. 44 (1917–18); translated as Joseph A. Schumpeter, "Money and the Social Product," trans. A. W. Marget, *International Economic Papers*, no. 6 (1956), 627–715; as well as Howard S. Ellis, *German Monetary Theory, 1905–1933* (Cambridge, MA: Harvard University Press, 1934), 42.

91. Weber returned to a more detailed discussion of Knapp later in the second chapter. Max Weber, *Economy and Society*, trans. Keith Tribe (Cambridge, MA: Harvard University Press, 2019), 159–68 and 284–319; Max Weber, *Wirtschaft und Gesellschaft: Grundriss der Sozialökonomik. III. Abteilung* (Tübingen: J.C.B. Mohr, 1922), 38–42 and 95–114. On the excursus on Knapp and Weber's difficult use of neologisms in the section, see Keith Tribe, "Introduction," in Weber, *Economy and Society*, 68n198 and 141. As Tribe puts it, Weber's discussion here becomes "progressively derailed by a casuistry more deliberately impenetrable than his own" (5).

92. Weber, *Economy and Society*, 160; Weber, *Wirtschaft und Gesellschaft*, 39. Weber described Knapp's book as "the greatest achievement of monetary economics" (163; 40). Weber found himself "*entirely* in agreement with Knapp. His book is formally and substantively one of the great masterpieces of German literary style and scientific acumen" (302; 105). Original emphasis.

93. Weber, *Economy and Society*, 284; Weber, *Wirtschaft und Gesellschaft*, 97.

94. Weber, *Economy and Society*, 286; Weber, *Wirtschaft und Gesellschaft*, 98.

95. Keynes, *Treatise on Money*, vol. 1, CW 5, 4. See also Ingham, *Nature of Money*, 39.

96. Keynes, *Treatise on Money*, vol. 1, CW 5, 4.

97. Keynes, *Treatise on Money*, vol. 1, CW 5, 4.

98. Keynes, *Treatise on Money*, vol. 1, CW 5, 20–43; Ingham, *Nature of Money*, 51.

99. Keynes, *Treatise on Money*, vol. 1, CW 5, 27.

100. Keynes, *Treatise on Money*, vol. 1, CW 5, 20–27, 176–78. For Wicksell and his influence on Keynes, see Robert Skidelsky, *Money and Government: The Past and Future of Economics* (New Haven, CT: Yale University Press, 2018), 67–70, 102. See also Keynes's earlier engagement with the credit theory of Mitchell Innes, whose work Keynes had already reviewed for the *Economic Journal* in 1914. See J. M. Keynes, "Review of A. Mitchell Innes, 'What Is Money?,'" *Economic Journal* 24, no. 95 (September 1914): 419–21. Strikingly though, Innes is neither cited nor mentioned in the *Treatise*; instead, Keynes frequently invoked Wicksell.

101. Keynes's account here reflected his close engagement over the previous years with his King's College colleague Dennis Robertson, whose *Banking Policy and the Price Level* had appeared in 1926, but also the work of the fellow Apostle Ralph George Hawtrey who had similarly dropped the old neoclassical "real balances" analysis in the course of the 1920s. As Robertson put it, "I have had so many discussions

with Mr J. M. Keynes on the subject-matter of chapters v and vi, and have rewritten them so drastically at his suggestion, that I think neither of us now knows how much of the ideas therein contained is his and how much is mine." D. H. Robertson, *Banking Policy and the Price Level* (London: P. S. King & Son, 1926), 5. See also CW 13, 29. For Hawtrey, see in particular his *Currency and Credit* (1919) as well as *Trade and Credit* (1928) and for a discussion, CW 13, 76–77, 126–39.

102. Ingham has made this point most forcefully in Ingham, *Nature of Money*, 50–51. Keynes at the same time lamented after the book's publication that readers had insufficiently appreciated the ways in which his account differed from prior credit theories. Keynes, *Treatise on Money*, vol. 1, CW 5, preface to the German and Japanese editions (dated April 5, 1932), xxiii.

103. Treasury Papers, the National Archives, London, T 208/153.

104. Bruce Caldwell, *Hayek's Challenge: An Intellectual Biography of F. A. Hayek* (Chicago: University of Chicago Press, 2005), 173.

105. The first part of Hayek's review appeared in August 1931, just before the British suspension of gold. F. A. Hayek, "Reflections on the Pure Theory of Money of Mr. J. M. Keynes," *Economica* 11, no. 33 (August 1931): 270–95.

106. John Maynard Keynes, "A Reply to Dr. Hayek," *Economica* 11, no. 34 (November 1931): 387–97.

107. F. A. Hayek, *Prices and Production*, with a foreword by Lionel Robbins (London: George Routledge & Sons, 1931).

108. Keynes, "Reply to Dr. Hayek," 394. Keynes also described (in the margins) Hayek's essay on "Capital Consumption" as "the wildest farrago of nonsense." Skidelsky, *Economist as Savior*, 459. See also Nicholas Wapshott, *Keynes Hayek: The Clash That Defined Modern Economics* (New York: W. W. Norton, 2012), 124.

109. Skidelsky, *Economist as Savior*, 457.

110. Hayek, "Reflections," 271.

111. Keynes, *Treatise on Money*, vol. 2, CW 6, 189–367.

112. Keynes, *Treatise on Money*, vol. 2, CW 6, 194.

113. Keynes, *Treatise on Money*, vol. 2, CW 6, 195.

114. Keynes, *Treatise on Money*, vol. 2, CW 6, 195.

115. Keynes, *Treatise on Money*, vol. 2, CW 6, 195.

116. Keynes, *Treatise on Money*, vol. 2, CW 6, 194, 198.

117. Keynes, *Treatise on Money*, vol. 2, CW 6, 200.

118. Keynes, *Treatise on Money*, vol. 1, CW 5, 26. See also Ingham, *Nature of Money*, 28.

119. Keynes, *Treatise on Money*, vol. 2, CW 6, 195.

120. Keynes, *Treatise on Money*, vol. 2, CW 6, 189. Original emphasis. See also Keynes, "Credit Control," for the *Encyclopaedia of Social Sciences*, written in February 1930, CW 11, 420–27. Skidelsky, *Money and Government*, 102 and 401n12.

121. Keynes, "Credit Control," CW 11, 424. As cited in Skidelsky, *Money and Government*, 102.

122. Keynes, *Treatise on Money*, vol. 2, CW 6, 190.

123. Keynes, *Treatise on Money*, vol. 2, CW 6, 261. The opening section of the chapter was also reprinted as "Auri Sacra Fames" in *Essays in Persuasion*, CW 9, 161–63, at 163.

124. Keynes, "Alternative Aims in Monetary Policy" [1923], CW 9, 180.

125. Keynes, *Tract on Monetary Reform*, 40; CW 4, 36. See also Keynes's comments in the Chamberlain-Bradbury Committee in the summer of 1924, CW 19, 272. As discussed in Morrison, *England's Cross of Gold*, 179.

126. Managed in the sense of left to discretionary decisions concerning the level of inflation and employment in the economy, rather than semiautomatically guided by the rules of the gold standard.

127. Keynes, *Treatise on Money*, vol. 2, CW 6, 261. See also Geoff Mann, *In the Long Run We Are All Dead: Keynesianism, Political Economy, and Revolution* (London and New York: Verso, 2017).

128. Walter Bagehot, *The English Constitution* (London: Chapman & Hall, 1867); originally published in serialized form between May 1865 and January 1867 in the *Fortnightly Review*. His influential account of central banks as a lender of last resort was advanced in Walter Bagehot, *Lombard Street: A Description of the Money Market* (London: Henry S. King, 1873).

129. Alexander Zevin, *Liberalism at Large: The World according to the Economist* (London and New York: Verso, 2019), 86.

130. Bagehot, *Lombard Street*, 330. The Bank of England was of course nationalized in 1946.

131. Bagehot, *Lombard Street*, 68. As Zevin observes, this "analogy between the function of credit and that of a constitutional monarch was deliberate—and revealing. Bankers had faith in the Bank of England as implicitly as 'Queen Victoria was obeyed by millions of human beings.' There was no good reason to accept either, in other words." Zevin, *Liberalism at Large*, 85.

132. Keynes, "Auri Sacra Fames" [September 1930], CW 9, 163.

133. The Bank of England itself was of course only too aware of the ways in which the interwar exchange standard required active management and how that management had to be shielded from politics. The main difference lies, I think, in Keynes's insistence that the Bank nonetheless had to acknowledge much more openly that it was in fact engaged in managing the currency while exposing itself to critique from outside experts. For Montagu Norman learning from Keynes, see Morrison, *England's Cross of Gold*, 175–77.

134. Keynes at the same time always tended to overstate his outsider status for good effect. See the discussion in Morrison, *England's Cross of Gold*, 176.

135. Originally the book was to be entitled *Essays in Prophecy*, which then turned into *Essays in Prophecy and Persuasion*, before finally being published in November as *Essays in Persuasion*. See also CW 20, 622.

136. Keynes, "Preface," *Essays in Persuasion*, CW 9, xvii.

137. Morrison, "Shocking Intellectual Austerity," 175–207.

138. John Maynard Keynes, *The Economic Consequences of the Peace* (London: Macmillan, 1919), CW 2. See also Keynes, *A Revision of the Treaty*, CW 3.

139. Keynes, *Economic Consequences of the Peace*, CW 2, 169, 188–89.

140. Jamie Martin, *The Meddlers: The Origins of Global Economic Governance* (Cambridge, MA: Harvard University Press, 2022).

141. Michael A. Heilperin, *Studies in Economic Nationalism* (Geneva and Paris: Publications de l'Institut Universitaire Hautes Etudes Internationales, 1960), 82–128.

"The views of Fichte on national self-sufficiency," Heilperin explained, "were rediscovered, or, rather, re-invented, by John Maynard Keynes in 1933" (63).

142. Isaac Nakhimovsky, *The Closed Commercial State: Perpetual Peace and Commercial Society from Rousseau to Fichte* (Princeton, NJ: Princeton University Press, 2011), 3.

143. Partially as a result, Keynes's interventions in the spring of 1933 attracted great attention around the world. They marked, in Skidelsky's words, "the start of public understanding of the Keynesian Revolution" and "begat an enormous debate which went on in several countries." Skidelsky, *Economist as Savior*, 473.

144. Keynes gave the lecture at University College, Dublin, on April 19, 1933. Four versions of it were subsequently printed: the full lecture in *Studies: An Irish Quarterly Review* (22, no. 1 [June 1933]: 177–93) and shortened versions in the *New Statesman and Nation* (6, no. 124 [July 8 and 15, 1933], 36–37; 65–67) and the *Yale Review* (22, no. 4 [June 1933]: 755–69). The *New Statesman* version of the lecture is also reprinted in CW 21, 233–46.

145. On the Anglo-Irish trade war, see Kevin O'Rourke, "Burn Everything British but Their Coal: The Anglo-Irish Economic War of the 1930s," *Journal of Economic History* 51, no. 2 (June 1991): 357–66.

146. John Maynard Keynes, "National Self-Sufficiency," *Studies: An Irish Quarterly Review* 22, no. 1 (June 1933): 177–93, at 186. The content of the Dublin lecture seems to have surprised an audience that had somehow expected a denunciation of tariffs and of the Irish position during the ongoing trade war between Britain and Ireland. Skidelsky, *Economist as Savior*, 479.

147. Amazingly, it was in the middle of the celebratory dinner following the Dublin lecture in April that Keynes received a phone call informing him that President Roosevelt had officially suspended the dollar's convertibility into gold. When he came back, Keynes announced to the room: "You may be interested to know that the United States has just left gold." Eric Rauchway, *The Money Makers: How Roosevelt and Keynes Ended the Depression, Defeated Fascism, and Secured a Prosperous Peace* (New York: Basic Books, 2015), 260n50; Ahamed, *Lords of Finance*, 461; Skidelsky, *Economist as Savior*, 480.

148. Keynes, "National Self-Sufficiency," 193.

149. In the *Treatise*, Keynes first also considered two parallel questions in the domestic realm: the desired relationship of the central bank to its member banks (ch. 32) and the legal limitations that should be placed on the discretion of the central bank (ch. 33).

150. JMK Papers, King's College, Cambridge, TM/1–4; CW 13, 28–50.

151. See especially chs. 36 and 38 of the second volume of the *Treatise on Money*, CW 6, 270–303, and 348–67.

152. Keynes, *Treatise on Money*, vol. 2, CW 6, 358.

153. Keynes, *Treatise on Money*, vol. 2, CW 6, 361–64. For a new history of the BIS as part of a larger quest for global economic governance during the interwar years, see Martin, *The Meddlers*; and Adam LeBor, *Tower of Basel: The Shadowy History of the Secret Bank That Runs the World* (New York: Public Affairs, 2014).

154. Even Skidelsky has described Keynes's international proposal from March 1933 as "conceding to orthodoxy." Skidelsky, *Economist as Savior*, 472.

155. Keynes, "Letter to the Editor of *The Economist*," March 20, 1933, CW 21, 186.

156. Keynes, "Letter to the Editor of *The Times*," April 7, 1933, CW 21, 185. Meltzer quotes a slightly different letter to the same effect from March 1933. Meltzer, *Keynes's Monetary Theory*, 230.

157. Keynes, "Should Britain Compromise on the Gold Standard?," *Daily Mail*, February 17, 1933, CW 21, 229–30.

158. R. H. Brand, *The Times*, April 7, 1933.

159. Skidelsky, *Economist as Savior*, 476.

160. Keynes, "Letter to the Editor of *The Times*," April 7, 1933, CW 21, 187.

161. On "Keynes's dilemma," see also Jonathan Kirshner, "Money Is Politics," *Review of International Political Economy* 10, no. 4 (2003): 645–60, at 647–49.

162. Skidelsky, "Keynes's Road to Bretton Woods," 134.

163. On fiscal policy, see John Maynard Keynes, *The General Theory of Employment, Interest and Money*, in *The Collected Writings of John Maynard Keynes*, vol. 7, ed. Austin Robinson and Donald Moggridge (Cambridge: Cambridge University Press, 2013), 94–96. See also Skidelsky, "Keynes's Road to Bretton Woods," 137. On the reception of the *General Theory*, see Geoff Tily, *Keynes Betrayed: The General Theory, the Rate of Interest and "Keynesian" Economics* (London: Palgrave Macmillan, 2010); and Michael S. Lawlor, *The Economics of Keynes in Historical Context: An Intellectual History of the General Theory* (London: Palgrave Macmillan, 2006).

164. I am indebted to James Morrison for extended discussions on this point and the argument below.

165. Keynes, *Treatise on Money*, vol. 2, CW 6, 270–303.

166. As Susan Howson suggested in this context, Keynes may have simply been too impatient since the monetary stimulus did eventually lead the United Kingdom out of the Great Depression, just not fast enough for Keynes's taste. Susan Howson, *Domestic Monetary Management in Britain, 1919–1938* (Cambridge: Cambridge University Press, 1975).

167. Rather than flowing from Keynes's pen, the figure of speech seems to have originated in US congressional hearings concerning the Banking Act of 1935. John Wood credits the appropriately named congressman Thomas Alan Goldsborough of Maryland with having coined the phrase. John Harold Wood, *A History of Central Banking in Great Britain and the United States* (Cambridge: Cambridge University Press, 2008), 231.

168. John Maynard Keynes, "Open Letter to Mr. Roosevelt," CW 21, 289–97, at 294. An abbreviated version of the letter was printed in the London *Times*. See John Maynard Keynes, "Mr Roosevelt's Experiments," *The Times*, January 2, 1934, CW 21, 297–304, at 301.

169. As Keynes had already put it in his Halley-Stewart Lecture in 1931, "There will be no means of escape from prolonged and perhaps interminable depression except by direct state intervention to promote and subsidise new investment." John Maynard Keynes, "The World's Economic Crisis and the Way of Escape," Halley-Stewart Lecture, February 1932, CW 21, 50–62; see also Skidelsky, *Money and Government*, 116.

170. Skidelsky, *Money and Government*, 114. Already in the *Tract on Monetary Reform*—dedicated after all to the governors of the Bank of England—Keynes had

remarked that "nowhere do conservative notions consider themselves more in place than in currency; yet nowhere is the need of innovation more urgent." Keynes, *Tract on Monetary Reform*, CW 4, xiv.

171. Macmillan Committee (1929–31), T 200; Committee on Finance and Industry: Minutes of Evidence, the National Archives, London, qq.7690. Also cited in Skidelsky, *Money and Government*, 115.

172. Keynes, "The Monetary Theory of Production," CW 13, 408–12, as well as 381; Keynes, *General Theory*, CW 7, xii.

173. Keynes, "Monetary Theory of Production," CW 13, 408–9.

174. Keynes, "Monetary Theory of Production," CW 13, 408.

175. Keynes to R. F. Harrod, August 30, 1936, CW 14, 85.

176. Keynes, *General Theory*, CW 7, xv–xvi.

177. One crucial point of continuity was, for example, the discussion of bank money. Keynes, *General Theory*, CW 7, 167n1.

178. For a lucid analysis of Keynes's take on Abba Lerner's functional finance, see Tony Aspromourgos, "Keynes, Lerner, and the Question of Public Debt," *History of Political Economy* 46, no. 3 (2014): 409–33. Aspromourgos helpfully foregrounds Keynes's distinction between theory and practice in this regard. While functional finance was not a necessary extension of Keynes's theory, it also did not rule it out; instead, whether functional finance's theoretical coherence translated into prudent policy was a question of politics.

179. Keynes, *General Theory*, CW 7, 164; Skidelsky, *Money and Government*, 125.

180. Keynes, *General Theory*, CW 7, 378.

181. Keynes, *General Theory*, CW 7, 267.

182. Keynes, *General Theory*, CW 7, 267.

183. "It is not the ownership of the instruments of production which it is important for the State to assume. If the State is able to determine the aggregate amount of resources devoted to augmenting the instruments and the basic rate of reward to those who own them, it will have accomplished all that is necessary." Keynes, *General Theory*, CW 7, 378.

184. Keynes, *General Theory*, CW 7, 378. As Morrison has perceptively observed, in the *General Theory* Keynes presented himself no longer merely as the iconoclast who called on others to take a leap with him into an unknown future but instead also as a restorative force who returned economic common sense to an earlier mercantilist wisdom that had been repressed since Ricardo. Morrison, *England's Cross of Gold*, 286, 365n45. See also James Morrison, "Thinking Backwards? Keynes versus Burke on the Competition of Continuities," paper presented at Georgetown University, April 24, 2021.

185. Keynes, *General Theory*, CW 7, 376.

186. Keynes, *General Theory*, CW 7, 376.

187. Keynes, *General Theory*, CW 7, 349.

188. As Keynes wrote to George Bernard Shaw on New Year's Day 1935: "To understand my new state of mind, however, you have to know that I believe myself to be writing a book on economic theory which will largely revolutionize—not, I suppose, at once but in the course of the next ten years—the way the world thinks about its economic problems." Keynes to George Bernard Shaw, January 1, 1935, CW 14, 492.

189. Keynes, *General Theory*, CW 7, 349.

190. Keynes, *General Theory*, CW 7, 335.

191. Keynes, *General Theory*, CW 7, 336.

192. Keynes, *General Theory*, CW 7, 350.

193. Keynes, *General Theory*, CW 7, 343, 342.

194. Keynes, *General Theory*, CW 7, 349.

195. Keynes, *General Theory*, CW 7, 349.

196. For discussion on this point I am grateful to David Grewal and Robert Hockett who have elegantly formulated the underlying "n+1" problem. Unpublished working paper on file with the author.

197. John Maynard Keynes, "Proposals for an International Currency (or Clearing) Union" [February 11, 1942], in Keith Horsefield, ed., *The International Monetary Fund, 1945–1965: Twenty Years of International Monetary Cooperation* (Washington, DC: International Monetary Fund, 1969), 3–18 and 19–36. See also the documents collected in CW 25, as well as his Treasury Papers in the National Archives, London. For an excellent overview, see Robert Hockett, "Bretton Woods 1.0: A Constructive Retrieval for Sustainable Finance," *N.Y.U. Journal of Legislation and Public Policy*, no. 16 (2013): 401–82.

198. CW 25, 28; see also Skidelsky, *Money and Government*, 127.

199. Keynes, "International Currency (or Clearing) Union," par. 16. Already the League of Nations had contained provisions to force deficit countries to adjust.

200. Keynes, "International Currency (or Clearing) Union," par. 19.

201. Keynes, "Not Utopia but Eutopia: The International Clearing Union," JMK Papers, King's College, Cambridge, W/6/1 (August 4, 1942). This plan—including Keynes's intriguing title—was also sent to Washington. Ed Conway, *The Summit: Bretton Woods, 1944: J. M. Keynes and the Reshaping of the Global Economy* (New York: Pegasus Books, 2015), 135; Robert Skidelsky, *John Maynard Keynes: Fighting for Britain, 1937–1946* (London: Macmillan, 2001), 247.

202. As cited in Conway, *The Summit*, 127.

203. As cited in Conway, *The Summit*, 127.

204. Conway, *The Summit*, 128. Bob Brand, a former Lazard banker on the British Treasury negotiating team, particularly pushed this concern. Keynes himself was at least initially convinced that the advantages of an international reserve currency were so great that even the United States would have an interest in seeing its trade credit recycled for the benefit of the world economy.

205. Keynes, "International Currency (or Clearing) Union," pars. 15, 26, 34, 72.

206. Conway, *The Summit*, 140.

207. Harry Dexter White Papers, Princeton University, Rare Books and Special Collections, Box 8/24. As cited in Conway, *The Summit*, 131.

208. "These things are too early," Roosevelt admonished Morgenthau. "We haven't begun to win the war." Morgenthau Diary 622, 8–9. As cited in Conway, *The Summit*, 139.

209. Conway, *The Summit*, 135–9.

210. CW 25, 269–80, at 269.

211. The most severe criticism came, inevitably, from almost all the Wall Street banks as well as the New York Federal Reserve. As the New York Fed put it, "The

plans for an International Monetary Fund . . . are not only based on mistaken principles but risk eventual failure which would bring further discredit upon the cause of
internationalism." In response, the US government launched what the *Herald Tribune* described as "the most high-powered propaganda campaign in the history of
the country." Conway, *The Summit*, 297–98.

212. Keynes to Wilfrid Eady, October 3, 1943, CW 25, 362–64. See Moggridge,
Keynes, 730.

213. "Speech by Lord Keynes in Moving to Accept the Final Act at the Closing
Plenary Session, Bretton Woods, 22 July 1944," CW 26, 101–5, at 102.

214. For the historiography of Bretton Woods, see Benn Steil, *The Battle of Bretton
Woods: John Maynard Keynes, Harry Dexter White, and the Making of a New World
Order* (Princeton, NJ: Princeton University Press, 2013); Eric Helleiner, *Forgotten
Foundations of Bretton Woods: International Development and the Making of the
Postwar Order* (Ithaca, NY: Cornell University Press, 2014); and the vivid account
in Conway, *The Summit*. Transcripts of the conference have recently been published
as Kurt Schuler and Andrew Rosenberg, eds., *The Bretton Woods Transcripts* (New
York: Center for Financial Stability, 2013).

215. CW 26, 17.

216. Henry Morgenthau, letter to President Truman, quoted in *New York Herald
Tribune*, March 31, 1946. Also quoted in Metzler, *Lever of Empire*, 265.

217. Skidelsky, "Keynes's Road to Bretton Woods," 150; Armand Van Dormael,
Bretton Woods: Birth of a Monetary System (London: Palgrave Macmillan, 1978),
228, 237; CW 26, 134.

218. Conway, *The Summit*, 349. Keynes was consequently the only one to vote
against the proposed salary packages.

219. CW 26, 215–17. As cited in Conway, *The Summit*, 346.

220. CW 26, 217.

221. Keynes, "Am I a Liberal?" [1925], CW 9, 305.

222. Keynes, "Am I a Liberal?" [1925], CW 9, 306.

223. This can read be read as a more or less explicit response to Carl Schmitt, "The
Age of Neutralizations and Depoliticizations," [1929] in Carl Schmitt, *The Concept of
the Political* (Chicago: University of Chicago Press), 80–96.

Chapter 6. Silent Revolution

1. Daniel Bell, *The Cultural Contradictions of Capitalism* (New York: Basic Books,
1976), 197.

2. Friedrich August Hayek, "The Pretence of Knowledge," lecture to the Memory
of Alfred Nobel, December 11, 1974; reprinted as Friedrich August Hayek, "The Pretence of Knowledge," in *The Market and Other Orders*, ed. Bruce Caldwell, *Collected
Works of F. A. Hayek*, vol. 15 (Chicago: University of Chicago Press, 2014), 362–72, at
362. For an account of Hayek's visit to Sweden, see Bruce Caldwell, "Hayek's Nobel,"
in Peter J. Boettke and Virgil Henry Storr, eds., *Revisiting Hayek's Political Economy*, Advances in Austrian Economics, vol. 21 (Bingley, UK: Emerald, 2016), 1–19.

3. Friedrich August Hayek, *The Road to Serfdom: Text and Documents—The
Definitive Edition*, ed. Bruce Caldwell, *Collected Works of F. A. Hayek*, vol. 2 (Chicago:
University of Chicago Press, 2007), 125.

For Keynes reading *The Road to Serfdom*, see his letter to Hayek dated June 28, 1944, and sent from Atlantic City, NJ. *The Collected Writings of John Maynard Keynes*, vol. 27 (*Activities 1940–1946: Shaping the Post-War World: Employment and Commodities*), ed. Elizabeth Johnson and Donald Moggridge (Cambridge: Cambridge University Press, 2013), 385–88.

4. Friedrich August Hayek, *The Constitution of Liberty* [1960], ed. Bruce Caldwell and Ronald Hamowy, *Collected Works of F. A. Hayek*, vol. 17 (Chicago: University of Chicago Press, 2011), 451–65. Whereas Hayek's defense of the rule of law was peppered with references to John Locke, in his discussion of the monetary framework he confined himself largely to twentieth-century references. But it was in these mid-century writings that Locke's status as intellectual forefather of liberalism was solidified. See Duncan Bell, "What Is Liberalism?," *Political Theory* 42, no. 6 (2014): 682–715.

5. For an extrapolated reading based on a brief reference, see Jens van 't Klooster, "Central Banking in Rawls's Property-Owning Democracy," *Political Theory* 47, no. 5 (2019): 674–98.

6. Consider, for example, the telling way in which recent critiques of commodification have been framed by opposing money to morality. Michael J. Sandel, *What Money Can't Buy: The Moral Limits of Markets* (New York: Farrar, Straus & Giroux, 2012); Debra Satz, *Why Some Things Should Not Be for Sale: The Moral Limits of Markets* (Oxford: Oxford University Press, 2010).

7. Jürgen Habermas, *The Theory of Communicative Action*, vol. 1, *Reason and the Rationalization of Society*, trans. Thomas McCarthy (Boston: Beacon, 1984), 359; Jürgen Habermas, *Theorie des Kommunikativen Handelns* (Frankfurt am Main: Suhrkamp, 1981), Band 1, 480.

8. G. A. Cohen, "On the Currency of Egalitarian Justice," *Ethics* 99, no. 4 (July 1989): 906–44.

9. The historiography of the Great Inflation is still remarkably thin once self-justifying practitioner histories by central bankers and conservative morality tales are excluded. For a historiographical overview and a first attempt at synthesis, see Stefan Eich and Adam Tooze, "The Great Inflation," in Anselm Doering-Manteuffel, Lutz Raphael, and Thomas Schlemmer, eds., *Vorgeschichte der Gegenwart* (Göttingen, Germany: Vandenhoeck & Ruprecht, 2015), 173–96.

10. Driven to its logical conclusion, this exposed the US to a dilemma between its domestic currency needs and global monetary stability. The classic statement is Robert Triffin, *Gold and the Dollar Crisis: The Future of Convertibility* (New Haven, CT: Yale University Press, 1960).

11. In addition, during the 1950s several countries—most prominently the United States and Germany—witnessed successful attempts by their respective central banks to regain some of the independence lost in the war. This added to the constraints imposed by Bretton Woods in removing monetary policy from the agenda of politics. Notable exceptions were of course instances in which a country came under pressure to devalue, as happened in Britain in 1967. For the Fed-Treasury relationship, see Allan H. Meltzer, *A History of the Federal Reserve*, vol. 1, *1951–1969* (Chicago: University of Chicago Press, 2010), 41–115.

12. David Singh Grewal and Jedediah Purdy, "Inequality Rediscovered," *Theoretical Inquiries in Law* 18, no. 1 (2016): 61–82.

13. John Kenneth Galbraith, *The Affluent Society* (Boston: Houghton Mifflin, 1958). For Galbraith's discussion of the "inutility" of monetary policy, see chapter 15: "Monetary policy is a blunt, unreliable, discriminatory and somewhat dangerous instrument of economic control. It survives in esteem partly because so few understand it" (176).

14. Katrina Forrester, *In the Shadow of Justice: Postwar Liberalism and the Remaking of Political Philosophy* (Princeton, NJ: Princeton University Press, 2019), 140, 272; Grewal and Purdy, "Inequality Rediscovered," 66–67; see also Stefan Eich, "The Theodicy of Growth: John Rawls, Political Economy, and Reasonable Faith," *Modern Intellectual History, First View* (2021): 1–26.

15. Rawls stepped outside of his self-prescribed agnosticism only when emphasizing the exclusive ability of markets to satisfy the first part of the second principle of justice: the right to free choice of occupation under conditions of fair equality of opportunity. John Rawls, *A Theory of Justice* (Cambridge, MA: The Belknap Press of Harvard University Press, 1971), 276.

16. For Rawls's extensive engagement with postwar economics, see Forrester, *Shadow of Justice*, 12, 30, 173.

17. There are two brief references to monetary policy in *A Theory of Justice* which implicitly suggest that Rawls regarded central banking as part of the responsibilities of a democratically elected government. Rawls, *Theory of Justice*, 271, 276. See Jens van 't Klooster, "Central Banking in Rawls's Property-Owning Democracy," *Political Theory* 47, no. 5 (2019): 674–98.

18. For a lucid commentary that combines proximity to the drama of the events with a clear-sighted mapping of it, see Susan Strange, "The Dollar Crisis," *International Affairs* 48, no. 2 (April 1972): 191–216.

19. Douglas Brinkley and Luke A. Nichter, eds., *The Nixon Tapes, 1971–1972* (New York: Houghton Mifflin Harcourt, 2014), 231–38.

20. Daniel J. Sargent, *A Superpower Transformed: The Remaking of American Foreign Relations in the 1970s* (Oxford: Oxford University Press, 2015).

21. As quoted in Harold James, *International Monetary Cooperation since Bretton Woods* (Oxford: Oxford University Press, 1996), 210.

22. Eich, "Theodicy of Growth," 6; Jan-Werner Müller, "Rawls, Historian: Remarks on Political Liberalism's 'Historicism,'" *Revue internationale de philosophie* 237, no. 3 (2006): 327–39, at 329; Grewal and Purdy, "Inequality Rediscovered," 66.

23. Angus Maddison, *The World Economy: Millennial Statistics*, available online: http://www.theworldeconomy.org (accessed June 20, 2021).

24. Daniel J. Sargent, "North/South: The United States Responds to the New International Economic Order," *Humanity* 6, no. 1 (Spring 2015): 203.

25. In 1982 and 1983, inflation was beaten only by high unemployment. See Robert J. Samuelson, *The Great Inflation and Its Aftermath: The Past and Future of American Affluence* (New York: Random House, 2008), 23.

26. Daniel Yankelovich, "The Noneconomic Side of Inflation," in Clarence C. Walton, ed., *Inflation and National Survival* (New York: Academy of Political Science, 1979), 20. As quoted in Samuelson, *Great Inflation*, 20.

27. Gerald R. Ford, "Address to a Joint Session of the Congress on the Economy (October 8, 1974)," in *Public Papers of the Presidents of the United States:*

Administration of Gerald R. Ford (Washington, DC: Government Printing Office, 1975), 228–38.

28. Adom Getachew, *Worldmaking after Empire: The Rise and Fall of Self-Determination* (Princeton, NJ: Princeton University Press, 2019); Mark Mazower, *Governing the World: The History of an Idea* (London: Penguin, 2012).

29. Albert O. Hirschman, "The Principle of the Hiding Hand," *Public Interest*, no. 6 (Winter 1967): 10–23.

30. Jürgen Habermas, *Legitimation Crisis*, trans. Thomas McCarthy (Boston: Beacon, 1975).

31. Jimmy Carter, "Anti-Inflation Program: Address to the Nation, October 24, 1978," *Public Papers of the Presidents of the United States: Administration of Jimmy Carter, June 30–December 31, 1978* (Washington, DC: Government Printing Office, 1979), 1840.

32. The report traced the crisis to an excess of democracy. Michel J. Crozier, Samuel P. Huntington, and Joji Watanuki, *The Crisis of Democracy: Report on the Governability of Democracies to the Trilateral Commission* (New York: NYU Press, 1975), 9.

33. Bell's book became "one of the mid-1970s' most important books of social theory." Daniel T. Rodgers, *Age of Fracture* (Cambridge, MA: Harvard University Press, 2011), 75.

34. Bell, *Cultural Contradictions*, 237.

35. Bell, *Cultural Contradictions*, 24.

36. Bell, *Cultural Contradictions*, 197.

37. Bell, *Cultural Contradictions*, 239.

38. Bell, *Cultural Contradictions*, 240–42. See also Fred Hirsch, *Social Limits to Growth* (Cambridge, MA: Harvard University Press, 1976).

39. Bell, *Cultural Contradictions*, 243. See also Stefan Eich, "The Double Bind: Daniel Bell, the Public Household, and Financialization," in Paul Starr and Julian Zelizer, eds., *Defining the Age: Daniel Bell, His Time, and Ours* (Columbia University Press, 2021).

40. Bell, *Cultural Contradictions*, 220–82.

41. Bell, *Cultural Contradictions*, 249n24.

42. Bell, *Cultural Contradictions*, 235.

43. Charles E. Lindblom, *Politics and Markets: The World's Political-Economic Systems* (New York: Basic Books, 1977).

44. The interview was conducted by Angelo Bolaffi at the Max Planck Institute in Starnberg and first appeared in *Rinascita*, the weekly journal of the Italian Communist Party (PCI), in issues 30 (July 28, 1978) and 31 (August 4, 1978). Two different English translations appeared as Jürgen Habermas, "Conservatism and Capitalist Crisis," *New Left Review*, no. 115 (May–June 1979): 73–84; and Jürgen Habermas, "Angelo Bolaffi: An Interview with Jürgen Habermas," *Telos*, no. 39 (Spring 1979): 163–72.

45. Habermas, "Conservatism and Capitalist Crisis," 81; Habermas, "Bolaffi: Interview with Habermas," 169.

46. A short version of the text appeared in *Merkur* in January 1976; the full version was published as Jürgen Habermas, "Legitimationsprobleme im modernen Staat," in *Zur Rekonstruktion des Historischen Materialismus* (Frankfurt am Main: Suhrkamp, 1976), 289. A partial translation appeared as Jürgen Habermas, "Legitimation Problems in the Modern State," in *Communication and the Evolution of Society* (Boston: Beacon, 1979), 195–96.

47. Habermas, "Conservatism and Capitalist Crisis," 80; Habermas, "Bolaffi: Interview with Habermas," 168.

48. *Report of the Deutsche Bundesbank for the Year 1974*, 16. Available online: http://www.bundesbank.de/Redaktion/EN/Downloads/Publications/Annual_Report /1974_annual_report.pdf.

49. Harold James, *Making the European Monetary Union* (Cambridge, MA: Harvard University Press, 2012), 62–88.

50. Michel Foucault, *The Birth of Biopolitics: Lectures at the Collège de France, 1978–79* (Basingstoke, UK: Palgrave Macmillan, 2008), 75–158. For the French transcript, see Michel Foucault, *Naissance de la biopolitique. 1978–1979* (Paris: Seuil, 2004), 77–164.

51. Foucault, *Birth of Biopolitics*, 86. Foucault never returned to Fichte.

52. On the foundational West German monetary reform of 1948, see Charles P. Kindleberger and F. Taylor Ostrander, "The 1948 Monetary Reform in Western Germany," in Marc Flandreau, Carl-Ludwig Holtfrerich, and Harold James, eds., *International Financial History in the Twentieth Century: System and Anarchy* (Cambridge: Cambridge University Press, 2003), 169–95.

53. For an account of the Franco-German and transatlantic politics of anti-inflationism, see Eich and Tooze, "Great Inflation," 185–91. As Habermas explained six months before Foucault's lectures, "In West Germany, the management of economic policy has been staged for the public in a very effective way. The immediate results of this staging have been on the one hand the processes of intimidation and discipline . . . and on the other hand a possibly reinforced cynicism towards the way the system redistributes its costs." Anyone who watched the news in West Germany could, according to Habermas, witness an economic policy that imposed discipline against workers while deflecting blame for doing so. Habermas, "Conservatism and Capitalist Crisis," 80; Habermas, "Bolaffi: Interview with Habermas," 168.

54. "The Sveriges Riksbank Prize in Economic Sciences in Memory of Alfred Nobel 1974." Available online: http://www.nobelprize.org/nobel_prizes/economic -sciences/laureates/1974.

55. Gunnar Myrdal, "The Equality Issue in World Development," lecture to the Memory of Alfred Nobel, March 1975.

56. See also Gunnar Myrdal, *Beyond the Welfare State: Economic Planning and Its International Implications* (New Haven, CT: Yale University Press, 1960).

57. Myrdal, "Equality Issue in World Development." For the NIEO resolution, see "Declaration on the Establishment of a New International Economic Order," resolution adopted by the United Nations General Assembly, A/RES/S-6/3201 (May 1, 1974).

58. Friedrich August Hayek, "The Use of Knowledge in Society," *American Economic Review* 35, no. 4 (September 1945): 519–30, esp. 526. See also Friedrich August Hayek, *Law, Legislation and Liberty*, vol. 1, *Rules and Order* (Chicago: University of Chicago Press, 1973), 103–4.

59. Hayek, *Road to Serfdom*, 87.

60. Hayek, *Constitution of Liberty*, 332.

61. Hayek, *Constitution of Liberty*, 451, 452.

62. "For the moment," he wrote in 1960, "the important fact is that, as long as government expenditure constitutes as large a part of the national income as it now

does everywhere, we must accept the fact that government will necessarily dominate monetary policy and that the only way in which we could alter this would be to reduce government expenditure greatly." Hayek, *Constitution of Liberty*, 452.

63. Friedrich August Hayek, *Denationalisation of Money*, Hobart Papers Special 70 (London: Institute of Economic Affairs, October 1976). Expanded version reprinted as Friedrich August Hayek, "The Denationalization of Money: An Analysis of the Theory and Praxis of Concurrent Currencies" [1978], in *Good Money, Part 2: The Standard*, ed. Stephen Kresge, *Collected Works of F. A. Hayek*, vol. 6 (Chicago: University of Chicago Press, 1999), 128–229.

64. Hayek, "Denationalization of Money," 202.

65. Hayek, "Denationalization of Money," 202.

66. Others, though sympathetic to Hayek's conclusions, were nonetheless more careful to distinguish between Keynes and postwar Keynesianism. See, for example, James M. Buchanan and Richard E. Wagner, *Democracy in Deficit: The Political Legacy of Lord Keynes* [1977], in *The Collected Works of James M. Buchanan*, vol. 8 (Indianapolis: Liberty Fund, 2000), 53.

67. Friedrich August Hayek, "Choice in Currency: A Way to Stop Inflation" [1975], in *Good Money, Part 2: The Standard*, ed. Stephen Kresge, *Collected Works of F. A. Hayek*, vol. 6 (Chicago: University of Chicago Press, 1999), 115–127, at 120.

68. Friedrich August Hayek, "Toward a Free Market Monetary System" [1977], in *Good Money, Part 2: The Standard*, ed. Stephen Kresge, *Collected Works of F. A. Hayek*, vol. 6 (Chicago: University of Chicago Press, 1999), 230–37, at 231 and 233.

69. "For in every country of the world, I believe, the avarice and injustice of princes and sovereign states abusing the confidence of their subjects, have by degrees diminished the real quality of the metal, which had been originally contained in their coins." Adam Smith, *An Inquiry into the Nature and Causes of the Wealth of Nations*, ed. R. H. Campbell and A. S. Skinner, 2 vols., Glasgow Edition of the Works and Correspondence (Oxford: Clarendon Press, 1976), bk. 1, ch. 4, 43. As cited in Hayek, "Denationalization of Money," 128.

70. Hayek, "Denationalization of Money," 186.

71. Friedrich August Hayek, "Preface," in *Law, Legislation and Liberty*, vol. 3, *The Political Order of a Free People* (Chicago: University of Chicago Press, 1979), xiii–xiv.

72. Hayek, *Law, Legislation and Liberty*, 3:113.

73. Friedrich August Hayek, "Consolidated Preface," in *Law, Legislation and Liberty: A New Statement of the Liberal Principles of Justice and Political Economy*, 3 vols. (London: Routledge & Kegan Paul, 1982), xx.

74. The proceedings were published as "The Arusha Initiative. A Call for a United Nations Conference on International Money and Finance," *Development Dialogue* (Uppsala), no. 2 (1980). The Swedish Dag Hammarskjöld Foundation had partially helped to fund the gathering.

75. See Getachew, *Worldmaking after Empire*, 142–75; as well as the special NIEO issue of *Humanity: An International Journal of Human Rights, Humanitarianism, and Development* 6, no. 1 (Spring 2015).

76. Vijay Prashad, *The Darker Nations: A People's History of the Third World* (New York: New Press, 2007), 191. For the Fund's perspective on the Arusha Initiative, see Jim Boughton, *Silent Revolution: The International Monetary Fund 1979–1989* (Washington, DC: International Monetary Fund, 2001), 588–601.

77. "Arusha Initiative," 12.

78. "The Terra Nova Statement on the International Monetary System and the Third World," Terra Nova Hotel, Kingston, Jamaica, October 5–7, 1979, *Development Dialogue*, no. 1 (1980). As cited in Prashad, *Darker Nations*, 66.

79. "Terra Nova Statement," 2.

80. For the notion of the post–Bretton Woods world as a "non-system," see Jacques de Larosière, "The Demise of the Bretton-Woods System Explains Much of Our Current Financial Vulnerabilities," speech delivered during the G7 High Level Conference at the Banque de France, *Eurofi Regulatory Update*, September 2019, https://www .eurofi.net/wp-content/uploads/2019/11/1.-the-demise-of-the-bretton-woods-system -explains-much-of-our-current-financial-vulnerabilities.pdf.

81. As Keynes had witnessed himself, American power was not just reflected in the Fund's voting shares and location but in particular in the decision to base the postwar financial architecture on the dollar instead of a new international currency.

82. Barry Eichengreen, *Exorbitant Privilege: The Rise and Fall of the Dollar* (Oxford: Oxford University Press, 2011). See also Benjamin J. Cohen, *Currency Power: Understanding Monetary Rivalry* (Princeton, NJ: Princeton University Press, 2015).

83. As Harold James has shown, early attempts to form a European monetary system during the late 1970s originate in this sense of collective vulnerability toward the swings of the dollar and US monetary policy. See James, *Making the European Monetary Union*, 9–10, 146–80. On "Eurodollars," see Jeffry A. Frieden, *Banking on the World: The Politics of American International Finance* (New York: Harper & Row, 1987), ch. 4.

84. On the leaks, see Boughton, *Silent Revolution*, 600.

85. James Ferguson, *The Anti-Politics Machine: "Development," Depoliticization, and Bureaucratic Power in Lesotho* (Minneapolis: University of Minnesota Press, 1994).

86. "Arusha Initiative," 14.

87. "Arusha Initiative," 21.

88. "Arusha Initiative," 11.

89. "Arusha Initiative," 21–22.

90. For an account of what it might mean to develop "just monetary arrangements" that fairly apportion burdens and benefits, see Sanjay G. Reddy, "Just International Monetary Arrangements," in Christian Barry and Thomas W. Pogge, eds., *Global Institutions and Responsibilities* (Malden, MA: Blackwell, 2005), 218–34. First published as Sanjay G. Reddy, "Developing Just Monetary Arrangements," *Ethics and International Affairs* 17, no. 1 (2003): 81–93. See also Sanjay G. Reddy, "International Debt: The Constructive Implications of Some Moral Mathematics," *Ethics and International Affairs* 21, no. 1 (2007): 33–48.

91. On the resulting political pressures when these implicit promises were inevitably disappointed, see Wolfgang Streeck, "Crises of Democratic Capitalism," *New Left Review*, no. 71 (September/October 2011): 5–29; as well as Streeck, *Buying Time*, 72–78.

92. See also Eric Helleiner, "Denationalizing Money? Economic Liberalism and the 'National Question' in Currency Affairs," in Marc Flandreau, Carl-Ludwig Holtfrerich, and Harold James, eds., *International Financial History in the Twentieth*

Century: System and Anarchy (Cambridge: Cambridge University Press, 2003), 213–38.

93. On Carter's self-fashioning and the "reification of technique" this entailed, see Stephen Skowronek, *The Politics Presidents Make: Leadership from John Adams to Bill Clinton* (Cambridge, MA: The Belknap Press of Harvard University Press, 1997), 365–74.

94. As quoted in Alasdair Roberts, *The Logic of Discipline: Global Capitalism and the Architecture of Government* (Oxford: Oxford University Press, 2010), 23.

95. As argued influentially by Finn E. Kydland and Edward C. Prescott, "Rules Rather than Discretion: The Inconsistency of Optimal Plans," *Journal of Political Economy* 85, no. 3 (June 1977): 473–92.

96. Bolstered by a Nobel Prize of his own and enjoying the esteem of his and Anna Schwartz's iconoclastic takedown of the Great Depression Fed, Friedman's monetarist beacon shone. Milton Friedman and Anna J. Schwartz, *A Monetary History of the United States, 1867–1960* (Princeton, NJ: Princeton University Press, 1963). On the rise of monetarism, see Daniel Stedman Jones, *Masters of the Universe: Hayek, Friedman, and the Birth of Neoliberal Politics* (Princeton, NJ: Princeton University Press, 2012), 180–272.

97. As quoted in Stedman Jones, *Masters of the Universe*, 180.

98. Besides Roberts, *Logic of Discipline*, see Mark Blyth, *Great Transformations: Economic Ideas and Institutional Change in the Twentieth Century* (Cambridge: Cambridge University Press, 2002) for a Polanyi-inspired account of this "disembedding of liberalism."

99. Hayek himself, pleased with the depoliticization of the 1980s, similarly put aside his monetary activism and focused instead on his final attack on socialism. Friedrich August Hayek, *The Fatal Conceit: The Errors of Socialism*, ed. W. W. Bartley III, *Collected Works of F. A. Hayek*, vol. 1 (Chicago: University of Chicago Press, 1988), 66–88.

100. For the concept of self-reflexive modernity, see Ulrich Beck, *Risk Society: Towards a New Modernity* (London: SAGE, 1992), 12–14, 155–236.

101. Roberts, *Logic of Discipline*, 23–46

102. Greta Krippner, *Capitalizing on Crisis: The Political Origins of the Rise of Finance* (Cambridge, MA: Harvard University Press, 2011), 142.

103. The Fed would later move toward a system of letting "the market" set interest rates or using intentionally abstract and convoluted language to turn an open-ended collective decision into a seemingly technical formality by an independent technocratic body without much room for maneuver. As Krippner perceptively points out, even the conscious discipline of monetarism eventually gave in to "market-led" monetary policy that though still politicized favored a more expansive credit policy. Krippner, *Capitalizing on Crisis*, 106–37.

104. Paul Volcker, *Keeping At It: The Quest for Sound Money and Government* (New York: Public Affairs, 2018), 113.

105. Peter Mair, *Ruling the Void: The Hollowing of Western Democracy* (London and New York: Verso, 2013). Wolfgang Streeck has described this phenomenon as "the de-democratization of capitalism through the de-economization of democracy." Wolfgang Streeck, *Buying Time: The Delayed Crisis of Democratic Capitalism*, trans. Patrick Camiller (London and New York: Verso, 2014), 5. See also Colin Crouch, *Post-Democracy* (Cambridge, UK: Polity, 2004).

106. As former Federal Reserve chairman Arthur Burns (in office 1970–78) insisted in 1979, it was simply "illusory to expect central banks to put an end to the inflation that now afflicts the industrial democracies." Arthur F. Burns, "The Anguish of Central Banking," Per Jacobsson Lecture, Belgrade, September 30, 1979 (Washington, DC: Per Jacobsson Foundation, 1979). See also John H. Goldthorpe, "The Current Inflation: Towards a Sociological Account," in Fred Hirsch and John H. Goldthorpe, *The Political Economy of Inflation* (Cambridge, MA: Harvard University Press, 1978), 195.

107. Michael Walzer, "Postscript (1980): Dissatisfaction in the Welfare State," in *Radical Principles: Reflections of an Unreconstructed Democrat* (New York: Basic Books, 1980), 52–53.

108. Habermas, *Legitimation Crisis*; Bell, *Cultural Contradictions*, 235.

109. Krippner, *Capitalizing on Crisis*, 107. Peter Burnham has set out this logic most explicitly and lucidly in his account of the politics of depoliticization in the British case. Peter Burnham, "New Labour and the Politics of Depoliticization," *British Journal of Politics & International Relations* 3, no. 2 (June 2001): 127–49.

110. The unlikely success of that vision had arguably much to do with its ability to deploy language successfully.

111. Krippner, *Capitalizing on Crisis*. On the related role of ideas in reframing the political options available, see Blyth, *Great Transformations*, 126–51.

112. Krippner, *Capitalizing on Crisis*, 141.

113. Karl Polanyi, *The Great Transformation: The Political and Economic Origins of Our Time*, 2nd ed., with a new introduction by Fred Block and a foreword by Joseph E. Stiglitz (Boston: Beacon, 2001), 147.

114. But as Brian Barry already asked at the time, what exactly was such local power worth in a modern economy? Walzer does not, Barry explained, "offer us any plausible explanation of the way in which participation in decisions taken in the workplace or the local community would be a way of achieving collective power over the most important economic decisions that shape people's lives." Brian Barry, "Review of Michael Walzer, *Radical Principles*," *Ethics* 92, no. 2 (January 1982): 369–73, at 373.

115. See his frequent pieces in *Dissent*, some of which were reprinted in *Radical Principles*.

116. See, however, his note in Walzer, "Dissatisfaction in the Welfare State," 52. Originally published as Michael Walzer, "Politics in the Welfare State," *Dissent*, January–February 1968, 26–40.

117. Michael Walzer, "Must Democracy Be Capitalist? Review of Charles E. Lindblom, *Politics and Markets: The World's Political-Economic Systems*," *New York Review of Books*, July 20, 1978.

118. Walzer, "Must Democracy Be Capitalist?"

119. Brian Barry, "Does Democracy Cause Inflation? Political Ideas of Some Economists," in Leon L. Lindberg and Charles S. Maier, eds., *The Politics of Inflation and Economic Stagnation* (Washington, DC: Brookings Institution, 1985), 280–317, at 317. See also Forrester, *Shadow of Justice*, 233.

120. Barry, "Does Democracy Cause Inflation?," 317.

121. Habermas, *Theory of Communicative Action*, 1:359; 2:171–72, 184, 264–73, 342–43; Habermas, *Theorie des Kommunikativen Handelns*, 1:480; 2:255–57, 274–75, 395–400, 503–4.

122. Habermas, *Theory of Communicative Action*, 2:171; Habermas, *Theorie des Kommunikativen Handelns*, 2:255.

123. Monetary exchange embodied "a block of more or less norm-free sociality" produced by the kind of functional differentiation that marked capitalist modernity. Habermas, *Theory of Communicative Action*, 2:171; Habermas, *Theorie des Kommunikativen Handelns*, 2:255.

124. Thomas McCarthy has even suggested that "one of the principal aims of *The Theory of Communicative Action* [is] to develop a more adequate version of the theory of reification." Thomas McCarthy, *Ideals and Illusions: On Reconstruction and Deconstruction in Contemporary Critical Theory* (Cambridge, MA: MIT Press, 1991), 152. Cited by Martin Jay, "Introduction," in Axel Honneth, *Reification: A New Look at an Old Idea*, ed. and with an introduction by Martin Jay, with commentaries by Judith Butler, Raymond Geuss, and Jonathan Lear (Oxford: Oxford University Press, 2008), 13n6.

125. Jürgen Habermas, *Between Facts and Norms: Contributions to a Discourse Theory of Law and Democracy*, trans. William Rehg (Cambridge, MA: MIT Press, 1996).

126. Habermas, *Between Facts and Norms*, 39, see also 343 and 500–501.

127. Habermas, *Between Facts and Norms*, 56.

128. Michael Walzer, *Spheres of Justice: A Defense of Pluralism and Equality* (New York: Basic Books, 1983). On Walzer's intellectual development, see also Rodgers, *Age of Fracture*, 193–98.

129. Michael Walzer, "'Spheres of Justice': An Exchange between Ronald Dworkin and Michael Walzer," *New York Review of Books*, July 21, 1983.

130. Walzer, *Spheres of Justice*, 18. Citing Karl Marx, "Economic and Philosophical Manuscripts" [1844], in *Marx and Engels Collected Works*, vol. 3, 325. Already in 1973 Walzer had drawn on Marx's early writings on money as the universal medium of exchange in a capitalist world to argue that the purpose of money was to function as a medium of economic exchange. "This is the proper function of money," Walzer explained, "and, ideally, its only function." Michael Walzer, "In Defense of Equality," *Dissent*, September 1973, 399–408.

131. Viviana Zelizer, *The Social Meaning of Money: Pin Money, Paychecks, Poor Relief, and Other Currencies* (New York: Basic Books, 1994); Nina Bandelj, Frederick F. Wherry, and Viviana A. Zelizer, eds., *Money Talks: Explaining How Money Really Works* (Princeton, NJ: Princeton University Press, 2017).

132. Nancy Fraser and Axel Honneth, *Redistribution or Recognition? A Political-Philosophical Exchange* (London and New York: Verso, 2003).

133. Michael Walzer, "Liberalism and the Art of Separation," *Political Theory* 12, no. 3 (1984): 315–30.

134. Beck, *Risk Society*, 191.

135. On this essential point, see Grewal, *Network Power*, 104–5.

136. What motivated this shift was, however, not a reorientation of priorities or a return of democratic politics but instead the liquidity demands of financial markets.

See Daniela Gabor, "Revolution without Revolutionaries: Interrogating the Return of Monetary Financing," *Transformative Responses to the Crisis* (2021). Available online: https://transformative-responses.org/wp-content/uploads/2021/01/TR _Report_Gabor_FINAL.pdf.

137. Adam Tooze, *Shutdown: How Covid Shook the World's Economy* (New York: Viking, 2021).

138. Philip Mirowski, "The Neoliberal Ersatz Nobel Prize," in Philip Mirowski, Dieter Plehwe, and Quinn Slobodian, eds., *Nine Lives of Neoliberalism* (London and New York: Verso, 2020), 219–54; see also Avner Offer and Gabriel Söderberg, *The Nobel Factor: The Prize in Economics, Social Democracy, and the Market Turn* (Princeton, NJ: Princeton University Press, 2016), 13, 48–49.

139. Mirowski, "Neoliberal Ersatz Nobel Prize," 225. Mirowski chronicles the political showdown over the Bank's daring move and the reticence of the Social Democrats to reveal that the Bank had essentially just staged an economic coup against the government (and won). For some background, see Mark Blyth, "The Transformation of the Swedish Model: Economic Ideas, Distributional Conflict, and Institutional Change," *World Politics* 54, no. 1 (October 2001): 1–26.

140. Friedrich August Hayek, "Speech at the Nobel Banquet," December 10, 1974.

141. Alan Ebenstein, *Friedrich Hayek: A Biography* (New York: St. Martin's Press, 2001), 385n6, 261.

142. Gunnar Myrdal, "Nobelpriset i ekonomi," *Dagens Nyheter*, December 14, 1976. Translated as Gunnar Myrdal, "The Nobel Prize in Economic Science," *Challenge*, March–April 1977, 50–52, at 52. See also Leonard Silk, "Nobel Award in Economics: Should Prize Be Abolished?," *New York Times*, May 31, 1977.

143. Juliet Johnson, *Priests of Prosperity: How Central Bankers Transformed the Postcommunist World* (Ithaca, NY: Cornell University Press, 2016).

Epilogue

1. Rudi Dornbusch, *Keys to Prosperity: Free Markets, Sound Money, and a Bit of Luck* (Cambridge, MA: MIT Press, 2000), 15.

2. Martin Luther King Jr., "I Have a Dream . . ." (1963). Spoken version of the speech. The version reproduced in King's collected writings and speeches misses the line oddly. James M. Washington, ed., *A Testament of Hope: The Essential Writings and Speeches of Martin Luther King, Jr.* (New York: HarperCollins, 1986), 217.

3. Adam Tooze, *Crashed: How a Decade of Financial Crises Changed the World* (New York: Viking, 2018), 162.

4. Andrew Ross Sorkin, Diana B. Henriques, Edmund L. Andrews, and Joe Nocera, "As Credit Crisis Spiraled, Alarm Led to Action," *New York Times*, October 1, 2008. As quoted in Tooze, *Crashed*, 162.

5. The key question of the crisis was thus in many ways: "Where is my swap line?" Brad W. Setser, as cited in Katharina Pistor, "Moneys' Legal Hierarchies," in Lisa Herzog, ed., *Just Financial Markets? Finance in a Just Society* (Oxford: Oxford University Press, 2017), 198–99. For an overview of the swap lines between central banks during the crisis, see Tooze, *Crashed*, 10–11, 211; and Aditi Sahasrabuddhe, "Drawing the Line: The Politics of Federal Currency Swaps in the Global Financial Crisis," *Review of International Political Economy* 26, no. 3 (2019): 461–89.

6. Tooze, *Crashed*, 197.

7. Robert C. Hockett and Saule T. Omarova, "The Finance Franchise," *Cornell Law Review* 102, no. 5 (July 2017): 1143–218.

8. These are the words of Phillip Swagel, then assistant secretary for economic policy at the Treasury. As quoted in Tooze, *Crashed*, 198.

9. Jacob S. Rugh and Douglas S. Massey, "Racial Segregation and the American Foreclosure Crisis," *American Sociological Review* 75, no. 5 (2010): 629–51. More broadly on the impact of the financial crisis on the widening racial wealth gap in the US, see Mehrsa Baradaran, *The Color of Money: Black Banks and the Racial Wealth Gap* (Cambridge, MA: Harvard University Press, 2017).

10. Tooze, *Crashed*, 449–70.

11. Timothy F. Geithner, *Stress Test: Reflections on Financial Crises* (New York: Crown, 2014), 18.

12. Adam Tooze, *Shutdown: How Covid Shook the World's Economy* (New York: Viking, 2021).

13. Daniela Gabor, "Revolution without Revolutionaries: Interrogating the Return of Monetary Financing," *Transformative Responses to the Crisis* (2021). Available online: https://transformative-responses.org/wp-content/uploads/2021/01/TR _Report_Gabor_FINAL.pdf.

14. Dipesh Chakrabarty, *Provincializing Europe: Postcolonial Thought and Historical Difference* (Princeton, NJ: Princeton University Press, 2000), 3.

15. Eric Helleiner, "A Bretton Woods Moment? The 2007–2008 Crisis and the Future of Global Finance," *International Affairs* 86, no. 3 (May 2010): 619–36; as well as Eric Helleiner, *The Status Quo Crisis: Global Financial Governance after the 2008 Meltdown* (Oxford: Oxford University Press, 2014). This does not mean that change can come only from a singular moment of founding. The "productive incoherence" (Hirschman) of the interregnum is itself a potent space for transformations that are more gradual but no less impactful. See Ilene Grabel, *When Things Don't Fall Apart: Global Financial Governance and Developmental Finance in an Age of Productive Incoherence* (Cambridge, MA: MIT Press, 2017).

16. Tooze, *Crashed*, 219.

17. As quoted in Tooze, *Crashed*, 215.

18. It was Zhou Xiaochuan, then China's central-bank governor, who in March 2009 surprised his colleagues by floating the idea of a new Bretton Woods based on Keynes's Bancor blueprint. Zhou Xiaochuan, "Reform the International Monetary System," *BIS Review* 41 (March 2009). For a similar move by the Indian central bank, see Prachi Mishra and Raghuram Rajan, "Rules of the Monetary Game," Reserve Bank of India Working Paper Series, no. 4, March 29, 2016. In October 2020, in the midst of the COVID pandemic, even the IMF managing director Kristalina Georgieva called for "A New Bretton Woods Moment," https://www.imf .org/en/News/Articles/2020/10/15/sp101520-a-new-bretton-woods-moment. For some of the earlier proposals and pleas, see Yanis Varoufakis, "Imagining a New Bretton Woods," *Project Syndicate*, May 4, 2016, https://www.project-syndicate.org /commentary/imagining-new-bretton-woods-by-yanis-varoufakis-2016-05; David Adler and Yanis Varoufakis, "The World Bank and IMF Are in Crisis. It's Time to Push a Radical New Vision," *The Guardian*, January 31, 2019, https://www.theguardian .com/commentisfree/2019/jan/31/world-bank-imf-bretton-woods-banking-keynes;

and Robert Hockett, "Bretton Woods 1.0: A Constructive Retrieval for Sustainable Finance," *N.Y.U. Journal of Legislation and Public Policy*, no. 16 (2013): 401–82.

19. For the original statement, see Henry Morgenthau Jr., "Bretton Woods and International Cooperation," *Foreign Affairs* 23, no. 2 (January 1945): 182–94. For a classic articulation, see G. John Ikenberry, "The Political Origins of Bretton Woods," in *A Retrospective on the Bretton Woods System: Lessons for International Monetary Reform* (Chicago: University of Chicago Press, 1993), 155–98.

20. Walter Bagehot, *Lombard Street: A Description of the Money Market* (London: Henry S. King, 1873), 20.

21. Christine Desan, "The Key to Value: The Debate over Commensurability in Neoclassical and Credit Approaches to Money," *Law and Contemporary Problems* 83, no. 2 (2020): 1–22, at 22.

22. Mark Carney, *Value(s): Building a Better World for All* (London: William Collins, 2021); Minouche Shafik, *What We Owe Each Other: A New Social Contract* (London: Bodley Head, 2021).

23. The former British central banker Paul Tucker has consequently called on political theorists to attend to the institutional questions of legitimacy posed by the unelected power of monetary policy. Paul Tucker, *Unelected Power: The Quest for Legitimacy in Central Banking and the Regulatory State* (Princeton, NJ: Princeton University Press, 2018), xi.

24. Jacqueline Best, "Bring Politics Back to Monetary Policy: How Technocratic Exceptionalism Fuels Populism," *Foreign Affairs*, December 2017.

25. For a critical account of "central-bank capitalism" that complements and overlaps with my conclusions here, see Joscha Wullweber, *Zentralbankkapitalismus: Transformationen des globalen Finanzsystems in Krisenzeiten* (Berlin: Suhrkamp, 2021).

26. Joseph Vogl has referred to this entanglement more broadly as "the sovereignty effect." As modern government has become financialized, finance has gained quasi-governmental powers. Joseph Vogl, *Der Souveränitätseffekt* (Zurich and Berlin: Diaphanes, 2015); Joseph Vogl, *The Ascendancy of Finance*, trans. Simon Garnett (Cambridge, UK: Polity, 2017).

27. Chiara Cordelli, *The Privatized State* (Princeton, NJ: Princeton University Press, 2021).

28. Elizabeth S. Anderson, *Private Government: How Employers Rule Our Lives (and Why We Don't Talk about It)* (Princeton, NJ: Princeton University Press, 2017).

29. El Salvador has in this context achieved the dubious honor of being the first country that has both dollarized and adopted Bitcoin as a parallel legal tender. Jude Webber and Eva Szalay, "El Salvador Approves Bitcoin as Legal Tender," *Financial Times*, June 10, 2021, 3.

30. Apart from Baradaran's *The Color of Money*, see also Keeanga-Yamahtta Taylor, *Race for Profit: How Banks and the Real Estate Industry Undermined Black Homeownership* (Chapel Hill: University of North Carolina Press, 2019); Destin Jenkins, *The Bonds of Inequality: Debt and the Making of the American City* (Chicago: University of Chicago Press, 2021).

31. Ana Patricia Muñoz, Marlene Kim, Mariko Chang, Regine O. Jackson, Darrick Hamilton, and William A. Darity Jr., *The Color of Wealth in Boston* (Federal Reserve Bank of Boston, 2015).

32. Akilah Johnson, "That Was No Typo: The Median Net Worth of Black Bostonians Really Is $8," *Boston Globe*, December 11, 2017, https://www.bostonglobe.com/metro/2017/12/11/that-was-typo-the-median-net-worth-black-bostonians-really/ze5kxC1jJelx24M3pugFFN/story.html.

33. Mehrsa Baradaran, "Banking and the Social Contract," *Notre Dame Law Review* 89, no. 3 (2014): 1283–342.

34. Mehrsa Baradaran, "It's Time for Postal Banking," *Harvard Law Review Forum* 127, no. 165 (2014): 165–75.

35. For a comprehensive blueprint for how money could be democratized by redesigning the central-bank balance sheet, see Saule T. Omarova, "The People's Ledger: How to Democratize Money and Finance the Economy," *Vanderbilt Law Review* 75, no. 5 (October 2021).

36. John Crawford, Lev Menand, and Morgan Ricks, "FedAccounts: Digital Dollars," *George Washington Law Review* 89, no. 113 (2021): 114–72. If the future of money is digital but not to be found in private digital currencies, one alternative possibility is thus that central banks or treasuries themselves issue their own form of digital currency in the form of Central Bank Digital Currency (CBDC) or some kind of "eCash." See the written congressional testimonies by Lev Menand for the hearing on "Building a Stronger Financial System: Opportunities of a Central Bank Digital Currency" in June 2021: https://www.banking.senate.gov/download/menand-testimony-6-9-21; as well as the written congressional testimony by Rohan Grey for the hearing on "Digitizing the Dollar: Investigating the Technological Infrastructure, Privacy, and Financial Inclusion Implications of Central Bank Digital Currencies," also in June 2021: https://financialservices.house.gov/uploadedfiles/hhrg-117-ba00-wstate-greyr-20210615.pdf.

37. Robert Meister has in this context recently argued for the need to construct new forms of political contestation based on the liquidity dependencies of finance. Robert Meister, *Justice Is an Option: A Democratic Theory of Finance for the Twenty-First Century* (Chicago: University of Chicago Press, 2021).

38. Hélène Landemore, *Open Democracy: Reinventing Popular Rule for the Twenty-First Century* (Princeton, NJ: Princeton University Press, 2020).

39. Anderson, *Private Government*; Hélène Landemore and Isabelle Ferreras, "In Defense of Workplace Democracy: Towards a Justification of the Firm-State Analogy," *Political Theory* 44, no. 1 (2016): 53–81.

40. Central bankers often respond to such proposals by insisting that while public deliberation is feasible and desirable for writing the rules of delegation, central banks' regular decisions cannot and must not be opened up to democratic deliberation. See, for example, Tucker, *Unelected Power*, 261. But how credible is this idealization of decision-making by committee when we have plenty of empirical evidence to the contrary?

41. As cited in Peter Conti-Brown, "Misreading Walter Bagehot: What Lombard Street Really Means for Central Banking," *The New Rambler*, December 2015.

42. The line serves as the epigraph to Tucker's introduction. Tucker, *Unelected Power*, 1.

43. As David Runciman has put it, for Hobbes both the state and money have a fictional character based on a form of collective acknowledgment that exceeds individual acts of recognition. David Runciman, "The Concept of the State: The

Sovereignty of a Fiction," in Quentin Skinner and Bo Stråth, eds., *States and Citizens: History, Theory, Prospects* (Cambridge: Cambridge University Press, 2003). On the complex meaning of "fiction" in Hobbes, see Quentin Skinner, "Hobbes and the Purely Artificial Person of the State," *Journal of Political Philosophy* 7, no. 1 (1999): 1–29; and David Runciman, "What Kind of Person Is Hobbes's State? A Reply to Skinner," *Journal of Political Philosophy* 8, no. 2 (2000): 268–78.

44. Jeremy Bentham, *A Fragment on Government*, ed. J. H. Burns and H.L.A. Hart (Cambridge: Cambridge University Press, 1988), 53. See also Quentin Skinner, "The Sovereign State: A Genealogy," in Hent Kalmo and Quentin Skinner, eds., *Sovereignty in Fragments: The Past, Present and Future of a Contested Concept* (Cambridge: Cambridge University Press, 2010), 26–46.

A NOTE ON THE TYPE

THIS BOOK has been composed in Miller, a Scotch Roman typeface designed by Matthew Carter and first released by Font Bureau in 1997. It resembles Monticello, the typeface developed for The Papers of Thomas Jefferson in the 1940s by C. H. Griffith and P. J. Conkwright and reinterpreted in digital form by Carter in 2003.

Pleasant Jefferson ("P. J.") Conkwright (1905–1986) was Typographer at Princeton University Press from 1939 to 1970. He was an acclaimed book designer and AIGA Medalist.

The ornament used throughout this book was designed by Pierre Simon Fournier (1712–1768) and was a favorite of Conkwright's, used in his design of the *Princeton University Library Chronicle*.

CPSIA information can be obtained
at www.ICGtesting.com
Printed in the USA
JSHW052028081022
31331JS00001BA/1/J